THE DERVISHES
OR
ORIENTAL SPIRITUALISM

THE DERVISHES
OR
ORIENTAL SPIRITUALISM

by

JOHN P. BROWN

THE MEVLEVEE SHEIKH OF PERA, CONSTANTINOPLE

With Twenty-Four Illustrations

GYAN

Published by

Gyan Publishing House
5, Ansari Road
Daryaganj, New Delhi-110002
Phone: 011-47034999, 9811692060
E-mail: books@gyanbooks.com

Distribution Network
gyanbooks.com
India, USA, Canada, UK, Australia, France

ISBN : 978-81-212-6160-9 (PB)
First Published, 1868

2nd Impression 2021

Printed at: Gyan Press, Delhi.

The Dervishes or Oriental Spiritualism
Author: John P. Brown

THE DERVISHES,

OR,

ORIENTAL SPIRITUALISM.

By JOHN P. BROWN,

SECRETARY AND DRAGOMAN OF THE LEGATION OF THE UNITED STATES OF AMERICA AT CONSTANTINOPLE.

THE MEVLEVEE SHEIKH OF PERA, CONSTANTINOPLE.

With Twenty-four Illustrations.

PREFACE.

THE object of this volume is to afford information in regard to the Belief and Principles of the Dervishes, as well as to describe their various modes of worshipping the Creator.

That the Spiritual Principles of the Dervish Orders existed in Arabia previous to the time of the great and talented Islam Prophet cannot be doubted. The historical portions of the Old and New Testaments were also well known among the Arabs, differing traditionally, however, in many respects from the narratives of the Sacred Writings; and if a conjecture may be made as to the starting point of Islamism, we would say that it originated in the act of perfect submission of Abraham to the will of the Almighty, when he determined to offer up his son Isaac in obedience to the Divine command.

The spiritualism of the Dervishes differing in many respects from Islamism, and having its origin in the religious conceptions of India and Greece, perhaps the information I have been enabled to collect together on the subject may not be without interest to the reader. Much of this is original; and having been extracted from Oriental works, and from Turkish, Arabic, and Persian MSS., may be relied upon as strictly accurate. In procuring materials from original sources, valuable assistance has been rendered me by personal friends, members of various Dervish Orders in this capital, to whom I would here express my thanks. Notwithstanding the unfavourable opinion entertained by many —principally in the Christian world—against their religious principles, I must, in strict justice, add that I have found these persons liberal and intelligent, sincere, and most faithful friends.

In the extracts from the works of other authors, some of whom are too well known to the public to require more than to be named by me—D'Ohsson, Sir William Jones, Malcolm, Lane, Ubicini, and De Gobineau—some differences will be perceived, mostly with regard to the estimate placed by each of these upon the character and influence of "The Dervishes" in the Mussulman world. To these eminent authors I am under great obligations, and take the present opportunity of acknowledging them.

To the kindness of Dr. Rost, the secretary of the Royal Asiatic Society, in getting my little work through the press, I am more deeply indebted than I can here properly express.

As a book of reference, I trust that this imperfect work will prove of some use; and travellers in the East will perhaps be enabled to learn from it much that would be otherwise obscure and hidden from their knowledge. Much more could have been added to it, especially with regard to the Dervish Orders in the more distant parts of Asia, India, and Africa; but I hope that some one more competent than myself will collect the information which was beyond my reach.

THE AUTHOR.

CONSTANTINOPLE, *October* 1867.

BERRAK, THE ANIMAL ON WHICH THE PROPHET VISITED HEAVEN.

CONTENTS.

A MEVLEVEE DERVISH OF DAMASCUS.

LIST OF ILLUSTRATIONS.

A KADIREE DERVISH.

THE DERVISHES.

CHAPTER I.

THE earliest form, or principle, of Religion is connected with an intuitive conviction in the mind of man of the possession of a soul or spirit, independent of his body, or corporeal existence. The soul is believed to survive the body, and refers to a superior Spirit, creative and providential in its character. A more perfect knowledge and communion with this greater Spirit, or God, is the object of man's continuous aspirations. The senses (or faculties) of man are possessed in common with other animals. These are all intimately connected with his intellectual faculty, so much so that, when they do not exist, as in childhood and advanced age, or are enfeebled by accidental causes, as in idiocy, it is seriously affected The reasoning faculty, and that of speech, seem to be those which distinguish man from ordinary animal nature, and yet both of these are possessed, in a greater and less degree, by most animals. It is supposed that the brain is the seat of the "intellectual faculty," and its operations are explained by its connexion with the nervous system and the other senses, such as hearing, seeing, and the touch. The size of the brain does not increase the reasoning faculty, nor that of the body the other ordinary faculties.

Man, thus, in his most degraded and least intellectual condition, in his most barbarous state, seems to have an "intuitive conviction" of the possession of a *soul*, and of a future existence after the death of his body. It seems not to be dependent upon mental culture, nor upon a knowledge of the greatness of this God, and the magnitude of His power and works. Does this perception extend to any other of His creatures, vegetable or animal, or is it restricted entirely to man?* I believe that the idea is always limited to the fact that there is *a* God, and that the belief in a plurality of Gods is a matter of pure imagination, dependent upon the varied convictions and wants of man in the several parts of the world.

Just as the soul of man thus leads him to believe in the existence of God, so does it likewise impress him with a conviction of the greatness of the Deity, and, in his helplessness, to supplicate Him in the hour of need, of suffering, and of danger. This, therefore, is the original means of communicating with the Creator on the part of the creature. Divine providences are not restricted to man only, but are experienced throughout all creation. The same laws of nature which affect him in this life extend also to all living beings, and the question may be again repeated, whether inanimate as well as animate creation, the vegetable as well as animal, have any perception of this fact?

Leaving the idea of the unity of the Deity, it is found that man has endeavoured to give to this simple conviction a place and a form. On the former there seems to be a belief in common among all men, that the Creator of all things exists far beyond the conceptions of the senses, and invisible to the ordinary senses; whilst the imagination ascribes to Him innumerable forms, all dependent upon the imagination and the fancied wants of ordinary life. With some He is all benevolence, with others avenging; whilst some believe that all His providences are unchangeable, and therefore constitute what is called destiny and fate, others regard them as merciful, and adapted to the needs of those who implore His compassion. Whilst He is considered omni-

* *Vide* Psalm cl. 6, and others.

potent in all things, it is held that He may, and does, alter His laws of nature, and so permit of occurrences which are called miracles. They even go still farther, and hold that He grants this power to those who invoke Him, so that they may effect equally surprising supernatural acts.

Besides this communion with God by spiritual means only, and a direct intercourse between the Spirit of the Creator and the soul of man, many—particularly in the East, the birth-place of humanity, according to the earliest history—believe it possible for him to *approach near to God.* This is effected by a devout adoration of Him, a frequent calling upon His Name; and the method of doing so has been established in a regular system. As this is peculiar to the East, the following account of the Dervishes will serve in some manner to explain it.

For most of the religious creeds of the Moslems I believe the source, or at least parallels, may be found in the Bible, and the history of Christian saints. The same thoughts give rise to a similarity of impulses and of acts; and this fact, with many, leads the mind to believe in their truthfulness.

A closer application to the contemplation of the Deity as the one Supreme Spirit, Creator of all things, and omnipotent Sovereign of the universe, and of the immortality of the soul of man, leads the mind to a disregard of the history of the human race as a Divine revelation. It places the *forms* of worship—sanctified in our estimation only by the assumption of their founder, that he possessed a position of devout communion with the Deity not possessed by his fellow-creatures generally—in a secondary, if not, indeed, in an unessential, point of view. They are valued only as the creation of the mind of one who commands our respect by his evident intention to benefit his fellow-beings, by elevating them from a meaningless idolatry to an adoration of the One only true Deity, and by wise moral laws and regulations to guide their ignorant and feeble intellects in a "pathway" leading from earth to heaven. Although we may be disposed to accept the idea that man has an "intuitive conviction" of the existence of God, this same intuition gives us no insight into the condition of the soul in its future existence. It nevertheless strongly suggests the fact of a right and a wrong, of good and evil acts, and of a future reward for the one, and a punishment for the other. The insignificancy of the historical part of the Bible, in comparison with that which relates to man's spirituality, becomes the more apparent as we pursue the latter. It is, in almost every instance, only the narrative of temporary human weaknesses,—of the empire of the passions, and of the feebleness of the soul, when unsupported by the Spirit of the Deity; often offering some of the worst deeds which darken and degrade mankind in his short career in this existence. These cannot be attributed to Divine inspiration, though the narrator may have been inspired to record them for a wise and useful purpose. The spiritual history of man only demands our deepest attention. In this we are led to regard with complacency, as non-essential to his future existence, the forms and particular rules of worship, established in modern as well as in ancient times, by the various individuals who fully considered the frailties of human nature, the necessity of external appearances, and the strength of whatever is mysterious upon the mind of men generally. How many men and women have believed themselves as especially called upon to assume the character of prophets and prophetesses, and to appeal to their fellow-beings in the language of Divine inspiration! We are struck by the strange mixture of good and evil which appears in the history of their own lives, and by the termination of their careers. We are lost in the vain endeavour to seize upon one fact calculated to procure a self-conviction of the truthfulness of their assumption. With some, we find youth and manhood devoted to mental instruction, in a religious point of view, and we are, therefore, led to give them our respect. And yet such instruction as this seems to command no claim to Divine inspiration, for the most unlearned have effected the most salutary results, the deepest and most lasting. Others, by the apparent purity of their lives, and the purely spiritual character of their administrations, place them high in our estimation; so that we do not care to call into question either their intellectual attainments or the grounds of their assumption, satisfied, as we are, by the evident benevolence of their designs to their fellow-beings.

In the East there is another class, who assume to have attained, by their own efforts, to a superior degree of spirituality, and to powers which come from Divine inspiration. These recognise the prophets and prophetesses who have preceded them, and who, through the purity of their lives, have become saints in the spirit-world, there filling positions of varied eminence and influence, which their followers invoke in their own behalf. This may be said also of some of the branches of Christianity, in which the theory of patron-saints is so far extended as to obviate the necessity of the worship and adoration of the Deity.

Revealed religion requires an unlimited degree of faith, and prescribes the exercise of reason, the same faculty, which, from its peculiar character, seems to have had a direct origin from the Creator, inasmuch as it places man above all other creatures. The simple religion of man, which is intuitive to his nature, is so perverted in modern times as no longer to inspire its principal feature, viz. that of universal benevolence; and, in its varied forms, is antagonistic to the evident will of the Supreme Deity, which cannot have any other object than that of justice, peace, and affection between all mankind. Revealed religion also teaches the existence of celestial spirits, who are supposed to be near the Deity, where they have been from a period the length of which cannot be even imagined. Of their origin nothing whatever is known: yet they must have been created in a manner different from that of man and his progeny. These are called Archangels and Angels, some of whose names we even know, such as Michael,

Gabriel, &c.; and, in more modern times, the abode of God has been peopled with saints, transformed from ordinary corporeal beings in this world to purely spiritual ones in heaven; and we still give them there the same names which they bore on earth.

Revelation relieves the mind of man of much of what is dark and concealed. It sheds a light upon the mysterious and the unknown, and, when accepted as a pure matter of faith, gives calmness and repose to the believer. A firmly-seated conviction, be it whatever it may, right or wrong, renders its possessor tranquil; and with it the Jew, the Christian, the Moslem, as well as even the idolater, or the fire-worshipper, passes through his career in life, satisfied with his faith, and meets the hour of his departure with cheerful confidence. *Religion*, in its ordinary signification, means the outward expression of a belief, accompanied by various forms of worship and external ceremonies. *Spiritualism* rejects these as non-essentials, and is the simple communion of the human soul with the Divine Spirit, by means of prayer and contemplation. The heart's adoration of the Supreme Creator may be audible or silent, and each be equal to the other, in point of value, with Him to whom nothing is secret. The inutility of forms and ceremonies is, therefore, evident, and at best may be regarded as human conceptions, or as symbols of mysteries having for object only an influence upon the mind and imagination of the worshipper. If these be considered as insignificant in the sight of the Almighty, they may also be regarded as innocent and harmless. These should not, however, tend to withdraw the worshipper from the Creator to the creature. It is impossible to suppose God unwilling to hear the supplications of any one who appeals to Him in a sincere and fervid spirit. It is equally impossible to believe that He has placed a barrier to this faculty, in the form of a multitude of intermediate creatures, or that He has given to any one a power to accept or refuse the salvation of another. The laws of God are equally over all and for all, and never can be otherwise than perfectly just. Any assertion to the contrary must, therefore, be attributed entirely to the imagination, the vanity, and the weakness of man. Some men have been good for their own sakes only; others have not only been themselves good, but have endeavoured to induce others to be equally good, so far as weak human nature and the power of the passions permit. Here, then, is an evident principle of benevolence, which alone renders its advocate superior to those who disregard it. That religion which is erected on this basis rests upon an eternal foundation, and possesses a Divine origin; whilst any other which inculcates strife and enmity, with all their attendant evils, must be held as antagonistic to the design of the Supreme Creator and Judge of the whole human race. The laws prescribed by the earliest legislatist of whom we have any knowledge, Moses, impressed upon the minds of those whom he designed to benefit, *first*, the unity of the Deity, to whom only man must address his adorations, and *next*, the principle of right and wrong towards each other,—or, in other words, the necessity of mutual benevolence.

The subject of Spiritual Powers is the principal object of the writer in collecting the materials of the present little work. No one, so far as he can learn, has devoted a book to the Dervishes exclusively. Some accounts of them, especially of the external forms of their worship, are found in various writings; but few have gone farther than these, or have given, at most, biographical sketches of their more prominent members.

The subject is not a new one. It can be traced in the Old and New Testament, as well as in the Koran, and, I fully believe, is peculiar to the learned ranks of the people of India, from whence it entered into Arabia and Persia. It has its origin in the belief that man's spirit is a Divine emanation, and, under certain peculiar circumstances, is possessed of a Divine faculty disconnected with his corporeal part, and, therefore, to be attributed wholly to his spiritual. The unity of the Deity was the principle of the Greeks and the Hindoos, and the other gods were supposed to be emanations from the One great Supreme Deity, called among the former Jove, and the latter Brahman. Among the Jews the unity was retained, and among the people of Arabia the same principle has not been forsaken, though that of emanations, or peculiar gifts of the Spirit of Allah to those who devotedly invoke and adore Him, is sustained to its fullest extent. The Trinity of the Christian creed seems to have been the chief object of Mohammed's abhorrence. In chapter cxii. of the Koran is found the whole basis of his doctrine: "God is one God; He begetteth not, neither is He begotten; and there is not any one like unto Him."

Whilst Moslems reject the divinity of Jesus Christ, they fully believe in His miraculous conception, and even call him, *par excellence*, the "Spirit of God" (*Rooh Ullâh*); they reject the theory of His mission as a Redeemer and Saviour, and of the Baptism, and yet admit him as one of the *saints* (Evlia) whose intercession with God is beneficial to those who implore Divine mercy.

I cannot do better than here quote the remarks of M. Garcin de Tassy, in his preface to the admirable translation of the poem "Mantic Uttaïr" (one of the most beautiful collections of ideas on the Spiritualism of the East), to demonstrate the subject before me:—

"The enigma of nature has been variously explained by philosophy. Great geniuses have arisen in different places and in different ages, and their varied suppositions on this subject have been reduced to systems and found millions of docile followers. However, an authentic explanation was needed for this great mystery which would satisfy the mind and the heart.

"Mussulmans have shown a remarkable subtlety in developing the mystery of nature. They have undertaken the most serious task of showing the alliance between philosophy and revelation. Placed between the Pantheism of the Indian Jogis and the Koran, which is sometimes an informal copy of the Bible, their philosophers, named the *Soofees*, have established a Pantheistic school appropriate to Islam ideas,—a sort of esoteric doctrine of Islamism, which must be distinguished from Indian Pantheism, though indeed it presents only the errors of the *Vedânta* and the *Sânkhya*. 'Pantheism, as a moral doctrine, leads to the same conclusions as materialism—the negation of human liberty, the indifference to actions, and the legitimacy of temporal enjoyments.' In this system *all is God, except God Himself*, for He thereby ceases to be God.

"The spiritualism of the *Soofee*, though contrary to materialism, is, in reality, identical with it. But if their doctrine is not more reasonable, it is, at least, more elevated and poetical. Among their authors, there are some who have endeavoured to form a concord between Mohammedan dogmas and their own principles, so as to establish for them a character of orthodoxy.

"The doctrine of the *Soofees* is ancient in Islamism, and is much spread, especially among the partisans of 'Alee (the fourth caliph). Out of it grew the belief in the infusion of the Divinity in 'Alee, and their allegorical explanation of all religious precepts and ceremonies. One Islam writer says that the first person who took the name of *Soofee* was Aboo Hâshim of Koofa, in the latter part of the eighth century; whilst another declares that the seeds of Soofeeism were sown in the time of Adam, germed in that of Noah, budded in that of Abraham, and the fruit commenced to be developed in that of Moses. They reached their maturity in that of Christ; and in that of Mohammed produced pure wine. Those of its sectarians who loved this wine have so drunk of it as to lose all knowledge of themselves, and to exclaim, 'Praise be to me! Is there any greater than me?' or rather, 'I am the Truth (that is to say, God)! There is no other God than me!'

"It is well to remember that the word *Soofee* does not come from the Greek word σοφὸς (*sage* or *wise*), as one might be tempted to suppose, but from the Arabic word *soof* (wool), and signifies a *woollen dress*, which forms the costume of the Dervishes and Fakeers, 'contemplatifs and spiritualists.' From this name comes that of the *Soofees*, *Mutasauwif*, and signifies especially a *Tâlib*, or novice, who desires to become a *Soofee*. They generally give the name of *Sâlik* to the *Tâlib*, as 'one who walks in a spiritual path.' This name also simply signifies 'a man.' They call *'Aboodiyat*, 'slavery' or 'servitude,' the service of God; and *'Abd*, he who devotes himself to His service. *'Ârif*, or the 'knowing,' is the devout contemplator; and *Ma'rifat*, the 'knowledge of God,' is the object of the contemplation. He who has reached this knowledge is called a *Wâli*, or one who is brought near to God; an expression which, in the end, signifies a *saint*. *Jezb* is the Divine attraction; the ecstatic state, which is the result of contemplation, is called *Hâl*, and its degrees, *Makâm;* the union with God is *Jam';* the separation *Fark*, and the continuation with Him, *Sukinât*. They call the ignorant or worldly individual *Jâhil*, and this expression signifies one who is not occupied with spiritual matters; and a distinction in fervour is thus defined, viz.:—Love of God, *'Ashk Ullâh*, differs from 'Affection;' Friendship, *Mohabbet; Shevk*, 'Desire;' *Ishtiâk*, 'Ardour;' and *Wejd*, 'Ecstasy.'

"These are the principal expressions used by Mussulmen Spiritualists, though there are many others, which cannot here be given."

The following extract from a mystical poem on Spiritualism, cited by the same author, will serve to develop the Dervish idea of God and man:—

"Man is the most perfect of God's creatures; he is the king of nature, because he is the only one in the world who knows himself,—knows, thus, the Creator, and possesses the intelligence of revelation. One may compare God to the sun reflected upon the waters; this reflection of light is nothing other than the light itself. For this reason, religious men, intoxicated with the cup of Divine communion, exclaim, 'I am God.' In fact, man's attributes are of a Divine character—what do I say?—his substance is that even of God. The only difference is, that he is a casual being, whilst God is the only necessary being." *

The following is a succinct account of the doctrine of the *Soofees* which is generally adopted in the Dervish Orders.

1. God only exists,—He is in all things, and all things are in Him.

2. All visible and invisible beings are an emanation from Him ("divinæ particula auræ"), and are not, really, distinct from Him. Creation is only a pastime with God.

3. Paradise and Hell, and all the dogmas of positive religions, are only so many allegories, the spirit of which is only known to the *Soofee.*

4. Religions are matters of indifference; they, however, serve as a means of reaching to realities. Some, for this purpose, are more advantageous than others, among which is the Mussulman religion, of which the doctrine of the *Soofees* is the philosophy.

(On this subject, Jelâl ed Deen er Roomee, the author of the Text Book of the Order of the Mevlevees, called the *Methnevee Shereef*, remarks in one of his verses:—"In whatever place we may set our foot, we are always, Lord, within Thy resort. In whatever place or corner we may entrench ourselves, we are always near to Thee. Perhaps, we say, there is a path which leads elsewhere, and yet, let our pathway be whatever it will, it invariably leads to Thee.")

5. There does not really exist any difference between good and evil, for all is reduced to unity, and God is the real author of the acts of mankind.

6. It is God who fixes the will of man, and he is therefore not free in his actions.

* St. Paul says in Hebrews xi. 3, "Through faith we understand that the worlds were framed by the word of God, so that things which are seen were not made of things which do appear." John of Parma, General of the Franciscans, the author of a celebrated Catholic work, called the "Eternal Gospel," and the author of the "Imitation," proclaim that "To lose oneself in God is the only object towards which man should strive."

7. The soul existed before the body, and is confined within the latter as in a cage. Death, therefore, should be the object of the wishes of the *Soofee*,—for it is then that he returns to the bosom of the Divinity, from which he emanated, and he obtains what the Booddhists call the *Nirvâna*, or, "annihilation in God."

8. It is by this metempsychosis that souls which have not fulfilled their destination here below are purified, and become worthy of reunion with God.

9. The principal occupation of the *Soofee* is meditation on the Unity, and progressive advancement, so as to gradually attain to spiritual perfection, and to "die in God," and whilst in this life to reach to a unification with God.

10. Without the grace of God, which they call *Faiz Ullâh*, no one can attain to this spiritual union; but this they assert is practicable, for it is held by them that God does not refuse His aid to those that fervently ask it.

M. de Tassy adds, that these doctrines have had their partisans in Christian Europe; for the Adamites teach that the human soul is an emanation of the Deity, imprisoned in bodily organs, from which it must be freed; and that the acts of the body are matters of indifference, which have no influence on the soul. In the seventh century, some held that God was in all nature, and that His essence gave life to it. Others maintained that it was necessary to disengage the soul from the weight of the faculties, so as to arrive at an absolute fusion with the infallible One, and that was only by contemplation.

The religious or mystical poems of the people of the East are mostly upon this subject. They serve to show that the writers, though nominally Mussulmans, were, nevertheless, not held by the ties of ordinary religion, its forms, dogmas, and ceremonies, to all of which they attached but little importance, when compared with the vast idea of the greatness of the Creator and Providential God of the universe. With them, there is but one book worthy of their research—that of Nature; in every page of which they read the unity and power and perfection of the Deity. In the journey of this life, there are many paths, all of which meet at the same goal,—the death of the body, the immortality of the soul, and its reunion with its First Great Cause. Many extracts and translations might be offered to explain the Dervish's idea of the Deity, but the following ode appears to me to convey it far more beautifully than anything else I have ever seen. It is also peculiarly Oriental in its chararcter.

GOD.

O THOU ETERNAL ONE! whose presence bright
All space doth occupy! all motion guide;
Unchanged through Time's all-devastating flight,
Thou only God! There is no God beside.
Being above all beings! Mighty One!
Whom none can comprehend, and none explore;
Who fill'st existence with Thyself alone;
Embracing all—supporting—ruling o'er—
Being whom we call God—and know no more!

In its sublime research, Philosophy
May measure out the ocean deep—may count
The sands, or the sun's rays; but, God! for Thee
There is no weight nor measure; none can mount
Up to Thy mysteries. Reason's brightest spark,
Though kindled by Thy light, in vain would try
To trace Thy counsels, infinite and dark;
And thought is lost ere thought can soar so high,
E'en like past moments in eternity.

Thou from primeval nothingness didst call
First Chaos, then Existence. Lord, on Thee
Eternity hath its foundation; all
Sprung forth from Thee; of Light, Joy, Harmony,
Sole origin—all life, beauty, Thine.
Thy word created all and doth create:
Thy splendour fills all space with rays Divine.
Thou art, and wert, and shalt be glorious! great!
Life-giving, life-sustaining Potentate.

Thy chains the unmeasured universe surround,
Upheld by Thee, by Thee inspired with breath!
Thou the beginning with the end hast bound,
And beautifully mingled Life and Death!

As sparks mount upward from the fiery blaze,
So suns are born, so worlds spring forth from Thee!
And as the spangles in the sunny rays
Shine round the silver snow, the pageantry
Of Heaven's bright army glitters in Thy praise.

A million torches lighted by Thy hand
Wander unwearied through the blue abyss;
They own Thy power, accomplish Thy command,
All gay with life, all eloquent with bliss:
What shall we call them? Piles of crystal light?
A glorious company of golden streams?
Lamps of celestial ether burning bright?
Suns, lighting systems with their joyous beams?
But Thou, to those, art as the noon to night.

Yes! as a drop of water in the sea,
All this magnificence in Thee is lost:—
What are a thousand worlds compared to Thee?
And what am I, when heaven's unnumbered host,
Though multiplied by myriads, and arrayed
In all the glory of sublimest thought,
Is but an atom in the balance, weighed
Against Thy greatness—is a cypher brought
Against Infinity? What am I, then? Nought.

Nought! but the effluence of Thy light Divine,
Pervading worlds, hath reached my bosom too;
Yes, in my spirit doth Thy Spirit shine,
As shines the sunbeam in a drop of dew.
Nought! but I live and on hope's pinions fly,
Eager towards Thy presence; for in Thee
I live, and breathe, and dwell; aspiring high,
E'en to the throne of Thy Divinity.
I am, O God, and surely Thou must be!

Thou art! directing, guiding all, Thou art!
Direct my understanding, then, to Thee;
Control my spirit, guide my wandering heart;
Though but an atom 'midst immensity,
Still I am something fashioned by Thy hand!
I hold a middle rank, 'twixt heaven and earth;
On the last verge of mortal being stand,
Close to the realm where angels have their birth,
Just on the boundary of the spirit-land!

The chain of being is complete in me;
In me is matter's last gradation lost,
And the next step is spirit—Deity!
I can command the lightning, and am dust!

A monarch, and a slave ; a worm, a God !
Whence came I here, and how ? so marvellously
Constructed and conceived, unknown ? This clod
Lives surely through some higher energy ;
For from itself alone it could not be.

Creator ! Yes ! Thy Wisdom and Thy Word
Created me ! Thou Source of Life and Good !
Thou Spirit of my spirit, and my Lord !
Thy Light, Thy Love, in their bright plenitude
Filled me with an immortal soul, to spring
O'er the abyss of death, and bade it wear
The garments of Eternal Day, and wing
Its heavenly flight beyond this little sphere,
Even in its Source, to Thee, its Author, Thee.

O thought ineffable ! O vision blest !
(Though worthless our conceptions all of Thee,)
Yet shall Thy shadowed image fill our breast,
And waft its homage to the Deity.
God ! thus alone my lowly thoughts can soar,
Thus seek Thy presence. Being wise and good !
'Midst Thy vast works, admire, obey, adore ;
And when the tongue is eloquent no more,
The soul shall speak in tears of gratitude.

Just as some of the Dervishes use internal incentives to religious fervour, such as the *Hashish*, hereafter described, and believe that the imagination, excited by such physical means, obtains a glimpse of future spiritual felicity, so others enliven the mental faculty by corporeal excitements. In this view, they inspire each other with increased fervour by the agitation of the body and the continued exercise of the powers of speech, which they call invoking the Deity or the *Zikr.* With some, such as the *Mevlevees*, the sense of hearing is excited by the sound of a sweet or harmonious music. At least, such to themselves is the performance of their little orchestra, and it is used more as a calming or soothing element than as an exciting one. If, by certain means, the senses can be excited almost to a point of frenzy, by others they may be lulled into a condition almost of inertia. The power of the moral influence of the "spiritual guide" (*Sheikh* or *Murshid*) is fully explained in the system of the Dervishes, and the submissive deportment of his *Mureeds*, or pupils, or disciples, is so visible to the observer that he is almost led to believe in the theory of the power of the superior will over the inferior and willing spirit, which is so important an element in their system. Nature and its laws are studied and understood, whilst life and the soul are inexplicable, as much so as is their great Author Himself. The latter may possess qualities yet unknown to the most learned in the sciences, yet of which some persons, often the least instructed, imagine they have glimpses, from which theories are formed totally at variance with natural science, and must, therefore, be qualified as "spiritual."

The following extract from the Oriental work called "Fusoos," by Muhi ed Deen el 'Arabee, will serve to give the ideas of a Mussulman on the preceding :—

"Man having been formed, by the hand of his Creator, out of the best of the soil of the earth, became composed of all of the varied natures which characterise the diversities of vegetable matter, which is the natural product of soil, and of all that partakes of the four distinct elements of nature, fire, air, earth, and water, and also possessing the three properties, animal, vegetable, and mineral; he received the most noble of forms, and his human material was formed with the finest traits that adorn the living creature. God blessed His work with the gift of His own Holy Spirit, and endowed man with the powers of intellect and of speech; so that he possessed the attributes of his own Creator. These precious gifts were bestowed upon him, so as to enable him to comprehend the wondrous works of his Divine Originator and to speak His praises.

"Adam, thus blessed with Divine gifts, was permitted to speak to his own posterity in the language of prophecy, and to direct it to the worship of his Creator. The knowledge which he possessed of his creation and his Creator has been transmitted to us through his descendants. God also gave him power over the whole vast universe in which he was placed, and an intellectual capacity requisite for the acquisition of a knowledge of all that surrounded him.

"As to those more elevated beings who occupy the upper celestial abodes, God has given them that knowledge which it pleases Him for them to possess. They worshipped in Adam an intellectual capacity and power superior to their own, notwithstanding that they do possess a knowledge of the hidden and the veiled secrets of the Divinity which was not known to him. They are permitted to behold the attributes of the Most High, of which man only knows the names; and, from their position near Him, are able to see the exercise of them over all His creation throughout the vast and interminable universe. Man was gifted with a mental capacity, because he possessed a knowledge of his own creation and of the exalted attributes of his Creator. Why it pleased the Almighty to create him, except it be to serve Him, is unknown to him, and it does not become him to seek to penetrate into the mysterious Will of Him who said, 'Be,' and it was."

Among mankind differences of opinion have arisen with regard to the ways of God in this world, as well as respecting the hereafter, and the condition of those who exist in His heavenly abode. Whilst some believe that there is nothing in existence but what is visible to the sight, and to the ordinary organs of vision, others consider that there is much that is veiled from sight, and which can only be seen through a nearer approach to their Divine Creator; and that this faculty is only to be obtained by a life of deep contemplation and adoration of Him, and a close spiritual communion with His eternal and all-pervading Spirit. They are, consequently, divided into two classes, viz.:—1. Those who attach themselves to whatever is clear and external. 2. Those who seek to penetrate into the veiled and mystical,—otherwise into what is purely "Spiritual."

Of these, the first explains all that is external, as well as what is secret, by means of the ordinary human intellect, or reason; they are called the *As-hâb i' Ilm i Zâhir:* and the second devote themselves to the ways of Mysticism, and to pointing out the *paths* by which a knowledge of the veiled and the hidden may be obtained; these are called the *As-hâb i' Ilm i Bâtin:* and God, in His merciful compassion, teaches them, through the power of His names and attributes, in Divine and spiritual visions. The beginning of their hopes is based upon the verse of the Koran which says, "Ye are of those who are near (to Me)," and their termination, "Ye are of those who are the inheritors of them who inherit Paradise, and remain there perpetually."

It would be interesting to trace the growth of the belief in saints and other human beings to whom man has assigned a position in the other life. The oldest record of history, the Bible, shows clearly that the earliest conviction of mankind,—that which was doubtless handed down from Adam, to whom it no doubt was a Divine revelation, vouchsafed at the period of his creation,—was, strictly speaking, in the Unity of God, and in the existence of angelic beings, created previous to this world, or to the first progenitors of the human race. To this may be added a perfect knowledge of good and evil, and the consequent belief in rewards and punishments. A conviction, however, based upon the preceding, of a future condition of happiness or misery after this life, nowhere gives to any one a place superior to another. Each individual is held responsible by the Creator for his own acts, and the Omniscient and All-Just rewards or punishes them, according to their respective merits. To the truly repentant His mercy endures for ever. God alone is the Judge and Arbitrator, and His decisions are beyond appeal or intercession in the life to come. At a later period, the sinfulness of the human passions and the feebleness of the mind of man are apparent in the necessity of a Mediator between God and man, as shown in the symbolic sacrifices prescribed in the laws of Moses.

Among the Romans and Greeks, to whom revealed religion was unknown, the system of celestial hierarchy seems to have been a matter of poetical imagination, which supposes that each element must be under the especial direction of a titular deity. These from time to time becoming more and more numerous, some were placed in higher, and some in lower positions; and all connected, as emanations from a One Supreme Deity, who reigned over and commanded all of the others. To these, however, were ascribed human attributes and human passions; so that the whole system is readily seen to be wholly inconsistent with the character and attributes of the One Divine Creator. Besides that the existence of the greater part of these gods is due to human imagination, assemblies of men believed that they could confer honour upon individuals by deifying them, or, in other words, conferring upon them positions of eminence in the heavens. Such is the ruling principle of what we call Mythology. To these gods were ascribed various characteristics, and varied powers over certain elements. In the hour of danger men appealed to them for succour and safety; and even consulted them when desirous of penetrating into the dark and hidden Future. The gods and goddesses became the patrons and patronesses of credulous mortals, and to each was assigned certain distinct forms, which have been handed down to our times in the masterly works of art now existing.

It would therefore appear that the system of modern saints and saintesses—so to speak—is totally different from the original faith of Adam and his descendants possessing revelation, and this is a continuation only of that of Mythology. The resemblance, at least, is so striking that it is impossible to attribute it to any other origin.

This modern system of "saints" varies among different people, and the degree to which it has attained among the Dervishes, and Mussulmans in general, is seen in the following chapters. Among these, prayers are offered to the saints for their intercession with the prophets; and prayers are also presented to them in the view of increasing their influence over the Deity. As it is not generally supposed that the souls of mankind will remain for ever in a condition of wretchedness, far from the presence of a merciful God, prayers are offered up to Him in behalf of those who, it is supposed, are still. expiating their sins in unhappiness, in the hope that the offering of supplications will be acceptable to the Almighty, and induce Him to pardon and forgive. Prayers for those still in life seem to be only for their worldly happiness and prosperity, without any reference to their future existence; though they may be in the desire and hope that they lead lives of purity, so as to merit happiness hereafter. Revealed religion teaches, by examples, that the sincerely devout may pray for the living, in the full expectation that their prayers will be heard and accepted; whilst I believe it does not admit of the efficacy of supplication for those who, having departed this life, have entered upon the responsibilities of their mortal career. This may, therefore, have given rise to the belief in the necessity of possessing patron saints and saintesses, already in heaven, and therefore near to the Deity, whose intercession may be invoked.

A study of the subject to which the following chapters relate has given rise to the preceding reflections, all of which are not, necessarily, those of the Dervishes. Perhaps I should apologize for thus expressing them, and for not having allowed the patient reader to form his own conclusions from the perusal of what I have collected.

In conclusion, these may be summed up in the idea that there is but One God, the Creator of all things. When God created man, He was pleased to give him faculties which He did not give to any other of His creatures; these were given him in the perfect vigour of manhood, and not in infancy, to be developed and strengthened in after years, as is now the case; they consisted of Reason and Speech. Man was created with a perfect knowledge of his own creation; possessed the faculty of reasoning thereon, and of communicating that knowledge to his posterity, which he did, and it has in this manner come down to our time. God also was pleased to gift man with an existence which, we may suppose, He did not give to any other of His creatures. He gave him an existence like His own, which will not only live in the present life, but will continue to exist hereafter in another. It is said that he was created even superior to the angels, but in what respect we know not; whether it refers to the power which he is enabled to exercise over other creatures of a secondary character, and even inanimate nature, in this world. This part of man's existence is called his *Spirit* or *Soul.* The peculiar character of this existence is such as to lead to the conviction that it is more than human, and must, therefore, be *Divine.* Oriental Spiritualism believes that its origin is due to a direct emanation from the Deity; and differs from the ordinary breath of life, which all other animated nature received on its creation.

We next are led to ask the question which remains unanswered, Is the spirit of man cut off entirely from that of its First Source and Origin, or has it still a connexion with it? When we sincerely and ardently pray to God, we feel that we approach Him—that we commune with Him; that He hears and answers our supplications; and that in this manner we re-unite our spirit to His. On the other hand, we feel that all evil acts—those which are the produce of our human passions—separate us from God, and destroy in us that pleasing conviction of the benefits to be derived from the influences of His Spirit, all of which are for good and wise purposes, such as tend to render man happy in his present life, and hold out for him a hope of continual happiness in that future life of which he knows almost nothing.

It is evident that the history of man's creation—such as has been written by Moses—is the only correct one, because it is that which the original man has handed down to his posterity. Why parts of it were veiled in allegory we scarcely dare to ask, and may only suppose that the knowledge was withheld from a good and wise cause. This history may be regarded more as a *revealed* than as an *inspired* one. We need not inquire in what manner God revealed or made known to man (Adam) a knowledge of his own creation. If God did not make it known to him, how did he learn it? To deny that

God made it known to him is to deny the existence of God and His creation of man, and leaves the imagination to wander, without any guide, in search of a spontaneous creation, or a self-creating nature, which ultimately, nevertheless, terminates in the conviction of the absolute necessity of a "Great First Cause," which is none other than the Almighty.

With this knowledge of our own creation, we are led also to believe that man originally possessed a profound conviction of evil and good, of right and wrong, unbiassed by the influences of the human passions. When these began to affect him, he lost much of the knowledge with which he was originally gifted. Just as these tend to withdraw him from God, so his spirit influençes him to approach Him. To call upon His holy name, and to praise Him, is what renders man in this life similar to the angels in heaven. We need not ask why God was pleased to create him with two such adverse characteristics; for it is evident that they are inherent to knowledge and ignorance, to good and evil, to merit and demerit. Without them he would have been perfect in knowledge; have been perfectly good and pure; would have had no duty to perform towards his Divine Creator other than to praise Him; in fact, he would have been possessed of all the characteristics of God Himself, and have been entirely a *spirit* dwelling upon earth.

Inspiration is a subject upon which depends the whole theory of the prophets and of the saints, and consequently opens upon a vast field for the imagination. Independent of the influences which the Divine Spirit is believed to exercise upon that of man, Oriental Spiritualism fully teaches that good men do not only have an influence upon him whilst an occupant of this life, but that the former may and do exercise one upon those who invoke their spirits after their departure, by inspiring them for beneficial purposes. This is therefore a subject only considered secondary to that of the creation of man, and of his being gifted with an ever-existing soul.

To possess the gift of approaching God in prayer, and to entertain the conviction that He will and does hear as well as answer our prayers, does not necessarily imply that God *inspires* any one. The powers of the passions are allayed; and the purer impulses of the Spirit are unrestrained. A conviction of our own helplessness and insignificancy—of our impotence to help ourselves under circumstances of need or of peril—naturally leads us to seek for some one who is able to aid and protect us. That One we feel can only be God. We therefore call upon Him, not only for ourselves, but for those whom we desire to benefit or to succour, as the Creator and Dispenser of all providences. Is this impulse to be attributed to a direct influence of the Spirit of God, or, in other words, to His inspiration? In reply it may be said that revealed religion teaches us that the Spirit of God does even *strive* with man, evidently so as to induce him to withstand the temptations of the *flesh*, and obey Divine influences, all tending towards his present and future welfare. Do those who accept and obey these influences become thereby gifted with characteristics of a superhuman nature in this life, and are consequently peculiarly holy? If we analyse the history of the "prophets," we find that, even if they were not always themselves pure and faultless, they endeavoured to benefit their fellow-men, and forasmuch received what is called inspiration. That God loves whatever is good, and abhors what is evil, cannot be doubted by any one who entertains a proper conception of His character; but the whole history of man shows us, by innumerable examples, that the benefits to be derived from a submission to His influences are not of this life, but of the future. The most holy men have prospered but little in this world, and met with the most cruel and painful of deaths. If, therefore, men acquired superhuman powers through "inspiration," it is natural to suppose that they would exercise them for their own preservation. In our entire ignorance of the future, we pray to God for our necessities and protection; or, in other words, to bless our own labours and those of others who labour for us, and when we receive them we attribute the results as an answer to our prayers. When they are not granted, we must either suppose that God has not heard us, or not been pleased to grant our requests. We even believe in the efficacy of the prayers of others in our behalf. Are these more efficacious when the prayers are of a good than when of a bad person? If the former, we are led to believe in the intermediation of those whom the world calls "living saints;" or of human beings who, on account of the purity of their lives in this world, possess a superior degree of influence with the Creator of all mankind. To deny this is to deny the many examples offered in support of it in revealed religion. Not only among the Dervishes, but other religions, holy persons are held to possess and exercise spiritual powers which appertain only to the Omnipotent Creator, and are worshipped accordingly by their followers, disregardful of the fact that, at the most, they are only the mediums of Divine providences. They are supposed to be able to perform what are called *miracles*. These superhuman powers are even attributed by many persons of great intellectual attainments to the bones of the departed, and these are believed to possess the power of changing and arresting the providences of God. Thus we see that "inspiration" leads even to the belief in the power of the animal portion of man—that which belongs not only to dumb brutes, but to inanimate creation—over the spiritual, thus reversing the whole theory of spiritual religion.

The Dervishes hold the saints in exalted estimation. They fully believe that some holy individuals possess great "spiritual powers," whilst yet in this life, and that those who follow in the "paths" pointed out by them, all, however, bowing to the same universal Creator, may profit by their intercession with Him. They believe that blessed spirits are ever around them, and, like that of the Omnipresent Deity, know no particular place of abode, and may therefore be invoked anywhere. They nevertheless venerate the places of their interment, as localities sanctified by the presence of their remains. They do not, however, attribute any miraculous powers to their bones. With them, "inspiration" is the fruit of prayer and devotion, in connexion with holy lives; and that it is mostly during slumber, when the physical faculties are lulled in an incomprehensible manner, that the sleeper sees visions and receives Divine influences. It was at such times as these that the prophets were spoken to by God, and commanded to proclaim certain Divine truths which were necessary to the future welfare and happiness of mankind. These "truths" are held to be incontrovertible, and are therefore declared in succinct terms, having the form of proverbs and maxims, and have therefore the force of commands.

ABRAHAM AND MOHAMMED.

In the course of the observations offered in the present work, allusion is sometimes made to certain principles contained in or deduced from the Koran, which, not being either originally taken from the Old or New Testament, remain a matter of speculation. To a good Mussulman, for whose mind the Koran offers a distinct field of belief, these are naturally attributed wholly to inspiration. Some of these ideas are certainly very sublime. The prophet of Islamism entertained the most elevated and exalted ideas of the Deity, akin to those so beautifully expressed in the Psalms of David. He called himself of the Sect or Faith of Abraham, thus forming a distinction between what he considered to be the religion of this patriarch and the Jews personally. In the second chapter of the Koran, it is stated :—

"Say, We believe in God, and in what has been sent to us from on high,—to Abraham, Ismail, Isaac, Jacob, and the twelve tribes. We believe in the books given to Moses and Jesus,—to those given to the prophets by the Lord. We make no difference between them, and we give ourselves up to God."

"Would you say that Abraham, Ismail, Isaac, Jacob, and the twelve tribes, were Jews or Christians? Tell then, Who is more knowing—God or you? And who is more culpable than he who conceals the truth confided to him by God? He is not indifferent to what you do."

"These generations have all gone by. They have received the fruits of their works, as you will of yours. No one will ask you an account of what they may have done."

And in the third chapter:—

"Abraham was neither Jew nor Christian. He was pious, and given up entirely to God, and did not associate any other person than One in the Godhead."

"Those who hold to the Faith of Abraham are those who follow him; such is the Prophet of the True Believers, and God protects those who are faithful to him."

In the verse preceding this latter, the word Jew is *Yahood*, and Christian *Nasrânee*, or Nazarene; whilst that which expresses the idea that Abraham was pious and submissive to God is the *Hanefee* Mussulman, or as by some translators, a Mussulman of the *Hanefee* (orthodox) rite.

The question thus arises, Was there a people in the prophet's time who were neither Jew, Christian, or Idolater, and whose dogmas formed the basis of his peculiar principles? If so, what were those principles, and from what source derived?

Oriental traditions contain much more minute details about Ibrahim (Abraham) than the Bible. He is supposed to have lived in the reign of King Nemrood (Nimrod), one of whose confidential officers his father Âzar was. This king and all his people were idolaters. It was a tradition of those times that a child would be born, who would be the cause of the destruction of his kingdom. To prevent this, the king ordered, on a particular occasion, all of the men of his city of Babel to be removed outside of its walls, and the females to remain within; but, as Âzar was one of the king's officers, and was stationed inside one of the gates, his wife joined him there. The king's astrologers, however, having been able to learn this fact, communicated it to him; and consequently, the child born to Âzar was concealed in a cave, until he reached the age of puberty.

"On issuing from this confinement, he was struck with the grandeur of the world and the celestial bodies, and impressed with contempt for the absurdity of the worship of idols. He, therefore, refused, at all times, to worship them, and became the object of the anger of King Nemrood. Called before him, he boldly told the king that his idols were only the work of man's hands, whilst the Great Creator of the Universe was the only true God, and Author of man's own existence; and, consequently, the proper object of his adoration. Finding an opportunity, he destroyed all of the idols, except one, the largest; and, having placed the axe with which he had knocked off their heads in the mouth of this one, said that probably he had destroyed the others, which argument rather forcibly struck the worshippers. On another occasion he asked the king to afford him an exhibition of his power, saying that the God whom he adored not only brought man into existence in this world, but gave him another in the life to come. The king produced two criminals, and having put one to death, pardoned the other; meaning thereby, that he could take away and bestow life. Abraham next asked him to cause the sun to rise and set, and the planets to appear, which were the daily works of his God; and this the king being unable to effect, the king's anger became increased, and he determined to put Abraham to death. For this purpose he had an immense fire prepared, and cast him into it. God, however, did not forget His faithful servant, and sent His celestial messenger, the angel *Jebrâil* (Gabriel), [signifying the 'power of God'] to his rescue. After the king and his people saw that Abraham was protected by a power hitherto unknown to them, many of the latter adopted his faith, and worshipped the only One true God.

"This fidelity of Abraham to the Creator, amidst a large number of idolaters, acquired for him the title of the *Khaleel*, 'the friend' or 'sincere advocate of God,' by which he is still known among Mussulmans.*

"In the course of time he took *Sarâh* or *Sarah*, a name signifying 'the pleasant,' or 'agreeable,' to wife; and as she proved to be barren, according to the Oriental custom, still in practice, she gave him her handmaiden *Hajir*, or Hagar, from *Hejere*, to fly from, or escape; the same root from which is derived the well-known word, *Hejira*, or 'Flight of the Prophet,' and from which the Mussulman period is taken. Hajir having borne him a son named Ismâ'il or Ishmael, or the 'heard of God,' from *Sémâ'*, to hear, and *Alâ*, God, she became the object of the envy of her mistress, and Abraham was compelled to remove her into a remote part of the country (Arabia). There God heard her voice, and protected her from death by thirst and starvation. The well, so much revered by Mussulmans, called *Zemzem*, at Mekkeh, was erected for her especial benefit. Ibrahim, when conveying Hajir and Ismâ'il from the Land of Sham, where he resided, to the spot on which Mekkeh stands, was guided by the angel *Jebrâil*, and directed to stop precisely where this celebrated well still exists. A tree sprang up at the time, to shelter them from the heat of the sun, and there he left them. Hajir implored him not to abandon her and her helpless child in so desolate a place; and, though he was much affected by her appeal, he told her that such was the will of God, conveyed to him during his sleep in a dream. She, on hearing this, resigned herself up to God's supreme will. He left her near to the *Bait el Harâm*, and to the spot designed for the *Ke'beh;* neither of which were yet in existence. The first simply signifies the 'Holy House,' and the latter 'The Cube.'"

The destitute condition of Hajir and her child is one of the most touching narratives of the Orient; only surpassed by that of the intended sacrifice of Ismâ'il by Abraham, in obedience to the command of God.

"It is related that, having consumed all of the food left with her by Abraham, hunger and thirst caused her milk

* James ii. 23.

to dry up, and her child, as well as herself, was apparently doomed to die a most cruel death, far from those who might come to her relief. She ascended Mount Safâ, and looked around her. No sign of cultivation or of water could be seen within the extent of her vision. Seated there, she wept, and in the anguish of her heart, at the sight of the starving child, cried out aloud for assistance. Descending from the mountain, she hurried across the intervening valley, and ascended Mount Meroeh, which also offered a wide field to her vision. She still was unable to see any habitation, or any fountain of water. In her grief she went seven times to and fro between these mountains, in the spot where the pilgrims of our times still encamp. At each passage, she would stop to see her child, and guard him against the wild animals of the desert. At length, from Mount Meroeh she thought she heard a voice. It seemed so distant and vague that she was unable to ascertain whence it proceeded. At length she became aware that it was from the spot on which she had left her son. Hastening to the spot, she became delighted with the sight of a running stream of pure water. By some it is supposed that the water gushed out of the spot where the child lay; whilst by others it is said that the same angel which accompanied them in the flight still watched over them, and that God, in answer to the cries of the mother and her suffering boy, touched the earth, and let a spring of water gush up from the sources which it everywhere contains. After both had drunk of the refreshing stream, she designed to fill her jug for future use, but the same unseen voice forbade her, saying that the stream would for ever afterwards continue to flow. She also designed to erect a dam of earth, so as to raise up the stream; but this was likewise forbidden to her, and she was told that Abraham would return and build a house there, which should become the *Kibleh*, towards which millions of sovereigns and subjects would turn their faces in adoration of God. She was also told that her son should become a prophet, and guide men in the true path of religion.

"Hajir was not long left in this condition. A tribe of Arabs called the *Beni Jerhem*, whilst on their way from Yemin to Shâm, attracted by the unexpected appearance of birds hovering around the stream, were delighted to find so useful a provision for themselves and their animals. These were distant relations of Abraham, but possessed no knowledge of his flight with Hajir and Ismâ'il, and much less of the well of Zemzem, on a spot where they had previously only found dry soil.

"Soon after this, and after hearing the history of Hajir and her son Ismâ'il, Jerhem, with all his people and flocks, established themselves on the spot now known as *Mekkeh*. With them came the tribes called *Katira* and *Mezamen bin 'Amru*, the chief of which was *Semedâ bin 'Âmir*, and thus formed the earliest residents of that city, among whom Ismâ'il grew up and found aid and sustenance. From them he learned the Arab tongue.

"Abraham was informed, through a visit of the angelic visitor, Jebrâil, of the prosperous condition of Hajir and Ismâ'il, and once a year paid them a visit, on a swift-footed animal called *Berâk*, from *Berk*, or Lightning."

This is the same name which the prophet gave to the animal on which he proceeded from earth to heaven in the night called the *Mi'râj*, or Ascension. In the shortest imaginable space of time, he saw and heard much in the seven heavens through which he passed, and the whole affair is now supposed by the more intelligent Mussulmans to have been only a vision, like the revelation of St. John.

"On the fleet-footed *Berâk*, Abraham annually made a visit to Hajir and her son. The latter had reached the age of fifteen when his mother died, and, aided by the Beni Jerhem, he laid her beloved remains in Mekkeh, close by the black stone which is so much revered by all the faithful, and was deeply affected by the loss of so affectionate and devoted a mother. After this he planned the design of emigrating from that country, and to prevent this his friends married him to one of the most noble of the daughters of the afore-named tribe.

"It is a matter of tradition that Ismâ'il was an excellent

cavalier and an adroit hunter. It happened that Abraham, according to his habit, that year made his annual visit to Mekkeh, and during Ismâ'il's absence in search of game arrived at his door. Knocking at it, his son's wife made her appearance, and, not knowing the stranger, failed to offer him the usual tokens of respect and hospitality due to him, which, giving him offence, he departed, bidding her describe his appearance to her husband on his return, and that he recommended him to change the sill of his door. Ismâ'il, on learning what had occurred, immediately recognised his father Abraham, and in the advice to change his sill a command to dismiss his wife, which he forthwith did. He next married another wife from among the maidens of the same tribe, and on the return of his father he was gratified by his dutiful obedience to his wishes. On the second occasion Ismâ'il's wife was most attentive to her guest—offered him hospitality, and pressed him to partake of a meal got ready for him. This latter Abraham, however, declined dismounting to partake of, and so had to dine seated on his animal. The cause of this was that he had formally promised Sarah, when he visited Hajir and Ismâ'il, not to dismount. After dining as aforesaid, his daughter-in-law brought water and washed his hands and feet, and combed his hair. Much as she begged him to descend from his animal, he persisted in his refusal, but so far gratified her as to rest one of his feet on a stone near her door, and the print of it remained upon it. On departing, Abraham bade her tell her husband, on his return from the chase, that the sill of his door was good, and he must be careful not to change it. On hearing what had occurred, Ismâ'il was extremely gratified, and informed his wife that the unknown stranger whom she had entertained was none other than his father Abraham. In conformity with his recommendation, he never during his lifetime married any other wife."

Connected with the history of Abraham, whose religion, the Islam prophet declares in the Koran, was his own, mention may be made of the children borne to him by Sarah, viz., *Is-hâk* (Isaac) and *Ya'koob*, or Jacob. The same work from which the present Arabian tradition is derived (*Revzet es Sefâ*), adds that by the great favour of the Almighty, Hajir was made illustrious among women, and Sarah ardently also desired to have a son, so that the prophetship might be continued in her offspring.

"About this time the angel *Jebrâil*, or Gabrail, was sent with several other celestial messengers to destroy the people of Lot, called *Loot*. They became the guests of Abraham in the form of men, and he killed a fatted calf for their entertainment. They refused, however, to partake of it until they should be made acquainted with its price. Abraham, in reply, said that in the beginning its price was the benediction still used by all Mussulmans, especially by Dervishes, 'In the name of God, the merciful and the clement,' and in the end, 'Blessed be God' for His bounties. Notwithstanding this act of piety, which Gabrail greatly applauded, the angels persisted in not partaking of the food, much to the alarm of their host; for in those times, whenever a guest entertained hostile designs, he would refuse to eat with their object. Fully aware of Abraham's fears, they informed him who they were, and the object of their Divine mission. Gabrail also gave good news to him, that God, in His great mercy, would give him and Sarah a son. Now Sarah heard this from behind a curtain, and smiled, and this circumstance is alluded to in the Koran: 'His wife was standing by, and laughed. We gave her the good news, that (she should bear) *Is-hâk*, and afterwards *Ya'koob*.' By some it is said that she laughed on account of the utter improbability of her bearing children; and by others, because she knew they were angels, and was rejoiced that they were sent to destroy the sinful people of Lot. Be this as it may, the angels knew what was passing in her mind, for, addressing her, they observed, 'Do you not know how the Almighty created Adam without father or mother, and that from him all his race is descended?' Soon after this Sarah bore Is-hâk, in the hundredth year of her husband's age, and it is traditioned that on the night of his birth he beheld a thousand shooting stars pass before his sight in the firmament, and having asked of the angel Jebrâil the meaning of so uncommon an occurrence, learned that from his son then born a thousand prophets would descend. Abraham praised God, and begged that his other son, Ismâ'il, should also be the object of His Divine favour. A voice was heard to reply, 'O Abraham, from Ismâ'il shall proceed one prophet, whose intercession mankind, to the end of time, will implore, and who will be the crown of all prophets.' Abraham blessed and thanked God for His mercies (Koran xiv. 41): 'Praise be unto God, who hath given me in my old age Ismâ'il and Is-hâk, for my Lord hears supplications.' It is related that Abraham was ninety-nine years of age when he was directed by inspiration to circumcise himself, and that he circumcised Ismâ'il at thirteen and Is-hâk at one year of age: some say that the former was three years older than the latter, whilst others say fourteen. It was after the Divine intimation that through these the prophetship would be carried down, that he was directed to offer one of them up as a sacrifice."

THE SACRIFICE OF ISMÂ'IL.

"On this subject there exist conflicting statements regarding which of the two sons, Ismâ'il or Is-hâk, it was. Some of the *As-hâbs* of the blessed Prophet, the commander of the faithful, 'Omar bin el Khattâb, 'Alee bin Abu Tâlib, and others of the *Tâbi'een* (those who were their followers), Ka'bel Ahbâr, Sa'id bin Jebeer, Mesrook, Abu-l Zeheel, Zehree, Sa'd, and others narrate that it was Is-hâk. On the other hand, some of the *As-hâbs* and *Tâbi'een*, such as 'Abd Allah bin 'Abbâs, Abu Huraireh, 'Abdullah bin 'Omar, 'Âas, and Abu Tofail 'Âmir bin Vaileh, as well as one of the eminent of the latter, Imâm el Hudâ Ja'far bin Mohammed bin Sâduik, Sa'id bin el Museeb, Yoosuf bin Mihrân, Mujâhid, and Sha'bee, all declare that it was Ismâil. Many proofs are brought to sustain the two statements. The composer of the present work says that, after having examined them all with much care, he has concluded (though God only knows the truth) that the son to be offered up was Ismâ'il.

"It is narrated that Ibrahim had vowed that if the Most High should favour him with a son, he would offer up to God a sacrifice, and that after this both Ismâ'il and Is-hâk were borne to him. He had, however, forgotten his vow; and one night, when sleeping at Mekkeh, or The Place of Sacrifices, he had a dream, in which some one said to him that it was the command of God he should offer up his son as a sacrifice. Waking up, he collected his thoughts, and, after pondering over the occurrence, decided in his own mind that it was not obligatory upon him. On the following night, however, he had precisely the same dream, and the same again during the third, and at the same time he heard a voice asking him how he could permit Satan (*Shaitân*) to mislead him from his obedience to God. On awaking, he bade Sarah to wash Ismâ'il's head, and anoint it, and dress him neatly; and to Ismâ'il he spoke: 'My dear boy, take some cord and a sharp knife, and accompany me, for the purpose of collecting wood on the mountain.' After this they set out together, and on the way *Iblees* (or The Tempter) went to Ibrahim in the form of an aged man, an adviser, who inquired of him where he was going, and the former replied that he was going to the foot of the mountain, where business called him. Iblees remarked, 'O Ibrahim, Satan has tempted you, and induced you to offer up Ismâ'il as a sacrifice to no purpose, whilst the whole world will become filled with his race alive.' Notwithstanding these words, Ibrahim knew, through his own spiritual powers as a prophet, and by the aid of Divine Light, that the speaker was Satan in disguise, and he exclaimed, 'O enemy of God, depart from me, for I must obey the commands of the Most High.' Iblees, both disappointed and scornful, departed, and having found Ismâ'il, he addressed him, 'Do you not know where your father is taking you? Under the pretence of cutting wood, he intends to sacrifice you, misled by Iblees, who has induced him to believe that his slumbers were of the Merciful.' Ismâ'il to this replied, 'Can any father sacrifice his own son? Whatever God has commanded, and my father decided to execute, I shall most cheerfully conform to.'

"Thus Iblees was unable to mislead either the father or the son, and he now returned to Hajir (Hagar), to whom he related how that Ibrahim, with the pretext of cutting wood on the mountain, had taken Ismâ'il there for the purpose of sacrificing him. Hajir replied, 'Can Ibrahim be so cruel as to kill his son, he who is so humane even to his enemies? But be this as it may, let your statement be false or true, it concerns himself, and my duty is to submit to his will.' On this Iblees, desponding, left, and thus the Most High preserved Ibrahim and his family from the tempter.

"Now it is narrated that Ibrahim reached a place called *Shâb*, and there he told Ismâ'il of his dream, in the following words: 'O my dear son, I saw in my dream that I should put you to death; reflect upon it, and tell me your opinion.' Ismâ'il answered, 'O my father, whatever you have been commanded to do let it be done.' 'How can you, my son, resign yourself thus to so dreadful an end?' asked Ibrahim; and Ismâ'il only replied, 'My father, God will enable me to bear it with patience,' and added, 'Tie my hands and my feet, so that when I am struggling in death, my blood may not fall upon you; sharpen, also, well the knife, that I may soon be freed from life; turn my face downwards, that lest you, beholding my struggles, may be deterred from the Divine commands, through paternal pity, and so deviate from your duty. Console my aged and beloved mother, Hajir, for my death, with the assurance that I terminated my earthly career in the path of God!'

"On this, Ibrahim was greatly affected, and cried out aloud: 'O God, during all my life, the mention (*Zikir*) of my petition and devotion to Thee has ascended up to Thy abode; in my old age, Thou hast given me a son; many months and years I have grieved for his absence; if this deed be according to Thy divine will, who am I, that I should oppose it? but if it be not, I will repent of so sinful a design.'

"All the angels and spirits upon earth, and in the heavens, beheld the submission (*Islâmiet*) of Ibrahim and Ismâ'il, and heard the devotion of the parent; and they wept, and cried aloud. Ibrahim pressed his knife to the throat of his son, but it would not cut, and turned upon its side, and just then an unknown voice was heard, saying, 'Thou hast verified thy dream!' and another, bidding him look behind him, and directing him to sacrifice whatever appeared to his sight, in the place of his own child.

"Turning round, Ibrahim perceived a large ram descending the mountain. This ram, it is said, had pastured for forty years in the garden of Paradise (*Jennet*); while others state that it was the same animal that the martyr *Habeel* (Abel, from *Hebele*, or any one taken away by death) had offered up in sacrifice, and which God had preserved for this occurrence. Ibrahim ran after the ram, and so performed the solemnity observed at the present time, called the *Jemreh*, by the pilgrims to the *Ke'beh*, when they throw stones (at the devil), for he also cast stones at the animal as he pursued it. The *Jemreh* of the people of Mohammed (the Prophet) has its origin in this occasion. There are, however, three *Jemrehs*, called the first, second, and third.

"It is related that Ibrahim threw seven stones at the ram, and at the third *Jemreh* he caught it. He then conveyed it to the spot of sacrifices at Mekkeh, called *Minâ*, and prepared to sacrifice it. The angel Gabriel now appeared, and freed the hands and feet of Ismâ'il, and said to him, 'Whatever you may desire to ask of God, ask it now, for this is a holy moment;' and so, raising up his hands, he prayed: 'O Lord of the universe, I implore that Thou wipest away from Thy registers the sins of any of Thy servants about to die who believe in Thee and in Thy unity.'

"When Ibrahim had finished his sacrifice, he came back to his son Ismâ'il, and beheld that the angel Jebrâil had loosed his hands and feet, and learned that he had prayed in behalf of the believing; he was greatly rejoiced, and said to him: 'My son, thou art surely protected and aided by God,' and at the same moment an unknown voice was heard to say: 'O Ibrahim, thou art the truthful of those who speak, and the best of those who are patient; thou art above all trial in temptation; thy devotion is perfect, and under all troubles thou showest submission. I have, therefore, prepared for thee an exalted place in Paradise, and made thy fidelity to be eminent in both worlds; this is the recompense which we give to those who do well' (this latter expression meaning *devotion*), 'for God sees every one, whilst no one is able to see Him. Thou, Ibrahim, art my faithful one (*Khaleel*) and my prophet (*Paighamber*); I have clothed thee with a pre-eminence superior to that of all creation. And thou, Ismâ'il, thou art pure and my prophet (*Resool*); I have made thee eminent above all the world's inhabitants for the purity of thy heart.' Both Ibrahim and Ismâ'il hereon offered up thanks and praises to the Most High for His great goodness, figurative and explicative in nature.

"The historian *Tabaree* states that when Ibrahim heard the voice declare, 'Thou hast verified thy dream,' he was greatly frightened, and trembled, and so let the knife fall from his hand. Jebrâil caught the ram by the ear and brought it with him from Paradise, at the same time exclaiming, '*Allâhu Ekber!*' (God is the greatest of all gods,) and Ibrahim hearing this repeated the *Tekbeer;* for on seeing the ram he cried out, '*Lâ ilâha illâ Allah,*' and '*Allah Ekber*' (there is no God but Allah, and Allah is the greatest). He then added to Ismâ'il: 'My dear son, raise up your head, for the Most High has gladdened our hearts,' which he did, and they both beholding Jebrâil and the ram, exclaimed, '*Allâhu Ekber vè el Hamd*' (Allah is the greatest of gods, and is the praised). In the work entitled the *Menâhij et Tâlibeen,* it is narrated that *Ja'fer es Sâdik* stated that God relieved Ibrahim from the sacrifice of his beloved son through that ram, as a great atonement. Khaleel was deeply afflicted by the Divine command, and God, by inspiration, said to him, 'O Ibrahim, the reason of my preserving Ismâ'il from being sacrificed is, because the Light of the prophetship of that seal of all prophets, Mohammed, was on the brow of that fortunate youth; that all of the prophets, from Adam down to that Seal (Mohammed), should be of his race.' Khaleel prayed to God, and a message was sent to him, by revelation, saying that all of the prophets which he beheld should surely spring from the loins of his son. Among these Ibrahim saw Mohammed 'Alee bin abi Tâlib, and the sons borne to him by the pure Fâtimeh. Ibrahim inquired who it was that he saw near to Mohammed filling so eminent a position, and was informed that it was Hosain, the son of 'Alee bin abi Tâlib, the prophet of the latter times and the light of all the prophets, the son of the daughter of Mohammed Mustafa. 'I have a greater affection,' replied Ibrahim, 'for that figured soul than for Ismâ'il, though the son of my own loins;' and God thereon continued: 'I have accepted of Hosain on account of the devotedness of Ismâ'il.'

"Thus, according to the statement of the Imâm Ja'fer, the great sacrifice was Hosain bin 'Alee, and the ram was figurative of that sacrifice which was to come in after years; for, he remarks with much correctness, what could a simple ram be, that God should call it the Great Sacrifice in the Holy Koran? The second application of this remarkable occurrence is that Adam was the original builder and founder of the *Ke'beh*, that, after his death, Seth (Sheeth) repaired it, and all mankind performed the solemn ceremony of the *Tawâf* (walking round) around it, just as the people of Mohammed do at the present time, on the occasion of their pilgrimage—a duty commanded by the Most High. When the deluge of Noah approached, by God's permission angels descended from heaven, and removed to the summit of the mountains both the Black Stone which Adam brought out of Paradise (*Jennet*), and the other stones which he collected for the *Ke'beh* in the mountains.

"It is related that when Adam became bent with the blows of his disobedience to God (Koran xx. 119) he descended from the Blue Paradise to this world, and for a great length of time wept tears of regret; and in his affliction prayed,—'O Thou who hearest the cries of those who weep, under all circumstances: I no more hear the voices of the angels, and this affliction is greater than all others.' The voice of God was heard saying, 'O Adam! out of regard for thy posterity I have caused a house of joy to descend from heaven to earth, around which always make it your duty to perform the *Tawâf* (or circuit), just as the angels in heaven make circular processions around the Great Arch (or Throne). It is, at this moment, thy duty—even obligatory—to go at once to that house; there let thy heart be free from all other imaginations than those of love and affection for me.' Adam immediately proceeded to the *Ke'beh Allah* (Verse in Persian). 'The pilgrim on the Ke'beh road seeks for a sight of the Divine countenance of Him who is the master of this house.'

"Filled with reflections as he went, he made no less than fifty Farsangs between each of his steps, so that, in this way, he soon passed over a great distance, and, reaching the object of his desires, beheld a house constructed out of one red ruby, the two doors of which were of green emeralds, the one looking to the east, and the other to the west. By Divine command an angel appeared, and taught Adam the ceremonies required at that holy spot. Whilst Adam was thus engaged, the angel showed himself to him, and said, 'O Adam! the Most High has been pleased with your conduct, your performance of the holy *Hajj*, or pilgrimage, and has forgiven your sins.'

"It is said that, on the occasion of the Deluge, the angels conveyed this house up to the heavens; and another narrative relates that after it had subsided a small mound of red earth pointed out its location, around which the people performed the *Tawâf*, on which account the Great Judge of all necessities (God) answered their prayers, until the time when Khaleel (Ibrahim), by Divine command, reconstructed it. In the view of having this pious service remain in the family of Khaleel, God commanded the angel Jebrâil to accompany him from Shâm to Mekkeh, and employ Ismâ'il and his mother on that edifice. Thus both the father and the son, who are the very best of the human race, renewed the foundations of that House of Mercy, and invited all mankind to visit it.

"On Khaleel's arrival at Mekkeh, he found Ismâ'il employed in making arrows, and having made known to him God's commands, he cheerfully accepted them. Ibrahim designed to reconstruct the house in its previous dimensions. He was aware of what these were at the time of Adam; but on this subject there are various accounts, each of which are given in the work called the *Revzet el Ahbâb*, and from all of them it would seem that the angel Jebrâil made them known to Ibrahim. Ismâ'il brought the earth and clay, and his father constructed the House of God; and in this way it reached such lofty dimensions that the latter was no longer able to raise the stones as high as its walls. He therefore had to mount upon a stone for that purpose, and the print of his feet has still remained on it. The stone in question is, at the present time, called the *Makâm i Ibrahim* (a place of Abraham). Upon reaching the elevation of the 'Black Stone,' which the angels had preserved from the effects of the Deluge by conveying it to the summit of the mountain called *Abu Kebees*, they went and brought it thence, and, taking it from them, Ibrahim put it in its place. When this stone first came from *Jennet*, it was whiter than snow or milk, but it has been discoloured by contact with the hands and faces of the disobedient to the Almighty.*

"Another tradition states that when the edifice had reached a certain elevation, Ibrahim bade Ismâ'il bring him a stone of an excellent and agreeable form, which should remain as a sign to the people, and that, though the latter brought one, his father did not like it, and was about departing for another, when he heard a voice saying, 'O Ibrahim! on Mount Abu Kebees there is

* Near the *Ât Maidân*, an ancient hippodrome of Constantinople, there is a small mosque, called "Mehmed Pasha Jamassi," which was originally a Greek church. In this mosque is a fragment of the celebrated *Hajir el Eswad*, or "Black Stone," brought from Mekkeh, and placed here by its founder.

one deposited.' So, proceeding to the spot, he found and brought away, himself, the Black Stone; and as Ismâ'il was absent at the moment, he only learned the facts from his father on his return. On the termination of their work they both prayed to God to bless and accept of their labours, which He was pleased to do. It was then that the angel Jebrâil appeared and taught them the solemnities of the *Tawâf*, of the *Menâsik* (sacrifices), of Mount 'Arafât, the *Remee Jemreh* (casting of the stones), the *Saee* and the *Shayee* (sacred symbols), all of which are *Sunnet* (commanded by the Prophet) to the pilgrims of Mohammedan people, to the present time.

"Before Ibrahim departed from Mekkeh for Shâm, he appointed Ismâ'il to be his *Khaleefeh*, or Caliph (successor), and it is said that he reached the age of 120 years."

THE DECEASE OF IBRAHIM.

By some it is said that, after the death of Sarah, Ibrahim took another wife from the land of Canaan, by whom he had six sons. From these sprang so many individuals as to greatly increase the number of his children and grandchildren, as well as of the tribes. The prophetship, however, remained with Is-hâk and Ismâ'il. Ibrahim became excessively wealthy in flocks and herds. He is supposed to have been the first person whose beard became white with age, a circumstance so much to his surprise as to cause him to ask God, in prayer, the cause of so extraordinary an occurrence, and, in reply, heard that it was a sign of seriousness of mind, and respect. He thereon asked that the former might be increased.

Ibrahim is said also to have asked of God that he might not be required to leave this life before he himself requested it; and that his prayer was granted. Now when the time approached for his departure, the Angel of Death appeared to him, in the shape of an aged man; and when, according to his principles of hospitality, he had food placed before him, he remarked that the hands of his guest trembled very much, so that he was unable to partake of the provisions, and through feebleness, he raised them even to his nose and ears, in place of carrying them to his mouth. Ibrahim, surprised at such a spectacle of human weakness, inquired of the aged man its cause, and was told that it was the consequence of advanced age. He next asked him how old he was, and the old man replied that he calculated his years were even less than those of Ibrahim; the latter thereon observed that there was not much difference between their ages, and he wondered whether or not he would be subject to the same degree of feebleness. "Yes, you will," said the guest; and Ibrahim, after some moments of reflection, having prayed to God to relieve him of this life and its infirmities, the Angel of Death conveyed his soul to Paradise (or *Ferâdees*—the plural of the Arabic noun Ferdoos).

Another tradition is, that, when the Angel of Death (*'Azrâil*) appeared to Ibrahim, the latter asked him whether it was possible for one friend to wish to take away the soul or life of another friend; and that this question having been, by the angel, conveyed to God, he was commanded to reply,—"Is it not natural that a friend should ardently desire to see the face of his friend?" On this, he consented freely to depart, and was buried in the fields of Khairoon, by the side of Sarah.

"In those days, hospitality was much exercised, and not only were the guests treated with great generosity in the houses of their hosts, but were provisioned on their departure. It is narrated, that once Ibrahim entertained an aged individual, whom he conducted to his residence; but, as he ascertained that his guest was an infidel (*Kâffir*), he did not lay before him the choice providences of God, and drove him away. The Most High thereon addressing Ibrahim, said: 'O Ibrahim, this infidel has, for many years, enjoyed my bounties, and yet served idols; and not for even one day have I deprived him of them. How much less, then, does it become you, as my friend and apostle, to cut him off from the use of my mercies?' On hearing this, Ibrahim made haste to follow after the old man, and related to him what he had learnt. The aged infidel was greatly affected, and wept; and having made the reflection that if a sovereign reproaches his own friend for his conduct to his foe, how great must be his goodness to his friends! thereon became a true believer.*

"It is said that ten books were sent down from heaven to Ibrahim, all filled with pious injunctions and wise commands. Of these, the following is one:—'O ye who are the rulers, judges, and sovereigns over the poor, be not misled by the temptations of worldly enjoyments, by those of the body, nor by Satan; I did not select you from the others of my creatures for the purpose of depriving the public of their goods and stores; perhaps you even think that I did so, that you might prevent the helpless from praying to me? Know then that I do not reject the prayers of the poor and the helpless—even if these be infidels.'

"To Ibrahim, it is related, are attributed many of the *Sunnets*, or religious observances, of the present day;" and the same author adds, that "the best of all is that the 'Pride of the Universe' (Mohammed) was a subject of his nation, or community (one of it), and many of his *Sunnets* are now practised in the Mohammedan religious laws."

The preceding suffices to show the connexion which exists between the faith of Abraham and that of Mohammed. The essence of the latter (*Islâm*) is, perfect submission to the will of the Almighty; and of this, the most striking exemplification in the record of man's history is the obedience of Abraham, when he prepared to offer up his own son as a sacrifice to his Creator. This figures largely in the principles of the Bektâshees, as will be seen in the account given of them hereafter.

Regarding the term or expression *Haneefeeya*, the cele-

* This is evidently the origin of Franklin's celebrated story to the French of Paris.

brated "Histoire des Arabes," of Cousin de Perceval, states, that it simply signifies "Orthodoxy, or the religion of Abraham." In the same work (vol. i. p. 323), there is the following:—"'Obaidallah, son of Jahsh, though established at Mekkeh, was not a Koraishite; but on his father's side descended from Asad, son of Khozaima, and belonged to the Koraish tribe through his mother Omaima, the daughter of 'Abd el Mottalib. After fruitless efforts to reach the religion of Abraham, or Orthodoxy (*El Haneefeeya*), he remained in doubt and uncertainty, until Mohammed commenced preaching. It was then that 'Obaidallah decided to recognise Islamism, as the true religion which he sought after. He therefore embraced it, but soon after abjured it, as will be seen elsewhere, to devote himself definitively to Christianity."

He was one of four persons who, on the occasion of the festival of the Arab idols, publicly denounced all participation in such a faith, saying, "Our countrymen walk in a false path, and are far from the religion of Abraham. What is this pretended divinity to which they immolate victims, and around which they make solemn processions? A mute and insensible block of stone, incapable of doing good or evil. Let us seek the true faith of our father Abraham; and to find it, let us, if it be necessary, even wander over foreign lands."

M. de Perceval adds, with regard to the new doctrine proclaimed by Mohammed:—"This was not a new religion which he announced, but the ancient religion of Abraham restored to its primitive purity."

Thus, the researches into the history of the Arabs, by this eminent writer, fully establish the fact that, in the traditional accounts possessed by them of the patriarch Abraham, Mohammed found the basis of his new faith; and that whatever is not clearly of this origin must be sought for in other traditions, drawn from India and Greece; or, as he so repeatedly declares in the Koran, in "Divine Inspiration."

THE "ÂTMBODHA," OR "KNOWLEDGE OF THE SPIRIT."

In the chapter on the *Soofeeism* of the Dervishes, as well as the others relating to them, the reader will find a strong analogy of doctrine with that of the people of India, as shown in the *Vedânta*. An interesting article of the *Journal Asiatique* of Paris (January, 1866), contains much on this subject, clearly showing that the peculiarities of the *Tareekats* have their origin in the writings of the Sanskrit authors; and it may not be amiss to quote some of the more striking of these parables.

Brahma, the chief divinity of the *Vedas*, or sacred writings of India, is the great spirit from which all the others are emanations. He is the source of all the Pantheistic doctrines of the believers in him.

Mîmânsâ is the desire to know, or the "Divine science;" in other words, the contemplative and mystical theology of Brahma. The fundamental idea of the *Vedânta* is that *Brahma* is the Absolute Spirit, and the Pure Being. It is also the doctrine which any one must know and deeply study who desires to aspire to the fourth degree of a religious life,—or who wishes to become *Sannyâsee*, a perfect ascetic. The religion of *Brahma* is too compendious and complicated to be explained in detail, and such is not the object of the present short notice. Indeed, there has been, of late years, so much written on the subject by the philologists of Europe, that it would be presumptuous to do more than refer the reader, for more minute information, to the many interesting works now existing in its various languages. Suffice it to say, that these point out the source and origin of whatever is Pantheistic and mystical in the doctrines of the Dervish *Tareekats*, which are not strictly Mussulman; and that, after penetrating through Northern India into Persia, they have spread over Asia, wherever these sects have been established. It would even seem that the Polytheism of India is the origin of all the fabled gods and goddesses of the people of Northern

Europe. The Pantheism of the one becomes the mythology of the other, shaped into varied forms, dependent upon the climate, the character of the seasons, and the varied productions of nature of each of the degrees of latitude through which it passed. The influence of language over the human mind is greater than at first seems apparent. The *Sanskrit*, a dead language of India, is one particularly adapted for the expression of the most minute details of mystical ideas,—quite without a parallel in the great family of idioms used by mankind. In it the human imagination found an able and willing servant, so capable of photographing—so to speak—the least tangible of its productions, that it in time became the sacred language of India,—that of its books, and not that spoken by its people. India has rivalled Greece in her philosophers—each has had her teachers and her schools, both undirected by Divine Light, though the intuitive reflections of reason and intelligence seem to have penetrated into the remote and misty future which so deeply interests mankind. Their "ancient wisdom" is still the object of the studies of the curious, even in modern times; and the human mind, still fettered and unfreed from the weight of long centuries of slavery in matters of religious faith, is unable to cast off the dogmas of a spiritual and mystical character, which, like the clouds, obscure the light of the One only true Divinity. Mankind deified at one period, is sanctified in another; and both in *Vedantism* and *Soofeeism*, we find the idea carried so far as to declare that the spirit of man, when properly purified by contemplation, religious fervour, and ecstatic love, becomes even that of God, from whom it is declared it is an emanation. Even the most reasonable of the Dervish *Tareekats* hold that by means of a certain form of worship, differing with each one, the creature *approaches* his Creator, and that this is the object of his adorations. His spirit becomes even absorbed in that of the Divinity. The soul is a Divine emanation incorporated in a human form. It exists in five conditions, viz. it is awake, it dreams, it is plunged in slumber, it fills a state of half death, and finally, even perfectly separated from the body. During the third state, it is re-absorbed already in the Divine Spirit. After death, it must pass through several new existences. Virtuous souls occupy spheres superior to that of this world, and enjoy the fruits of their good works, whilst the guilty ones are condemned to fill conditions inferior to that of humanity. The Dervish thus interprets the verse of the Koran lxviii. 18 :—"My people in the eternal life will rise up in companies;" and holds that wicked people who have degraded humanity in this life will live again in the shape of animal existence, to which it has become debased. The final effort of man in the *Vedânta* is his passage to the world of Brahma, when his soul will be delivered from all human ties, and return to its original source and be confounded with his principle. The Dervish, by a series of mental contemplations and fervid efforts, returns to the divine spirit of Allah ;—and even, for example, the *Mevlevee*, as he whirls round, according to the *modus* prescribed by his founder or *Peer*, believes that he is spiritually drawn nearer to God; or the *Rufâ'ee* as he howls the *Zikir* supposes that he becomes holy, and is absorbed in the spirit of the Allah whom he thus invokes. The *Cravana*, *Manana*, and *Nididhyâsana* (condition, meditation, and contemplation), are nothing other than the *Semâ*, *murakebeh*, *Tevedjuh*, and the *Zikr*, of the Dervish *Tareekat*. The *Bodha* of the Brahman is the *'Ilm*, and the *Jnâna* is the *Me'rifet* of the Dervish, without which it is not possible to emancipate and free the soul. The *Bektâshees* believe that God is in all things, and that the soul, after its separation from the human frame, may enter into the body of an animal, for which reason they are unwilling to kill any living creature, lest it contain the soul or spirit of a late human being. This is the principle of the Supreme Master Brahma, who penetrates all things. The *Manas* is the *'Anâsir Erbe'* of Soofeeism, viz. the four great elements of fire, air, earth, and water, which are supposed to compose the body, and constitute the internal faculty of comprehension; whilst the *upâdhi*, or subtile fluid, is the invigorating element of life, different from the *prânâs*, or *breath*, which is known to the

Dervish as the *Neffes*, or *Nefs*, the original emanation from the Creator, and which, after a serious and impressional invocation of Him, becomes so holy. The *'Âlem i Mesâl*, or "world of fancy,"—the *'Âlem i Kheyâl*, the "world of illusion," form an important part of the Brahmanic system. All is said to be transitory in this world—illusory; and there is nothing true and real but *Brahma*, which word, with Soofeeism, is equivalent to *Allah*. "Brahma has no resemblance with the world—nothing really exists but he; if anything else be produced other than he, it is vain and illusory, like the mirage in the desert." "The eye of science (spiritual) contemplates the Living Being (with the Dervish *Hay ve Kayyoom*, the 'Living and the Eternal'); but the eye of ignorance cannot contemplate Him, no more than a blind man can behold the sun." "He who undertakes the pilgrimage of the Spirit, which is in himself, penetrates all, without regard either to the state of the sky, the country, or time; dissipating cold and warmth, securing to himself a perpetual happiness, free from all impurity; frees himself completely from works, becomes omniscient, penetrates all, and is immortal." "He who, renouncing all labour, reaches the state or condition called *paramahansa*, or the ascetic of the last degree, frequents the *teertha* of the Spirit, knows all, in all things through the proper nature of the sovereign Spirit, becomes immortal, viz. absolutely free."

Such is the parallel between the principles of Brahmanism and Soofeeism, and which have evidently become engrafted on the ex-Mussulman systems of some, if not indeed all, of the modern Dervish sects. The *Mantik et Tair* of Fareed ud Deen 'Attar, and the *Mesnevee Shereef* of Jellâl ed Deen er Roomee, furnish much to corroborate the conviction that these Mussulman authors drew their inspiration from the religious reveries of the Hindoos. Even the mystical *Ghazals* of Hafiz are deeply imbued with the same.

CHAPTER II.

ON THE ORIGIN OF THE DERVISH ORDERS.—THE ORIGINAL ORDERS; FORMS OF PRAYER; CAPS, ETC.—TRADITIONS OF THE ORDERS.

THE word *Derwish* or *Dervish* is from the Persian language, and is written درويش. It is composed of two syllables, *Der* and *Vish*. The first, or *Der*, is the same as the English word "door," and has the same signification. *Vish* is probably from the Persian verb *Vihten*, to beg.

Various meanings are assigned to the two syllables taken together. Some say it means the "sill of the door;" others, "those who beg from door to door;" whilst there are many who declare that it signifies "in thought" or "deep meditation," using the *der* as a Persian preposition *in*, and not as a substantive, and the *vish* as "thought."

I am inclined to give to the word the signification now almost universally accepted, which is, "a poor fellow who goes from door to door for assistance." This is evidently the one in use all over the East, in India, Bokhara, Persia, Turkey, Syria, and Egypt,—in fact, wherever this class of people are known; though in those countries where the Arabic language is spoken, Dervishes are known as *Fakeers*, plural *Fukirâ;* and in Turkey the latter is often used, though of course erroneously, in the singular sense.

The Dervishes say that their original orders were twelve in number. They trace back their source as follows:—

Allah (God).
Jebrâil (Angel Gabriel).

Mohammed (the Prophet).
'Alee (the fourth Caliph).
Abu Bekir (the first Caliph).

From the Caliph 'Alee, they say, descended—

Hassan el Bahree.
Marufi Kerhee.
Surayee Sakattee.
Daudee Taee.
Junaydee Bagdadee.
Habeebee 'Ajemee.
Abu Bekir Shiblee.
Abu'l Mubârek Mahzumee.
'Abd ul Kâdir Ghilânee.

And from Abu Bekir, the first Caliph—

Selmânee Fârsee.

The twelve original Orders are:—

1. The Rufâ'ee.
2. The Sa'dee.
3. The Suhraverdee.
4. The Shibânee.
5. The Mevlevee.
6. The Kâdiree.
7. The Nakshibendee.
8. The Vaisee
   (which latter, they say, are *anti*-Mohammed).
9. The Jelvettee.
10. The Khalvettee.
11. The Bedawee.
12. The Dussookee.

The Dervish from whom I derived the preceding is a member of the order of the *Kâdirees;* and as there is much *esprit de corps* and rivalry among the various Orders, he may have been biassed in favour of those whom he placed highest in the list.

'Abd ul Kâdir Ghilânee was the founder of the sect to which my friend and assistant belongs, and I may here add, as a word of information regarding Arabic surnames such as the present, that *'Abd* signifies the *servant; ul* is the Arabic article and preposition, *the* and *of the;* and *Kâdir*, the *Powerful*, which is one of the Islam

attributes of God; so that his name is the "Servant of the Almighty." *Ghilânee* shows that he was a native of the province of Ghilân, in Persia. The Islam names of Mohammed, Ahmed, Mahmood, Mustapha, Ismâil, 'Alee, &c. have each a distinct signification, more or less connected with God, and most Mussulmans have properly two names, though neither are family names in our sense. The Prophet's names were *Mohammed el Mustapha*, or "Mohammed the Chosen."

Ahmed Sa'eed Rufâ'ee was the founder of the Order of the *Rufâ'ees*, generally known among European travellers as the "Howling Dervishes," from their peculiar mode of worship. He was the nephew of 'Abd ul Kâdir Ghilânee, and, therefore, also from the same part of Persia. His own followers considered him peculiarly holy; so much so, that they say he even declared regarding himself, "This foot of mine is over the necks of all the saints of Allah."

Among the *Kâdirees*, the office of *Sheikh*, or Chief of a *Tekkieh* (convent), is hereditary, and descends from father to son; and in case the latter be a minor, the brethren select one of themselves to act for him until he becomes of the age of twenty.

Among the traditions of the Order of the *Kâdirees* I would quote the following, as it sustains the saying of his nephew *Rufâ'ee.*

"It is related that once the daughter of the Prophet of God, Fâtimah, saw in a dream, that a man came out of her father's apartment, holding a large candle in his hand, the light of which extended from the East to the West. She mentioned this to her father, in the presence of her husband 'Alee, who was the nephew of the Prophet. The latter interpreted it, that 'one would come after him ('Alee), whose sanctity would resemble the candle, and be the chief of all saints.' 'Alee exclaimed against this, on the ground that he himself was the chief. 'No,' said the Prophet, 'the one I allude to will have his foot on the neck of all the saints, and all will come under his rule; those who do not bear his feet on their shoulders, and bend before him, will bear bags on their shoulders.' 'Alee would not admit this, and declared that for one he would refuse to bear him. Just then, the Prophet miraculously created a child; and as there was some fruit on a high shelf of the room, he asked 'Alee to reach it down for the child. 'Alee attempted to do it, but was not high enough, and the Prophet placed the child on his ('Alee's) neck, so as to reach the fruit. 'Alee having submitted to this, 'See, see!' exclaimed the Prophet, 'you already bear the person I allude to on your neck.' This child was 'Abd ul Kâdiree himself."

If there be really but twelve original Orders, these have many branches. The principal branches are said to be descended from *Hasan el Basree*, and it is these which are prevalent now in the Ottoman Empire. Some others are from *Selmân i Fârsee*. The *Mevlevees*, the *Nakshibendees*, and the *Bektâshees* are thus said to be descended from *Abu Bekir es Sidik*, the first Caliph. The *Bektâshees* are all deemed to be *Sayyids*, or descendants from the family of the Prophet. The *Tesleem tâsh* (a white stone), worn on their necks, has its origin from Abu Bekir, who, they say, once having used language which gave offence to the Prophet, repented of it, and in memory of his fault fastened a small stone around his neck, and when he came to chapel put it, in the presence of the Prophet, into his mouth to prevent himself from speaking improperly. The *Bektâshees* are all *'Aleeide* (Dervishes).

The *Khalvettees* wear leggings, called *Somâk*, in memory of those worn by the Prophet in the battle of *Bedr i Uhud*, and great care is taken by them not to soil them. They are in the form of boots, and made of black leather.

In the earlier times of the Dervishes, their Orders have names or titles different from those of the present. These were mere explications of their tenets or principles, and it was only at a later period that they took the names of their founders.

I will therefore mention a few of these titles, but refrain from digressing on a part of my subject foreign to the object in view.

1. The *Hulullieh*, or those who, by devout contemplation, became inspired by God.

2. The *Ittihadieh:* or those who deem God ever present, and fill the mind of His worshippers with no other idea than of Himself.

THE HULULLIEH.

3. The *Vusoolieh:* or those who believe that by constant devout contemplation of God they become peculiarly connected with Him, even in the present life.

4. The *'Ashkieh:* or those who keep their minds constantly filled with a devout love for God.

5. The *Telkeenieh:* or those who reach God by prayer, and by the means of constant devotion.

6. The *Zureekieh:* or those who by constant contemplation of their founder, or their immediate *Sheikh*, enter into his spirit, and dwell with it.

7. The *Wahdettieh:* or those who constantly contemplate the unity of God.

I have much endeavoured to find a sensible cause for the peculiar forms prescribed by the founders of the various Orders of prayers and costumes, but without success. Some wear caps of peculiar shapes, many made up of gores, or sections, called by the Dervishes *Terk*, a word signifying *abandon*, varying in number in different Orders. For instance, whilst the *Bektâshees* wear five or seven *Terks*, the *Nakshibendees* have eighteen. Some of their caps bear inscriptions, mostly verses of the Koran, and some are made in the shape of a rose. Others wear a turban of black, white, or green colour. The colour of their mantles also varies. They have a variety of prayers, though generally these are the same as those of all other Mussulmans, and are followed by one for the Prophet, his family, and friends, their founder, and the reigning sovereign. In fact, I have only been able to learn that they all owe their origin to the will of their founder, called by them the *Peer*, a Persian name signifying *Elder*. To some of their customs and parts of their dresses also a miraculous origin is assigned, which, I do not doubt, is perfectly satisfactory to themselves.

Some of them stand upright when performing the *Zikir*, or "call upon the name of Allah;" others sit; some form a circle, and put their hands on the shoulders of their companions to the right and left, and shake their bodies forward and aft, to the right and to the left, their animation and excitement increasing as the ceremony proceeds. Some cry out the *Zikir* with a loud voice, as also the Mussulman "Confession of Faith" (*Lâ ilâha illâ Allah ve Mohammed Resool Allah*), "There is no God but Allah (*the God*), and Mohammed is *the* prophet of Allah;" whilst others, like, the *Mevlevees* (called by travellers from Europe the Dancing or Turning Dervishes), move round in a *quasi*-mystic circle, in profound silence, mentally reciting the same. I have been told that the custom of these latter refers to the harmonious movement of the universe, and that the soft music of their order is symbolic of that of the spheres; but I am inclined to doubt it.

These two distinctions of *vocative* and *contemplative* Dervishes are said to refer to the command of the Prophet to Abu Bekir, the first caliph, whilst concealed together in a cave, "to recite the *Zikir* in silence," so as not to be heard by their pursuers; and to 'Alee, the fourth caliph, when he inquired of him what he ought to do so as to receive Divine assistance—"to call loudly God's name without ceasing."

All of these forms of worship are of Mohammedan origin, whilst many of the principles of the Orders date back to a much more remote period, and may be therefore designated as *Soofeeism*, of which more will be said hereafter.

As a general rule, no Dervish who has not been the *Sheikh* (chief or master) of a *Tekkieh*, can wear a turban folded round his cap. The turban is called *Sarik*, *Imâmeh*, and *Destâr*. A *Sheikh* may, however, name a large number of *Khaleefehs*, or " deputies" (successors), all of whom can wear the turban around their caps. These are consequently considered as honorary *Sheikhs*, or masters. The cap is called by most of the orders *Kulah*.

The *Rufâ'ees* wear twelve *Terks*, and the colour of the Sheikh's turban is black. They perform the *Zikir* standing upright. The hall in which they worship is called the *Serheed Khâneh*.

MEVLEVEE.

The *Mevlevees* wear a tall white or yellowish cap, without any *Terks*, and the colour of the *Sheikhs'* turban is green, because these are generally *Sayyids*, or descendants of the Prophet. As afore-stated, they perform their prayers standing upright, and in silence, turning round from east to west. On Sunday and Friday they perform a prayer called the *Ismi Jellâl*, seated in a circle,

1,001 times. This prayer is simply the word *Allah.* Their hall is called the *Sem' Khâneh.*

MEVLEVEE.

The *Kâdirees* wear four *Terks* in their cap, embroidered. Their *Sheikhs* have each seven *Terks*, and the colour of their cap is white if they be not *Sayyids.* They move round the hall standing upright, their hands placed on the shoulders of their neighbours. Their hall is called the *Terheed Khâneh.*

The *Bedavees* have twelve *Terks* in their cap; the colour is red, and they perform their religious exercises like the *Rufâ'ees.* Their hall is also called the *Terheed Khâneh.*

The *Dusookees* have no *Terks;* the colour is white, and they perform on foot.

The *Sa'dees* have twelve *Terks;* they wear turbans of a yellowish colour, and perform on foot.

The *Khalvettees* have no *Terks* in their *Kulah*, or cap; it is, however, divided into four angles; the colour is white, yellow, green, or other, and they pray on foot.

The *Nakshibendees* have four *Terks;* colour generally white, though they may wear any other: the cap is always embroidered, and originally contained a verse of the Koran. They perform seated a prayer called the

NAKSHIBENDEE.

Ikhlâs 1,001 times. One remarkable peculiarity of this order is, that when they assemble to perform this prayer they divide among their number 1,001 pebbles; and as each one recites an *Ikhlâs*, he lays down in the circle one of these as evidence of the fact, until all are recited.

The *Jelvettees* wear twelve *Terks:* the colour of their cap is green, and all may wear turbans. They perform on their knees the *Zikir* and the *Ismi Jellâl.*

The *Hamzâvees*, or otherwise called the *Melâmeeyoons*, have no distinction of costume, cap, nor belt. They all perform seated, and in silence, contemplating the Divine Spirit, and seeking for *Noor*, or "Divine Light."

The *Bairâmees*, *Sha'bânees*, &c. all are like the *Khalvetees.*

The *Bektâshees* have four and twelve *Terks;* their colour is white and green. They have no special form of prayer, nor position; but it is said that they perform like the *Nakshibendees.*

Some say that there are as many as sixty different Orders of Dervishes, and others even a hundred, each bearing the name of its founder. It would scarcely repay one the trouble to endeavour to enumerate them, and their shades of difference. In the Order of the *Bektâshees*, there are branches from the original stock, some more pantheistic than the others, and I presume that the same may be said of some of the other Orders. A few have been prohibited at Constantinople, such as the *Bektâshees*, on account of their too intimate connexion with the Janissaries; though, at the present time, they are not molested. They do not generally bear a good reputation, and are said to be quite atheistic, and not much attached to the principle of the Koran, nor firm believers in the prophetic mission of Mohammed. They generally are warm *'Aleeides*, or followers of the Caliph *'Alee*, and are therefore *Soofeeists*, or "Islam Spiritualists," which will be alluded to later in this work.

I am not aware that any one has written either a history or an account of the various Mussulman religious orders known under the title of *Dervishes*. The subject seems to be one of an original character, and interesting to the public, and especially to the travellers in the East, who have no means of acquiring any information regarding a class of individuals whose forms of worship strike their curiosity.

The difficulty which lies in the way of collecting facts respecting the Dervish orders will be apparent to Oriental students, and indeed I feel that I have been presumptuous in venturing to assume so serious a task. To all things there is, however, a beginning, and, though my humble sketches may appear imperfect, nevertheless they will serve as a nucleus to the labours of those who succeed me.

I have endeavoured to obtain my information from the most authentic sources within my reach, both oral and written, as well as printed. To offer a criticism on the belief of my Mussulman friends (for among the Dervishes of Constantinople I have several estimable and valued friends), to draw comparisons between what may be called the religious superstitions of Mohammedanism and

Christianity, forms no part of my plan. The enlightened reader is left to draw his own conclusions thereon, and to receive whatever impressions, favourable or unfavourable, which the recital may make upon his mind.

It has been thought by some persons that Freemasonry existed among the Mussulmans of Constantinople under another title, and consequently in other parts of the East. This I do not find to be the case, though, like in most secret fraternities, there may be points of resemblance accidentally. I have had an indirect intercourse with a Mussulman, who asserted that Freemasonry does exist there, and he gave even a list of the places in which lodges were held in various parts of the Empire, adding that the Grand Lodge existed on the Lake of Tiberias, in Palestine, where it had been taken after the destruction of Jerusalem. It must, therefore, have existed, and does still exist, among the Jews. I regret to have to state that, notwithstanding all my researches to verify this declaration, I have not found any trace of the fact on which I could rely. My opportunities of inquiry here have been numerous, and my desire to meet with brethren amongst Mussulmans led me to use all proper zeal in the pursuit of this desirable object. Others may, perhaps, meet with more success. The title by which, it is said, Mussulman Freemasons are known is *Melâmeeyoon;* and, when I come to speak of this order of Mussulman Dervishes of the 'Aleeide sect, the reader may judge how far the statement is incorrect.

I may here add that there are a few Mussulmans of my acquaintance, some of them in high official positions, who have become Masons in Europe, mostly in France. There are also others who belong to lodges in Constantinople and other cities of the Ottoman Empire, and there are many lodges in India, to which Hindoo Mussulmans belong.

It is rather strange that the Dervishes of the *Bektâshee* order consider themselves quite the same as the Freemasons, and are disposed to fraternize with them. The name of Freemasonry in the Turkish language is *Fermâson,* and is one of great reproach. It signifies atheism of the most condemnable character, and this may be said of the *Bektâshees*, who, from some reason or other not quite clear to me, are held in small repute among other Mussulmans, even those belonging to the other Dervish orders. No one in Constantinople may consider himself at all complimented when he is called a "Fermâson" or a "Bektâshee," no more than a Protestant is when called a *Methodist* by a devout Catholic, or a *Voltairean* by an ordinary Christian.

Inspired with the most laudable desire to withdraw his people of Arabia from the worship of idols, Mohammed proclaimed to them the adoration of an Universal Deity, the Creator of all things, and a perfect resignation to His Divine will.

This Deity must have been already well known in Arabia, previous to the advent of Mohammed as a prophet, under the name of *Allah;* a word most probably derived from the Hebrew of *Elohim.* It is composed of two Arabic words, *al*, the article *the*, and *lah* or *Alah*, which together is now written *Allah*. It is formed in Arabic of only four letters, *A*, *l*, *l*, *h*, called four mystical letters, marking in a peculiar manner the Divine Essence.

I need no more than remind the reader that the Arabic language is derived from the Hebrew, and that it is a Semitic tongue. It is therefore composed of radical letters, two, three, or four of which forming all the words of the language, under certain grammatical rules.

The definition which Mohammed gave to this Deity, when interrogated thereon by the Jews and Christians, the Magi, and other idolaters, is seen in one of the chapters of the Koran—the book containing his inspirations—and called the *Ikhlâs*, or the "most pure." He there says:—

"It is that God, who is unique, self-existing, from whom all creatures receive their existence; who does not beget, nor was begotten; and who has no equal amongst all that exists."

The latter part of this definition shows that he understood the Christians of Syria and Arabia as believing in more than one God. Whether or not the nature of the Trinity was ever properly explained to him, cannot now be ascertained, but it is clearly seen that it was unsatisfactory to him ; so much so, that during the whole of his career he condemned, in the strongest terms, the Trinity, as a system of false religion, as much to be avoided as the worship of fire and of idols. He denominates the Christians in the Koran as *Mushrikeen*, or those who associate others with God. The idolaters he calls *Sanâim*, or those who actually worship idols made by the hand of man.

This comprises all that he had in view to combat or refute in other religions, and it has thus been explained by an eminent writer on his faith :—

"The God whom I adore, and who should be adored by all, is a unique Deity, simple in His essence, and separated from all other beings by attributes peculiar to Himself. He is self-existing, and has no need of anything for His existence ; and all things exist by Him. He does not beget (this is against the opinion of the Jews, who believe that 'Ozair or Esdras was the son of God) ; He was not begotten (which is against the Christians, who believe that Jesus Christ, born of the Virgin Mary, is the Son of God, and is God), and that He has no equal (which replies to the Magi of Persia, followers of Zoroaster and Manes, and believers in the two equal principles of power—Oromasdes and Ahriman—the Good and Evil Spirits and Deities ; as well as against the Arabian idolaters, who sustained that there were certain spirits called the *Benau Hasha*, which were the companions and associates of God)."

This God he declared to be without beginning or end, and so far superior to His creatures that no one could have any conception of His immensity. Though His power and essence pervades every part of His creation, He is wholly invisible to ordinary mortal eyes, and His power and magnitude can only be comprehended by witnessing His works. One eminent writer says, "All that the mind, the sense, and the imagination of man can fancy regarding Him, be it ever so solid, falls at once before His majesty." Another declares, "Do not fatigue yourself with any ideal conceptions of Him, for it is all a useless labour." A celebrated Mussulman writer says it is impossible to form any idea of God, because He is superior to all comparisons, and there are no terms of human language which can convey any idea of His magnitude. 'Alee, the fourth Caliph, who among the Arabs was a man of much education, and served as an amanuensis for the Prophet, whose daughter he married, is said to have observed that "he who knows himself knows God;" and the same idea is confirmed in the words,—

"Thy soul is a cunning proof, and an invincible argument, of the existence of God.

"By reflection thou knowest thyself, thou knowest that thy existence is the work, and that there must be a worker."

Another states,—

"The existence of God being the same as His essence, know then that thy being, which receives its existence from Him, is the proof of thy existence."

The Founder of the Order of the *Mevlevees*, and the author of a celebrated mystical work, called the *Methnevee Shereef*, says:—

"To what purpose are all the efforts of the human mind to comprehend that Being who is above all combination, all distinction?

"He is a tree without branches or body, or roots, to which the mind can be attached.

"He is an enigma for which no natural nor metaphysical meaning can be found; nor of whom a satisfactory explanation can be given.

"Who has ever found in His existence any mystical, symbolical, or demonstrative comparison?

"He is infinitely above the capacity of our understanding—of our imagination; and we lose ourselves in vain conjectures whenever we seek to comprehend Him, or even to suspect what He is.

"It is, therefore, in vain for us to seek for words by

which to discuss properly His being. All that we may do is to adore Him in respectful silence."

In the view of still further explaining what Mohammed understood by *Allah*, I may be permitted to add that the unity of God is alluded to in the 89th chapter of the Koran, where God is said to have sworn by the *pair* and *impair;* the first are His creatures, and the second Himself; and one of its verses says,—"We have created all things double; but we say that God is one and unique."

A Persian writer states that no one should say *I*, because that property belongs alone to God; and a Turkish proverb adds that—"Whoever, other than God, says *I*, is a Satan; because he who says *I* must be a demon; for none but God can use that word with truthfulness, as all things came from Him, all are in Him, and obey Him. He only is self-existent."

A pious Mussulman, and an author of celebrity, used to declare,—"When I say *God*, I have said all things; for all else is but folly, or the fancy of foolish desires."

Another states,—"Since my heart is turned towards God, speak to me of nothing else than Him."

Allah is therefore defined as Omniscient and Omnipotent, and pervades all His creation. It is not held that He is in any particular place. I would, nevertheless, express my conviction that Mohammed was not pantheistic, in the modern sense, and much less that he believed in the modern metempsychosis. He, however, believed that the spirit of man was of a Divine origin, but made a wide distinction between the life which all creation enjoys, and the breath of life possessed by human beings. In this sense a writer tells us as a tradition, that Moses having asked of God where He was, he received the reply, "Know that when you seek for me you have already found me."

It is related that an Arab of the desert being asked how he knew there was a God, answered :—

"By the same by which I know from the traces in the sand that a man or an animal has passed over it. Is not the heaven decked with its bright stars, the earth with its fertile fields, the sea with its numerous waves sufficient proofs of the existence and the greatness of a Creator?"

Another child of the desert, in reply to a similar question, said:—

"Is there any kind of a torch to behold the brightness of the Aurora?"

And, to a companion who had met with a serious misfortune against which his own cares were unavailable, he said:—

"There is no other recourse or refuge from God than in Him."

In the Dervish acceptation of *Allah*, He is their All in all. To think of Him at all times, to contemplate His majesty and power, and to call upon His name for aid and succour during their mortal existence; to adore and worship Him in the most devout manner, and thereby increase their own sanctity and consequent spiritual power,—is the basis of all their belief. They consider it highly meritorious to pronounce audibly, or mentally,

His holy name most frequently, and even go so far as to strive to do this in a short space of time. If any one can call upon the name of *Allah* a hundred times in a minute, it is held to be still more meritorious to do so double that number of times in the same period of time. They believe that God, or *Allah*, will, and does, manifest Himself to the devout worshipper in a special manner whilst so occupied, and that around the heart a Divine light, or *Noor*, is shed in answer to his frequent calls. Also that the word *Allah* becomes distinctly impressed upon the heart in letters visible to the spiritual eyes of the devotee.

The faith or religion which Mohammed proclaimed to his brethren of Arabia he called the *Deen el Islâm*, or the obligation of perfect submission to the Divine will and decrees of *Allah*. He considered the word *Deen* to be the only true and correct faith, the right path leading to eternal happiness.

The word *Islâm* is fruitful in definitions, all derived from the same radical letters, *s*, *l*, *m*, *Salama*, among which is *Salâm*, "compliment" or "salutation," and peace; and *Salâmet*, salutation or safety. From it also is framed the past participle, *Moslem*, and its plural, a noun of multitude, *Musalmân*, and the feminine noun, *Moslimeh*, all signifying those whose faith is a belief in Divine decrees, and humble submission to the will of *Allah*.

The author of the *Methnevee Shereef* afore-mentioned says :—

"In whatever place we may be, we are, Lord, subject to Thy commands; be we wherever we may, we are always with Thee. We say to ourselves, 'Perhaps we may find a path leading elsewhere.' How vain is this idea, for all paths lead ever to Thee."

The opening chapter of the Koran commences, "Lead us, O Lord, in the right path," that is, in the true path of *Islâm;* and in the chapter called *An'am*, the Lord says, "This is the true path, follow it, and seek none other, for they will mislead you."

This mention of a *Path* is evidently the origin and

basis of the paths (*Târikât*) of the Dervishes. I mention them as Orders, or Sects, but the proper and correct term is *Paths*. All these are different pathways leading to the same *Allah*, just as an Oriental poet says, "Though we may each look out of different windows, we all see the same one great sun, source of light and warmth."

In the chapter of the Koran called "Ibrâheem," there is the following :—

"Religion is like unto a tree—like the palm-tree, the roots of which are in the depths of the ground, and its branches raised towards heaven, and which, by Divine order, gives fruit in its time. On the contrary, impiety is a wicked plant, like the coloquint, which is out of the ground, for it is easily pulled up on account of possessing no roots to sustain it."

An Islam author says there are four kinds of persons who serve God :—"The wise through a spirit of obedience, the penitent through fear, the devout through desire, and the just from a sincere love for Him."

In one of the chapters of the Koran it is forbidden to compel any one to abandon his own faith for that of *Islâm*; but in another, produced at a later period of the Prophet's mission, it is ordered that war should be carried on against all those who did not believe in it—the Jews, Christians, Magi, and Sabeans,—either to compel them to embrace it, or pay him (Mohammed) tribute as a temporal sovereign.

So intimately is an account of the Dervishes connected with the history of Mohammed, the prophet of the Arabs, and now of the whole Mussulman world, that some particular allusion to him seems to me here necessary. No one can peruse the Koran without being impressed with a high estimate of his character as a religious reformer and a law-giver, especially when they remember him only as a *camel-driver* (the title of reproach generally given to him by Christian writers). How different his origin and early history when compared to that of Moses, who was brought up at the court of Pharaoh, among the learned and wise of Egypt! All Mussulmans say that he could neither read nor write, and we have no knowledge of his early education in any religion whatever, much less in the deeply spiritual principles which appear in the Koran. Under these circumstances, it is but common justice to admit that he was certainly a very extraordinary *man;* indeed one of the most remarkable that the world has upon its records. When arrived at an age when man can feel and judge for himself, he was fully impressed with the deeply seated conviction that he was specially designed by the Creator of the Universe to reform his brethren the Arabs, and withdraw them from the most absurd belief in the power of idols, the work of human ingenuity, and lead them to the worship of one only God. This conviction he entertained to his last hour, and he never presumed to ascribe to himself any other character than a *Resool*, or envoy of Allah to call the misled into the true path. We call him a *Prophet*, signifying one inspired by God, and the question is open only as to his inspiration. With the convictions which he fully entertained of the errors of a Christian faith in a Trinity, and of the Arabs in the worship of their idols, his intentions were salutary, honest, and benevolent; and we are led to ask whence he received these impressions, these impulsions, to do good, if not from the great Source of all good designs? To plead for him a want of education, of a more intimate and correct acquaintance with the contents of the Old and New Testament, is to admit the falsity of his inspiration, for it is proper to suppose that God would have supplied this deficiency in a prophet.

We must, therefore, take him as he was,—an Arab, an uneducated man, a strong-minded human being, gifted with an extraordinary intellect, and of a strength of will and purpose which sustained him through an eventful career. Still the weaknesses of humanity were strong in him: he had many of the frailties of the flesh, and was filled with a strong ambition to carry out what he had designed to effect. He showed much ability in managing the various people upon whom he wished to exert an influence for their own spiritual good, and he stood perfectly alone in the opening of his career. That he succeeded in correcting their abuses, and withdrawing them from their idols, cannot be denied; and his religious principles are still honoured by a vast portion of the human race in Asia, Africa, and Europe. There are reflections in the Koran which would do honour to an educated theologian, and his followers are taught to expect only his intercession as a saint in heaven with the *Allah* whom he himself adored and worshipped. Although many of the Arabs of his time possessed much mental ability—many of them were even poets—they possessed no literature, and had but small means of extending and perpetuating knowledge. Thrown at an early age upon his own resources, Mohammed evidently acted upon principles of honesty and uprightness, and it has never been shown that he deviated from them, or abused the confidence of his employer, who subsequently married him. He grew up to manhood, possessing the respect of all of his acquaintances and relatives, and it is only a matter of surprise that, knowing the value and utility of letters, he never applied himself to learn them. As a merchant he is said to have made several journeys into Syria. During these he became acquainted with the Christianity of the Greeks and the faith of the Jews. His unfavourable impressions of the former are seen from his continual condemnation of it in the Koran. He probably visited their churches, and witnessed the reverence paid there to the images of the saints of the Greeks; he there learned the doctrine of the Trinity, without, however, being able to comprehend it, and in his own conscience denounced both as unworthy of his respect.

There is no reason to believe that Mohammed received any religious instruction either from the Jews or the Christians. The Arabs doubtlessly possessed a knowledge of the Old and New Testaments, especially of the former, and many traditions regarding the earlier history of mankind, some of which differ widely from the accounts given in the Bible. Few copies of the New Testament must have existed among them, judging from the little allusion to any of its characters by the Koran.

Mohammed's innumerable mystical and philosophical reasonings are totally distinct from the writings of those who composed the Bible. The story that he procured the Biblical knowledge which is comprised in the Koran from a Jew is too baseless for belief, and evidences its origin in the malice and hatred of the earlier denunciators of his faith. There is really no proof existing to show that the Koran is due to any other source than his own inspiration; and whatever it contains of good or evil must, therefore, be attributed to no one else than himself.

Mohammed does not reject either the Old Testament or the New. He believed in the Prophets who preceded him, and that those who were so directed left each his own book. Whatever in their books did not agree with the information possessed by him, he attributed to the perversion of more recent copyists. As to the New Testament of the Christians, it would seem that he believed these had perverted its original contents on important points, and so made Jesus Christ to say many things regarding Himself which are not true. This has led many Mussulmans to believe that there exists another New Testament, containing none of the changes introduced, they say, by modern Christians, and I do not doubt but that they really entertain this conviction.

Mohammed declared that Jesus Christ was of a miraculous origin—that he was born of a virgin, and that he was both a Prophet and the "Spirit of God," *Rooh Allah*, yet he denies in strong terms that He is God. He says, moreover, that Christ foretold his coming when He said, "I will send a Comforter," &c. This appears in the chapter of the Koran called *Saf*, when Christ says to the Jews, "O children of Israel! I am He whom God has sent to verify and accomplish all that has been revealed before me in the law of Moses, and to announce another envoy who is to come after me, and who will bear the name of *Ahmed*."

Mohammed declares himself to be the *last* of the Prophets, and that his mission is the *seal* of all those who preceded him. In the third chapter of the Koran it is said that the angel Gabriel was sent to Mary to announce to her, "God announces to you His *word* (*Kelâmet*, or Word), whose name will be Christ, or Messiah Jesus, and who will be your Son, worthy of all respect in this world and in the other."

Again, it is stated therein, "O Mary, God has elevated, purified, and very particularly chosen you among all the women in the world. O Mary, submit to your Lord; prostrate yourself before Him, and worship Him with all those other creatures who adore Him. This is a great secret which I reveal to you."

In another chapter, called the *Nesâ*, are these words: "The Messiah is Jesus, Son of Mary, the Envoy of God, His *word*, which He announced to Mary, and the same Jesus is the *Spirit* proceeding from Him."

By the word *Spirit* an eminent Oriental author says is meant, "He is endowed with a 'Spirit,' which proceeded immediately from God, without the medium of any other cause."

In the chapter last alluded to there is the following statement, which shows that Mohammed considered the Messiah in the light only of one of God's creatures, and not as God Himself:—"The Messiah does not disdain to be and to call Himself the Servant of God, as do the angels, the nearest to Him."

Mohammed commenced proclaiming his mission in the fortieth year of his age. His inspirations were retained in his memory, and, long after they were forgotten by those to whom he delivered them orally, he not unfrequently renewed them, showing thereby the great strength of his memory. They were, however, written down by his son-in-law and nephew, 'Alee, and by 'Othmân, both of whom became caliphs, or vicars of his mission, after his death. Thus the Koran was only completed in twenty-three years. The elegant construction of the Koran, its perfect grammatical formation, and the almost poetical beauties which it contains, have always been the admiration of its readers; and though in prose, it is susceptible of an intonation which almost amounts to a rhythmical measure.

science called *'Ilmi Remel*, or of sand, and by cabalistic calculations, generally of the numerical value of the letters forming the name of the party interested. The four elements, *Anâsir i Erb'a*,—viz. Fire, Air, Earth, and Water,—are also consulted, to ascertain which of them predominates in the person's system; this found, a *Nuskha*, or charm, is written out and delivered to the applicant. One of these four elements is supposed to be destroyed by the others, and the one which predominates in the system to its injury must be got rid of. The *Nuskhas* are composed of verses from the Koran, to which is connected a belief of peculiar power in especial cases, and are hung about the necks. When the verses are not from the Koran, they are the original handwritings of certain holy men of high repute. One kind of such writings is called *Istakhâreh*, and are placed under the pillow to influence the dreams of the sleeper. They even are supposed to be the cause of visits from benevolent spirits to the sufferer, or the troubled in mind, and to respond to the wishes of the applicant.

These persons are likewise often seen manipulating the faces, heads, shoulders, and arms of invalids, and, after praying over them, blow in their faces, or gently breathe upon the limbs affected. The invocation of the names of Allah has, it is supposed in such cases, sanctified his breath, and enabled him to exercise a salutary effect upon the sufferer.

CHAPTER IV.

TRANSLATION OF A TRACT ON THE COSTUMES AND TENETS OF THE DERVISHES.

RESPECTING the costumes and tenets of the *Tareeks*, or Orders of the Dervishes, the earliest mention is found made by *'Abdallah Ansâree*, a faithful friend and companion of the blessed Prophet, on the occasion of his flight from Mekkeh to Medineh.

By this person it is related that Mohammed Bâkir, the fifth Imâm, and a successor as well as a descendant of 'Alee, the fourth direct caliph, gave the name of *Irshad i Kisveh*, or Robe of Uprightness, to one of the garments worn at this period by pious and holy men; and that Ja'fer Sâdik, the sixth Imâm, also a lineal descendant of the same 'Alee, and son of Mohammed Bâkir, gave the name of *Erkiân i Evliâ*, to those good men who wore that garment. For the correctness of this relation, however, we can only place our trust in Allah.

The perfect *Murshids*, or Superiors, of Dervish *Tekkiehs*, or convents, were bound to make this known to the *Erkiân i Evliâ*, or "Columns of Saints;" and to their youthful disciples the *Mureeds*, they should point their appropriate places in the *Tekkiehs*, and explain to them how to wear, and the meaning of, their *Tâj*, or cap, and their *Khirka*, or mantle. They should only put them on after having been invested by the *Erkiân i 'Ain*, or Elders of the *Tekkieh*, so that the use of them would be legitimate. Should the latter be ignorant of this knowledge, the *Murshid* must expose them as impostors; and, in that case, to intercede for them is a crime equal to blasphemy.

On being publicly selected as the *Murshid* of a *Tek-*

or "God's Law as revealed by His Prophet;" the second signifies the *Tareekat*, or "Path of the Order;" the third signifies the *Ma'rifet*, or "Knowledge of God." The three together are a sign that their acquisition has bestowed the Hâl, or condition, known as the *Hakeekat*, or "Truth." The holy word *Hay*, or "The Living God," manifested to one Sheikh, has for its colour *green*, and for this reason the rose is made on cloth of that colour. The circles are white, and the reason is that this same is a sign of perfect submission to the Sheikh, according to the traditional words of the Prophet, "The Divine law is my word; the path is my acts (practices); the Knowledge is the chief of all things; and the Truth is my condition." Whoever knows these secrets must assume the disposition of the moral laws of God, and the character of the Divine nature. The blessings which will accompany him in eternal life are those of everlasting felicity and never-ending aid.

"The axis of the Lord, the Sheikh Ismâ'il er Roomee, —may God bless to him his secret!—was originally of the Khalvettees. In a dream or vision, he became the *Khaleefeh* or successor of 'Abd ul Kâdir Ghilânee. He adopted this rose as a sign of the seven Names of God, and their branches. The seven colours adopted by him are emblems of the *Envârs*, or Lights of these same seven Names; its eighteen *Terks*, or gores, are emblems of the eighteen numeral values of the two letters of the Arabic word *H*, *y*, or the Living (God). The roses given to the Sheikhs of the Order have nineteen *Terks*, emblems of the letters of the *Bismillah Shereef* and *Jennet el Esmâ* (used as *Nuskhas* or charms). In its centre is the *Muhur i Soleemân* (Soliman's seal), the *Belief of the Unknown*, which has six letters, *S*, *l*, *i*, *m*, *a*, *n*, signifying that the holy Sheikhs are blessed with six peculiar qualifications, viz.—*S* means freedom from all defect; *L*, gentleness of disposition; *Y*, the power of spiritual vision; *M*, familiarity with his companions; *A*, the pious character of praying at midnight; *N*, that his prayers and his rectitude all belong to God. This latter he calls the *Na'bidu Nesta'een*, a part of the fourth verse of the first chapter of the Koran,—'Thee do we worship, and of Thee do we ask assistance.'"

The same writer adds, on the subject of the mystical Rose of the Order of the Kâdirees, that "He who reposes in the cradle of Divine pardon, the Sultan of Sheikhs, Eshreefzâdeh Roomee,—may Allah bless his secret!—states,—'The emblems of the Most High, comprised in said rose, are as follows: There are three series of leaves; the first has five leaves; *H*, *y*, *a*, *z*, refer to the five virtues, which he said belong to the followers of Islamism. The second series has six leaves, emblems of the six characteristics of Faith; and the third series has seven leaves, referring to the holy crown — that mother of the Koran—*i.e.* the seven verses of the *Fâtiha*, or first verse of the Koran. The full number, eighteen, all allude to the circumstance that the blessed Prophet brought mercy to eighteen different worlds. It has four colours, yellow, white, red, and black, all chosen from other roses, signifying the same as aforesaid, Holy Law, the *Tareekât* (Paths), knowledge, and truth. In the centre are the seven petals, all alluding to the seven names of Allah. The entire rose must be embroidered on felt of camel's hair, in reference to the felt mantle (Hirkah) presented by the blessed Prophet to that Sultan of faithful lovers, *Vais el Korânee.* The green cord surrounding the rose is an emblem of the one living God.'"

The description is followed by a prayer, of which this is a translation:—

"Bless us, O Lord, with Thy blessings in both worlds. Amen. O Thou, who art the blessed of all the blest; Thou best of all aiders—on whom be the Divine satisfaction!—our Lord and Master, Mohammed, who created the rose (Al Verd) by his own knowledge,—on his family and companions, give peace to them on the Great Day of Judgment,—to all the prophets, those sent from God,—the saints,—the pure in heart,—the martyrs,—and those who follow in the right path; and raise us up with them all, through Thy great mercy."

The copyist calls himself,—"The *Fakeer*, the *Hakeer*,

was this same *Mehdee*, and that, having disappeared in a mysterious manner, he will reappear in some new form hereafter.

Not satisfied with the contents of the Koran, his followers, soon after his decease, collected all of his sayings together, under the title of *Hadeethât*, or traditions, which have now a value in their eyes almost equal to the verses of that book. They were collected, not only from the mouths of his immediate friends and companions, the *Ansârs* and the *As-hâbs*, but from others, who declare that they heard them maintain them as coming from the Prophet.

The friends of 'Alee have also collected his sayings, independent of the remarks made by the Prophet, and they hold them in high estimation. I cannot see in them anything peculiarly mystical, or even religious, so as to warrant him to be placed in the elevated position assigned to him by the 'Aleeide Dervishes. The following are a few of his sayings :—" I am a servant of whoever has taught me one letter." "A secret known to ten persons is no longer a secret." "Benefit your offspring with the blessings of learning." "Any service ever written is perpetuated." "When you are troubled by worldly affairs, remember the pleasure existing between ease and difficulty."

In concluding the present chapter, I will add that the earlier commentators on the Koran deduced from it the laws and precepts which still form the basis of Mussulman jurisprudence. They are comprised in a small work entitled the *Multikâ*. These were—*Hanefee*, born in Koofa, A.H. 80, and died in prison at Bagdad, in A.H. 150; *Shâfee'*, born at Ghaza, in Palestine, A.H. 150, and died in Egypt, A.H. 204; *Han Bellee*, born in A.H. 164, at Bagdad, and died there in A.H. 241; and *Malekee*, born at Medineh, A.H. 95, and died at the same place A.H. 179.

Each has his advocates and followers, who differ from each other quite as much as do the Dervish Orders.

CHAPTER III.

An author of much celebrity for his Oriental studies (Von Hammer) says, in reference to the Dervish Orders, that "the tombs of the Sheikhs and Dervishes who have acquired a certain celebrity by the foundation of an Order, or by the sanctity of their lives, are not less important in the Ottoman Empire than those of heroes and conquerors.

"During the reign of the Sultan 'Othmân, these Islam monks formed a community more powerful and redoubtable than that latterly of the '*Ulemâ*, or Doctors of Holy Law. 'No monks in Islamism,' an expression of the Prophet which should have been sufficient to prevent all innovations and imitations of the monachæism of the Hindoos and the Greeks; but the natural disposition of the Arabs for a solitary and contemplative life caused them soon to forget this precept, and the other phrase of the Koran, 'Poverty is my pride,' was the argument which, thirty years after the death of the Prophet, is that on which his sectarians based the origin of their numerous monasteries; since the Order of Fakeers (poor) and of Dervishes (sills of the door) so multiplied in Arabia, Turkey, and Persia, that they reached the number of seventy-two, exclusive of an equal number of heretic sects."

The following are the names which this writer gives to the *Tareeks*, or Orders existing previous to the foundation of the Ottoman Empire:—

1. Uwais.
2. Olwanee.
3. Edhemee.
4. Bestainee.
5. Sakettee.
6. Kâdiree.
7. Rufâ'ee.
8. Noorbakshee, or Suherwerdee.
9. Kubrawee.
10. Shadallee.
11. Mevlevee.
12. Bedâwee.

After the foundation of the Empire, there were the

13. Nakshibendee.
14. Sa'dee.
15. Bektâshee.
16. Khalwettee.
17. Sainee.
18. Babayee.
19. Bairâmee.
20. Eshrefee.
21. Waifayee.
22. Sunbullee.
23. Gulchennee.
24. Yagitbashee.
25. Ummee Sinannee.
26. Jelvettee.
27. Ushakee.
28. Shemsee.
29. Sinan Ummee.
30. Neyazee.
31. Muradee.
32. Nooreddeenee.
33. Jemâlee.
34. Eshrakee.
35. Ni'metullâhee.
36. Haidaree.

Of the thirty-six Orders, twelve are anterior to the foundation of the Ottoman Empire; the twenty-four others have been instituted since the commencement of the fourteenth century, down to the middle of the fifteenth. The first, viz. the Nakshibendees, was founded by 'Othmân, in A.D. 1319, and the Jemâlees under Ahmed III. in A.D. 1750.

KHALWETTEE.

Thirty-seven years after the "Flight," or "Emigration" (*Hejrah*) of the Prophet, the Archangel Gabriâl or Jebrâil appeared to Uwais, a native of Karu, in Yemin, and commanded him in the name of the Lord to renounce the world, and to devote himself to a life of penitence. In honour of the Prophet, who had lost two teeth in the battle of Ohod, Uwais had all of his teeth extracted, and required the same sacrifice of his disciples, from which it may be readily understood that he made few proselytes among the fanatics of Arabia. The Sheikhs Olwan, Ibrahim Edhem, Bayazid of Bestain, and Sirree Saketty, followed the example of Uwais, and founded the Orders which took their names, giving them the several rules of discipline. The most celebrated of these religious persons is the Peer of the Kâdirees, named 'Abd ul Kâdir Ghilânee, who had been proposed as guardian of the tomb of the great Imâm Abu Haneefeh of Bagdad. After the decease of 'Abd ul Kâdir his mausoleum was surrounded by those of the most renowned mystical Sheikhs. These tombs are those of Junaid, Shublee, Hasan Kerhee, Hosain Mansoor, Sirree Sakettee, and others. Of the most celebrated followers of 'Abd ul Kâdir are Juwaid of Bagdad, Abu Bekir Shublee, and the great mystical writers Muhee ed Deen al 'Arabee and Sadr ed Deen of Kaniah in Asia Minor. These tombs have given rise to the name of the "City of Saints," possessed by Bagdad, and, no doubt, to the religious fanaticism of its inhabitants. Bagdad has always been the object of the veneration of Mussulmans in general, and the various Dervishes in particular, and these often wander from Constantinople through Syria or Asia Minor, to pray over the tombs of the pious and holy men whose remains are there interred.

The Order of the *Rufâ'ees*, named after the founder, *Sa'eed Ahmed Rufâ'ee*, is the most generally known to the foreigners visiting Constantinople. The members of this sect offer the spectacle of the most startling self-torture; they perform acts of jugglery, such as swallowing swords and fire, expose parts of their body to the flames, dance in the most grotesque positions, and frightfully contort their limbs. The lives of these recall the ancient Etruscan priests of the sun, mentioned in the eleventh chapter of the Æneid, and twenty-eighth verse.

BRANCHES OF THE ORIGINAL ORDERS OF DERVISHES AT CONSTANTINOPLE.

Of the twelve original Orders there are a number of branches called *Ferru'*, at Constantinople, whose the *Kitmeer* (or dog of the seven sleepers) of the gate of the Sultan of the saints who dwell by the rivulets of Paradise—a Kâdiree Dervish."

The founder of the Order of the Kâdirees, the Sheikh 'Abd ul Kâdir Ghilânee, represents the *Etvâr i Seb'a*, or Seven Paths, as the following:—

"There are seven names of Allah which the brethren pronounce when performing the *Zkir*,—

"1. Lâ illâhé ill' Ullah. (There is no God but Allah.) Its light is blue, and must be recited 100,000 times, and has its own peculiar prayer.

"2. Allah, called the *Ismi Jeleel*, or 'beauteous name.' Its colour is yellow; it must be recited 78,586 times, and has its peculiar prayer. He says that after reciting it that number of times, he himself saw its Light.

"3. *Ismi Hoo.* (His name.) Its light is red, and number 44,630, and has its peculiar prayer.

"4. *Ismi Hay.* (Name of the Eternal.) Its light is white, and number 20,092.

"5. *Wâhid.* (The one God.) Its light is green, and number 93,420.

"6. *'Azeez.* (The dear or precious God.) Its light is black, and number 74,644.

"7. *Vedood.* (The loving God.) It has no light, and its number is 30,202."

It formerly was the rule that no one should be made a Sheikh until he had recited these names of the Deity according to their numbers, but it is now disregarded. After becoming a Sheikh, he must recite the following branches, called Ferru', viz.:—

"*Hakk*, or the Just.
"*Kâher*, or the Avenging.
"*Kayyoom*, or the Everlasting.
"*Vahhâb*, or the Giving.
"*Mahâmin*, or the Protecting.
"*Bâsit*, or the Extending God."

A young Mussulman friend informs me that when he desired to join the Order of the Kâdirees, he had already been in the habit of attending at one of their *Tekkiehs*, or convents,—the same to which he now belongs. He was then twenty-two years of age. Any one, he explained, can be admitted at eighteen. The Sheikh of the convent had a *Dèddé*, or old man, his servant, also a Dervish. To this person he had made known his intention, and he had promised to mention it to the Sheikh. "One day the latter called me into his private room, and directed me to perform two *Rik'âts* or genuflexions, and to recite the *Istaghfâr*, or Prayer of Pardon, one hundred times, as also the *Sallât i Salâm*, or prayer to the Prophet for his intercession, the same number of times, and then be attentive to what I should behold in my dreams. I did this that same night, and then lay down to sleep, when I dreamed that all the brethren of the *Tekkieh* had assembled in it, and were performing the *Zikr*, I amongst them. They led an individual to the Sheikh, who put an *Arrakieh*, or felt cap, on his head; they next did the same to another person, and then led me to the Sheikh. I said to the person who conducted me, that I already had become a Dervish. Not satisfied with my assertion, he persisted in leading me on, and the Sheikh having put the same cap on me, made me a Dervish.

"On the following morning, after performing my prayers, I went to the Sheikh, and told him my dream. He directed me to procure an *'Arakieh*, and having put it on my head, I truly became a Dervish, in the presence of the whole fraternity,—they all performing the *Tekbeer*, in which he joined.

"The Sheikh now presented me with a copy of the *Evrad*, or Litany of the *Peer*, or founder of the Order, and directed me to read it. It was the one usually used by all of the fraternity,—especially during the 'holy nights.' I next performed the usual prayers, such as the *Zikr*, &c. and used the *Tesbeeh*, or Rosary; and, whenever I had a dream, told it to my Sheikh, who directed me to recite such or such prayers, indicated by the nature of the dreams.

"I remained thus for five years. The number is not fixed for the *Mureed*, or neophyte, as this part of his career depends upon his ability, and the nature of his dreams. At the close of that time, the Sheikh gave me

"The Sheikh next offers the following prayer, called the *Istighfâr*, or for 'Pardon:'—

"'I beseech Thee, O Great God, to pardon me, Thou, like whom there is none other; I repent of my sins to Him; I ask of Him to pardon me, and accept of my repentance; to lead me in the true path; and to have mercy on all those who repent of their sins.'

"After this—

"'Accept my oath of fealty, or the same oath which the Prophet of God administered to the *As-hâbs* (Companions) of his mission.'

"The Sheikh next resuming his instructions, bids the Mureed—

"'All Mussulmans are bound to offer up their devotions, to give alms, to give religious advice, not to believe in any association with God (Father, Son, and Holy Ghost), not to drink wine, not to waste their means, not to commit adultery, not to kill for food what God has forbidden, and not to calumniate any one. I command you now to observe these as implicitly as the dead body is submissive to the hands of the one who prepares it for interment. Rebel not against what you know has been commanded thee of God, nor commit what is forbidden. Make no innovations in your prayers, commit no sins, and distinguish between the wrong and the true path, and that which leads to salvation. Bear your Sheikh ever in mind, in this world and in the other. The Prophet is our prophet, and the Sheikh 'Abd ul Kâdir Ghilânee is our *Peer;* the oath of fealty is the oath of God; this hand is the hand of the Sheikh 'Abd ul Kâdir, and the Director of the True Path is in your hand.'

"The Sheikh adds:

"'I am the Sheikh of 'Abd ul Kâdir; I accepted this hand from him, and now with it accept of you as one of his disciples.'

"The Mureed rejoins:

"'And I also accept of you as such.'

"The Sheikh responds:

"'I therefore do now admit you.'

"The Sheikh next pronounces the *Zikr*, which the

Mureed repeats after him three times. The Sheikh next bids him recite the *Fâtiha*, which he does with the Sheikh, together with a prayer for the Prophet, called the *Salât i Salâm*. The Mureed kisses the hand of the Sheikh, which act is called the *Musâfaha*, and does the same to all of the Dervishes present. The Sheikh now offers up a prayer (the *Istighfâr*) for the pardon of the sins of the new disciple, and, addressing the company, adds :—

"'The acceptance of this initiation by the Mureed is a source of future advantage to him ; the Prayer which we have offered up for him is for the submission of his body to his Spiritual Will, just as when the Angels, before addressing the Creator, prostrate themselves humbly before Him. So, in like manner, has he, by his acceptance of this *Bai'at*, submitted to my rule. Our Sheikh has said : It is not proper for the Sheikh to sit in the *post* of pillage, nor to gird on the sword of benevolence, until he becomes qualified by the following twelve qualities :—

"'1. The qualities of Allah (each having two).
"'2. Those of the Prophet ditto.
"'3. Those of Abu Bekir (Caliph) ditto.
"'4. Those of the Caliph 'Omar ditto.
"'5. Those of the Caliph 'Othmân ditto.
"'6. Those of the Caliph 'Alee ditto.

"'The qualities of Allah are to cover up and forgive.

"'Those of the Prophet to intercede and accompany.

"'Those of Abu Bekir, truthfulness and benevolence.

"'Those of 'Omar, to command and forbid.

"'Those of 'Othmân, to feed the poor, and to pray when others sleep.

"'Those of 'Alee, to be knowing and brave.

"'If these qualities be not possessed by the Sheikh, he is unworthy of the submission of the Mureed, and the public needs to have recognised them in him. You must follow under his banner when he does ; and if he does not, Satan has made him his friend, and he will not participate in the benefits of this life, or the one to come. It is related of the blessed Prophet, that when a Sheikh gives spiritual individuals depend upon their favour; for if they do not favour them, unexpected obstacles will arise to frustrate them.

Besides the preceding, there are other spiritual beings, called the *Abdâls*, people whose intellects are supposed by the public to be weak, and that they are even maniacs of a harmless character. Many of these are in this world, where they often exercise a strong influence, though unknown in their true character. Their number is limited to seventy, and they succeed to the forty *Rijâl el Ghaïb*. There are also eighty others, called the *Nukebâ* (plural of *Nakeeb*), or magistrates, who succeed to the seventy, and are all taken from the most worthy of mankind.

ABDÂL.

There have been, and it is supposed still are, many persons bearing the title of *Abdâls*, though it is not known with any degree of certainty whether or not they belong to the seventy. These are sometimes to be seen in the public streets, wandering about in a state of nudity—or nearly so—and seem to be idiots. Others possess all their faculties, and are very intelligent, but retire from the ordinary intercourse with mankind, and live on mountains, in caves, and other deserted places, cultivating intimacy with wild beasts, over which they exert a remarkable spiritual power, so as to render them perfectly harmless; and they are much revered for their sanctity. There were several celebrated Abdâls in Asia Minor during the earlier Ottoman sultans.

WANDERING DERVISHES.

The Dervishes whom one meets in Constantinople and throughout the East, generally dressed either peculiarly or shabbily, and wearing either a tiger or leopard's skin over their shoulders, and bearing a cup, called *Keshkool*, in their hand, are from India and Bokhara. They are not always Dervishes, but are simply *Fakeers*, or men who prefer to remain poor and miserable than to devote themselves to an honest calling. They are supposed to have abandoned the pleasures and attractions of the world, and to be totally divested of all human ambition, for the love of God. Sometimes, if questioned as to the object of their vagabond life, they represent that they are, in the fulfilment of a vow, visiting certain holy tombs, and spend much of their time in prayer and meditation. Many of them, however, belong to the orders of the *Keshtees* and *Suherverdees*, and those from Bokhara to the Nakshibendees and Kâdirees. Beggary is forbidden in nearly all of the orders. Some of these pious Dervishes go as far as Hungary to visit the tomb of a Santon, named *Gûl Bâbâ*.

The Kalenders are not an Order. One of the Dervishes of the *Kâdirees* was named *Shehbâz i Kalenderee*, as also another of the *Mevlevees*, called *Shems ed Deen Tabreezee Kalenderee*. Those who carry with them a crooked horn, called the *Liffer*, and call out *Yâ! Vidood*, belong to the Order of the *Bektâshees*.

There are still another class, supposed by many to be Dervishes, but who are not so. They are known in Constantinople by the name of *Khavâsjeelar*. These may be seen sitting in small shops, often dressed somewhat like Dervishes, and wearing green turbans. They are *Diviners*, and tell where lost objects may be found, how the affections of erring husbands may be restored to their wives, &c. The drawings on an open hand, stuck up in the windows, represent the hand of the Prophet, in which are written *Âyats*, or verses of the Koran. Their divinations are made by means of the

The word Koran is from the Arabic radical *k*, *r*, *a*, to read, and, conformably with the grammar of that language, the object read is *Kur-ân*, or otherwise a "book." Mohammed declared that its contents, in the form of inspirations, commenced descending from heaven, under the charge of the angel Gabriel, during the moon or month of Ramazân, in the night called the *Lailet el Kader*, or the "Night of Power." It has always been the subject of discussion among pious Mussulmans, whether or not the *Koran* was created, or emanated directly from God, and this especially during the times of the Abbaside caliphs. His own son-in-law, 'Alee, believed that it was created like any other of God's creations, and, having acted as the Prophet's amanuensis in writing it out, he ought to know best.

After Mohammed's death, the chapters and verses of the Koran were much dispersed, and Abu Bekir, the first caliph, had them collected in one volume, which he named the *Mashâf*, a title still used by many when alluding to it. There are seven original copies mentioned by its commentators,—two made at Medinah, one at Mekkeh, one at Koofa, one at Bassora, and one in Syria, and another called the *Vulgate*. That made by Abu Bekir is considered the primitive, and was referred to for corrections by others. The Caliph 'Othmân copied it off himself, and so did the Caliph 'Alee (the original), aided, however, by another friend of the Prophet. Several chapters were abrogated, and these now form a volume into which they have been collected, called the *Mensuhat* (or "the Abrogated"), one of which, a Dervish friend assures me, is now in the library of the Royal Mosque of Sultan Bayazid of Constantinople. There are also other copies of it in existence,—one at Bassorah ; and it would be worthy of translation into one of the European languages.

Mohammed died without any male heir. It is uncertain whether he had any desire to form a dynasty. He was evidently warmly attached to his son-in-law and nephew, 'Alee, the fourth of the direct caliphs or vicars of his mission. The regular caliphs were Abu Bekir, 'Omar,

'Othmân, and 'Alee, called the *Khulafâ Râshideen*, or the direct or regular caliphs. They were all elected by the Moslems of Medineh, and were men of great mental abilities,—of simple and frugal habits, and worthy to follow their illustrious Prophet, and carry out the principles which he had inculcated.

Oriental writers represent that 'Alee aspired to become the successor of his uncle, and there is no room to doubt but that such would have been satisfactory to his deceased relative, to whom he had rendered the most confidential and important services, both with his pen and his sword. But republics are apt to forget the claims of their great men to their suffrages, and popular favour is often carried away by the current of events, and to be bestowed upon those who neither expect nor merit it. Eminent men are allowed by them to descend to their graves in disappointment, too often carrying with them even the memory of their great deeds, and, in the hour of peril and misfortune, these cry out, like the blood of Abel from the ground, to the hearts of their countrymen, who thus neglected them whilst living. So it was with 'Alee, and the wrong done to him still divides the Mussulman world into two distinct sections. Most of the Dervishes, however, are '*Aleeides*, who, as will be shown hereafter, revere his memory, as well as deplore his fate.

The most influential members of the citizens of Medineh were the *Ansârs*, or those who had been the faithful "assistants" of the Prophet. The widow of the Prophet also still resided there, named *Â'yisha*, and her influence was very great among the devoted followers of her late husband. This lady was the daughter of the second caliph, 'Omar. It is worthy of remark that the Prophet, as well as his direct successors, had Christian and idolatrous servants in their service, and that it is nowhere mentioned that any violence was ever used to induce them to become Moslems.

The Dervishes declare that the Prophet designed 'Alee as his successor, and they attach a mystical signification to the intimate connexion which existed between them. They say, that the Prophet on many occasions declared,—

kieh, the guide of a painful career, and the depositary of all the secrets and traditions of his Order, he must hold the following discourse :—

"Brethren! Ye who are designed to become in eternal life the heads of the Assembly of the Believers in the blessed Prophet, and of the Water Carriers of the fountain of *Kevser*, the blessed martyr 'Alee,—elevate the standard of your Order in every seat, and in the Council of Heaven. Be careful, above all things, to learn who are impostors, and who are genuine members of your Order, so that none but the latter be found amongst you."

He must inquire for his duties of the most eminent *Khalâfats*, or Vicars of the Order, and so become fully acquainted with its chief secrets. In the eyes of the All-Just poverty is preferable to worldly advantage. He will cause him to drink of the waters of *Selsebil* and *Kevser*; put on him apparel made of the satin and silk of Paradise, and enjoy the delightful pleasures of the *Hoorees* and Gholâms of eternal Paradise—intoxicated with the delights of that exalted abode.

As to the *Muklids*, or impostors, the Prophet of Allah has said, "They shall suffer anxious desires for this world and for eternity." Yet, through the grace of God, and by faith in the Prophet, they shall also be shown favour and spiritual direction. The impostor is one who is not known to the good *Murshid;* this latter has never taken him by the hand, and he is one who does not follow the commands of the *Erkiân i 'Ain*, or superior officers of the Order, who do not die spiritually before their physical death, and who only wear the rags of indigence for personal gratification. Of such, it has been said, "They die before the close of their lives."

THE HOLY MANTLE OF THE PROPHET.

It is said that the holy Prophet had a particular friend, named *Owais*, to whom he commanded that his mantle should be given. This mantle is made of a coarse woollen material. It is a long robe, with a collar, and wide sleeves reaching low beneath the knees.

This person was much beloved of the Prophet; and when the latter had a tooth knocked out in a battle with the Arabs, Owais had all of his, thirty-two in number, pulled out in token of sympathy for the loss sustained by the Prophet. He felt no pain from the operation. On this occasion God caused to grow in Arabia a fruit called *Mooss*, until then unknown, as a provision for Owais.

The charge of this mantle has ever since remained in the family of Owais, and a descendant of his, now a youth (A.D. 1860), and consequently a minor, has charge of it at Constantinople. Until he reaches the age of puberty, a *Vekeel*, or deputy, appointed by the Sultan, as caliph, acts for him. Once a year it is carried in procession to the Old Seraglio, where it is exhibited to a few select Mussulmans, and, after receiving their adorations, is replaced in its particular building.

The mantles of the Dervish Orders are all symbols of that of the Prophet.

THE "KULAHS," OR DERVISH CAPS.

Before the present world existed there is said to have been a spiritual world, called in the Arabic tongue *'Alemi Ervâh*, or "World of Spirits." In the same belief a soul is considered as being a *Noor*, or "Light," without body or substance.

The soul of Mohammed, the blessed Prophet, is said to have already existed in that world of spirits, and the Creator there placed it in a vase also made of light, in the form adopted by the Dervishes, especially those of the Order of the *Mevlevees*, for their *Kulah*, or cap. It therefore is held to be of a Divine origin. As aforestated, the *Kulah* is made of a certain number of gores, called *Terk*, each signifying a sin abandoned, and the last one is called the *Terk i Terk*, or the abandonment of all sins. The *Kâdirees* wear a rose in their cap, embroidered, to which they attach the following legendary history, translated from a Turkish MS. :—

"O ye who pursue the path of the *Kâdirees!* O nightingale of the rose-garden of the path of the *Eshrifiehs!* Have ye made choice of the meaning of the rose of our Order, known throughout the land of Fars (Persia) as the *Gul*, a rose?

"Know ye that every *Tareek*, or path, has its particular sign, and that of the noble *Kâdiree* is the rose, the origin and colours of which have thus been explained by the great Sheikhs and *'Âshiks* of our Order. May they be visited with the especial favour of Allah!

"The present humble Dervish, *Ibrâheem el Eshremee el Kâdiree*, was once in the service of the beloved Sheikh *'Alee el Vâhidee el Kâdiree*, the 'Axis of the Lord,' the 'Centre of the Eternal,' the 'Bestower of the Cup of Him who bestows light,' the 'Splendour of Evidence,' the '*Ke'beh* (*Caaba*) of the glorious Eternal.' The Sheikh el Sa'eed 'Abd ul Kâdiree Ghilânee was directed by *Khizir* (Elias) to proceed to Bagdad. On his arrival there, the Sheikh sent him a cup filled with water, the meaning of which was that the city of Bagdad was full of holy people, and that it contained no place for him. This occurred during the winter season, and no flowers were in bloom. The Sheikh put a rose in the cup, signifying that Bagdad would afford a place for him. Seeing this, all present exclaimed, 'The Sheikh is our rose,' and going to meet him they conducted him to the city, and showed him marked respect. This is the real origin of the rose of the *Kâdirees*.

"So far as I know, our Sheikh performed the following unusual acts through the power of the All-Just. He descended from the family of the blessed Prophet, of whom it is related that he once called his two grandsons, Hasan and Hosain, his 'two eyes' and his 'two roses,' and it is to his connexion with the Prophet that we must ascribe his power to produce, miraculously, a rose. How great should, therefore, be the love and respect of his disciples! Suliman Effendi, in his work on the *Mevlad*, or birth of the blessed Prophet, has the following verse in relation to the Sheikh *Kâdiree*:—

> " 'Whenever he perspired, each drop became a rose.
> Each drop, as it fell, was gathered as a treasure.'

" The rose of the Sheikh is therefore a sign of the Prophet himself, like in the proverb:—'The son is the secret of his father.'

" On the death of my Sheikh 'Alee al Wâhidee, his successor was Eschref Zâdeh, a follower of 'Abd ul Kâdir. One night, whilst in my cell after sunset, employed in reciting the *Zikr*, the rose of my Order came into my mind, and I reflected that there was a difference between the roses of Bagdad and Stambool, and I tried to comprehend the cause. By divine favour it became clear to me. I thought why the Eschrefees have no rose, and suddenly the form of one appeared before me. After terminating my prayers, I hastened to trace out its shape, and decided in my own mind that it should be their rose. I wrote out also some of its secrets, and drew the colours of various roses, and named my little work, 'The Resâlah of the Gulâbâd' (Treatise of the Home of the Rose).

> " 'The rose on the head honours the wearer,
> It points to the path of Kâdir Ghilânee.' "

The word *Gul*, or rose, is written in the Oriental characters with only two letters, named *Kaf* and *Lam*, or *K* and *L*. These are the first letters of the two lines of the verse of the Koran (thirty-seventh verse of the thirty-ninth chapter):—" Is not God above all to protect His servant? The infidels will seek to alarm thee with the idols: but he whom God leads astray will never more find a guide to the true path. God is full of goodness towards His servants; He gives food to whom He wishes; He is strong and powerful."

The form of the rose of Bagdad is as follows:—It has two outside and two inside rings, and three circles, and is made of green cloth. The first circle signifies *Shir'at*,

"I am the House, and 'Alee is my Door." They ascribe to 'Alee all that is metaphysical in their faith,—that is, *mystical* and *spiritual*, and some go so far as to declare him superior in this respect even to the Prophet. The warmer devotees of Soofeeism call him *'Alee el Ilâhee*, or "'Alee, the Divine."

On the decease of 'Omar, the Moslems were again called upon to elect his successor, and their choice fell upon 'Othmân, though 'Alee still refused to waive what he considered to be his right. Seeing, however, the will of the people, he acquiesced in their decision, and paid homage to his more fortunate rival. His partisans were greatly disappointed, and, aided by the widow of the Prophet, fermented trouble to the new caliph. Now commenced the first dissensions amongst Moslems, which have had so direful an effect upon their political and religious career. It is not improbable that differences of interpretation had now also begun on passages of the Koran, and that sectarianism had its origin at this early period.

On the final succession of 'Alee, the fourth caliph, he began his administration by removing from office all those who had been appointed by his predecessor, without any regard to their past eminent services, elevated characters, and distinguished qualifications. This he did, contrary to the advice of his friends and the wiser of the citizens of Medineh, who saw, in such a course, the seeds of future party strife, as well as disregard of the welfare of the whole community, by men ambitious only of attaining to power, so as to punish others for the wrongs done to themselves.

The sad fate of 'Alee is well known to most readers of Eastern history. He, and nearly all of his family, were put to death by an Arab general named Mu'âvieh, who seized upon the caliphat without asking to be elected to it. This violence is the origin of the present two Islam sections, the *Shee'as* and the *Sunnees*, as well as their varied subdivisions — among which are the Dervish Orders.

It seems to me necessary to add a few remarks on the

personal character of the Caliph 'Alee, with whose history is connected so much that is interesting in an account of the Dervish Orders. It is, however, desired to limit them, as much as possible, to his position as a seceder from the original principles of the Prophet. His biography is so made up by them of the marvellous and the incredible, that it rivals the position assumed by the Prophet himself, and strongly conflicts with his own remarks concerning him. If but a small portion of what they relate about him be correct, the Prophet would certainly have clearly stated his desire for him to succeed him, and even proclaimed him as such previous to his decease.

'Alee is my *beau idéal* of the most chivalrous of warriors in the times of the Prophet, who, in consequence of his valour, called him the "Lion of God," and his sword, the gift of the Prophet, is revered throughout the Islam world under the name of *Zil farkain*. In the coat of arms of the Shah of Persia, a lion is seen holding a sword in his paw, in memory of 'Alee. The Prophet is said to have, on one important occasion, wrapped his own mantle around himself and 'Alee, and declared that they were one spirit.

On another occasion he is said to have declared—"'Alee is for me, and I am for him; he is to me what Aaron was to Moses; I am the city in which all knowledge is contained, and 'Alee is its portal."

It is from among the descendants of 'Alee that the more devout Moslems expect the *Mehdee*, who is to reappear on earth in company with the Prophet Elias, on the second coming of Christ. This belief is connected with the partisans of the metempsychosis,—among whom the most prominent of the Dervish Orders are the *Bektâshees*.

The *Shee'a* Moslems reject the caliphats of Abu Bekir, 'Omar, and 'Othmân, and commence directly with that of 'Alee, whom they call the first *Imâm*. After him are eleven others, completing the full number of twelve,—the last being the *Mehdee* afore-mentioned. The Druses declare that the founder of their religion, *Hâkim bi Emr Illah*,

Peers or Founders are buried there; among these are the *Sunbullees*, at Khoja Mustapha Pasha, and at Psamatia.

The *Erdebellees*, between the gates of the city, Topkappu and Selivria Kassussu, on the roadside.

The *Ummee Sinan*, at the Mosque of Eyub, in the quarter of the *Dukmajilar*.

The *Ushakees*, at *Kâsim Pasha*, and the valley of *Uzun Yolda*.

The *Hudayees*, or *Jelvettees*, at Scutari.

The *Kâdirees*, at Topkhaneh, and the name of the Peer was Ismâ'il er Roomee.

The *Mellamiyuns* have a sheikh at Psamatia now living. Once a year they go to the *Oke Madan* above the Navy Yard, to the grave of *Idreesee Muhtâfee*, where a sheikh meets them. They have also another at Scutari who, it is said, never goes out of his premises. They are now called *Hamzavees*. They pray over the graves of the "Holy Dead." It may be here mentioned that Mussulmans in general pray at the tomb of those whom they repute Saints (Evliâ), and implore their intercession in their own behalf. If at an ordinary grave, it is for the benefit of the soul of the deceased, the place and actual condition of which is unknown to the prayer. If the deceased, however, be in Paradise, the prayer is conveyed as an offering to the happy soul from the prayers; if it be in hell, it aids it out of that place of punishment.

There is a *Hadeeth*, or traditional saying, of the Prophet to this effect: "If your hearts be oppressed with sorrow, go, seek consolation at the graves of the holy dead." Many of the *Tekkehs* of the Dervishes are erected at, or even over, the tombs of eminently pious sheikhs, or other holy men. Their remains offer additional attraction to the public. Great care is taken of them, and much respect evinced for them by the costly shawls and embroidered cloths spread over the tombs, wholly irrespective of the civil or official position which the deceased may have occupied. Lamps are kept burning before them, as an emblem of the spiritual light which they shed around them, and vows are offered up at them by passers-by or visitors, called *Nezer*, in the view of procuring relief through their saintly intercession, from sickness, misfortune, sterility, &c. With each vow a common rag is tied on the iron bars of the tomb, as an earnest of the vow. Miraculous results are declared to have occurred at these tombs, quite equal to those of the greater Christian saints. Lights are often seen to float over them, or to lead to them, and the living holy sheikhs, by means of their spiritual powers of vision, acquired by long meditation and prayer, often are enabled to discover the graves of deceased holy men, long after they have been lost to human knowledge.

PECULIAR TITLES GIVEN TO THE FOUNDERS OF SOME OF THE ORDERS OF DERVISHES.

Kâdirees.—'Abd ul Kâdir Ghilânee is called the "Sultan el Evliâ," or the Sovereign of the Saints.

Mevlevees.—Ahmed er Rufâ'ee is called "Abu el 'Âlemain," or the Parent of the Two Worlds, which alludes to the temporal and spiritual worlds.

Bedâwees.—Ahmed el Bedâwee is called "Abu 'l 'Ainain," the Parent or Father of the Two Sources, in reference to his connexion with the two original Orders of 'Alee and Abu Bekir.

Sa'dees, or *Jebâwees.*—Sa'd ed Deen el Jebâwee is called "Abu 'l Futooh," or the Father of Victims.

Doosakees. — Ibrâheem ed Doosakee is called the "Sheikh ul 'Arab," or the Sheikh of the Arabs.

THE "SÂHIB I TESÂRRUF," OR "SPIRITUAL OWNERS" OF THE DERVISHES.

"I left Medineh," so related to me one of my Dervish friends, "and went to the *Meshhed i Ullâ*, or the Holy Tomb of the fourth Caliph 'Alee ; I remained there three days, visiting and performing my prayers over it. I had read in a work called the *Tabakât i Shervalee*, mention of those the *Bai'at*, or giving of the hand in a peculiar manner, viz. his right hand clasped in mine, with the two thumbs raised up against each other. He bade me also repeat after him the tenth verse of the forty-eighth chapter of the Koran, as follows :—'Verily, they who give thee their hand, and take an oath of fidelity, swear it to God; the hand of God is upon their hands; and whoever violates such an oath, does it to his own hurt; and unto him who keeps it faithfully will be given a magnificent recompense.'

"I truly believe," he added, "that I have frequently seen the *Peer* of my Order in my dreams. Spirits see each other, though not with the eyes; we may see, in our dreams, persons whom we have never seen in our lives, and know them distinctly. I have never seen, once, the portrait of my *Peer*, and yet I would know his portrait among a thousand others, in consequence of having seen him so often in my visions. I fully believe in dreams; they all have a meaning. For instance, if one dreams that he becomes rich in worldly stores, it means that his prayers will be accepted in the other life; and if he dreams that he has fallen in filth, it signifies that he will eventually become wealthy. To dream that any one has received base and vile treatment from another, signifies that he will receive great benefits from the same person."

My friend related the following to me :—

"In the year of the Hejra 1268 (A.D. 1851), I left Constantinople with a brother of my own Order for Egypt, by steamer, intending to visit the two Holy Cities (Mekkeh and Medineh). This was done, on the recommendation of our Sheikh, in consequence of a dream which both of us had seen, in which we clearly and distinctly beheld the blessed Prophet of Islamism. I still retain a vivid impression of his appearance, dressed as an Arab, wearing a mantle over his shoulders, and of a thoughtful and deeply intelligent countenance. He looked at me with a stern, though pleasing gaze, and then gradually disappeared from my sight.

"We took goods with us for sale, and from Alexandria

and Cairo went to Suez, whence we sailed for Jidda. From this place we travelled to Mekkeh, and performed the pilgrimage. We next went to Medineh, and remained there three years, opening a shop for the sale of our goods. We left Medineh for Bagdad, with Ben Rashee, an Arab Sheikh of the Jebbel Shemmar tribe. He was also the Emeer, or commander of the *Hajjees*, or pilgrims, who had come from Bagdad, the most of whom were Persians on their way to the Holy Cities. Such pilgrims hire camels of the Sheikh to come and return; and he makes much money from such persons in the following manner. On reaching a spring of water in the desert, he encamps, and tells his pilgrims that he cannot proceed farther without purchasing the right of passage from a neighbouring tribe, which threatens to rob them unless a certain sum is made up by the company for it. We all expected this, and accordingly were prepared for it; the sum was collected, but the Sheikh kept it for his own use. We had with us food for ninety days. We finally reached the country of the Sheikh, called *Nejd*, famous for its fine breed of horses. It is a fine, fruitful land, very cold in winter, and having an abundance of water. I reached Bagdad in some ninety days, and remained there three years, in the *Tekkieh* of my own Order, where is the tomb of our *Peer*, 'Abd ul Kâdir Ghilânee. We did not engage in any business, but lived on the bounty of the *Nakeeb*, or Sheikh of the *Tekkieh*, who is a lineal descendant of our *Peer*. From thence, we returned to Constantinople, through Kerkoot, Mosul, Dyarbekir, Urfa, Halep, and Escanderoon, where we took ship for Stambool.

"When I was at *Kerkoot*, in the province of Shehrazor, near to Mosul, I visited a *Tekkieh* of the Kâdiree Order, for the purpose of seeing a Sheikh of much repute, and great spiritual powers. The Sheikh presided over the *Tekkieh* in question.

"When I reached the *Tekkieh*, a large number of *Mureeds*, or neophytes (disciples), were present, all appearing to be much excited by the power or the spell of the Sheikh; so much so as to rise and dance, sing or cry out involuntarily. On entering the hall where they were assembled in the presence of the Sheikh, I was also much affected by the spectacle, and, retiring to a corner, sat down and closed my eyes in devout meditation, mentally praying to the Sheikh to send away those persons, and to permit me to enjoy, alone, his society. The Sheikh was several paces distant from me, and, as I did not speak, could only have known what was passing in my mind by means of his wonderful spiritual powers, by which expression I mean the faculty which one spirit has of communing with another, and the power which a superior spirit has over the will of another spirit.

"On opening my eyes, I was amazed to hear the Sheikh address me in the following words,—'In a few minutes' time your prayer, young man, will be granted, and you will commune with me alone.' To my surprise, in a few minutes, the Sheikh, without speaking a word to any one present, had dismissed all his disciples from the hall, and so I remained with him alone. One by one each had ceased to be affected by his spell, and withdrew. I then experienced an impulse beyond my power of refusal, to arise and approach him,—which I did. I threw myself, helpless, at his feet, and kissed the hand which he extended to me. We next sat down together, and I had a long and most instructive conversation with him."

The following is a translation of a small *Resâleh*, or treatise on the Mubâya'eh, or initiation of a Dervish of the *Kâdirees*, which same was appointed by its *Peer*, the Sheikh Muhee ed Deen 'Abd ul Kâdiree—on whom be the Divine Satisfaction!

"In the name of Allah, the Merciful, and the Clement,—

"Abul 'Abbâs ('Abd ul Kâdiree) taught me, Ahmed bin Abu 'l Feth Abu 'l Hasan 'Alee el Damashkee, the following from the rules established by the Sheikh el Imâm Jemâl el Islâm, the Kudvet us Sâlikeen, the Tâj el 'Ârifeen, Muhee ed Deen Abu 'l Kâdiree, ibn Ebi Sâlih bin 'Abd Ullah el Hasanee (from Hasan, son of 'Alee, and grandson of the Prophet), of Ghilânee in Persia, of which he was a native—on whom be the Divine Satisfaction!

"When the Mureed, or disciple desirous of becoming a Dervish, is seated with his hand in that of the Sheikh, and is desirous of expressing his repentance, and take upon himself the engagement ('Ahd) from the Sheikh, it is necessary that the *Fakeer* be of an active mind, brilliant in thought, of good repute, near in approach to God, of a good heart, of a meek demeanour among men, of serious deportment, easy to acquire knowledge, prepared to teach others who are ignorant, disposed to trouble no one, though they trouble him; to speak only of those things which belong to his faith; generous of his means; to avoid what is forbidden and wrong; to be careful in refraining from what is doubtful; to aid those who are strangers; to be a parent to the fatherless; to be of a pleasant countenance; to be gentle of heart, joyful of spirit; to be agreeable and happy even in poverty; not to expose his secrets to others, nor to destroy them; to be gentle in conduct, and of intercourse; to be bountiful of his benefits, kind in language, few in his words; to be patient with the ignorant, and to refrain from doing them any wrong; to show respect to great and small; to be faithful to those who confide in him, and to keep aloof from all duplicity; to be strict in his religious duties; to refrain from sloth and slumber; to speak ill of no one; to be sedate and easily satisfied; thankful for benefits bestowed; much in prayer and fasting; truthful of tongue; permanent in abode; to curse no one; without calumny, hatred, or stupidity; of a pure heart, and careful of the perfect performance of all the religious duties of his order; and to be as correct in thought as in deed.

"After uttering this advice to the Mureed, the Sheikh should, holding his hand in his own, recite the *Fâtiha* once (1st Chapter of the Koran); the tenth chapter, entitled 'Assistance;' the first ten verses of the 48th chapter, called the 'Victory;' the 56th verse of the 33d chapter, called the 'Ahzâb;' and the 180th, 181st, and 182d verses of the 37th chapter of the Koran.

persons who are called the *Sâhib i Tesârruf*, and wished to learn something about them. I had heard that there was one of these, named *Jemel ed Deen Koofee*, who frequented the tomb of 'Alee.

"On leaving Bagdad, I passed by Koofa, where the Imâm (Caliph) 'Alee was martyrized by *Ibn Meljen*. I met Jemel ed Deen, on his way out to the Desert, and immediately got off my horse and approached him, for the purpose of kissing his hand. I was behind him, at the distance of a dozen paces; he turning round, looked up at me, and cried out in a loud voice, '*Arruh el Allah*,' *Go to God.* I was frightened and trembled from emotion, and stopped, so that I was unable to kiss his hand.

"He was a person of middle stature, perfectly naked; his beard was scanty, only a little hair on his chin, of a feeble frame, and of some forty to forty-five years of age. His hair was also scanty. I returned to Koofa, so as to visit its *Mesjid*, or chapel, erected on the spot of 'Alee's martyrdom. I inquired, at the door, where the person slept whom I had seen, and he showed me a spot near to the tomb of the son of the brother of 'Alee, named *Muslim ibni Okail*, adding that he always slept there on a mat made of date palms, with a stem for a pillow. I next asked what he did, what he ate and drank, and he answered that he really did not know, for every evening he came in to sleep, and early in the morning left again for the Desert, without ever speaking to any one. In A.H. 1260, this person died, and in his place another, named *Beder ed Deen es Sabir*, filled his place. His native place is called *Dâr es Soor, ve Hadd el Ard*, and he will live to A.H. 1280. After him another will come, named *Husain ed Deen Mekkehee*, who will then be the *Khâtem i Evliâ*, or *Vellaya*, 'the last of the saints.'"

My friend explained to me that these persons are considered as being the chief of the numerous *Sâhib i Tesârrufs*, who live in the world, and to whom is given a spiritual command over souls, similar to the temporal authority of sovereigns and other rulers over the bodies of mankind.

In connexion with this belief, he explained to me that the chief of all these individuals is called the *Kutub*, centre or axis; he is unique of his kind; on his right and left are two persons called the *Umenâ*, plural of *Emnee*, or *Emeen*, the "Faithful." When the one in the middle dies, the one on his left succeeds him, and the one on the right takes his place. The latter place is then filled up by a person called the *Evtâd* (plural of *Vetted*). These are four in number. There are also five others, called the *Envâr* (plural of *Noor*, or light), who succeed to the *Evtâd*, or *middle*. There are also seven *Akhyâr* (plural of *Khair*, or "the good"), who succeed to the *Envâr*. There are forty others called the *Shukedâ* (plural of Sheheed, the "Martyrs"). By some they are called the *Rijâl-i-Ghaïb*, or the "Absent Ones." These have a *Dâïreh*, or circle, divided into thirty parts, equal to the days of the month. The circle has a North, South, East, and West, and on each day they all together wander over the surface of the globe, which is the *Dâïreh*, in a certain direction of the compass, fixed for each day of the month, of which they all possess a perfect knowledge, through the *data* written in this circle.

The celebrated author, Muhee eddeen el 'Arabee, has written a detailed account of these, and Mollâ Jâmee, one of the most celebrated of the Persian poets, comments upon them in the book called the *Nufahât el Uns*, or the "Breath of Man."

Any one consulting the tables of the circle, so as to ascertain where the *Rijâl i Ghaïb* are proceeding, and thus look to them for spiritual aid, will, it is said, be sure to meet with success. My informant assures me that Dervishes believe firmly in their existence. Mekkeh is their centre and point of departure, and to which place they return daily. All the transactions of mankind come under their jurisdiction, and are decided upon spiritually, previous to being carried into execution temporally by the rulers of the earth. They are the *Nâibs* and *Vakeels*, or deputies of the prophets and saints who have left this world, and God makes known to them His supreme will, with regard to the actions of men. Even the designs of advice to one of his disciples, and he refuses to abide by it, God abandons him. The Sheikh 'Abd ul Kâdir has also said, on the subject of the *Istighfâr* (prayer of pardon): When any of my disciples is oppressed with affliction, let him walk three steps to the eastward and recite these lines:

"'O Thou who art much desired; Thou who art the aid of all things in the hour of trouble;

"'In the deepest of darkness, as in the dangers of the desert, Thou seest all things;

"'In the hour of shame and confusion, Thou only canst protect me;

"'When I am overcome with affliction,—in the hour of danger, Thy supreme intelligence will support me;

"'O Thou who art ever present, I implore Thee to free me from my grief.'"

Among the *Kâdirees*, this is a much used prayer, and is generally addressed to their *Peer* ('Abd ul Kâdiree Ghilânee).

From another source I have obtained the following account of the affiliation of a Mureed into the Order of the *Kâdirees*,—perhaps of a more modern character than the preceding.

Whenever any one desires to enter this *Tareek*, and feels an affection for the Sheikh of a *Tekkieh*, he seeks for a Mureed already belonging to it, and expresses his wish to become a disciple of his Sheikh. In reply, the Mureed enjoins upon him to continue frequenting the *Tekkieh*, and to wait upon its members and visitors. The service required of him is of a domestic character, and must, however, be performed by the pupil, whatever may be his social or official position. It lasts for several months, or a year, and serves to increase his love for the order of the Sheikh, and prevents his falling off, or joining any other *Tekkieh*. He is not, however, under any obligation to continue in it, and may leave it and join another if he so chooses.

At the expiration of this period the pupil, on the direction of his friend the Mureed, brings with him an '*Arakieh*, or small felt cap, without any gores. When this is done the Mureed carries it to the Sheikh, who consents to receive him, and orders the Mureed to attach a *Gul* or rose to it. This is a rose of eighteen points, called *Terks*, which are the number of the letters of the words "Bismillah er Rahmân er Raheem," (In the name of God, the Clement and the Merciful,) or the numerical value of the letters of the word *Hy* (Living God): *h*, 8, and *y*, 10. In their centre is the figure of the *Muhur i Solaimân*, or Solomon's Seal, which is two triangles crossed The rose to be attached to the cap or *Kulah* is placed by the Sheikh in his bosom; he takes it with him to a mosque, or to his *Tekkieh*, the day or night at which his disciples assemble to perform the *Zikr*. Whilst seated on the *postakee*, or sheepskin mat, the Mureed conducts the pupil before him; the Mureed kisses the hand of the Sheikh, the pupil does the same, kneeling before the former, who is also on his knees. The Sheikh now takes off the cap usually worn by the pupil, and, putting in its place the '*Arakieh*, recites the *Allahu Ekber* three times.

If the *Tareek* be the *Kâdiree*, this is the customary form of investiture of a neophyte; if the *Rufâ'ee*, the Sheikh fills a coffee-cup with water from the sacred well, called Zemzem, at Mekkeh, or in its place with any other water, —prays over it, and gives it to the pupil to drink; if the *Sa'dieh*, the Sheikh orders an oke of dates to be brought to him, and places them on the *postakee* beside him. He next takes one of these dates in his hand, and after taking out its seed, breathes on it and recites a prayer, and puts the date into the mouth of the pupil. On each side of the latter is a Mureed, balancing him and themselves from right to left, reciting the prayer, "La ilâhé illâ Allah." The Sheikh also balances or rocks himself at the same time, and in the interval the pupil swallows the date.

They all now rise, and the pupil, having become a Mureed or Dervish, kisses the hand of the Sheikh.

In all *Tekkiehs*, there are but three grades of Dervishes:

1. The Sheikh.
2. The Khaleefeh (vicar of the former).
3. The Mureeds.

There is no fee required for the initiation; yet all the Mureeds are supposed to aid in the support of the Sheikh, and the other expenses of the *Tekkieh*, and they seldom visit him without bringing him a present. There are no officers whatever to any *Tekkieh* except the Sheikh; he alone directs and commands absolutely, and must use all his influence for the interests and welfare of his Mureeds. There is no purser, or clerk, nor any sum for the public use or charitable purposes in or out of the *Tekkieh*. The Mureeds live in the world, and gain their livelihood as they please; but the Sheikh has no other occupation than the service of his own *Tekkieh*, and trusts to Providence for a support,—as the Dervishes express it—*Alà bâb ullah*, "on the door of Allah."

I may here add that of the two hundred, or more, *Tekkiehs* in Constantinople, some fifty only are possessed of sufficient wealth for their support. By far the greater number are poor. Their resources consist in *Wukoofs*, or real estate bequeathed to them by private individuals, or gifts from the sovereign. It has frequently happened that the reigning Sultan becomes an honorary member of an Order of Dervishes, and sometimes attends its religious exercises. They are more disposed to join the *Mevlevees* than any other Order, on account of the connexion of this Order with the earliest Sultans of the Ottoman family.

The *Bai'at*, or election of the Mureed, by placing of hands on his head, or the hand of the Sheikh in his hand, in some cases, only takes place several years after his original admission to the Order. The period much depends upon the will of the Sheikh, and the degree of knowledge and spiritual acquirements of the Mureed. The Sheikh or the Mureed is held to see in a vision, either the Prophet 'Alee, or the *Peer* of the Order; and this ceremonial is the only one of which the secret, if indeed one exists, has not been divulged to me. The Mureed, at that time, takes an oath never to divulge it, and not to commit certain ordinary sins. I believe there is no secret sign of recognition by which one Dervish can tell another. The costume fully explains the Order to which the Dervish belongs, and the *Kulah* or cap, and the *Khirka* or mantle, as well as the *Kewer* or girdle, are the principal parts which designate him. Among the *Bektâshees*, an arm is left out of the sleeve on certain occasions, signifying, "I come to you in pure amity, and without any desire to seek profit."

PENITENCE.

Of the *Kâdirees*, the cap is called *Tâj* or crown, and the belt, *Kemer*. These may be of any colour; green is, however, mostly used. The cap is also called *Muzzân*. At their devotions, after reciting the *Fâtiha*, the Dervishes take each other by the shoulder, and turn round in the hall of the *Tekkieh*, calling out, "*Hay Allah!*" This ceremony is called the *Dewân*, or turning. Its originator was *Hazret i Ismâ'îl i Roomee*, who is interred in the *Kâdiree Khâneh*, or *Tekkieh* of Topkhâneh. All Dervishes say grace at their meals, called the *Gul benk*, which differs in different Orders. That of the *Kâdirees* is the following prayer :—

"Praise be to God. May He increase His bounties. By the blessings of Khaleel (Abraham); by the Light of the Prophet,—the grace of 'Alee; by the war-cry of Mohammed (Allah! Allah!); the secret of the Sultan Mahee ed Deen 'Abd ul Kâdir Ghilânee, we beseech Thee to be of good favour to our Lord (the Peer of the Order). O! Allah Hoo!"

Whilst the Sheikh is occupied, after the meal, in reciting the *Tekbeer* (*Allahu Ekber*), or even in repeating this grace, his disciples simply exclaim, "Allah! Allah!" and, at its conclusion, all cry out, "Hoo!" (Him, signifying God.)

I am informed that nearly all the Orders use this form, the only difference being that each one uses the name of its own *Peer*.

CHAPTER V.

THERE is much in the belief of the Dervishes which has its origin in the ordinary religion of Islamism. None venture to separate themselves from the tenets promulgated by the Prophet in the Koran, but rather seek to spiritualize its language, and evoke hidden and concealed meanings from isolated verses, without consulting the sense of the entire chapter, or the occurrences which gave rise to it. They declare that most parts of the Koran have a hidden, inner, or spiritual significance, called by them, *Ma'ânde Batenee*, in addition to the ordinary conception, called *Ma'ânde Zâhiree.*

From a repeated and careful perusal of some of their mystical or spiritual writings, I conclude that their appreciation of the Koran, and religion in general, is as follows. The Koran and all other pious books, including, of course, the Bible and Testament, are divided into three, or even more divisions, viz. what is historical, biographical, and purely spiritual. Religion is considered to be the external parts of the worship of God, and is liable to change, according to the teachings of individual prophets or other pious men, such as the *Peers* of their numerous *Tareeks* or Orders. These are conformed to, in consequence, more out of personal regard for those who established them, and whose good will in the spiritual world will be propitiated by their observance, than as a duty to God. The historical and biographical portions of these books may even comprise errors, omissions, and exaggerations, and even may have been more or less changed from time to time by copyists; whilst that which is purely spiritual and essential to the soul of man commenced with his creation, has always existed unchanged, and will so continue to the end of time.

In various verses of the Koran it is clearly enunciated that the soul or spirit of man has a Divine origin, and emanated directly from the Great Spirit of God; whilst the body of man was created from the earth on which he dwells. After God had created Adam, he breathed upon him the breath of life, and that differs widely from the life or existence of ordinary animal nature. The former is eternal, whilst the latter is temporary, and ceases with the flesh of which the body is composed. All bodies, therefore, come from the earth, of which they are made, and return to it after death; whilst the spirit of man came from the Great Spirit of God, and returns to Him, after the decease of the body.

With regard to creation, their best writers state that there are four distinct ones:

1. The creation of Adam from the clay, or mud, of which the earth is composed.

2. The creation of Eve from a rib, or part of Adam.

3. The creation of the human species,—that is, the children of Adam and Eve, by natural propagation.

4. The creation of Jesus Christ by a special breath of God conveyed to a virgin—Mary—by the angel Gabrâil.

It is believed that the spirit of man communes directly with the Holy Spirit of God—and that the latter, also, communes with the former, not only in visions, but even in wakeful hours, always for good, and never for evil. Holy and pious men hold frequent intercourse with God, by contemplation, meditation, and prayer; and there is no more sacred duty than the invocation or "calling" upon His name, called the *Zikr*, already frequently alluded to in preceding chapters. This frequent invocation renders the breath of man additionally holy, and gives to it a spiritual or superhuman power. By this intercourse with God, men reach a superior and more sublime character; leading holy and, as it were, sinless lives, they become friends of God, and assume an intimate connexion with Him, even in the present life. A man fully impressed with the possibility of attaining to such a position naturally enough regards all that is connected with the transient existence of this world as insignificant, and unworthy of any serious consideration and regard. He becomes indifferent to the ordinary pleasures and gratifications of life; his mind is supposed to be continuously absorbed in the one whole object of his life, and to revert at all times to the contemplation of God. The more destitute he is of worldly goods, the less his mind is connected with the ordinary cares of life, and he is left free to devote his entire existence to communion with the Creator and His Divine Spirit. He is proud of a destitute and impoverished condition, as it is a sure outward proof of his spiritual superiority and excellence. This is in strict accordance with a remark of the Prophet: "My poverty is my pride," and is the origin of all those wandering Orders of Dervishes, or, more correctly, simple *Fakeers* of the East.

THE "EVLIÂ" OR SAINTS.

The Dervish Orders put full faith in all the grades of spiritually superior men and angelic beings. The former compose what are ordinarily termed saints or friends of Allah. These in the Koran are designated as "the friends of God who fear nothing; they are not subject to any affliction, because they entertain the true faith; they have lived consistently with it, and in exact obedience with God, from whom they receive a reward in this life and in the other." "They are those who among men are the nearest united to God, and who consequently enjoy His most intimate presence." "Those who, having been the enemies of themselves in this life, become the friends of God in the other." "They are the title of the book of the law of God; the demonstration of all the truths and mysteries of faith; their external appearance leads us to an observance of the laws of God, and their interior incites us to abandon and detach ourselves from all the pleasures of this world." "They commenced their career before the beginning of time, and labour only for eternity." "During their lives, they never left the portals of the sacred palace of the Divinity, and finally enter therein." "They discover and behold the spiritual secrets which God reveals to them, and maintain therein a religious silence."

It is held that holy men do not fear the evils of life, nor the terrors which surround death and the judgment. The calm which they possess in this life is only a foretaste of the happiness prepared for them hereafter, of which they are allowed a foresight. A part of their recompense in this life is the love and respect of their fellow-men, and the veneration shown to their memories after death. They are favoured with spiritual visions and apparitions, and frequent intercourse with angelic visitors, who appear to them in that semi-existence called a state of bodily slumber. In this world, the saint hears the will of God, and, in the other, he understands it.

The Dervishes and ordinary Mussulmans possess many biographies of the saints (*Evliâ*), and the pure (*Sâliheen*), from which much may be learned with regard to the spiritual visions and spiritual powers, attained by lives of great purity and constant meditation on the Divinity. These put the reader on his guard against impostors and hypocrites, who, for worldly purposes, pretend to a degree of piety and consequent purity of character which they do not possess.

These saints commence with the earliest period of the world's existence. Adam was superiorly a holy man, and on his creation the angels were commanded by God,—who had animated his earthly body with His own holy breath,—to worship him, which all did save one—Satan—and he was in consequence expelled from the presence of God, for his disobedience. Abraham was the "friend of God" *par excellence*—and Jesus Christ owns His existence as a saint to the special breath of His Divine Creator—but is not, nevertheless, considered as being God. He is held to be only a Divine Emanation of the most sublime character.

It is also held by some that the spirits of some men

return again to this world, and animate new human forms; and even that the spirits of others existed among celestial beings in the Divine presence, previous to their coming to this world. Mohammed is supposed to have been one of these; and the faithful admirers of 'Alee, the fourth Caliph, attribute to him a similar distinction. This is the origin of the metempsychosis—or the transmigration of souls—a point of doctrine which has been greatly abused, and changed from its original interpretation. Among the *Bektâshee Dervishes*, a belief is generally entertained that those spirits which have during their existence in man never loved nor obeyed God, are degraded to continue in this world, in an animal form of existence, and, on the decease of their human form, enter the bodies of certain animals; but their condemnation to this kind of existence is not defined, and is hidden from mortal comprehension. God alone is said to fix and know the extent of its continuance. Man, thus, by a sinful and vicious life, actually debases himself to a brute; and, it is held, at the death of the body, or at the final day of judgment, rises up again in the form which he held in this world.

Mohammed called himself the *Resool*, or "Sent of God." He is also now called by his followers in Arabia, the *Nebee*, or Prophet, and in Persia and Turkey, the *Paigamber*, or "He who bears a message" from God to mankind. The Turkish language, as far as I know, has no other word sufficiently significant of his mission, and so has adopted that of the Persians. His mission was to call men from the errors of idolatry—the worship of fire, and the belief in the existence of Three Gods (Father, Son, and Holy Spirit)—to the adoration of One God only, *Allah*. He declared that each of the others who preceded him with Divine messages, was sent for special purposes, and, having accomplished his mission, returned to God. Jesus Christ, he declared, was not killed by the Jews; that another person, resembling Him, was put to death in His stead, and that He will return again, at the Judgment Day. Of the family of 'Alee, the fourth direct Caliph, his followers, in particular, believe that the twelfth Imâm, called the *Mehdee*, or "Spiritual Director," will reappear for the benefit of the faithful. They say that he disappeared in a mysterious manner in a cave, and that he will come again into existence, together with Christ, for the purpose of overthrowing the Antichrist, and uniting Christianity and Islamism. It is this belief in the reappearance of holy personages which gave rise to the religion of the Druses, whose founder, *Bi Emir Allah*, after having already existed in this life in another form, returned as the Caliph and Reformer of Egypt, and, having mysteriously disappeared, will reappear at a future period.

As to the Prophet Mohammed, all Mussulmans and the Dervish Orders assert that he existed before the creation of this world, and that had it not been for him it would never have been created; that he was created out of light, or *Noor*, referring, I presume, only to his spirit. They declare that his coming was fully predicted by Christ, and the following is supposed to be an extract from the *Injeel*, or New Testament :—

"In the latter times a child will be born, who will be a bearer of a message from God (Paigamber), and never utter an untruth. His birthplace will be Mekkeh, and he will emigrate to Medineh; his name will be Mohammed, and his character praisable. Those who incline to him, I believe, will go to the paradise, or *Jennet*, of the faithful; he will be in this world an avenger and a conqueror. He will conquer the lands of the *Kaiser i Room*, or the Emperor of Constantinople."

A pious commentator on the preceding says that this extract, taken from the real and true Testament, has been copied and widely spread; that among the Jews and Christians some said that he had not yet come, and others that, though he had truly come, they did not put faith in him, and so blasphemed against the prediction of Christ.

Another extract from the real Testament is said to be the following :—

"A child will come into the world, of the Koraish family, who will be the Lord of the two worlds. Those whom he will call to the true faith will never enter the fires of hell (Jehennem). He will be the messenger of the latter times, and his name be Mohammed, on whom will be the peace and satisfaction of the Most High God."

Both of these extracts were given to me by a Dervish friend, and in his note he added that a monk having perused them was convinced of their truthfulness, and embraced the true faith. What language they are in I am unable to say.

CHAPTER VI.

THE RUFÂ'EES (HOWLING DERVISHES).

THIS Order of Dervishes commence their devotions by reciting the *Fâtiha*, the chapter of the Koran called the *Bakra* (or *Lâm Elif*), the *Evrâd*, and the *Tevheed.* Those prayers for their *Peer* and the Sultan are simply *Du'â*, or supplications.

Their belt is called *Alif-lâm-end.* Their mantle is called the *Ridâlee Khirka*, and may be of any colour; its edging, however, is green. The latter colour has its origin in the circumstance that the angel Gabrâil once brought some good news to the Prophet, who, from joy, turned round like the *Mevlevees*, and let fall his cloak. His disciples cut it in pieces, and sewed the strips around their own. Its colour was green.

The cap is called *Tâj*, and is made of white cloth, with eight *Terks*, each signifying a carnal sin abandoned. Some are of twelve *Terks.* The turban is black, and is called *Shemla*, or *Siâh i Shereef.* Most of these Sheikhs wear black garments: the mantle of the Prophet was green or black, and they follow his example. The black cloth thrown over their shoulders is called *Shed.*

Reâ is a principle followed by them and all Dervishes in general, and signifies a retirement from the world, and abandonment of all the pleasures of life, entirely satisfied with Allah alone. These abandonments are four in number, *Reâ* being the chief of all. They are *Shereè at*, *Tarikat*, *Hakeekat*, and *Ma'rifat.*

The *Tâi* of their Sheikh has twelve *Terks*, four of which are called *Kapu*, or doors. The twelve refer to the twelve Imâms, and the four to the *Reâs.*

The Mureed, or neophyte, is held to bring with him to the *Tekkieh* a sheep or lamb for a sacrifice; it is sacrificed at the sill of the door by one of its Mureeds, and its flesh is eaten in common by all the members of the *Tekkieh.* The wool is made into a belt, called *Taybend*, for the use of the neophyte.

Mengusay is the name of the ear-rings of the new Dervish. If only one of his ears is drilled, he is called a *Hasanee*, from Hasan, one of the sons of 'Alee; if both, he is called a *Husainee*, from his second son. This is left optional with him.

Kan'at tâshee is the name of the stone which they wear in the centre of their belts. This is figurative of the means which poor Dervishes use to appease the cravings of their stomachs for food. In place of one stone, there may be as many as four in number, though it is supposed that before the Dervish is called upon by hunger to compress his stomach with so many, the one over the other, Providence will have procured him food.

The shape of the cap of the Rufâ'ee previous to his making the *Bai'at*, or final initiation,—when he accepts of Hazret i Rufâ'ee as his *Peer*, and the actual head of the *Tekkieh* as his *Murshid* or Sheikh,—is a perfect circle, or rather two circles, the one within the other, and between the two are the initial letters of the words composing his six *Terks.* Within these is another circle, much resembling a wheel with its spokes. After the initiation, a cap somewhat similar, differing only in form, is used.

Their Prayers are as follow:—

"In the name of Allah, the Merciful and the Clement. Say, Allah is One; He is the Eternal God; He was never begotten, nor has He ever begotten; nor has He any one equal to Himself."—Koran, cii.

"In the name of Allah, the Merciful and the Clement. Say, I seek a refuge in God, from the break of day; against the wickedness of those beings whom He has created: against the evils of the dark night when it comes upon us; against the wickedness of sorcerers who breathe upon knots; against the evils of curious who envy us."—Koran, ciii.

"In the name of Allah, the Merciful and the Clement. Say, I seek a refuge in the God of mankind; the King of men; the God of all men; against the wickedness of him who suggests evil thoughts, and develops them; who breathes evil into the hearts of mankind; against the genii (evil spirits), and against men."—Koran, civ.

"In the name of Allah, the Merciful and the Clement. Praise be to God, the sovereign Master of the universe,—the Clement and the Merciful: the Sovereign of the day of retribution. It is Thee whom we adore, and it is of Thee that we implore help. Direct us in the true path; in the path of those on whom Thou bestowest Thy blessings, and not those who have incurred Thy displeasure; nor those who have wandered away from Thee into darkness."—Koran, i.

"In the name of Allah, the Merciful and the Clement. This is the book of which there is no doubt: it is the direction pointed out to those who fear the Lord; of those who put their faith in hidden things; who observe exactly their prayers, and give bountifully of the good things which have been bestowed upon them; of those who believe in the revelation which has been given to thee (Mohammed), and to those who have preceded thee (the other prophets); of those who believe in the truth of the life to come. They only will be led by their Lord (to heaven); they will be of the happy."—Koran, ii.

The 157th verse of the same chapter:—"Your God is the unique Allah; there is none other; He is the Clement and the Merciful."

The 256th verse of the same:—"Allah is the only God; there is no other God than Him; He is the living and the everlasting; He knows no drowsiness nor slumber; all that is in the heavens, or upon the earth, belongs to Him. Who can intercede near Him, without His permission? He knows who is before thee, and who is behind thee, and no man learns of His knowledge except that which He wishes him to learn; His throne extends throughout the heavens, and over the earth, and the charge of them gives Him no trouble whatever. He is the most high, and the most exalted."

The 286th verse of the same:—"All that is in the heavens and upon the earth, belongs to God; whether you expose your acts in the great day (of judgment), or whether you conceal them, He will surely call you to an account for them; He will pardon whom He pleases, and punish those whom He pleases. God is all-powerful. The prophet believes that the Lord has sent him; the faithful believe in God, His angels, books, and the prophets whom He has sent. They say, 'We have heard, and we obey,—pardon our sins, O Lord, we will return to Thee.' God imposes upon each soul a burden according to its strength; that which it has done will be alleged against, or in favour of it. Lord, punish us not for the sins of forgetfulness, or of error. Lord, do not place upon us the burden which Thou hast imposed upon those who lived before our times. Lord, do not burden us beyond what we are able to support; blot out our sins,—pardon us—have pity on us—have pity on us, and pardon us, Thou art our Lord, and give us victory over the infidels."

(I am) "That God, beyond whom there is none other." —Koran, lix. part of 22.

Then follow the various titles of God, for which, Koran, vii. 179, is cited as authority.

Esmâ el Husnâ, or the "Beautiful Names of God;" ninety-nine in number.

1.	Allah	God.
2.	Er Rahmân . . .	The Merciful.
3.	Er Raheem . . .	The Clement.
4.	El Malik	The Possessor.
5.	El Kudoos . . .	The Holy.
6.	Es Salâm . . .	The Saviour.
7.	El Mumin . . .	The Giver of faith.
8.	El Muhaymin . .	The Giver of safety.
9.	El Azeez	The Strong.
10.	El Jebbâr . . .	The Absolute.
11.	El Mutakebbir . .	The Giver of greatness.
12.	El Khâlik . . .	The Creator.
13.	El Bâree	The Producer of souls.
14.	El Musavvir . . .	The Giver of forms.
15.	El Ghaffâr . . .	The Pardoner.

16.	El Kahhâr . . .	The Avenger.
17.	El Vehhâb . . .	The Bestower.
18.	Er Rezzâk . . .	The Provider.
19.	El Fettâh . . .	The Opener (of His will).
20.	El 'Aleem . . .	The Knowing One.
21.	El Kâbiz	The Holder (of hearts).
22.	El Bâsit	The Rejoicer (of hearts).
23.	El Hâfid	The Restrainer.
24.	Er Râfi'	The Elevator.
25.	El Mu'izz . . .	The Honorer.
26.	El Muzill . . .	The God who looks down upon all things.
27.	Es Semee'	The Hearer.
28.	El Baseer . . .	The Seer.
29.	El Hâkem . . .	The God who judges.
30.	El Âdil	The Just.
31.	El Lateef . . .	The Gracious.
32.	El Khabeer . . .	The Knowing.
33.	El Haleem . . .	The Meek.
34.	El 'Azeem . . .	The Great.
35.	El Ghafoor . . .	The Pitying.
36.	Esh Shekoor . .	The Thankful.
37.	El 'Alee	The High.
38.	El Kebeer . . .	The Great.
39.	El Hafeez . . .	The Protector.
40.	El Mukeet . . .	The Supplier of wants.
41.	El Haseeb . . .	The Esteemed.
42.	El Jeleel	The Beautiful.
43.	El Kereem . . .	The Gracious.
44.	Er Rakeeb . . .	The Envious.
45.	El Mujeeb . . .	The Acceptor of prayers.
46.	El Vasee' . . .	The Extensive.
47.	El Hakeem . . .	The Decider.
48.	El Vedood . . .	The Loving.
49.	El Mejeed . . .	The Glorious.
50.	El Bâ'ith . . .	The Sender.
51.	Esh Shâhid . . .	The Testifier.
52.	El Hakk	The Just.
53.	El Vakeel . . .	The Procurer.
54.	El Kavee . . .	The Strong.

55.	El Meteen . . .	The Solid.
56.	El Valee . . .	The Friend.
57.	El Hameed . . .	The Praisable.
58.	El Muhzee . . .	The Calculator.
59.	El Mubdee . . .	The Commencer.
60.	El Mu'eed . . .	The Resuscitator.
61.	El Muhayyee . .	The Reviver.
62.	El Mumeet . . .	The Destroyer.
63.	El Hayy	The Eternal.
64.	El Kayyoom . .	The Everlasting.
65.	El Vâjid	He who finds.
66.	El Mâjid	The Glorious.
67.	El Wâhid . . .	The Unique.
68.	Es Samed . . .	The Everlasting.
69.	El Kâdir	The Powerful.
70.	El Muktadir . .	The Giver of power.
71.	El Mukaddim . .	The Preceder.
72.	El Muâkhir . . .	The Follower.
73.	El Evvel	The First.
74.	El Akhir	The Last.
75.	Ez Zâhir	The Clear.
76.	El Bâtin	The Secret.
77.	El Vâlee . . .	The Governor.
78.	El Muta'âl . . .	The Most High.
79.	El Berr	The Benign.
80.	Et Tevvâb . . .	The Cause of repentance.
81.	El Muntakim . .	Who takes vengeance.
82.	El 'Afoov . . .	The Forgiving.
83.	Er Raoof . . .	The Propitious.
84.	Mâlik el Mulk . .	The Possessor of possessions.
85.	Zoo'l Jelâlee ve'l Ikrâm	The Possessor of greatness and honour.
86.	El Muksit . . .	The Equitable.
87.	El Jâmi'	The Assembler.
88.	El Ghanee . . .	The Rich.
89.	El Mughennee . .	The Bestower of wealth.
90.	El Mâni	The Preventer.
91.	Ed Dârr	The Harmer.
92.	En Nâfi'	The Benefiter.
93.	En Noor	The Light.

94. El Hâdee . . . The Guide.
95. El Bedee'a . . . The Commencer.
96. El Bâkee . . . The Ender.
97. El Vârith . . . The Heir.
98. Er Resheed . . . The Director.
99. Es Saboor . . . The Patient.

These "*Ismi Jelâl*," or the "Beautiful Names of God," are used as invocations, or as calls upon Him. They are ninety-nine in number, and figure in the *Tesbeeh*, or Rosary of all Mussulmans. There is still another list, reaching to as many as 1,001. It is possible that I have not, in some few cases, given their exact interpretation, and some of them differ but slightly from the others in meaning.

A RUFA'EE DERVISH IN AN ECSTATIC STATE.

The following is a common prayer of many of the Dervish Orders, and especially of the Rufâ'ees :—

"Thy attributes, O God! are holy, without any doubt; I abstain from comparing Thee to anything else; I declare that Thou art our Lord,—that Thou art One, and all things prove it. Thou art One, and knowest no diminution; Thou art subject to no disease; Thou art known by Thy goodness and Thy knowledge; to Thy knowledge there is no limit; none can praise Thee too much; Thou art the First—the Everlasting, and without any Beginning; Thou art the Last, and the Benevolent, and without any end. Thou hast no genealogy,—no sons; Thou canst never do wrong; Thou revolvest with the cycles of time; Thou never weakenest with age; all Thy creatures are submissive to Thy greatness and to Thy commands; Thy *fiat* is the letters B and E, '*Be;*' the pure in heart behold Thy beauty by means of the *Zikr* (the recital of His name), and bless Thee with the *Thirties* (the rosary is divided into thirty-three parts, together making the full ninety-nine); Thy guidance directs them in the right path, through the same means; they live in perfect love in Thy beneficent paradise; Thy science is everlasting, and knows even the numbers of the breaths of Thy creatures; Thou seest and hearest the movements of all of Thy creatures: Thou hearest even the steps of the ant when in the dark night it walks on black stones; even the birds of the air praise Thee in their nests; the wild beasts of the desert adore Thee; the most secret, as well as the most exposed thoughts of Thy servants, Thou knowest; Thou art security for Thy faithful ones; Thou strengthenest and givest to others victory, and rejoicest their hearts; Thy *Zikr* gives power, and overthrows concealed harms, and so do the *Âyats* (verses) of Thy book (when borne on the person as charms); Thy commands uphold the heavens, and support the earth; and Thy science has circumvented the entire globe; and Thou art merciful and beneficent to Thy sinning creatures.

"Like unto Thee, O God, never has anything existed; Thou hearest and seest all things. O Lord, preserve us from evil (this is repeated three times). Thou canst allow even the occurrence of evil things—great and good God! blessed be Thy holy councils. Have mercy upon us, O Lord, and give us victory, for there is no power or strength but in Thee. Blessings without number be upon Thee,—Thou who doest all that Thou deemest best. Thou art great, and great is Thy glory; Thy power extends to all things; Thy glory is manifested by Thy will. Living and inventing God, everlasting Lord, and merciful Creator of the heavens and the earth, none is worthy of adoration but Thee; hear and accept of our prayers, O merciful God, for the sake of Thy blessed Prophet; give us peace of soul, and freedom from all sin; may Thy mercy rest, and its blessings be upon us, and in our families and friends—for Thou art the great, the glorious, and the clement God of all (Koran, xxxiii. 33). 'God does not wish other than to deliver you all from the abomination, and to love his family, and to secure to you a perfect purity' (xxxiii. 56).. 'God and the angels are precious to the Prophet. Believers! address your prayers to the Lord, and pronounce (*Zikr*) His name with salutation confidently.'

"O Allah! give praise and peace to our Lord Mohammed and to his family, conformably with what Thou hast said of him,—in Abraham (Ibrahim) and his family, bless Mohammed and his offspring, as Thou didst Ibrahim, preserving him from fire in both worlds; for Thou art the glorious and the merciful! according to the numbers of Thy creatures and Thy holy will; be clement to the arch of Thy heavenly abode,—to each letter of Thy word; to the number of those who call Thy Name (*Zikr*); according to the number of those who forget Thee, O Lord, praise with the choicest of Thy praises, the best of Thy creatures, our Lord Mohammed, his offspring and his companions (the *As-hâbs*), according to the number of Thy science,—the number of Thy words, and of those who mention (*Zikr*) Thy holy name, as well as those who forget Thee. O Allah! praise our Lord Mohammed, Thy secret, and Prophet and friend, and him whom Thou hast sent; he who was illiterate (the Dervishes say that none of the Prophets could read or write, and their knowledge therefore came directly from above), his family and friends, according to the number of Thy heavens and earths, and all things which are between them. Have mercy on our affairs, and upon all Mussulmans, O Lord of all worlds.

"O God, may Thy praises be upon our Lord Mohammed, and his family and friends, according to the number of years of this world's existence, and of those worlds which are to be, and of all that Thou knowest relative to this, Thy world. O God, may Thy praises be upon the soul of our Lord Mohammed, amongst all the other souls, in his body, among all the other bodies, and in his illuminated grave, and upon his name, amongst all other names.

"O God, may Thy praises be upon our Lord, the possessor of the sign of the Prophetship upon his back (a mole), and the cloud (which always accompanied and preserved him from the heat of the sun); on the intercessor and the pitying, and the embassy (the Koran); on him who is more beauteous than the sun and the moon, according to the good deeds of Abu Bekr, 'Omar, 'Othman, and Hyder ('Alee); to the number of the plants of the earth and the leaves of the trees; on the good one—the possessor of the place in Paradise (*Makâm i Mahmood*), and of the tongue of eloquence; he who comes with preaching and intelligence and pity, and upon his family and friends. May the best of Thy praises be upon him, according to the vast amount of Thy great knowledge,—to the number of the words which Thou hast written,—the mentions made of Thy name, and of those who make mention of Thee (*Zikr*); of those who forget Thee; of those who in assemblies bless Thee with innumerable breaths (*nefs*); upon Thy Prophet who enlightened the hearts of those who pointed out a path (*Tareek*) to each friend; who came in tenth; who was sent in mercy to the world, to intercede for sinners; according to the merits of the blessed Prophets, and their greatness; according to his (Mohammed's) influence with Thee, the all-powerful; on him, the most blessed of all the prophets; of those who are resigned to Thee; on him, who is Thy Friend (such is the blessing of all Mussulmans); on his fathers; on Ibrahim, the sincere friend of Allah; upon *Moosà* (Moses), his brother, who spake with Thee; and upon Israel (Jesus), the Faithful (*El Emeen*), who was the Spirit of God (*Er Rooh Allah*); on Thy servant and prophet Soliman, and his father, David, and on all the other prophets and envoys, and all those who submit to Thee; on all those who people the heavens and the earth; those who call upon (*Zikr*) Thy name, as well as those who forget Thee. Praises be upon the fountain of Thy mercy (the Prophet), the amount of Thy judgment day,—on the measure of Thy path (*Tareek*), on the ornament of the crown of Paradise,—the bride of the other world,—the sun of holy law,—whose words are deeds,—the intercessor for all mankind,—the Imâm of all,—the Prophet of pity, our Lord Mohammed; upon Adam and Noah; on Ibrahim, the intimate friend of God,—his brother Moses, and the Spirit of God, *Jesus;* on David and Soliman, Zekeriah, Yahya (Isaiah), and Sheb (Seth ?), and on all their offspring,—those who call upon Thee, as well as those who forget Thee.

"O our Eternal God of mercy, Thy praises be upon Thy people, who spread open their hands to glorify Thee,—Thou bestower of all good things; Thou pardoner of all things, sins, and faults; Thy praises be upon our Lord, who is the best of all those having good dispositions,—upon his offspring and friends, and the good men of this world; pardon us who are now present. There is no God than Allah, and Mohammed is the Prophet of Allah, and Ibrahim is the intimate friend of Allah.

"O our Lord! O Prophet of God,—He whom we desire,—who gives us from out of His abundance; the Possessor of time; Thou helper in the hour of need,—Thou purest of all prophets,—the Jewel of the Universe; who elevates atoms into worlds; Thou refuge of the poor (*Fukerâ*); the Eye which beholds all the past; Thou all-seeing, I have praised Thee, O Prophet of God; I have believed in Thee, and in Thy sufficiency; Thy goodness comes upon us kindly, and with Thy excellence it invites us to call upon Thee, approaches us to Thee.

"Thousands of prayers be upon Thee (three times

repeated),—upon the 100th, 80th, and 1090th (this refers to the belief that in the 2280th year of the Hegira the world will end); praises be upon him who is the true light, *Ahmed el Mustapha* (Prophet),—the Lord of all prophets, his offspring and all his friends. O God, have mercy upon all the faithful. One thousand prayers, and one thousand salutations, be in the great secret of Thy Prophet. O Thou affectionate, beneficent, lead us in our belief; Thy praise be upon Thy perfect Son (the Prophet) in the judgment day,—during the length of days,—in the mode (sign or seal) of his prophetship,—on him who was shielded by a cloud, on Mustapha,—for the sake of Allah,—Thy secret,—on his secrets; bestow upon us thy favour, O Mustapha, bestow thy countenance upon us, for His sake, and thy own; pity our weaknesses,—elevate us through thy peace (three times). O Prophet! help us (three times); we believe in thee. O thou friend of God! intercede for us,—we know that He will not reject thy intercession. Thou, O Lord, art Allah,—favour us as Thou knowest best (three times). There is no God but Allah, and Mohammed is the Prophet of Allah."

The patient reader will have perceived much in this lengthy prayer peculiar to the belief of the Dervishes generally, though a great part of it is purely Mussulman.

THE NAKSHIBENDEES.

The Order of the *Nakshibendees* is one of the most extensive which exists in the East, and particularly in the Ottoman empire. They have a work in Turkish, called the *Reshihât 'ain el Heyât*, or "Drops from the Fountain of Life," which is not only a perfect biography of their founder, Mohammed Bahâ ed Deen, but also a detailed account of his peculiar spiritual doctrines. M. D'Herbilot states that *Nakshibend* was his surname; that he was the author of a work entitled *Makâmât* (*Sittings*), on various subjects connected with eloquence and academic studies; and another called *Avrâd el*

Bahiyyât, "Prayers of Bahâ," taken from his own name, and that he died A.H. 791.

In the addendum of the work called the *Shekkaik Numânieh*, the *Silsileh*, or successor of Nakshibend, it is thus related, and the detail will serve as an example of the descent claimed by all of the Dervish Orders. "The Sheikh Bayazid Bestâmee has it from the Imâm Ja'fer Sâdik, who has it from the Imâm Mohammed Bâkir, who has it from the Imâm Zain el 'Abideen, who has it from the Imâm Husain, who has it from 'Alee (fourth caliph), who has it from the Prophet of Allah,—that Bayazid Bestâmee was born after the decease of the Imâm Ja'fer Sâdik, and, by the force of the will of the latter, received spiritual instruction from him. Imâm Ja'fer also spiritualized Kâsim bin Mohammed bin Abu Bekr es Sâdik. He was one of the seven doctors of Divine Law, and derived his spirituality through the mystic will of Selmân Fârsee. The latter enjoyed direct intercourse with the blessed Prophet of God, and beside this peculiar honour, received instruction (*Terbiyet*) from Abu Bekr es Sâdik (second caliph). When these were concealed together in the cave, and there conversed with the Prophet, they all performed the secret *Zikr* (called upon God's name mentally), seated on their hips, with depressed eyes, repeating it three times.

"After the decease of Bayazid Bestâmee, Abul Hasan Kharkânee was born. Sheikh Abul Kâsim Kerkiânee has connexion with both of these. According to this statement, Abul Hasan Kharkânee was employed in their service. Sheikh Abul 'Othman Maghrebee received from them,—Abu 'Alee Reduharee from them also; from them came the spiritual powers of Junaid Baghdâdee, from him to Sirree Sâketee, from him to Ma'roof Kerhkee. The latter also had two sources of descent,—the one, Daoud Tâyee; from them came Habeeb Sajemee; from him Hasan Basâree, and these all received their spirituality from the Commander of the Faithful, 'Alee. Ma'roof Kerkhee drew from 'Alee Rizâ; he from the Imâm Musa Kiâzim,—he from Ja'fer es Sâdik.

"The continuation of the descent is as follows:—Abul Kâsim Kerkiânee left his powers to his pupil, *Khoja* 'Alee Fermendee; his *Khaleefeh* (successor) was *Khoja* Yusoof Hemdânee,—that of the latter was his own servant 'Abd ul Khalik Gajdivânee; after him Khoja 'Ärif Rivkeree—after him Mohammed Fagnavee,—after him 'Alee Rametnee—after him Mohammed Bâbâ Semsasee—after him the Emir Sa'eed Gulân—after him the Khoja Bahâ ed Deen Nakshibend—after him, Allay ed Deen el 'Attar—after him Nizâm ed Deen Khamush—after him Sultan ed Deen al Kashgâree—after him 'Obayd Ullah Samarkandee—after him Sheikh 'Abd Allah al Lahee—after him Sheikh Sa'eed Ahmed al Bokhâree—after him Sheikh Mohammed Chelebee, nephew of Azeez—after him Sheikh 'Abd el Lateef, nephew of Mohammed Chelebee—may Allah bless their secrets!"

From the *Nakshibendee* Order evidently sprang the Order of the *Noorbakhshees;* for the same author adds that the Emir Sultan Shems ed Deen derived from Sa'eed 'Alee, father of Mohammed bin 'Alee el Husainee el Bokhâree; they derived from the Sa'eed Mohammed Noorbakhshee. The *Khaleefeh* of Emir Bokhâra, Hasan Khoja Van's Khalefeeh Valee Shems ed Deen, are all mentioned in the *Shekaik.* These derived from Is-hak Jelâlee, he from Sa'eed 'Alee Hemdânee, he from Mohammed Kherkânee, he from Allay ed Devlet Semenânee, he from 'Abd ur Rahmân Asfarânee, he from Ahmed Jurkânee, he from 'Alee bin Sa'eed Lalla, he from Nejm ed Deen Kubrâ, he from 'Omar bin Yasserbedlissee, he from Abul Nedjeeb Sherverdee, and down through the whole succession."

The same author, in alluding to the author of the *Nakshibendees*, says:

"This people (*Tâifeh*) polish the exterior of their minds and intellects with pictures, and being free from the rust and wiles of life are not of those who are captivated by the vain colourings of the world, as varied as those of the changeful chameleon; and as Nakshibend drew incomparable pictures of the Divine Science, and painted figures of the Eternal Invention, which are not imperceptible, his followers are become celebrated by the title of the *Nakshibendees*, 'The Painters.'"

From the work before alluded to, called "Drops from the Fountain of Life," it would appear that the originator of this order was 'Obaid Allah, and that Bahâ ed Deen Nakshibend was only a learned writer on its principles. The members of the order are called *Khojagians*, or the teachers. The Khaleefehs (or successors) and the disciples of 'Obaid Allah were *Valees*, and their holy tombs are scattered over various parts of the farther East, in Merv, Samarkand, Sind, Bokhara, and throughout Persia, where they are much visited for the purpose of seeking spiritual inspiration from the revered remains of the sainted men which they contain. Various members of the Order gave rise to varied points of belief, and one declared that the soul would, and does, return to this world in a new body. As this borders closely upon the theory of the metempsychosis, it is treated upon in various ways—all spiritually. Another teaches the necessity of the *Khalvet*, or profound meditation on the Deity, which he says must be so perpetual and continuous, as to absorb completely the mind; so much so, that when even in the midst of a crowd, the meditator can hear no voice or other sound. Every word spoken by others will then appear to him the *Zikr*, and so will even his own words, when spoken on other subjects. But to attain to this the greatest attention and labour is necessary.

As advice to a Mureed, or disciple, the following instructions are given by a member of the Order respecting the *Zikr*, which he says is a union of the heart and the tongue in calling upon God's name. In the first place, the Sheikh, or teacher, must with his heart recite, "There is no God but Allah, and Mohammed is the Prophet of Allah," whilst the Mureed keeps his attention fixed by placing his heart opposite that of the Sheikh; he must close his eyes; keep his mouth firmly shut, and his tongue pressed against the roof of his mouth; his teeth tight against each other, and hold his breath; then, with great force, accompany the Sheikh in the *Zikr*, which he must recite with his heart, and not with his tongue. He must retain his breath patiently, so that within one respiration he shall say the *Zikr* three times, and by this means allow his heart to be impressed with the meditative *Zikr*.

The heart, in this manner, is kept constantly occupied with the idea of the Most High God; it will be filled with awe, love, and respect for Him, and, if the practiser arrives at the power of continuing to effect this, when in the company of a crowd, the *Zikr* is perfect. If he cannot do this, it is clear that he must continue his efforts. The heart is a subtle part of the human frame, and is apt to wander away after worldly concerns, so that the easier mode of arriving at the proceeding is to compress the breath, and keep the mouth firmly closed with the tongue forced against the lips. The heart is shaped like the cone of a fir-tree; your meditations should be forced upon it, whilst you mentally recite the *Zikr*. Let the "*La*" be upward, the "*Illahé*" to the right, and the whole phrase "*La Illahé*" (there is no God but Allah) be formed upon the fir-cone, and through it to all the members of the whole frame, and they feel its warmth. By this means, the world and all its attractions disappear from your vision, and you are enabled to behold the excellence of the Most High. Nothing must be allowed to distract your attention from the *Zikr*, and ultimately you retain, by its medium, a proper conception of the *Tevheed*, or "Unity of God."

The cone-shaped heart rests in the left breast, and contains the whole truth of man. Indeed it signifies the "whole truth," it comprises the whole of man's existence within itself, and is a compendium of man; mankind, great and small, are but an extension of it, and it is of humanity what the seed is which contains within itself a whole tree; in fine, the essence of the whole of God's book and of all His secrets is the heart of man. Whoever finds a way to the heart obtains his desire; to find a way to the heart is by a heartful service, and the heart accepts of the services of the heart. It is only through the fatigues of water and ashes that the Mureed reaches the conversation of the heart and the soul; he will be then so drawn towards God that afterwards, without any difficulty, he may without trouble, in case of need, turn his face from all others toward Him. He will then know the real meaning of the *Terk*, the *Hakeekat*, the *Hurreet*, and the *Zikr*.

It is through the performance of the *Zikr*, by *Khalvet* (pious retirement for purposes of deep devotion), by the *Tevejjuh* (or turning the face or mind devoutly towards God in prayer), by the *Murâkebeh* (or fearful contemplation of God), the *Tesarruf* (or self-abandonment to pious reflection and inspiration), and the *Tesavvuf* (or mystical spiritualism), that the fervent Dervish reaches peculiar spiritual powers, called *Kuvveh i roohee bâtinee* (a mystical, internal, spiritual power). The life, or biography, of every eminent Sheikh, or *Peer*, details innumerable evidences of this power exercised in a strange and peculiar manner. This exercise is called the *Kuvveh Irâdât*, or the "Power of the Will," and, as a theory, may be traced historically to the Divine Power—the soul of man being connected with the Divine Spirit—from which it emanates, and with which, through the means before mentioned, it commences. Some Sheikhs are more celebrated than others for their peculiar and strange powers, and it is to their superiority that their reputation and reverence in the Mussulman world in general, and among Dervishes in particular, is to be attributed. With the supposition that the details given of them by their biographers, disciples, or successors are not invented, or even exaggerated, their powers are certainly very remarkable. Whilst among them, an implicit belief in them is firmly sustained, sultans and princes have evidently doubted them, and being alarmed with the influence the possessors acquired and sustained among the public generally, they have often shown a direful exercise of their own arbitrary will and power, which resulted in the untimely end of the unfortunate Sheikh. Many, on the other hand, have survived the frequent exercise of their "spiritual powers," and either because they acquired a power and influence over the minds of their temporal rulers, or whether they used them for their own private purposes, so as to conciliate the more religious or fanatic, they succeeded in reaching advanced ages and a peaceful end of their remarkable careers. When the ruler of the country has not cared to order the execution of the Sheikh who declared himself possessed of these "spiritual powers," he has simply exiled him from his capital, or his territory, and permitted him freely to exercise his powers and renown in some less objectionable locality. These powers can only be acquired through the long instruction of a superior spiritual director, or Murshid, or *As-hâb i Yekeen*, for whom the disciples ever retain a most grateful remembrance and attachment.

Among the practices of these powers is the faculty of foreseeing coming events—of predicting their occurrence—of preserving individuals from the harm and evil which would otherwise certainly result for them—of assuring to one person success over the machinations of another, so that he may freely attack him and prevail over him—of restoring harmony of sentiment between those who would otherwise be relentless enemies—of knowing when others have devised harm against themselves, and through certain spells of preserving themselves and causing harm to befall the evil-minded; and even of causing the death of any one against whom they wish to proceed. All this is done as well from a distance as when near.

In other parts of the world, and among other people, these attainments would have been attributed to sorcery and witchcraft; in modern times they would be ascribed to Spiritism, or magnetic influences, either of the spirit or of the body; but to the instructed Dervish they all derive their origin in the spirit of the holy Sheikh—the special gift of the great Spirit of God, which commences with the spirit of man from which it directly emanated. The condition or disposition necessary for these effects is called the *Hâl* (state, or frame), and is much the same as that required by the magnetized, and the object of his operation. The powers of the body are enfeebled by fasting and mental fatigue in prayer, and the imagination kept in a fervid state, fully impressed with the conviction that such powers are really possessed by the Sheikh, and that he can readily exercise them over the willing mind and body of the disciple. How the Sheikh can produce such strange results on a distant and unconscious person is left to the admiration and imagination of the faithful disciple, as an incentive to exertions in the same true path as that of his Sheikh.

To exercise the power of the will, it is necessary to contract the thoughts suddenly upon the object designed to be effected, so perfectly as to leave no room for the mind to dwell, possibly, upon any other. The mind must not doubt, for an instant, of the success of this effort, nor the possibility of failure; it must, in fact, be completely absorbed by the one sole idea of performing the determination strongly taken, and firmly relied upon. The person must, from time to time, practise this; and as they proceed, they will be able to see how much propinquity exists between themselves and the *Hazret i Asmâ* (God ?), and how much they are capable of exercising this power.

As an example, the author of the *Reshihât* narrates the following :—

"In my youth, I was ever with our Lord Molânâ Sa'eed ed Deen Kâshgharee at Hereed. It happened that we, one day, walked out together, and fell in with an assembly of the inhabitants of the place who were engaged in wrestling. To try our powers, we agreed to aid with our 'powers of the will' one of the wrestlers, so that the other should be overcome by him; and after doing so, to change our design in favour of the discomfited individual. So we stopped, and turning towards the parties, gave the full influence of our united wills to one, and immediately he was able to subdue his opponent. As the person we chose, each in turn conquered the other. Whichever we willed to prevail became the most powerful of the two, and the power of our own wills was thus clearly manifested."

On another occasion, two other persons, possessed of

these same powers, fell in with an assembly of people, at a place occupied by prize-fighters. "To prevent any of the crowd from passing between and separating us, we joined our hands together. Two persons were engaged fighting; one was a powerful man, whilst the other was a spare and weak person. The former readily overcame the latter; and seeing this, I proposed to my companion, to aid the weak one by the power of our wills. So he bade me aid him in the project, whilst he concentrated his powers upon the weaker person. Immediately a wonderful occurrence took place; the thin, spare man seized upon his giant-like opponent, and threw him upon the ground with surprising force. The crowd cried out with astonishment, as he turned him over on his back, and held him down with much apparent ease. No one present, except ourselves, knew the cause. Seeing that my companion's eyes were much affected by the effort which he had made, I bade him remark how perfectly successful we had been, and adding that there was no longer any necessity for our remaining there, we walked away."

Just as it is impossible to conflict with the Koran, so is it to conflict with an *'Árif*, or "knowing person," possessed of the power of the will. His power conflicts with that of others, but there is no confliction in his designs; nor is it essential that the person to be assisted should be a believer; he may be, even, an infidel, for faith is not needed to the performance of the design of the willer. Just as is the influence of the pure heart, so is that of the breath of the wicked. Even the most powerful princes of this world do not prosper without assistance. The Sheikh once left for Samarkand, for the purpose of holding a conversation with the sovereign of that place, Mirza 'Abd Ullah bin Mirza Ibrahim bin Mirza Shahrokh. "I," says the writer, "was then in his service, and went with him. On arriving, an officer of Mirza 'Abd Ullah waited upon him, and the Sheikh explained to him the object of his visit, and added, that he did not doubt but much advantage would be derived from the interview.

"To this the officer impertinently replied, that his Mirza was a youth without any fear, and would excuse him from waiting upon him, and that he could well do without the demands of Dervishes. This language displeased the Sheikh so that he replied that he had an order to communicate with sovereigns, that he had not come of his own accord, and that if his Mirza was fearless, he could retire and give place to one who was fearful. The officer departed, and so soon as he had left, the Sheikh wrote his name upon the wall of the house wherein he was then dwelling, and a moment afterwards wiped it off with his own mouth, remarking that he could not receive hospitality from either the sovereign of the place, or from his officers. He, the same day, returned directly to Tashkend. A week afterwards, the officer died, and within a month Abu Sa'eed Mirza Akza appeared from Turkistan against Mirza 'Abd Ullah, and killed him. From this occurrence, it is readily seen that Abu Sa'eed owed his success to the spiritual aid (Himmet) of the holy Sheikh.

"On another occasion, the Sheikh was at a place called Farkat, when he asked us to furnish him with pens and ink, with which he wrote several names upon a paper. Among these was the name of the Sultan, Abu Sa'eed Mirza, and he placed the paper in his turban. At that time no such person as this was anywhere known to exist. Some of those present asked the Sheikh why he was pleased to favour the names so greatly as to keep them in his revered turban. He replied, that they were the names of certain persons, whom he and we, and all of the people of Tashkend, Samarkand, and Khorassan, should respect. Very soon after this, Sultan Abu Sa'eed Mirza appeared from Turkistan. He had seen, in a dream, that our beloved Sheikh, together with the Khoja Ahmed Tessevvee, had recited the *Fâtiha* (first chapter of the Koran), with especial reference to himself. He inquired of Khoja Ahmed the names of our Sheikh, and retained them in his memory, and made diligent search for him throughout the whole country. He soon learned that, of a truth, there was just such a person dwelling at

Tashkend ; and he immediately set out to find him there. So soon as our Sheikh heard of his approach, he set out for Farkat. The Mirza came to Tashkend, and, not finding the Sheikh there, proceeded to Farkat. As he approached the latter place, our Sheikh went out to meet him. When the Mirza saw the Sheikh, his countenance changed, and he exclaimed : 'By Allah! you are certainly the same person whom I saw in my dream.' He threw himself at the Sheikh's feet, and with much anxiety implored the aid of his prayers. The Sheikh was extremely gracious to the Mirza, so that the latter became greatly attached to him.

"Later, when the Mirza desired to collect a force, and march against Samarkand, he revisited our Sheikh, and begged his permission and assistance in favour of his campaign. The Sheikh asked him with what object he designed making it : 'If,' he added, 'it is to enforce the law of God, and to act in a humane manner, you will be successful.' The Mirza declared that it was, and the Sheikh then bade him depart with his commendable intentions. By some it is related that the Sheikh told the Mirza : 'When you are opposite your opponents, do not attack them until you perceive a flight of crows coming up from your rear.' In consequence of this admonition, when the Mirza Abu Sa'eed was opposite the forces of Mirza 'Abd Ullah, the latter ordered his cavalry to make an attack upon the troops of the latter ; but Abu Sa'eed did not attempt to meet them, until a large flight of crows came up from behind them ; and so soon as these appeared, his troops' hearts became filled with joy and courage, and falling upon those of Mirza 'Abd Ullah, completely overcame them. In the defeat, Mirza 'Abd Ullah was thrown off his horse, and taken captive, and his head cut off."

"From the preceding may be seen the spiritual powers of a holy man, who can by their aid commune with persons widely separated from him, predict coming events, and aid those in whose welfare and success he feels a pious interest for good.

"Hasan Bâhadur was one of the chiefs of the country

of Mamen, in Turkistan, and the people of Mamen formed a numerous tribe. He relates that 'When Sultan Abu Sa'eed marched with his forces from Tashkend to Samarkand, I was with him; we met Mirza 'Abd Ullah on the banks of the river Bulungoor, drawn up in array: I was near to the Mirza, and our troops numbered some 7,000 only, whilst those of the Mirza were well armed, and in excellent condition. At this moment, some of our men went over to the Mirza, which troubled greatly the Sultan, and alarmed him, so that he called out to me, "Ho! Hasan, what do you see?" and I replied that I saw the Khoja (the Sheikh) preceding us. The Sultan, on this, swore by Allah that he likewise saw him. I bade him be of good cheer, for we would prevail over our enemies. At the same moment our troops made a charge against their opponents, and in half an hour all of the forces of Mirza 'Abd Ullah were beaten, and he, falling into the hands of his enemies, was put to death. On that same day, Samarkand was taken.'

"The Sheikh himself states that, when Mirza 'Abd Ullah was taken prisoner, 'I was on my way to Tashkend, and saw a white bird fall from a height to the ground. This was caught and killed, from which circumstance I knew that Mirza 'Abd Ullah had just met his fate.' The Khoja after this proceeded, on the request of Sultan Abu Sa'eed, to Samarkand.

"Mirza Baber bin Mirza Baiker bin Mirza Shahrokh came with 500,000 troops from Khorassan against Samarkand. Sultan Abu Sa'eed went to the Sheikh, and told him: 'I have not sufficient troops with which to meet him,—what shall I do?' The Sheikh quieted his apprehensions. When Mirza Baber crossed the Âb Amooee, Sultan Abu Sa'eed Mirza sent a charge of troops to meet him, and having repulsed him, the Mirza fled to Turkistan, and fortified himself. In this view, he loaded his camels to depart, which becoming known to the Sheikh, he hastened to go to the drivers, and, in great anger, commanded them to put off their loads; then going to the Mirza, he asked him where he was going. 'Do not go anywhere,' he said to the Mirza, 'for there is no need of such a proceeding; your business is here, and I will be responsible for the result; be of good cheer, for it is my business to overcome Baber.' Abu Sa'eed's officers were much troubled by this language on the part of the Sheikh, and some of them, throwing their turbans on the ground, declared that they would all be sacrificed. The Mirza, however, had entire faith in the Sheikh, and would not listen to any one else; he stopped his forces, and prepared to meet those of Baber, whose officers, nevertheless, thought that Abu Sa'eed would certainly fly before him.

"The Sultan Abu Sa'eed conformed to the words of the Sheikh, and commenced fortifying himself. Mirza Baber came near to Samarkand, and sent forward Khaleel Hindoo with his ordnance as far as its gates. A few Persians came out of the city and fought them. Mirza Baber had no men in armour, and Khaleel Hindoo was taken prisoner, and whenever he sent men against the strong walls of Samarkand, the inhabitants made sallies, and cut off the ears and noses of all the captives who fell into their hands, so that many of his people having returned to his camp in this mutilated condition, spread alarm among the others. In the course of a few days a disease broke out among his cavalry, from which many died, and spread a malaria throughout the camp, greatly to the distress and annoyance of his own people, so that very shortly he sent the Molânâ Mohammed Mu'ammâ (a Sheikh) to our own Sheikh to treat for peace. Molânâ Mohammed, on meeting our Sheikh, greatly praised the Mirza Baber, and said he was a prince of the most exalted sentiments; and our Sheikh, in response, told him that the acts of his forefathers had done him much harm, and without this he might have effected great things; that, in their time, he himself was a poor Fakir in Herat, together with a great number of similar persons, all of whom suffered much from their persecutions. Finally, peace was made, and Mirza Baber made it a matter of stipulation that he should be permitted to conciliate the goodwill and profit by the prayers of our pious Sheikh, from whose spiritual powers he had met with so much loss and discomfiture."

In the same work there are farther statements regarding the spiritual powers of this celebrated Sheikh. He claimed to be able to affect the minds of the sovereigns in such a manner as to compel them to conform to his will, and even to leave their thrones and seek a refuge at his feet. This power is called *Teskheer*, or the "subduing faculty." The Sheikh says of himself: "Were I to live as a Sheikh, none other would have any Mureeds or disciples; but my business is to preserve Mussulmans from the evils of oppression. On this account I am in conflict with sovereigns, and must therefore compel them to conform to my demands, and so promote the welfare and interests of the true believers. Through the especial favour of the Most High, a strength or power is given to me by which, should I desire it, the Sovereign of Khatay, who assumes to be a god, would obey a letter from me, and, leaving his kingdom, come barefooted after forsaking his kingdom, and seek the sill of my door. Although I possess so much power, I am wholly submissive to the will of the Most High; and whenever it is a matter referring to the will, His command reaches me, and it assumes a bodily form. For this great moral sentiment is essential, and it is this which subdues my will to the superior one of the Most High, so that it is His will which ensures justice."

A person relates that he was once a spectator of a scene between the Sheikh and Sultan Ahmed Mirza, in the village of Mâtreed. The latter had called to make a visit to the Sheikh, and they were both seated near to each other, the Sheikh composedly conversing with the Sultan, but the latter was so much under the influence of his "subduing power" that great fear and alarm were clearly visible in his features, and large drops of perspiration flowed down his face, whilst his whole frame was singularly convulsed. This fact has been sustained by the testimony of witnesses, and its truthfulness is strongly corroborated. Then follows an account of the reunion of three princes through the powers of the Sheikh, and the subduing to peace of these and all their forces by a kind of spell. The warlike spirits of these were wonderfully calmed, and kept in perfect subjection, until a formal document of pacification was drawn up by the Sheikh and signed by the princes.

On another occasion an *employé* of the Sheikh, whilst travelling in Khatay with a *Kervan* (caravan) laden with goods, was attacked by Kalmucks, and through the wonderful powers of a sword belonging to the Sheikh, his pious master, he put the whole band of robbers to flight when all of his companions had given themselves up as lost. On his return, having related this surprising affair to the Sheikh, the latter explained it to him, by the fact that, having submitted his own feeble will to that of the Most High, a superhuman "power of the will" was granted him, by which he overcame his enemies.

Many individuals who have seriously wronged and oppressed his friends received punishments through the powers of the Sheikh. Several instances are related wherein some such even fell sick and died, or were only restored to health by open declarations of repentance, and imploring his prayerful intercession with God. His spirit seems to have accompanied those in whose welfare he took an active interest, and enabled them to commune with him, though far distant from him. His power of hearing them was well known to his friends, and several instances are cited to prove the fact. His power of affecting the health of those who injured him or his friends was greatly increased whilst he was excited by anger, and on such occasions his whole frame would be convulsed, and his beard move about as if moved by electricity. On learning details of cruelty done to innocent individuals, the Sheikh would be strangely affected, so much so that no one dared to address him until the paroxysm was passed; and on such occasions he never failed to commune spiritually with the sovereign or prince in such a mysterious manner, as to inspire him to deal justly with the guilty person, and secure his merited punishment.

Through his "mystical powers" many persons were impressed with the unrighteousness of their course, and having repented of the same, became good and pious and firm believers in his spiritual influences. These powers were always connected with his prayers, and it was during these that he was enabled to assure the parties interested of their salutary results, and the acceptation of their desires. It scarcely needs to be added, that these prayers were in conformance with Islamism, and were offered up to Allah, whom he adored, and to whose supreme will he attributes his powers. He constantly performed the *Zikr Jehree*, or "audibly called God's name," and the frequent repetition of this practice fitted him for such holy purposes. Sometimes he would affect the mind of the individual upon whom he exercised his powers, in such a manner as to throw him into a species of trance, after which he could remember nothing that he had previously known, and continued in this state until the Sheikh chose to restore him to the enjoyment of his ordinary faculties. Notwithstanding all of these eminent powers, this great Sheikh is reputed to have spent the latter days of his life at Herat in extreme indigence, much slighted and neglected by those who had so admired him whilst in the vigour of his career. All fear of his mystical influences seems to have disappeared, and it is narrated that these greatly declined with his ordinary strength of mind and body.

CHAPTER VII.

THE BEKTASHEES.

THE Dervishes bearing this denomination, derived it from the name of the founder of the *Tareek*, or Path. He was a native of Bokhara. It would seem that there were two persons of this name, *Bektâsh*, the preceding one adding to his name *Koolee*, or servant (of God), and was the author of a mystical work called *Bostân al Khiyâl* ("The Garden of Mental Reflections"), in much repute among spiritual Mussulmen. The other is called *Hâjee Bektâsh*, and lived in Asia Minor during the reign of the Ottoman sovereign, Sultan Murad I. in A.H. 763. As this Order of Dervishes was intimately connected with the Ottoman militia, known as the *Janissaries*, now destroyed, some particular notice of him seems necessary, even in a work like the present.

Historians narrate that Hâjee Bektâsh or *Begtâsh* blessed the newly instituted troops, and named them *Yani Cheree*, or "New Troops" (the signification of the word *Janissaries*), whilst others dispute it. Von Hammer says they adopted for a head-dress the white felt cap of the Dervish Hâjee Begtâsh, the founder of an order spread over the Ottoman empire; that the Sultan Orkhan, accompanied by the new renegades (of whom the Janissaries were composed), met him in the village of Sulijay Kenariyoon, near to Amassia, to implore his benediction, and the gifts of a standard and a flag for his new forces. The Sheikh put the sleeve of his mantle over the head of one of the soldiers in such a manner that it hung down behind his back, and then declared the following prophecy :—"The militia which you have just created shall be called *Yanee Cheree*,—its figure shall be fair and shining, its arm redoubtable, its sword cutting, and its arrow steeled. It shall be victorious in all battles, and never return except triumphant." In commemoration of this benediction, the white felt cap of the Janissaries was increased by the addition of a piece of the same pendant on their backs, and ornamented with a wooden spoon. As most of the Janissaries were incorporated into the Order of the Begtâshees, they formed a military fraternity, of which all the members were, at the same time, monks and soldiers, differing but little from the Knights of the Temple, the Hospital, and of Malta. It is possible that the approximity of the Knights of Rhodes, whose galleys aided the first crusaders to seize upon Smyrna during the reign of Sultan Orkhan, may have inspired this prince with the idea of uniting the renegade soldiers into a monical-military corps, under the patronage of the Sheikh Hâjee Begtâsh. There was also this remarkable fact connected with his Order, that the Sheikh who directed it was at the same time Colonel of the 99th Regiment, and that eight of his Dervishes established in the barracks of the Janissaries offered up prayers there day and night for the prosperity of the empire and the success of the arms of their companions, who called themselves of the family of Hâjee Begtâsh.

The preceding is, however, denied in the Ottoman history of 'Âshik Pâshâ Zâdeh, of which the following extract has been furnished me by Dr. Mordtmann :—"I have not included *Hâjee Bektâsh* among the list of the *Ulemâ*, and *Fukerâ* of *Room Vilâyet*, because, unlike the others, he had never any connexion with the Ottoman Sultans. *Hâjee Bektâsh* came from Khorassan, with his brother Mentish, and they established themselves at Siwas (in Asia Minor), near to Baba Ilias. At a later period, they went to Caisarieh, from which place his brother returned to their own country by Siwas, and was killed on the way. Begtâsh, whilst on his way from Caisarieh to the Kaza Ujuk, died, and was interred there, where his holy tomb still exists. The people of Room are divided into four classes of *Musâfirs* (guests),—one *Ghâziyân-i-Room*, or the 'Heroes of

Room;' one *Akheeân-i-Room*, or the 'Brothers of Room;' and the other, the *Abdâlân-i-Room*, or the '*Abdâls* or Ascetes of Room.' There is also one more branch, called the *Hem-Bâjiyân-i-Room*, or the 'Sisters of Room.' Hâjee Begtâsh chose the *Bâjiyân-i-Room* among the *Bulaurs*, and made over his principles of spiritual power to the *Khâtun Anâdur* (a lady of the latter name), and then died. Although it is stated by the Bektâsh Dervishes that he gave the *Tâj* (crown or cap) to the *Janissaries*, the assertion is certainly false. This white cap already existed in the time of Orkhan himself at Balejik. I do not wish to gainsay what I have already related in the preceding chapters, and persist in the assertion that the white felt cap of the Bektâsh Dervishes was taken from the Janissaries. The impulsion for its adoption was given by a Sheikh of the Order of the Bektâshees named 'Abdel Moosà, who, having formed the desire to make a campaign, joined the Janissaries, and one day begged from them an old felt cap, which one of them loaned him. This he put on his head, and after having made the campaign, returned to his own country, wearing it, so as to show that he wore the same head-dress as those who fight for the Faith. When he was interrogated as to its name, he said it was called *Bûkmeh-Alif-Tâj*, *i.e.* a cap which never bends, and is ever upright, and worn by those who fight for the true faith. This is the true orign of the cap of the Janissaries."

Near the city of Angora, in a village called *Bektâsh-kyooy*, is the tomb of *Bektâsh*, much revered by all of his numerous followers scattered over the greater part of the Ottoman empire. Over it has been erected a pretty mausoleum and a *Tekkieh*, the object of veneration and visits from pious Mussulmen generally.

The Sheikh Hâjee Bektâsh received his spiritual education from Ahmed Yessevee Balkhee, a native of the city of Balkh. The lineal descent of the Order is as follows:—

Ahmed Yessevee from
Yoosuf Hamadânee, he from
Ebi 'Alee al Fermadee, he from

Abu'l Kâsim Kurkanee, he from
Abu'l Hasan Harrakianee, he from
Abu Yazeed Bestâmee, he from
Ja'far ibn Mohammed Sâdik (who was of the race and family of the Imâm Husain, one of the unfortunate sons of the fourth and last of the direct Caliphs, 'Alee), he from
Mohammed ibn Abu Bekr, he from
Selmân i Fârsee, he from the Sheikh of the two different *Tareeks*, viz.—the one of
Abu Bekr es Siddeek (first Caliph), and the other of
'Alee (the assumptive fourth Caliph).

Abu Bekr es Siddeek received his education direct from the holy Prophet.

This *Tareek* is therefore called the *Siddeekieh* (Faithful), from Abu Bekr, and the *'Aleevieh* ('Aleevide) from 'Alee.

All of these persons are known as the *Sheikhs*, or "Elders," and as the *Murshid i Kâmil*, or "perfect spiritual instructors," who teach to others the "true path" which leads mankind to Allah. There are, however, said to be many such paths, for the holy Prophet said in a *Hadees*, or traditional assertion, collected and preserved by his earlier followers :—

"The paths leading to God are as numerous as the breaths of His creatures."

Hâjee Bektâsh, Jân Noosh, Shahbâz i Kalenderee, Jellâl i Bokhâree, Lokmân Kalenderee, were all disciples of Ahmed el Yessevee. Of these, all were of the Order of the Nakshibendee, and at a later period founded each a separate Order.

Jân Noosh is buried at Khorâsân; Jellâl Bokhâree and Shahbâz i Kalenderee, at Simna, near Kurdistan and the Persian frontier. With the exception of Jellâl Bokhâree, they all wore the costume of the Order of Hâjee Bektâsh; and the only difference is that Jân Noosh wore twelve *Terks* or gores in his cap, Jellâl Bokhâree one, Shahbâz seven, and Lokmân Kalenderee four.

Regarding the principles of the Order of the Bektâshees, the following will serve to give some explanation.

There are six *Ahkiâm*, or "Commands."

1. Liberality.	4. Holy Law.
2. Knowledge.	5. Submission.
3. Truth.	6. Contemplation.

There are six *Erkiân*, or "Columns."

1. Science.	4. Thankfulness.
2. Meekness.	5. Calling on God.
3. Contentment.	6. Retirement.

The Constructions are six (*Benâ*).

1. Repentance.	4. Increase of Spirituality.
2. Submission.	5. Contentment.
3. Fidelity.	6. Seclusion.

The Wisdoms are also six (*Hukum*).

1. Knowledge.	4. Fidelity.
2. Liberality.	5. Reflection.
3. Approach to Divine Science.	6. Faith in God.

The Evidences of the Order are six (*Espât*).

1. Benevolence.	4. Abandonment of Passions.
2. God's Praise.	5. Fear of God.
3. Abandonment of Sin.	6. Cheerfulness of Spirit.

Regarding the cap, cloak, and girdle, called by the Bektâshees the three points, or principles, the following is legendary.

The angel Gabriel once visited the holy Prophet, during the war called the *Ghazâ i Ahwet*, and asked him what he was occupied in, and he replied in reciting the verses of the Koran, shaving his beard and cutting his hair. — *Vide* Koran, xlviii. 27. By Divine permission, the angel brought a razor from heaven, and cut the hair and shaved the beard of the prophet. He next put a cap on his head, a cloak over his shoulders, and a girdle around his waist. He had already done this to two other persons, viz., to Adam when he left the

Garden of Eden, and to the patriarch Abraham, when he dwelt in Mekkeh, which was built by him. The Prophet next did for 'Alee what the angel of God had done for him; 'Alee did the same, by the Prophet's permission, to Selmân i Fârsee, and 'Omar Ummieh Bilâl Habeschee, and these did the same for twelve other persons.

One of these twelve, named Zeenoon Misree, was sent into Egypt, Selmân to Bagdad, Sohailee to Room (Asia Minor), Dâood Yamanee to Yaman (Arabia Felix), for the purpose of imparting instruction on these points. The people of Bagdad call the girdle the letter Alif, *a*, of the alphabet; those of Room call it Lâmalif, *lâ;* and those of Egypt *Berlâm.* The people of Yaman wear the girdle next to the skin, and not over the clothes.

On the girdle brought to the Prophet by the angel was written, "There is no God but Allah, and Mohammed is His Prophet, and 'Alee is His friend."

The Bektâshees relate that Adam was the first to wear the girdle used by them; after him sixteen other prophets wore it in succession, viz. Seth, Noah, Idrees, Shu'aib, Job, Joseph, Abraham, Husha', Yoosha', Jerjees, Jonas, Sâlih, Zekaree, Khizr, Ilyâs, and Jesus. God said of Moses in the sixty-fifth verse of the eighteenth chapter of the Koran: "May I follow thee, said Moses to Him, so that Thou mayest teach me what Thou knowest regarding the *true path?*"

Moses learned the secrets of the *True Path* from Khizr. Khizr, or Khezer, is a mythical character, who figures largely in Oriental Spiritualists. Some say he lived in the earliest times, and having drank of the fountain of life never has died; others, that he was Elias, St. George (of the dragon), and an officer in the army of Alexander the Great. The *place* of Khizr is equally mythical. The *Tareekats*, or paths, are 'Alee's, and the *Shir'at*, or holy law, is the Prophet's. Khizr is called the chief of all of the *Evliâs*, or saints.

In the girdle of the Order is a stone called the *Pelenk;* it has seven corners, or points, called *Terks*, in token of the seven heavens and seven earths which God created, also the seven seas, and the seven planets; for God has said, "We have created the seven heavens in seven folds, and seven earths in the same form, all out of light." He then commanded all of these to worship Him, which they do, continually revolving round His holy throne. The *Pelenk* is very useful, and the Sheikh of the Order puts it on and off, each seven times, saying,—

1. "I tie up greediness, and unbind generosity.
2. "I tie up anger, and unbind meekness.
3. "I tie up avarice, and unbind piety.
4. "I tie up ignorance, and unbind the fear of God.
5. "I tie up passion, and unbind the love of God.
6. "I tie up hunger, and unbind (spiritual) contentment.
7. "I tie up Satanism, and unbind Divineness."

When putting it on a disciple, he says to him, "I now bind up thy waist in the path of God. O, holy name, possessed of all knowledge! Whoever knows His name will become the *Nâib*, or successor of the Sheikh." He next offers up the following prayerful address: "There is no God but Allah, Mohammed is the Prophet of Allah: 'Alee is the *Valee*, or friend of Allah; Abu Muslim, the nephew of 'Alee, is the sword of Allah; Mehdee is the master of the *Imâmat*, and the *Ameen*, or confidant of Allah. Moses is the Word of God, Jesus is the Spirit of God, and Noah is the sword of God. It is not to be opened by 'Alee excepting with the sword called Zoolfakâr. Our first *Valee*, or Founder, is *Bektâsh*, the middle the Dervish Mohammed, and the last was Mustapha, the owner of the *Kitâbet*, or writing. The knowledge of the world is to know the *Shir'at*, or holy law; the *Tareekat*, or new path; and the *Ma'rifet*, or new science of spiritualism. These are the portals of our Order."

The Sheikh also adds as instruction—"There are 40 *Makâms*, or seats, 360 degrees, 28 *Menzils* (places of rest), 12 spheres, 24 hours, 4 *Fasls*, or chapters, 7 climes, 4 Karârs, 13,000 worlds, 7 *Sebul i Mesâvee*, or *Ayats* (verses), called the mother of the Koran, 7 Letters, 7 Fâtihas (first chapters, or openings) of the Koran; all of these are called *Hàl* (dispositions), and not *Kâl* (sayings). There is but one light; the truth is the moon, and these were given to Adam. He who has found the science of his own body, called the *'Ilm i Vujood* (or the counterpart of himself in a spiritual sense), knows his Lord; for the holy Prophet has said, 'To know thyself is to know the Lord.' In this is comprised a knowledge of thy own secret, and that of thy Creator."

The latter is a Mussulman idea that every one in this world possesses a *Peer* in the spiritual existence, called the *Mesâl*, or equal, who dies forty days previous to his temporal self. The *Mesâl* is supposed to know everything, and to teach the temporal body to which it belongs by visionary forewarnings. It is also believed (on a verse of the Koran) that God does not make saints of the ignorant. He first has them taught by the *Mesâl*, and then makes them to be *Evliâ* (the plural of *Vâlee*, or saint). It therefore fills the place of a guardian spirit, or angel. The temporal body thus becomes, by its means, freed from all darkness, and moreover is transferred into a *Noor*, or light to others. It is then a complainer for the woes of mankind (*Ehl i Derd*); its pledge of faith finds its place, and is a "faithful one" in God.

THEIR COSTUME.

Haideree is a vest without sleeves, and with a streak of a different colour, somewhat resembling in form a word, supposed to be that of the fourth Caliph 'Alee. It should, also, have twelve lines on it, signifying the twelve Imâms.

Khirka is a cloak, or mantle, without a collar, and with the same streak as the vest.

Taibend is a girdle which is worn around the waist, and is made only of white woollen materials.

Kamberieh is a cord, also worn around the waist, to which is attached a stone. This latter is round or oblong, mostly of crystal, called Nejef. The cord has three buttons or knots; the first knot is called *El bâghee* (hand-tie), the second *Dil bâghee* (tongue-tie), and the third *Bel bâghee* (rein-tie). These serve to remind the wearer that he must neither steal, lie, nor commit fornication.

Mengoosh are the earrings which are put in the ears of the new disciple. If only one ear is drilled it is called *Hasanee*, from one son of 'Alee; and if both are pierced they are called *Husainee*, from the other son of the same Caliph. It is optional with him.

Tâj is the name of the cap which all wear in common. It is made of white felt, and is in four parts. The first shows that the wearer has given up the world; the second, that he has abandoned all hopes of Paradise; the third, that he disdains all hypocrisy, and means that the Dervish cares not whether he is seen or not praying, and is wholly indifferent to public opinion; the fourth is the total abandonment of all the pleasures of life, and that he belongs to and is fully satisfied with Allah alone. Their names also, are *Sheree'at*, *Tareekat*, *Hakeekat*, and *Ma'rifat*.

The Sheikhs all wear the *Tâj*, with twelve *Terks*, which are of four *Kapoos*, or doors. These twelve allude

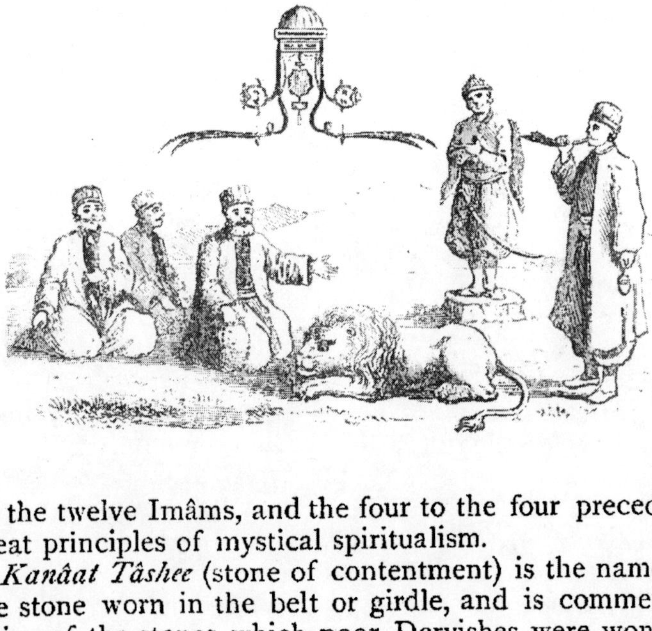

to the twelve Imâms, and the four to the four preceding great principles of mystical spiritualism.

Kanâat Tâshee (stone of contentment) is the name of the stone worn in the belt or girdle, and is commemorative of the stones which poor Dervishes were wont to put in their girdles to appease or allay the pangs of hunger. They used to be three in number, the one worn inside the other; but it is supposed that aid comes to their relief before the necessity arises of using the full number of three.

Terjumân, or interpreter, is the name of the secret word or phrase of the Bektâshees. It varies according to the occasion.

When a Mureed, or neophyte, is desirous of joining the Order, he goes to the *Tekkieh*, and at its sill a sheep is sacrificed by one of the fraternity. Its flesh is eaten by the members, and from its wool his *Taibend* is made.

It is related that the Caliph 'Alee had a horse called *Duldul*, on whose legs a rope was usually tied by his groom named *Kamberia*. The latter, when accompanying his master, used to tie the rope around his waist. It had three knots, called as aforestated *El bâghee*, *Dil bâghee*, and *Bel bâghee*.

Regarding the stone which was worn round the neck, the following tradition is given:—

"*Moosâ* (the Prophet Moses) was once bathing in the river Nile. He had laid his shirt on a stone, and the latter running away, followed by Moses, entered the city of *Misr* (Cairo). Moses reproached the stone for carrying off his clothes, but it told him that it did so by Divine command, and that he should ever after keep a stone suspended to his neck, in memory of the occurrence. He called the stone *Dervish-dervishân*, and it contained twelve holes. During all his travels, by means of this stone Moses performed miracles, among which was the producing of fountains of water, simply by striking it on the ground."

So much significancy is given to the *Tâj*, or cap, worn by this Order of Dervishes, that I may add some farther account of it.

They state that all the letters of the alphabet originated in the first one, called *alif*, or *a*. The original cap is said, in the same manner, to be of a similar source, and this is called the *Elifee*, or cap of A.

It is considered to be the sign of the *Khaleefat*, or succession of the blessed Prophet, and when he appointed a Sheikh to succeed him, he made a cap of the form of the celebrated sword of 'Alee, named *Zoolfakâr*. After this, the cap assumed other forms, peculiar to the four chief *Tareeks*, or Orders; one was called the *Malikee*, one the *Saifee*, one the *Shurhee*, and one the *Halawee.*

The cap of *Hâjee Bektâsh i Valee*, is of twelve Terks. He made a second called the *Tâj i Jannoosh* of nine Terks, and another was worn in Persia, of seven Terks, called the *Sayyid i Jelâl*, after the eminent man of that name. This person was the founder of the Order of the *Jelâlees*, who have no *Tekkiehs* in Constantinople, though members of it often go there from Persia as travellers. There is still another cap sometimes worn by the Bektâshees, called *Shahbâz i Kalenderee*, after the founder of the *Kalenderees*, made of seven Terks, of white felt, said to have been assumed by a Shah (king) of Balkh, named *Edhem*, and is called therefore the *Edhemee.* He is said to have abandoned his throne so as to become a Dervish. It is also said that to his time, the Dervishes were all called after *Junaidee*, a holy man of that name resident in Bagdad, and there was then but one *Tareek*, or Order.

As a detailed description of the cap, I may add, that the cap is called the *Peer* in honour of the founders of the various *Tareeks*, and that on it was originally written, "All things will perish, save His (the Omniscient's) face, and to Him will all return," taken from the last lines of the 28th chapter of the Koran.

Around the top was written the *Ayat al Kursee*, from the 2d chapter of the Koran, and ending with the 256th verse.

Around its edges was written the 36th chapter of the Koran, called the *Soora i Yasee.*

Inside was written the 41st chapter of the Koran; near its edge the 53d verse, "We will cause our miracles to shine over the different countries of the earth."

On its front, the 109th verse of the 2d chapter, "To God belongs the east and the west; turn to whichever side you will, you will meet His countenance; God is immense, and knows all things."

On the other side was written the Mussulman Confession of Faith, "There is no God but Allah, and Mohammed is the Prophet of Allah," and "'Alee is the *Valee*, or Friend of Allah."

Behind it was written the 29th verse of the 2d chapter of the Koran, "God taught to Adam the names of all beings, afterwards He brought them before the angels, and said to them, 'Name them to him if you are sincere.'"

A stone which the Bektâshees wear suspended on their necks is called the *Tesleem Tâshee*, or "Stone of Submission." One of the interpretations given regarding it is, that it is worn in remembrance of the bestowal of Fâtimeh, the daughter of the Prophet, upon his nephew 'Alee. It is said that, on this occasion, her father took her hair in his hand, and giving it into that of 'Alee, delivered her up to him.

In their ears they wore another stone called the *Mengoosh Tâshee*, of this shape ◡, or that of a new moon, in remembrance of the horse-shoe of 'Alee. Around their waists they wore belts called *Kamberia*, made of dark-coloured goats' wool or hair, with several knots, which, passing through a ring attached to one end of it, serve to fasten it. These knots are called as aforestated.

On their legs they wear leather gaiters, called *Dolak*, from one of the principal disciples of Bektâsh, named Baba 'Omar (Dolakee), who wore them.

Suspended from their belt is a small bag called *Jilbend*, made after the following form  on which is embroidered the name of 'Alee, and serves to contain papers and books. It is said that the Prophet gave such a bag to his uncle Hamza, in Mekkeh.

A Begtâshee is not allowed to beg; and if he ever does, it is after fasting three days, and then only at seven doors. If these give him nothing he must cease. When begging, they are called *Selmân*, after Hazreti Selmân i Fârsee, and must carry their *Keshgool*, or beggar's cup, under their clothes.

An Oriental friend gives the following extract from a

journal kept by him during an excursion in Asia Minor, referring to the founder of this Order.*

"Toozkyöy, *i.e.* 'Salt Village,' situated in a volcanic part of the country, contains about one hundred houses, the inhabitants of which are all grazers, and possess many cattle, sheep, and Angora goats. The name originates from the salt mines about a quarter of an hour distant, and which are still worked. According to tradition, they have been created by the famous Hâjee Bektâsh, the founder of the Order of that name, who on passing through this village was regaled with unsalted meat. When he asked the cause of the absence of savour to his meat, he was informed that the inhabitants had no salt, whereupon he struck upon the ground with his stick; and so produced, miraculously, a salt mine. Up to the present time, annually about 1,000 batmâns (17,000 lbs.) of salt are delivered to the *Tekkieh* opposite, on the river Kizil Irmak, near to the village of Hâjee Bektâsh, where also the shrine of this founder is to be seen. On the height which dominates the city, there is a number of buildings, among which is a Mosque, and the tomb of Sayyidi Ghâzee Battâl, a Medreseh, and a *Tekkieh*, inhabited by some four or five Dervishes of the Bektâsh Order. A verandah, built of marble, leads to the interior of this building, and the traveller is shown here two relics of Hâjee Bektâsh, viz.: in the well, the impression of his mouth and teeth, which, to judge from the size, must have been of the dimensions of those of a buffalo; and in the entrance gate, an impression of his hand and finger."

The hall of a convent or *Tekkieh* of the Bektâsh Order is always a square. In its centre is a stone with eight corners, called the *Maidân tâsh*, in which, on occasions of ceremony, stands a lighted candle; around this are twelve *posts* or *postakees*, seats consisting of white sheepskin. Whenever a Mureed is to be initiated, the candle is removed from the stone, and one is placed in front of each of the *posts*. Among the explanations given of this stone is the following:—"The Prophet used to put a stone in his girdle to suppress, by its pressure, the

* Dr. Mordtmann.

cravings of hunger, and that this one, as well as that worn in the girdle of the fraternity of this Order, is in remembrance of his practice. It is said that Hâjee Bektâsh called the candlestick which stands on this stone his eye, the candle his face and the room his body."

In the *Tekkieh* is a stick, called the *Chellik*, of this shape, with which the members are punished in case of need. It is in remembrance of the stick with which 'Alee punished his groom *Kamberia*, and the latter ever afterwards carried it in his belt.

The twelve *posts* are in remembrance of the twelve Imâms, and are as follows:

1. Is the seat of the Sheikh, who personifies 'Alee.

2. Of the cook, called the *post* of Said 'Alee Balkhee, one of the Caliphs of the Order.

3. Of the breadmaker, called after Baheem Sultan.

4. Of the *Nakeeb* (Deputy Sheikh), named after Gai Gusoos.

5. Of the *Maidân*. It is occupied by the Superintendant of the Tekkieh, who represents Saree Ismâïl.

6. Of the steward of the *Tekkieh*, called after Kolee Achik Hâjim Sultan.

7. Of the coffeemaker, called after Shazalee Sultan.

8. Of the bag-bearer, called after Kara Devlet Jân Baba.

9. Of the sacrificer, called after Ibrahim Khaleel Ullah, or the prophet Abraham of the Old Testament.

10. Of the ordinary attendant of the services, called after 'Abdal Moosà.

11. Of the groom, called after Kamber, the groom of the Caliph 'Alee.

12. Of the *Mihmândâr*, or the officer charged with attending upon the guests of the *Tekkieh*, called after Khizr.

The apartment of the Sheikh is called the *Sheikh Hudjrasee*, or "cell of the master." He seldom resides in the *Tekkieh*, but occupies a separate house with his family. He, however, sometimes makes a vow of celibacy, called the *Mujarred Ikrâr*, in which case he resides in the Convent. A Bektâshee Dervish on making this vow is asked by the Sheikh whether, if he breaks it, he is willing to come under the sword of 'Alee (the *Zoolfakâr*), and he answers in the affirmative, and adds that he may be cut asunder by the sword of our *Shâh i Velâyet*, or supreme "spiritual chief," who is 'Alee. This is one of the secret vows of the Order. The number twelve is a mystical one for the Bektâshees, for whenever any one makes a vow, called the *Nezr*, he always incurs the penalty of twelve punishments should he fail to keep it; he swears by the twelve, pays money in twelves, and strikes twelve blows as a punishment. This, I am told, is done simply in imitation of the practice of the Founder. The *Zikr Ullah*, or Prayers of the Brethren in the *Tekkieh* are always silent, and have, it is said, the following origin:

It is related as coming from 'Alee—may God bless him with His Divine Satisfaction!—"I once asked of the Prophet, 'O Prophet of Allah, instruct me in the shortest way to God, and facilitate me in the proper way to worship Him.' He replied, 'O 'Alee, the proper way is to mention, or call upon His Name.' I asked how I should mention Him, and he answered, 'Close your eyes, and listen to me, repeating after me, *Lâ illâha ill' Allah*, (there is no God but Allah). These words the Prophet uttered three times with his eyes closed, speaking with a loud voice, and I imitated him."

It is said that once when the Prophet and 'Alee were alone together, the former knelt, and 'Alee did the same before him, so that their knees met. The Prophet commenced reciting the preceding, three times; the first time with his face turned over his left shoulder, the second with his face over his breast, and the third with his face turned to his left shoulder; his eyes were closed, and his voice raised, confirming his *Hadees*, or saying, "The best of mentions or prayers is, 'There is no God but Allah.'"

This form of prayer is called the *Jehree*, or Audible, and is common to many other Orders also. The silent one is called the *Hiffee*, and had its origin in the commands of the Prophet to Abu Bekr when they were concealed together from their enemies in a cave. It may be added the 40th verse of the 9th chapter of the Koran is the basis of the form of prayer of all the Dervishes, *i.e.* "They were both in a cave, and he (the Prophet) said to his companion, 'Be not grieved, for God is with us, He has caused his protection to descend from on high, and sustained him with invisible armies, and he overthrew the word of the infidels. The Word of God is much the highest,—He is powerful and wise.'"

The members of a Bektâshee *Tekkieh*, who offer the name of an individual to the Sheikh for acceptance, are called *Rehpers*, or Guides; those who accompany him in the *Tekkieh* during the initiation, are called *Terjumâns*, or Interpreters, and the latter are armed with a weapon called *Tebber*, of this shape ⊢<. The cord which is put round his neck, when first entering the *Tekkieh*, is called the *Dehbend*, or *Taybend*. The horn which the Bektâshees blow is called the *Luffer*; it is also called after one of the titles of God, *Vedood*, or the Loving.

One of the secret signs of the Order are in the two words *Tebran* and *Toolan*, "Far and near," signifying "near in affection and far in conceit." The second *Tie* called *Bâgh*, or *Bend*, is in the words, "He was the Sovereign of the *Telkeen* (Spiritual or Mystical) instructors of all the *Peers*, or founders of Orders, and of their vows," and its execution is the *'Ahd i Vefâ* (performance of vow).

THE TWELVE IMÂMS OF THE BEKTÂSHEES.

"It is related that the blessed Prophet told his confidential companions (the *As-hâbs*) that he did not require of them either the performance of the *Namâz* (prayers), the *Savm* (fast,) the *Hajj* (pilgrimage to Mekkeh), or the *Zekyât* (bestowal of alms to the poor), but only that they should look after the members of his family."

The Prophet had but one daughter, Fâtimeh, whom he married to his nephew 'Alee. The 'Aleeide Dervishes, and especially the Bektâshees, declare that the Prophet designed him to be his successor (Kaleefeh) or "Caliph," whilst the orthodox Mussulmans deny it. This daughter bore two sons, named Hasan and Husain, to whom the Prophet, who had no male children, was warmly attached. These are the first Imâms of Islamism, for although many deny their rights of succession, their direct descent from the Prophet surrounds them with a halo of veneration, respect, and affection. Hasan was poisoned, and lies interred at Medineh, and Husain was killed by Yezeed bin Muavieh, and is buried at Kerbalay.

The fourth Imâm was Zain el 'Abedeen, and son of Husain; he was killed by Merwân, the son of Yezeed, and is buried at Medineh.

The fifth, Mohammed Bâkir, was killed by Hushâm, son of 'Abd ul Malik, and interred at Medineh.

The sixth, Ja'fer es Sâdik, was killed by Mansoor i Kufr, and is buried at Medineh.

The seventh, Moosà el Kiâsim, was killed by Haroon er Rasheed, with poisoned grapes, and is buried at Bagdad. The spot is still called *El Kiazzemain.*

The eighth was 'Alee Moosà er Rizâ; he was killed by the Caliph Maimoon, and is buried at Khorassan, now called the *Meshhed i A'lâ.*

The ninth, Mohammed Tâghee, was killed by the Caliph Mostakeem, and is buried at Semara, near Bagdad.

The tenth, 'Alee Nâkhi', was killed by the Caliph Mostakeem, and is interred at the same place.

The eleventh, Hasan el 'Askeree, was killed by the Caliph Muta'ammid, and is buried at the same place.

The twelfth, Mehdee, who is said to have mysteriously disappeared the 15th day of Sha'bân, and the 266th year of the Hegira, at Semara, and there is a cave at that place from which, it is supposed, he will reappear. All the Dervishes confidently expect this, and so do most devout Mussulmans and that he will reign as a temporal sovereign.

These were all sons of the Imâm Husain. Hasan also had children. The grandchildren of both escaped from these massacres, and from them descended the *Sayyidat*, or the *Sayyids* (Cids), who wear green turbans as a family distinction, a colour which, it is said, Allah commanded the Prophet to use. There were two kinds of *Sayyids* (sometimes called also *Emeers*, commanders);

they are *Sayyidat 'Aleevieh*, or those born to 'Alee by another wife, and not by Fâtimeh. They all have a jurisdiction, in many respects, separate from ordinary Mussulmans, under the direction of a functionary called the *Nakeeb el Eshref*, who resides at Constantinople. Every Mussulman claiming to be a Sayyid, is required to possess a document establishing his genealogy.

The following is a translation from a MS. of the Bektâshees, and is an account of their various prayers at their *Tekkieh.*

1. The *Tekbeer* (*Allahu Ekber*) "God or *Allah*, is the greatest of all Gods," on putting on the *Tâj* or cap.
2. Similar.
3. Ditto.
4. When he visits the *Tekkieh* as a guest.
5. On arriving at the sill of the inner door.
6. On entering it.
7. On taking the first step inside it.
8. " second "
9. " third "
10. " fourth "
11. On approaching the Murshid (Sheikh).
12. On offering him a present.
13. On standing before him, with the arms crossed on the breast, one hand over each shoulder, and the right toe over the left toe, called *Dar durmak.*
14. Similar, called the *Dar i Mansoor*, after Mansoor, who was killed.
15. On the same occasion.
16. For sins.
17. "
18. Called the *Kunâh i gulbenk*, or prayer for sins of omission, and to thank God for His bounties.
19. Called *Tekbeer i Khirka ve Post*, or for the mantle and seat.
20. Ditto, for the *Khirka* only.
21. "

22. For the *Fenâee*, or cap.
23. For ditto.
24. A *Terjumân*, of the Tesleemtâsh.
25. Ditto.
26. „
27. A Tekbeer, on the Alef-lâm-ed, the Tennooreh, the Pelenk.
28. On the Pelenk.
29. „ „
30. „ *Alef-lâm-ed.*
31. „ *Kamberia.*
32. „ ditto.
33. „ *Tennooreh.*
34. „ Mengoosh.
35. *Chirâg*, or candle, after the *Deleel*, or ceremony at the outer door.
36. Ditto.
37. „
38. „
39. On the *Chellik* or whip.
40. „ *Keshgool*, beggar's cup.
41. „ *Postakee* of the Nâib.
42. „ „ of the cook.
43. „ *Chahar Yâr*, or four direct Caliphs.
44. „ *Kurbân*, or sacrifice.
45. On asking permission of the Sheikh to go to the table.
46. On spreading the table.
47. On the table.
48. On his seat at the table.
49. On the *Maidânjee*, or sweeper of the hall of the *Tekkieh.*
50. *Terjumân*, or the *Gusul*, or ablutions.
51. On the door.
52. „ Dar i Mansoor.
53. „ Drink-giver.
54. „ *Salâm* (salutation).
55. „ Attendants.
56. „ Flag and Lamentations for the cruel fate of Hasan and Husain.

57. On the Flag.
58. „ Chirâg of the Centre Stone.
59. On emptying the *Keshgool* on the table.
60. On the *Tebber*, the *Fignee*, and the *Chellik*, peculiar instruments used by the Bektâshees when on a long journey.
61. When putting on the girdle.
62. On the *'Ashk i Mengoosh*, or love for the horse-shoe of 'Alee, used as an ear-ring.
63. On the *Jemjemeh*, or skin thrown over the shoulders of the Bektâshees when travelling.
64. On the *Terjumân i Dalak*, or leggings.
65. „ *Levenk*, or long shirt worn by them.
66. „ *Muliffeh*, a wide dress worn by them.

(These two latter refer to the garments worn by the Prophet when he declared "'Alee is my body, blood, soul and flesh: my light and his light are one.")

67. Of the *Dehbend*, or the rope which is put round the disciple's neck when first introduced into a *Tekkieh.*
68. On the *Sherbet*, or drink.
69. Ear-rings.
70. „ Sacrifice.
71. On Shaving.
72. On entering a *Tekkieh.*
73. „ the door.
74. „ some steps.
75. On approaching the Sheikh.

The following are translations of a few of the preceding prayers. Some of them are ordinary Islam prayers, and many so closely resemble each other as not to be of any particular interest as explicative of the Dervish Orders. The word *Terjumân*, or "Interpreter," has also the signification of a prayer, though only with relation to spiritualism.

1. *Terjumân* of the door sill:—

"I have placed my head and soul (heart) on the sill of the door of repentance, so that my body may be pure as gold. My request is that you, O Sheikh, deign to turn your eyes for an instant on this *Fakir.*"

2. *Terjumân* on presenting an offering to the Sheikh:—

"The ant brought as an offering to Soliman (son of David), the thigh of a grasshopper; thou, O Sheikh, art Soliman, and I am thy ant; pray accept of my humble offering."

3. *Terjumân* on saluting the Sheikh and Dervishes :—

"*Salâm alaik* (peace to thee), O ye followers of the true path; ye elders of the light of truth; ye disciples of true knowledge."

4. On asking forgiveness of a fault :—

"I have failed, O Sheikh,—pardon me for the sake of *'Alee el Murtezà*, with whom God was satisfied; for the sake of Hasan, the martyr of Kerbelâ. I have wronged myself, O Sheikh!"

5. On putting on the cap, called *Fenâee* :—

"Sign of the glorious Vais el Kurâ; of Kamber the groom of the sublime 'Alee,—of those who are dead, of the great family of the Imâm Rizâ—permit me to put on this cap; for I fully believe in its efficacy."

6. On putting on the eight-angular stone, called the *Tesleemtâsh* :—

"O Allah, the rites of the *Erenler* (disciples) have become my faith; no doubt now exists in my heart; on putting on the *Tesleem* I have given myself up to Thee."

7. Ditto on the ear-ring :—

"End of all increase, ring of the neck of all prosperity, token of those who are in Paradise, gift of the martyr Shah (Husain), curses upon Yezeed" (who killed him).

8. A *Tekbeer* of the *Tesleemtâsh* :—

"Allah! Allah! In the name of Allah, the Merciful and the Clement! God commanded him (Moses) to strike the stone with thy staff, and twelve fountains were suddenly opened by the blow (2d chapter of the Koran and 57th verse). We sent a cloud over your heads,—we sent you manna and quails, saying, Eat of the delicious food which we have sent you; you have more wronged yourself than me."—Koran ii. 54.

9. A *Tekbeer* of the *Alif-lâm-ed* and the *Pelenk* :—

"God has been satisfied with the believers who have given thee their hand under the tree, as a sign of fidelity. He knew the thoughts of their hearts. He gave them tranquillity, and recompensed them with a speedy victory," and ending with the exclamations, "O Mohammed! O 'Alee."—Koran xlviii. 18.

10. Ditto of the *Alif-lâm-end*, on taking the vow of celibacy:—

"I abandon all matrimony, and obligate myself with this belt to do so." (He then recites chapter cxii. of the Koran, and the Sheikh declares to the Mureed, "God does not engender nor bring forth, (and so may men tell of thee), and no one is equal to Him").

11. A *Terjumân* of *Kamber*:—

"I am become a *Kamberee* in the footsteps of thy steed. Under thy feet I have long suffered. 'I have become the leader of all prophets,' says Mohammed. Thou (the Sheikh) seest all things; thou knowest all things; thou art all things to me."

12. A *Terjumân* of the *Tennoorch*:—

"O thou who art devoted to the Path, cling to thy Peer, and wander not about. From thy heart follow the noble Hyder ('Alee); attach the stone to thy ear; be a servant; come to the Shah of the Erens, and become the ostler of the ostler of 'Alee."

13. A *Terjumân* of the *Chirâk* (Light).

This is given after a lesson from the *Peer*, on the proper method of extinguishing it.

"Allah is my friend. Hakh! Hoo! Erens! Ashik! Faithful! Those who burn with Love! The Awake! The 'Ain i Jem'!" (This latter is the name of the place where they meet.) "The abiders in Love! Splendid Light! The Pride of all Dervishes!" (This is said to refer to the custom of 'Alee, who caused his friends to meet him, and lit a candle in their midst.) "Laws of all Mankind! Shah of Khorassan! By the beauty of Mohammed! The perfection of 'Alee! Hoo! Dost!"

14. On the same:—

"Allah! Allah! We have lit this light—the pride of all Dervishes, for the love of God,—the love of the Lord of both worlds,—the seal of all prophets,—the love of Him who gives water from the fountain of *Kevther* (in Paradise),—'Alee, the chosen of Khadeejah, the best of women (the Prophet's first wife) of Fâtimeh,—the twelve hearts of the *Peers*,—the leaders of the Saints,—the sons of 'Alee, and the Imâms Hasan and Husain—for the fourteen pure victims, sons of the Imâm Husain, and the family of *El 'Abâ*." (This refers to the circumstance that the Prophet once collected under his *'abâ* or cloak 'Alee, Hasan and Husain, and Fâtimeh, himself being the fifth). "For the love of the *Hazret i Khonkiâr*, the *Kutub i Evliâ!* May it burn and enlighten to the last of days the love of Hâjee *Bektâsh Valee*,—by the beauty of the Prophet and the perfection of 'Alee! Hoo!"

15. Ditto:—

"Light of the saints! light of the heavens! May this spot be like the mountain of *Thoor* (Sinai), where Moses saw the divine light, and worshipped it! Whenever thou art lit, may the lighter offer up a prayer for Mohammed and 'Alee!"

16. Ditto of the *Chellik* (stick):—

"Death to all those who believe in the Trinity! Say it does not open, except by 'Alee,—there is no sword but that of *Zoolfakâr*." (This is from a verse of the Koran).

17. Ditto of the *Keshgool*:—

"Poor of the door of 'Alee; beggars of the *Keshgool* of the *Derkiâh* (*Tekkieh*); *Sened* (bond) of the lovers! In the name of 'Alee! Hoo! Dost! Ay Vallah!"

18. Ditto of the *Post*:—

"I look upon the face of a fair friend. O elevated man (the Sheikh), thou hast the two lines (the eyebrows), thy seat is the seat of the *Ellest*." (This refers to the 171st verse of the 3d chapter of the Koran. It is their belief that the light of the prophets descended from God upon the foreheads and between the eyes, and the pious Dervish, closing his eyes, becomes absorbed in thought, so as to produce, in imagination at least, on his own forehead, the form and figure of the *Peer* of his Order. This *Äyat* or verse is considered as forming an *Ikrâr*, or vow of faith. The *postakees* of the four angels are the seats of God,—these are, 1st, *Shereeʼat*, 2d, *Tareekat*. 3d, *Hakeekat*, and 4th, *Ma'rifet*). "By the present and the absent; the *Ain i Jem'!* Evenler! Hoo!"

19. Ditto of the *Kurbân* :—

"By the sacrifice of Ismâil (Ishmael), ordered by God through the angel Gabriel! Hoo! Dost! Ay Vallah!"

20. Ditto of the Table.

(This is entirely the 8th and 9th verses of the 77th chapter, and the 114th verse of the 5th chapter of the Koran).

21. Ditto, in entering the *Tekkieh* for the purpose of asking hospitality :—

"Allah is our friend! Joy to the dwellers in the *Tekkieh!* Love to those who are joyful! To all those *Fakeers* now present! To the *Peers* and the *Ustâds* (masters). To the *Nâyibs!* To the dwellers in this house of the Shah ('Alee)!"

22. The following is the *Gulbeng*, or grace before meals, of the Order :—

"O God! O God! by the horn of the archangel Isrâfeel!—by the meaning of Kamber!—by the light of the *Mesjid* (Prophet), and the *Mihrab* and the *Minber* (altar and pulpit, the former pointing towards Mekkeh),—by our Sovereign *Peer*, Hâjee Bektâsh Valee, *Server* (General),—by the Breath of the 3, the 5, the 7, and the 40 true Saints,—we thank Thee! Hoo!"

These numbers refer to the *Rijâl i Ghaib* (or the unseen men), who every morning are supposed to attend at the *Ke'âbeh* (Caaba) of Mekkeh, and who wander over the whole world, by Divine command, to superintend the affairs of mankind. Of the first three, one is called the *Kutb*, or Centre,—the second and third the *Umenâ*, or the Faithful. One stands on the right and the other on the left of the *Kutb*, and they all stand on the summit of the *Ke'âbeh*. They are also called the *Ehl i Tesarruf* (Owners or Masters of Destiny), and they never leave Mekkeh. There are also four others, called *Evtâd* (the Great or Eminent), who wander over the world. The seven are called the *Akhyâr*, or the Very Good, who equally wander over the surface of the globe. The 40 are called the *Shuhedâ*, or the Victims, and their mission is equally the same. There are also 70 others, called the *Budelâ* (plural of *Abdâl*), or the servants of Allah; also eight, called the *Nukebâ*, or the Deputies, and their duties are much like those of the others.

All of these go to Mekkeh every morning, and report the result of their previous day's peregrinations to the *Kutb* or Centre, offer up prayers, and set out anew.

The Horn of the Bektâshees, called the *Luffer*, alluded to in the prayers, is the shape of a wild goat's horn. It is probably in remembrance of the horn of the angel *Isrâfeel.* By it the fraternity are called to refreshment, and warned of danger. It is, as aforementioned, also called *Yâ Vidood* (O Loving God)!

On the Asiatic side of the Bosphorus, inland from the town of Cadi Kyöy (ancient Chalcedon), is a small village called *Merdeven Kyöy*, much visited by pious, as well as simply superstitious Mussulmans, on account of a tomb which it contains. This tomb contains the dust of a Dervish of the Bektâshee Order, named 'Azbi Châush, once a public messenger of the government in the time of the Sheikh ul Islam Vânnee, and the reign of Sultan Ahmed.

This *Châush*, or messenger, was ordered to carry into exile, to the town of Illimiyeh, an individual named Musree Niazzee Effendi. On their way the messenger perceived that, whenever his prisoner performed the *Bismillah* prayer, his fetters fell off his wrists, and, supposing he had a secret method of effecting this, doubled them. Notwithstanding this precaution, the same thing occurred. He therefore became aware that it was to be attributed entirely to his great sanctity, and his respect for him became in consequence very profound.

After reaching Illimiyeh, he resigned his office of Châush, and resided there with this pious man some fifteen years. At the expiration of this period, the exile told his companion that he was about to die. He presented him with his *Tesleemtâsh*, which he had always worn around his neck, and the *Kemer*, or girdle, from his waist, and begged him to return to Stambool, where his wife was about to marry another person, and to eat of her *Zerda Pilâff* (or wedding dish). He reached the capital just as the wedding was about to be consummated, and, having convinced his wife of his identity, was accepted as a husband in the place of the other person whom she had designed marrying. On his decease, 'Azbi Châush was interred at the village of Merdeven Kyöy, and, from having become an eminent Bektâshee, his grave is much visited.

All the various *Tareeks* of the Dervishes profess to base their creeds on the *Koran* and the *Hadeesât*, the latter being the sayings of the Prophet, collected after his decease from among the *As-hâbs*, or intimate friends, who enjoyed familiar intercourse with him. Many of these were procured from second and third, or even many more persons, who having had them the one from the other, enabled the compilers to trace them back to their prophetical origin. They consist in a great measure of axioms, some proverbial, others moral or religious, and others relating only to what men supposed to be his own private wishes, not expressed in the *Koran*, the contents of which were conveyed to the Prophet directly from God by the archangel Gabriel. Mystical as are many of the verses of the Koran, several of these traditional sayings of the Prophet are much more so; and to those who desire to learn the condition of the mind of the Arabs during his time, they offer a wide field for gleanings. They also serve to show the character of Mohammed, and the weight of his mental abilities. The collection exists in Arabic, and, I do not doubt, also in Persian, with commentaries and translations in Turkish. Whatever may be the wanderings of the Dervish Orders from the teachings of the Koran, they all profess to belong to one or the other of the four great commentators on that work. The peculiar devotion of the Bektâshees to the fourth direct caliph 'Alee is shown by the preceding account, as well as their strong attachment to the twelve Imâms, all descended from him. Among the "Sayings of the Prophet," which they quote, are the following:—

"I am the city of science (religious or spiritual), and 'Alee is its portal."

"'Alee is the portal of a vast country; whoever enters

therein is a true believer, and whoever departs from it is an infidel who disbelieves God."

This is said to be the spiritual signification of the 55th verse of the 2d chapter of the Koran. "Enter into this city, enjoy the wealth which is there to your entire satisfaction; but on entering, prostrate yourselves and say, Pity us, O Lord! and He will pardon your sins, for he has said, 'He will bestow our gifts upon the just.'"

"'Alee, and those who follow him, will find salvation in the Day of Judgment."

THE INITIATION OF A BEKTÂSHEE.

The Mureed must be well recommended to the Murshid (Sheikh) of the *Tekkieh* by two members of the fraternity, called the *Rehpers* or guides, previously mentioned. On the night appointed for his reception, he takes with him a sheep for sacrifice, and a sum of money according to his means, as an offering to the Sheikh, which is subsequently divided among the functionaries of the *Tekkieh*, twelve in number. The sheep is sacrificed at the sill of the door, and a rope is made from its wool, and put round his neck. The remainder is preserved for the purpose of being made into a *Taibend* for his subsequent use. The flesh is kept for the meal, of which all partake after the ceremony. As the meetings of the Order are all secret, care is taken that no listeners are concealed about the Tekkieh, and two of the fraternity keep guard outside the door. Three others are *en service*, inside the *Tekkieh*.

The Mureed is deprived of nearly all his clothing, and care is taken that he has nothing on his person of a metallic or mineral character, showing that, on entering the order, and offering himself to the Murshid, he makes a voluntary sacrifice of the world and all its wealth, and other attractions. If he designs taking the *Mujarred Ikrâr*, or Vow of Celibacy, he is stripped entirely naked, whilst, in case he does not, his breast alone is bared. The rope is put around his neck, and he is led into the hall of the Tekkieh by two *Terjumâns*, or spiritual interpreters, *en service*, inside of it. He sees before him twelve persons, all seated, one of them is the Murshid (Sheikh), and before each a lighted lamp or candle. He is led to a stone of twelve angles in the centre of the hall, called the *Maidân Tâsh*, and directed to stand upon it, with his arms crossed on his breast, and his hands resting on his shoulders. This is called *Boyun Kesmek*, or "bending the neck in humble respect and perfect submission." His right great toe is pressed over the left great toe, and his head is inclined towards his right shoulder, his whole body leaning towards the Sheikh.

One of the *Terjumâns*, addressing the Sheikh, announces to him that he has brought him a *Kool*, or slave, and asks whether he will accept of him, to which the Sheikh acquiesces. Addressing the Sheikh, he repeats the following prayer after the guide :—

"I have erred,—pardon my fault, O Shâh! for the sake of the accepted one ('Alee), of the exalted place,—for the sake of Husain, the martyr of Kerbelâ. I have done wrong to myself, and to our lord, and I implore pardon of him."

His fault is in having deferred becoming a member of the Order. The Sheikh recites the prayers prescribed in the Litany aforementioned, and the disciple responds to them from the same, taught him previously by the two *Rehpers*, who recommended him to the Sheikh. At their conclusion, the two *Terjumâns* lead him off the stone, and holding him by the arms, conduct him to the Sheikh, before whom he bows low, and then prostrates himself. He then kneels before the Sheikh in a peculiar position, the former taking his hand into his own.

The *Maidân Tâsh* represents the altar on which, in obedience to the Divine command, *Ibrâhim* (Abraham) was about to offer up his son Ishmâ'il (Isaac). The kneeling position of the Mureed is that which, it is said, was taken by 'Alee before the Prophet, his knees touching those of the Sheikh; each holds the other's right hand, the two thumbs raised up in the form of the letter *Alif* (*a*), the first of the Oriental alphabet. He places his ear near to the Sheikh's mouth, and the latter recites to him the 10th verse of the 48th chapter of the Koran :—"Those who, on giving thee their hand, swear to thee an oath of fidelity,—swearing it to God ; the hand of God is placed on their hands. Whoever violates his oath, does so to his hurt, and he who remains faithful to it, will receive from God a magnificent recompense."

The two *Rehpers* who conducted the Mureed to the *Tekkieh*, remain outside of the door, armed with the weapon formerly described, called *Tebber*.

Some say that, as the Bektâshees believe in a certain principle of a Pantheistical character, the Sheikh whispers in the ear of the disciple a doctrine to which he must consent, under the penalty of death, and that he must admit that "there is no God," meaning, however, that all living nature is God ; but others deny it, and from a good Dervish source I have learned that it is not correct.

I have also been told that there are other secrets of the Order which are imparted by the Sheikh to the Mureed, under a fearful penalty in case he imparts them ; but as these are not printed, nor even written, they are known only to those of the Order. These form the *Ikrârnâmeh*, or vows of the fraternity. The Bektâshees call the Sheikh "'Alee," and the *Rehper*, "Mohammed," thus placing, in their spirito-mystical category, the Prophet lower than the Caliph. It is also said, that the Mureed, before his acceptance, is placed under surveillance for a full year, and has imparted to him certain false secrets, so as to test his powers of fidelity. He is, during this period, called a *Mehakk, i.e.*, one who is being verified. In the meantime he frequents the *Tekkieh*, but learns none of the real mysteries of the Order. None are present at the initiation beyond the Sheikh, the representatives of the other eleven Imâms, and the *Terjumâns*. It is called the *Ikrâr ;* and whenever a Dervish is asked to whom he made his *Ikrâr* (vow), he names the *Peer* or founder of the Order, and not the Sheikh. No other reply is ever expected, or given.

I am also informed that each Sheikh establishes a particular sign by which the members of his own *Tekkieh* may be recognised when knocking for admittance, and that it is responded to from within. This is not general, but is local and conventional.

Among the *Ikrârs* which the Sheikh recites to the Mureed, and which by him are repeated, is the following. It throws some light upon the ritual :—

"In the name of Allah, the Merciful and the Clement.

"I beseech Allah's forgiveness" (repeated three times). "I have come to implore pardon ; I have come in search of the Truth ; I ask it for the sake of God" (the word used is *Hakk*, the "True" or "Just") ; "truth is the true path which leads to God,—the All True whom I know ; what you call evil is the evil which I also know, and will avoid taking with my hand what belongs to another. I repeat (three times) 'Repent of your sins unto God,—a repentance without any return to sin.'" (From the Koran).

The Sheikh adds, "Eat nothing wrong ; speak no falsehoods ; quarrel with no one ; be kind to those below you in life ; show respect to your superiors, and be good to those who visit you ; do not criticize the faults of others, if you see them conceal them ; if you cannot do this with your hand do so with your skirts, your tongue, and your heart. Be among the correct towards the twelve Orders of Dervishes ; we acknowledge each of the other eleven, for this is according to the precept of the Koran, 'A day will come when nothing will benefit you—neither wealth, nor family,—nothing except submission to God with a pure heart.'"

The Mureed replies by kissing the hand of the Sheikh, who continues :

"If you now accept me as your father I accept you as my son ; hereafter the pledge of God (*Emânet Ullah*) be breathed in your right ear."

Among the *Kâdirees*, *Rufâ'ees*, *Bedâwees*, *Mevlevees*, &c., all of the original twelve Orders, the *Ikrâr* is simply the *Telkeen*, or the name *Allah*.

The conclusion of the *Ikrâr* is the following : the *Murshid* says to the Mureed, who repeats it, "Mohammed is my *Rehper* (conductor)," "'Alee is my *Murshid* (spiritual guide)."

The Sheikh then asks him—

"Do you accept of me as your Murshid?" (in the place and as the representative of 'Alee.)

The Mureed replies,

"I accept of thee as my Murshid."

The Sheikh responds,

"I then accept of thee as my son."

These words may seem to be of little import, yet they have to devout Mussulmans a signification of an impious and awful nature; for they place the blessed Prophet and the Koran inferior to 'Alee, and the Sheikh, as his representative, in the place of the Prophet.

After having been once admitted as a Dervish, the only salutation on entering the *Tekkieh* is to incline the head gently towards the Sheikh, and lay the right hand across the breast, near to the neck, in sign of perfect submission to him. When meeting in public, I am informed, and have verified it by observation, that Dervishes recognise each other by placing the right hand, as if unintentionally, on the chin. Some, and I believe it is a general rule, on entering a *Tekkieh*, or meeting a brother, place the right hand upon the heart, and with a gentle inclination of the body, exclaim, "*Yâ Hoo, Erenler!*"

The reply is, "*Ay Vallah! Shâhim* (or) *Peerim.*"

The former means, "O! Him (God or Jehovah,) Erens" (noble fellows,) and the latter, "Good, by Allah, my *Shah*, or my *Peer.*"

On making an inquiry of the health, they say, "*Keifler Jumbushlerim!*" (Health, my Joys,) and the reply is, "*Ay Vallah Erenlerim!*" (Good, by Allah, my *Erens.*)

On meeting, they say, "*Hoo Dost Erenler*" (Him, friend, Erens), and the reply is, "*Ay Vallah, Erenler.*" On departing, to take leave, they exclaim, "*Ay Vallah!*" and the response is, "*Hoo Dost.*"

I may here add, that these salutations are common to other Orders than the Bektâshees, though generally, in private life, they all use the ordinary Islam one, of

"*Salâm Alaikum,*" "Peace be with you," and the reply is, "*Alaikum es Salâm,*" "With you be peace."

The following extract from the same MSS. is explicative of some of their forms. It is the address of the *Murshid* to the neophyte :—

"Come near and learn the manner in which we lead you in the True Path to Allah. Those who come to the Avowal, are well understood by us ; hearts respond to hearts ; one person is needed who knows the way to be pursued,—one to initiate,—and one to act the part of a friend ; those to be present will all be there (in the *Tekkieh*), and we then lead the Mureed in the Path ; one on his right and one on his left, who are called *Rehpers*, and remain by your side ; three persons act as servants, called *Pervânehs*, and so now we open the wonderful *Tekkieh* for labour. Twelve persons must be there, well knowing the four Columns of the Order ; give up all worldly knowledge, and confide your souls to us ; the *Rehpers* conduct you to the *Dâr* (or the *Maidân Tâsh*), and there you make your vow. You then know what a *Murshid* is, and we also know the same ; you enter by the four doors (the Columns,) and serve under them with warmth and fidelity ; be not a hypocrite, or we will know how to punish you ; the *Murshid* will address you from the texts of the '*Ahd* or Covenant (Koran, vii. 171); receive his words with all your heart, or he will cut off your head. If those who know not God, or the *Peer*, learn from you your secrets, you will be led by them to the prison, and the asylum of the insane, or cause your death, and we will be with you in the hour of merited punishment. Be careful not to follow the dictates of your personal passions, and so wrong the four Columns of our Order ; your place will at first be that of the lowest degree, and if you are faithful, we will raise you to the Pleiades ; associate only with those who, like yourself, have learned the secrets and taken the vow of our Order ; others will divulge what you tell them, denounce you to the public, and cause us to degrade you for your weakness. Follow in the path, and keep the secrets of the *Erens*, and so sustain the high standing of the Order ; whatever comes to your heart regarding the true path, keep it for communion with us; to us you have made your vow, and from us learn the knowledge which you and we must possess.

"Whenever your true friends, the *Rehpers* and the brethren present, are of one mind and heart, they become *Ehl i Bait*, or members of the family of the Prophet (a degree), such as those who were *Ehl i 'Abâ*,· or those who were covered by him with his mantle (a degree),—or all of the 3, the 42, and the 73 in number (a degree). The *Rehpers* must have a sword, the *Zoolfakiâr*; your offering to the *Murshid* must be consistent with your means, and will form your *Nizr* (votive offering); place this in the hand of the bearer of the *Tebber*, it is to cleanse your heart, and fill it with purer thoughts; one half of it is for the *Shâh* (Sheikh, who represents 'Alee), and the rest will be divided into four parts, of which the half is for the Erens, and the other half for the expenses of the *Tekkieh*."

The night of meeting is called that of the *'Ain i Jem'*, the five persons (the *Rehpers* and the *Pervânehs* or *Terjumâns*) must all be of one soul, and of the degree of the *Ehli 'Abâ*, for they are the lights of the congregation, and are called *'Alee*, *Zehrâ*, *Shepper* (or Hassan), *Shâh Peer* (Husain), and the *Hazret-i-Kubrâ* (the Mehdee).

They say that there are four distinct worlds,—the first, *'Âlem-i-Misâl*, or the world of dreams or assimulations; the second, the *'Âlem-i-Ejsâm*, the present, or world of bodies; the third, the *'Âlem-i-Melkoot*, or world of angelic beings; and the fourth, the *'Âlem-i-Nâsoot*, or the world of mortals. Man's existence is divided into three parts,—wakeful existence, when all the mental faculties are vigorous; sleep, when the faculties of life are lulled or annihilated, but the spirit is wakeful; and death, when the body has entirely ceased to possess animation or existence, and the spirit is freed from its mortal ties. The *'Âlem-i-Misâl* is also a state of ecstaticism, when the spirit or soul has perceptions, though the body is not lulled by sleep, of spirituality or of the beautiful in thought. It then may have wakeful visions, of which it is incompetent in ordinary hours, and consequently approaches its Creator.

In the work aforementioned, called the *Nâshihât*, the writer remarks, that the *Soofieh* Sheikhs are those who, through the medium of a perfect conformance to the blessed Prophet, arrive at a degree of approximity to the Divinity, and after this desire to return and inspire others with the wish for the same *Tareck* or path which led themselves to Him. These perfectly pious or devout individuals become, by the grace and favour of God, submerged in the '*Ain i Jem*' of His unity, and wrecked in the depths of the sea of the indubitable truth of the One God only, and their mission is to lead others from the snares of corruption and uncertainty to the exalted shores of perpetual safety. There is, however, another sect, who, having reached the shores of perfection, are not required to retire and seek the salvation of others. They only continue engaged in devout piety, and spend their precious lives in perpetual praises and calling upon the holy name of the Eternal. The former are the *Ehl i Sulook*, or advocates of the true path, and are divided into two classes, the *Mutasoofieh* and the *Melâmieh*,—the one aspiring to *Jennett*, or the celestial Paradise of spiritual felicity, and the other to the *Âkhiret*, or that last period of spiritual existence which never ends. The former, through their incessant adoration and praise of the Omnipotent Allah, become freed from some of the ordinary attributes of humanity, and gifted with some of the characteristics which belong only to spiritual beings, so that they naturally prefer to withdraw from the scenes of life, and spend their days in contemplating that Omnipresent Deity, who is hidden by the veil of mortality from ordinary sight, and to whom they have by this means approached. Though still hanging on the skirts of temporal existence, their souls become reunited, to a certain extent, with the all-pervading Spirit of the Creator.

The *Melâmiyoons*, on the other hand, strive to lead lives of strict virtue and benevolence towards themselves and all mankind. The performance of the virtues of this life, as well as of acts of supererogatory excellence, are deemed by them essential to the path which they adopt, and in this they care but little for the commendation and admiration of the public, for all their acts are performed in reference only to the Divine satisfaction. With them, sincerity, free from all hypocrisy, is the essential object of their lives, and God only is the judge of their conduct. They abstain from all possible rebellion against His commands, the idea even of which is a sin; they are said to expose good and conceal evil, and among them are persons of great excellence of character, commendable for all the virtues and excellences of life; but yet the veil or curtain of mortality is not withdrawn from their eyes, and their vision is that which belongs only to temporal existence. They, therefore, do not possess the same distinct perception as the Sooffiehs of the Divine unity.

CHAPTER VIII.

THE MELÂMIYOONS.

THE original founder of this order in Constantinople came from Broosa. His name is Sheikh Hamza, and on that account they are sometimes called Hamzavees. The author of the Order, *i.e.*, the *Peer*, came from Persia, and his tomb is in the cemetery of Silivria Capusu, beyond the walls of the capital. They say that the chief of all the Orders is Hasan Basree of Basrah, where he died, and that he received his spiritual powers directly from 'Alee.

The Melâmiyoons had a Tekkieh in Scutari, in the *Divijilers*, called that of Himmet Efendi; another in Stambool at Yanee Bakchee, near Nakkâsh Pasha. The latter is called "Himmet Zâdeh Tekkieh-see," and is in appearance like any common dwelling. It bears at present the name of *Bairâmieh.* Another at Kassim Pasha, near Kollaksiz, is called "Sachlee Hâshim Efendi Tekkieh-see." One of their great men is buried at the cemetery of Shahidler, above the Castle of Europe, on the Bosphorus; he was named Ismâ'il Ma'shookee. Another Tekkieh existed in Constantinople, at Ak Seray, called "Oglanlar Sheikhee." Its Sheikh was Ibrahim Efendi, and was immediately behind the *corps de garde* of that locality. He was put to death by order of Sultan Soliman I. on account of his writings, which were considered anti-orthodox. It is said that he had forty Mureeds, all of whom, voluntarily, were decapitated at the same time that he was put to death. On the tombs of the Melâmiyoons are peculiar signs, the origin and signification of which I have not been able to learn. For instance, on that of El Hajee' Omar Aga, deceased A.H. 1122, and that of Abbaji el Hajee' Abdullah Aga, deceased A.H. 1137, which have been shown to me, there is a double triangle of this shape ⧗. Others have a single triangle, thus △, and some with the addition of one or more dots above and beneath the angles. Many have also the "*Muhr-i-Suleemân*," or Soliman's Seal, thus, one triangle covering another, ✡, but without dots or points. Some say that the original Order was the *Khalvetees*, from whom descended the Bairamees, and from these the Hamzavees, by which name the Melâmiyoons are now known in Constantinople.

Like the Order of the Bektâshees, that of the Hamzavees is almost under prohibition at Constantinople, though from widely different causes. The latter, it is said, hold their meetings in secret, in houses in nowise resembling *Tekkiehs*, and for this reason it is thought by some persons that they are Mussulman Freemasons. It has even been said, that the Melâmiyoons have several lodges in the Ottoman Empire, under warrants from a Grand Lodge existing on the Lake of Tiberias, in Palestine, where it was taken after the destruction of Jerusalem.

The word "*Melâmiyoon*" signifies "the condemned," or "the reproached,"—a title assumed by this Order. Their Litany shows them to be a very sincerely pious sect, conscientious in all their dealings, and living much for themselves and their doctrine, without any regard for the opinion of the world. They even disregard external appearances, so much so, that any poor and miserable objects, as destitute of intellect as of the garments necessary to cover their persons, is now called in Stambool a *Melâmiyoon*.

Sheikh Hamza was put to death on a *Fetvâ*, or religious sentence of the Muftee Abu Sâoud, A.H. 969. His remains are buried near the Silivria Gate, in a spot known only to his brethren and particular friends. As his accusation was a strange one, and little understood by the public, he is generally considered either as a very revered martyr, or as an impious disbeliever in Islamism. His crime was that of neglecting to repeat in his prayers the full *Ismâ i Shereef*, which are seven in number, he always omitting the three last. Various traditions are still prevalent in Constantinople about his piety and wonderful spiritual powers ; and 'Abd ul Bâkee, the author of the following *Risâleh*, or pamphlet, has also composed a work, "The Serguzeshteh 'Abd ul Bâkee," giving an entire history of the Order.

He narrates that his grandfather, named Sâree 'Abdullah Efendi, and the writer of a celebrated commentary on the *Methnevee Shereef*, told him that his father, Hâjee Husain Aga, once addressing him, said, "'I am now an old man, and hope before leaving this world to make you acquainted with my friends of God.' I was then not yet arrived at the age of puberty. He told me, 'When you go to see them with me, and are asked what you came for, say, "My desire is God."'" So we both performed the *Abdest*, or Islam ablution before prayers, and accompanied him. We were perfectly alone, and without any servant to attend upon us; we went to a place called *Kerk Cheshmeh* in Constantinople, to the khan called the *Peshtimâl' Odalâree*, and there entered a chamber in which was an aged man engaged in weaving. My father saluted him, and kissed his hand; I did the same; my father told him that I was his son, and that he had brought me in so that he might 'look into my heart.' The old man asked my father whether he had the permission of the Sheikh to bring me, and he replied that he had not, but could bring me without it. On hearing this, the old man struck the wall with his hand, and all the *Ustâds*, or labourers in the khan, entered the room where we were, to the number of twelve, forming a circle, in the midst of which they placed me, and asked me why I had come there. I replied as previously directed by my father, 'My desire is God.' The old man then addressing me, said, 'If you have come for that purpose, drive away all else from your heart, and turn your thoughts entirely to Him, and we will see what our Lord the *Peer* will do in your behalf.' All of those present thereon commenced the *Murâkebeh* and the *Mutavejjeen*, 'contemplation' and 'supplication,' and the old man bade me do the same, which I did, thinking only of Allah. After some time I opened my eyes, and saw a light turning round the circle, and I cried out '*Allah!*' at the same instant the feeling that my heart was filled with the love of God became so impressed upon me that I swooned away, and was quite senseless for an hour. At the end of this time I revived, and looking round me found that all those who had been with me had disappeared, except the old man, who, as previously, was engaged at his work, and my father who sat near me. My father, so soon as I could rise, bade me go with him. My heart was still filled with *light;* I kissed the hand of the old man, and so as to conceal myself I wrapped my cloak over my breast, at seeing which the old man told me no one could see it, and that I must strive always to keep it there.

"On our way, I tried to think who our Sheikh was, and, though I had never seen him, wondered whether I should ever behold his face, at the same time feeling a warm affection for him. I was ashamed to ask my father who he was, but my affection for him increasing, I was, one Friday, requested to accompany my father to the mosque of *Ayâ Sofiâh*, and there perform our prayers. After these were terminated, we left the mosque; my father covered himself, and looked behind him with much respect on account of some person then present. Just then, I perceived an aged man come out of the mosque, who, in passing, saluted us, and inquired of my father who I was, and whether I was not his son. He looked fixedly at me, and immediately I felt like a *Jezbeh*, or crazed person; the people in the way collected round us, and my father told them that I was suffering under a complaint which at times thus affected me. I had to be conveyed home, where I remained in a state of insensibility. After my recovery, I asked my father who the individual was whose regard had so strangely impressed me, and he told me that he was our Lord and Chief, Idreesee 'Alee Efendi, the *Kutb i Zamân*, and the bestower of the *Jezbeh i Rahmân*, and that the brethren whom we had seen at the *Kerk Cheshmeh* were his disciples."

A Translation of the "Risâleh" (pamphlet or tract) of the Hamzâvees, otherwise known as the Melâmiyoon, written by La'lee Efendi Zâdeh 'Abd ul Bâkee, who is buried at the mosque of Eyoob el Ansâree,—on whom be the Divine satisfaction. He entered the Kalender Khâneh in the vicinity of the said mosque, near the Tekkieh of the Bhoharalees. His tomb is near to its doorway. He was originally of the Bairâmieh Order, and subsequently joined that of the Melâmiehs. This Risâleh contains, in detail, the rites of the latter Order, their intercourse, and great love for God.

CHAPTER I.

THE SECTARIAN RITES OF THE MUCH LOVING TAREEK OF THE MELAMIYOON.

The following is the advice which the *Fakeer*, or elder member of the Tareek, gives to the disciple :—

"If, after having performed the *Ahkiâm i Sheree'at*, or religious ordinances, the *Levâzim i Tareekat*, or exigencies of the Order, any one commits an act growing out of the feebleness of the human passions, and contrary to the *Sheree'at* and the Order, and permits himself to use improper language, or commits a sinful act, he will be expelled from the Order; he will not be permitted to re-enter it; but if, after this, he acknowledges his fault, and promises not to commit the same again, and begs to be restored to his place, the way to arrive at it will be pointed out to him, and he will renew his *Be'at*, or confirmation. He must conform strictly to the commands given him,—to the law of God,—the *Akvâl*, or directions of the inspired Prophet, and the *Tareekat* of the saints; he will undergo the disciplinary punishment of the Order, to be re-accepted as before in all love. If, on the contrary, he refuses to do this, he must remain for ever rejected.

"God forbid such an occurrence! Should any one who believes in the *Ehl i Tevheed*, or Unity of the Divinity, so far err as to admit the erroneous doctrine of the *Vahdet el Vujood*,* or the existence of the Divine Creator in all things of His creation, and thus fall from the true path into impiety, persisting, at the same time, in the correctness of his course, adding that *El bait bait Ullah* and *El zait zait Ullah*, it is the duty of every correct person to strive, by gentle means, to withdraw him from such an error, by showing him his fault and the dangers which he incurs, and telling him clearly that, so long as he continues in such a sin, he cannot be of us. He must also be cut off from all intercourse with his former friends and associates, so that no one will commune with him. They must even avoid his presence. Should the Almighty, in His bountiful mercy, again draw him into the true path, and he repent of his sin, the whole false doctrine of his heart will disappear, and he again become a bright light. He will come to his Sheikh, and admit his sins, and return to the discipline of the Order. The *Seâsât i Soofieh*, or punishments of the *Soofees*, are numerous, and are all well known to the Sheikh, so that he can prescribe them according to the fault which the erring one may have committed. After this, he is re-admitted, and the past is forgotten.

"Alas! that whilst at one time it was so necessary to be secret in the matters of our Order, everything has become public. Up to the time of the venerable Mohammed Hâshim, one of the Sheikhs of our Order, there was no need for secrecy: the *Adâb i Tareekat*, or moral rules of the Order, and the *Ahkiâm i Sharee'at*, or holy commands of the law, were brilliantly executed by the *Fakeers*, and no reference was ever made to the judges and governors of the sovereign; everything was done by the command of the Sheikhs of our Order; the faulty admitted their errors and sins, repented of them, and suffered their expiation in this world so as not to do so

* Pantheism.

in the other; their repentance was accepted of God,—their hearts were filled with the light of love, and, as before, they performed the *Zikr i Khefee*, or silent call upon God's name, whilst alone, and the audible call, or *Zikr i Jehree*, when in the midst of the congregation.

"By command of the Most High, after the occurrence of the saintly martyr Beshir Aga, who is interred in Scutari,—may his secret be blessed!—the hearts of the brethren became troubled and sorrowful; they diminished in number; few sought for the path of love; sloth overcame others; the 'Self Reproaching' and the 'Living Ones' (titles of the Order) fell into faulty habits,—daily they became degraded, and it was absolutely requisite to form systems of secrecy for the benefit of the Order. This necessity was declared by Beshir Aga as growing out of the *Asrâr i Kazâ*, or secret Providences, and yet it was hoped that a time would again arrive when the secret (*Bâtin*) would be known (*Zuhoor*), through the brethren who labour for that purpose."

The *Rooh i 'Alem* and the *Khaleefeh* of the blessed Prophet, who is the *Sâhib i Zamân*, receives his bounties and grace by the will of God. This person is called the *Kutb* (Centre), and is a spiritual being placed by Allah over the spiritual world. He sees every place, and knows all things by Divine permission. Of this there is no doubt; whatever be the will of God, he makes apparent, and the faithful must inevitably submit to that will.

The Sheikh must restore the feeble sinner to his original position; he must know the mental condition of each disciple, and this he is able to see through the light of the *Velâyet* (spiritual power of the Peer), and he must see and know all things through the light of the truth (*Hakk*). The light given by the blessed Prophet is peculiar to the Perfect; the holy body and precious heart of the latter become the mirror of God. All the sayings of the Prophet (*Hadeesat*) and his degrees (*Makâmât*) are revealed to the truly devout. These degrees are explained to me as being seven in number, of which there are also seven branches; in all fourteen. To each of them is prescribed one *Asmâ*, name or title of God, and they are also called the *Atvâr i Sebi'ah*. "O God, all favour is from Thee, so is the true path of love and sanctity; show then this true path to those who seek after the All-Just, to those lovers of the All-Beautiful, and lead them to the object of their desires; preserve them from shame and indifference; intoxicate them with the wine of reunion to Thee and love; open to their sight a glimpse of Thy perfect beauty; O thou Living One, Thou Aider, through thy Friend (the Prophet), and the Seal of the universe, on whom be prayers and salvation, and on his family and all his friends. Amen."

ON THEIR ASSEMBLIES.

Whenever those who follow in this path, and who love the unique God, to the number of two or three, or more, meet together and join in the *Tevheed* and the *Zikr*, and their hearts are occupied with their worldly affairs, they should, on their way to the place of meeting, employ their minds with thoughts of God, in all sincerity and purity, and also beg their *Peer* to lend them his spiritual aid, so that when they reach the meeting, they may all, small and great, with humility and contrition, embrace the hand of each other, and devoutly join in the contemplation of the Deity, and turn their faces towards the Grace of the All-Just (*Hakk*), the ever-rising love of Allah, without harbouring in the tongue, in the mind, or otherwise, any thoughts respecting worldly concerns, but, with perfect hearts and active spirits, take part in these pious ceremonies.

They must next offer up those prayers which are conformable with the rules of the Order, seat themselves, and, if there be among them any one possessing a pleasant voice, let him peruse ten verses of the great Koran, and interest the company with some account of the prophets and saints, or even of the Deity. No one must feel concern about his worldly affairs; all their remarks must be relative to the love of God, of pious fervour (here the name used is *Jezbeh*, which signifies craziness, or that condition in which the mind and intellect is taken away from the body by Divine favour, as in idiots); no one not of the Order must be admitted, and should any such be present, the peculiar gift of God (*Faiz Ullah*) will not rest there. After this the assembly must disperse, and each return to his proper worldly occupation. Every one must, even when thus employed, preserve in his heart the love for God. Should other thoughts than these enter his mind, he must forsake his occupation and seek converse with the *Ehl i Fenâ* (those who have abandoned the world) and the *Fukerâ* (Dervishes), and they must not be satisfied with themselves until they have in this manner freed their hearts. When they casually meet each other, let their conversation be always about God, and never consider themselves as being superior to any one else; but, on the contrary, regard themselves as poorer, lower, and more humble than all others—as insignificant, even, as an ant. Following this course, they must, as much as possible, withdraw from all intercourse with the world, seek to gain their living honestly, always endeavouring to lead spiritual lives. They must not divulge the secrets to their families (wives and children), nor to any one who is not a seeker of the truth (*Tâlib Sâdik*), and ask for assistance in attaining to the path of God (*Hakk*). In that case violence must not be used towards him who does divulge them to another in the view of engaging him to join the Order and finds that he refuses; but such cases are rare.

THANKS FOR FOOD.

It is one of the rules (*Erkiân*) of the Order, obligatory on all its members, whenever he is at meals with a brother, or even alone, to retain in his heart the remembrance of God, and, after the conclusion of his meal, to offer thanks to God in a devout prayer. For this purpose, he must sincerely turn his thoughts to Him, and pronounce the *Zikr Ullah* (Koran xxiv. 37, 38: "Men celebrate His praises, whose traffic does not divert their minds from remembrance of Him,—from the observance of prayer, and from the giving of alms, who fear the day wherein man's heart and eyes shall be troubled, so that God may recompense them according to the utmost merit of what they shall have wrought, and add unto them of His abundance a more excellent reward; for God bestoweth on whom He pleaseth without measure"), so that the food of which he has partaken may strengthen him with the love of God. Thus, each mouthful speaks with the tongue, and says, "O God, give us the favour of an humble and faithful believer." In case you do not do this, you will have done violence to the truth; the food will prove ungrateful to you, and seem to say, "This violent person has abandoned Him," and it will complain against you to the Giver of all bounties. Should the food be vegetables or meats, and you seem to ask whether they can speak,—learn from the verse (Koran xvii. 46), "The seven heavens, and all that they contain, as well as the earth, celebrate His praises. There is nothing which does not praise Him; but you do not comprehend their songs of praise. God is humane and indulgent." Those who do understand their praises are the spiritual, the devoutly loving, and the perfect—through the attributes of the prophets and the saints. In case of need, they cause even those who do not believe to hear His praises. When this occurs, and comes from the blessed Prophet, it is called a miracle; and if from the saints, a favourable demonstration. When the prophets call infidels to the true faith, they are ordered to perform miracles, as an evidence of their conversion. It is not proper to aspire to the performance of miracles, or favourable demonstrations (*Kerâmeh*), except when directly ordered by God, and He will decide as to the necessity. The saints are few in number; they are empowered to make animals, vegetable and even inanimate things, speak; and such are found in the history of their lives.

ACQUISITION OF THE MEANS OF EXISTENCE.

The faithful, who devoutly seek for the path of God and the love of Him, will find, regarding the acquisition of the means of existence, in the *Hadees*, the saying of the

Prophet, "The seeker of gain is the friend of God." Those who are busily engaged in the daily acquisition of their own existence in this world, must, in the event of their acquiring much wealth, return to their homes, reject from their minds the idea of the value of gold, and turn their thoughts, with deep piety and with a pure heart, towards God,—giving themselves up entirely for the time to feelings of devotion.

There is a difference in the sentiment of pious ecstasy. Ecstatic feeling is derived from a deep contemplation of the heart of God, and of the *Murshid.* A sense of sincere satisfaction is the result, and the person feels a conviction of personal helplessness, which he will enjoy immensely. This kind of feeling is most acceptable to God. Ecstasy is also that state of the heart which arises from a fervent desire to drive away from it all anxiety about worldly store. It comes from a profound contemplation and reflection of the Deity, and an absorption in sincere prayer to Him: from tears and a sight of repentance; from the performance of the *Zikr;* from a convulsive movement of the body; from a frequent repetition of the word *Hoo;* from a seeking devoutly after the same state (*Vejd*); and when in this search, from the opening of a door to the seeker, through which he receives what is called the *Jezbeh-i-Rahmân*, or the merciful attraction of God, and is filled with intense joy and delight. The termination of this ecstatic state is called *Vejd*, the close of this is called the *Vejdain* (two *Vejds*), meaning worldly and eternal ecstasies, which leads to the *Vujood*, or undying state of existence, in which there is no death. Regarding this subject, I have been given two *Hadeeses* of the Prophet. "*Jezbet*, or attraction, comes from the attraction of the All-Merciful, and the recipients of this grace abandon all care or thought of this world, and their future existence."

It is related that the Caliph 'Alee, when absorbed in this state, was told that he had lost his senses. He immediately fell down in prayers of thankfulness to God, declaring that he had at last reached the condition mentioned in the Prophet's Hadees above stated.

The second Hadees says: "The faithful do not die; perhaps they become translated from this perishable world to the world of eternal existence."

It is said that on this account Dervishes implore the help of the *Evliâ*, or Saints. This state, however, must not be shown to strangers or the public; it is proper to be enjoyed in private, amongst the lovers of the same.

When engaged in conversation about the *Tevheed* (unity of God) with the brethren, and the heart is in its appropriate state, there is no impropriety in exciting the occurrences of this ecstasy; but, among the brethren to excite it, in the view of having it spoken of to their praise, and that they are *Ehl i 'Ashk* (lovers of God), is hypocrisy equal to that of *Shirket* (saying that God has an associate), for it will have had its source entirely in the *personal* ambition of the individual, and not in the *spiritual.* It gives rise to all kinds of spiritual disease; and when your sins are taken into account at the Day of Judgment, the tricks of your body will, by the excellence of God, be made apparent, and seem like dark spots on the surface of pure milk. However, it may be added, that those who do fall into such errors are not fully perfected in the brotherhood. Besides these, the saints are the *Ehl i Fenâ*, who have given up all care for this world; and the *Mukhliseen*, or the freed from worldly anxieties, are pure and faithful, and not liable to this sin. They may even use those members of the body which provide for its wants; but their hearts must, nevertheless, be always occupied with God. They arrive at nothing through the medium of mental superiority (science or knowledge); no one can comprehend their real state through the ordinary sources of calculating intelligence, as they are only commissioned to be seekers of piety through the deepest sincerity of the heart, and through the spiritual guidance of the Sheikh, who, in consequence, keeps them always in his pious remembrance (his prayers).

"O God! facilitate us through the favour of the *Ehl i Fenâ* and the *Bakâ*."

This *Bakâ* (a condition in which there is no death) is

the source out of which the *Fenâ* originates. The *Vujood* is also that which is referred to in the verse of the Koran where God says—

"Be it known that those who search for the pathway of God, find it through the *Tevekkul*, or confidence in His mercy, and in the *Kesb*, or acquisition of the means of existence;" but the former is only proper to the *Ehli Fenâ*. The *Ehli Tevekkul* is that person who, on his admission to the Order, considers himself as dead, and regards all his worldly interests as wholly given up and perished, and abandons himself, spiritually and temporally, to the guidance of his Sheikh. He must not give any thought to himself; he must consider his wife and children, his servants and dependants, as lost to him, or as if they never existed. He must abandon all his sources of gain, and place his entire dependence and confidence in the Bestower of all gifts; he will then be shorn of all worldly connexions, so that he will be registered, by God's command, on his *Peer;* he will be in a state of annihilation; but this is a very difficult rule of conduct to pursue. Now, according to the "Hadees," *Elkiâsib Habeeb Ullah*, or the "Gainer is the friend of God," this condition is better than the former, and it is better to gain an honest livelihood by proper means, depending always upon Him for success in your endeavours. The "Lover" and "Faithful," in thus using the means necessary for gaining an existence, do this not simply with the idea of depending wholly upon God, but rather in obedience to the commands of the "First Cause of all causes." The servants of God in all things acknowledge their own poverty in the sight of God. Those who become faithful followers of the Prophet—on whom be the Divine satisfaction—were all, individually, occupied in the acquisition of an existence, and it is necessary that each person, in honour of God, should be thus engaged; yet there are some idle persons who employ their time in no useful occupation,—abandon even the name of Dervish, and call themselves *Zuhd*, or Ascetics. These give themselves up to idleness and inactivity. God has covered His saints with a veil—

such as are worldly employments—which conceals their real character from public gaze, so that those whose spiritualism has not been touched with *Kehl* (collyrium) of the light of Mohammedanism, are unable to distinguish them, and to recognise in them the true saints of God. Thus, it is only through the light of Mohammedanism that the saints recognise each other; none other can distinguish them; and for this reason the lovers of God (*'Ushshâk Ullah*) have abandoned all causes of hypocrisy.

CHAPTER IX.

REAL AND FALSE DERVISHES.

TRANSLATED FROM A MS.

THERE is as much difference between the real and false Dervish as between heaven and earth. The right-minded man can recognise them, and draw the distinction.

To the question, "What is true repentance shown by?" the reply is, "Goodness of heart;" and this is qualified by "the abandonment of all pride and pretension, and by following a line of straightforwardness in the Path of the Most High." The number of the columns of the Path are six—viz. 1. Repentance, 2. Resignation, 3. Fidelity to the Order, 4. Increase of internal devotion, 5. Contentment with your lot, and 6. Devout retirement from the world. The Precepts of the Order are also six in number—viz. 1. Knowledge, 2. Generosity, 3. Nearness to God, 4. Fidelity, 5. Meditation, and 6. Trust in God. The Rules of the Order are equally six—1. Knowledge, 2. Meekness, 3. Patience, 4. Submission to superiors, 5. Good breeding, and 6. Purity of heart.

The Rules of the *Tareeket* are six—viz. 1. Benevolence, 2. Calling upon God (the *Zikr*), 3. Abandoning evil (the *Terk*), 4. The abandoning of all worldly enjoyments, 5. Fear of God, and 6. Love of God.

The ablution of the *Tareeket* is a total abnegation of all worldly goods, and contentment with the will of the Sheikh. The truthful ablution is "to increase in love for God."

A question was once put to the Imâm Ja'fer as to the peculiar characteristics of a *Fakeer* (Dervish), and he replied, "It is the characteristic of the Prophet, and of love; for he has said in a *Hadees*, 'Bear the characteristics of God,' the tree of which is straightforwardness, and its fruit is to know one's self. Its jewel is utter poverty, or a total disregard of self. Now one who possesses these certainly knows himself, and can do anything he pleases, but abandons all for devotional retirement. The Caliph 'Alee has said, 'Whoever knows himself, knows his God.'"

The *Terk*, or abandonment required by the *Tareeket*, is thus explained :—To abandon the world, its comforts and dress,—all things now and to come,—conformably with the *Hadees* of the Prophet, *i.e.* "'The world is forbidden to those of the life to come; the life to come is forbidden to those of this world; and both are forbidden to the true servants of God," which is thus explained: —The true Dervish in heart not only willingly abandons all the joys and pleasures of the world, but he is willing also to give up all hope of the pleasures of Paradise, and to be satisfied with the enjoyment derived from a submissive and devout contemplation of the beauty of God, and the hope of attaining to that private Paradise, occupied only by the pious, the holy, and the prophets.

Abandonment of the world is also to neglect to comb the hair, to regulate the eyebrows, to cleanse the beard and moustaches; and whoever pays attention to these personal comforts has already determined to return to the world, and given up the hope of seeing God hereafter. Not to shave the head in the presence of the *Murshid*, shows that the Mureed knows himself. To suspend a *Cherkhâ*, or circle, to the neck, means, "I have resigned myself entirely to the will of God, for blessing or for punishment;" to suspend the *Menkoosh*, or earrings, to the ears, signifies, "I believe the language of the saints is that of the Most High, and that their words are my laws, or my *Menkoosh*, and is ever hung over my heart." If ever any one is asked whose son and Dervish he is, he must reply, "I am the son of Mohammed 'Alee," the proof of which is in the *Hadees*, "I am of that people to which I belong."

The *Erkiân*, or Columns of the Order, are based upon

the following:—When it is asked what Dervish means, the reply is, "One who asks nothing of any creature, and to be as submissive as the earth which is trodden upon by the feet, to serve others before yourself, to be contented with little, to do neither good nor evil, to abandon all desires, to divorce even his wife, to submit hourly to all occurrences of misfortune and accident, not to drink wine nor to lie, not to commit fornication, not to touch what does not belong to you, to know the true and the false, and to restrain the tongue and speak little."

The rules of the Tareek are thus explained:—1. To change the thing desired to whatever is wished for miraculously; 2. To divorce his wife and live secluded, because to become a true *Murshid* this must be done so as to enable the aspirant to that position to devote himself wholly to the love of Allah; the disciple, though married, must become a benedict if he hopes to be a good *Murshid.* (This is not now followed, for Sheikhs are favoured with visions, in which they receive permission to keep their wives, or to take one if they have none.) This is founded upon the principle contained in Koran xxvi. 87, 88—"Do not dishonour me in that day when all mankind will be resuscitated; that day when all riches and offspring will be of no value; it is only for him who comes to God with an upright heart that Paradise will be opened and approached by pious men."

In reply to the question as to what is a *Tâj* (crown or cap) it should be said, "Honour and respect;" to that as to their number, say, "There are two, the *Tâj i Jâhil* and the *Tâj i Kiâmil,*" viz. the "Crown of the Ignorant" and the "Crown of the Perfect" in spiritual knowledge. The principle of *Khalvet* and '*Uzelet* signifies retirement from the eyes of the world, and cessation from seeking the honour and respect of any one. The "Crown of the Ignorant" means to frequent the public streets and bazaars, and to possess the esteem and honour of every one, whilst that of the Perfect signifies to have the esteem of no one.

The form (turban) which is wrapped round a crown is called *Istivâ.* Its centre, or *Kubbeh;* its border; its diameter; the letters which form its name, *t a j;* its upper surface, *Kibleh;* its ablutions, its key, its religious duties, commanded by God; its services, directed by the Prophet; its soul, its interior,—all have their respective significations.

1. The *Istivâ*, "Parable," means to change evil deeds and actions to those of an exalted and pious nature.

2. The *Kibleh*, "The position facing you at prayer directing to *Mekkeh*," is the Peer, or founder of the Order.

3. The *Kenâr*, or "border," is the faculty of spiritual command in both worlds, viz. to pray with a devout heart to God for the release of any one in danger, for God accepts an intercession for the latter, and it relieves him from the danger.

4. The *Lenger*, or "capacity," means to point out (by the Sheikh) the true path to his disciples.

5. The *Kelimeh*, or "Letters of the word *Tâj*" (*t a j*), means to implore pardon from God according to the *Ayat*, or verse of the Koran, "God is the rich, but we are the poor."

6. The *Kubbeh*, or "Summit of the Cap," means the point of truth, which signifies that the owner knows all things; the "Summit of the Sphere of the Universe" (God) allowing the observer to see and know all things.

7. The *Ghusl*, "Ablution," means not to mingle with the public, and so remain pure.

8. The *Kileed*, or "Key," means to open the secret and difficult. The Sheikh interprets and explains by it all dreams and visions of his disciples.

9. The *Farz*, or "Obligation," means the conversation and communication with the Peers and the brethren (*Erens*).

10. The *Sunnet*, "Order of the Prophet," means honour and respect.

11. The *yân*, or "Soul," means to keep the commandments of the Peer or Sheikh, and to abstain from hurting the feelings of any one, and to withdraw from the world.

12. The *Muvât*, or "Dying," means to touch the living creature's hands, as on the initiation of a Mureed.

13. The *Fer'*, "Branch or Decoration," is to refrain from all females.

On the *Tâj* is written "There is no God but Him, the Living and the Eternal." In the front is written, "All things perish except the face of God." In the middle, "I swear by the learned book (Koran)."

There is another question as to the number of the *Tajs.* These, as aforestated, are two, viz. that of the learned and that of the ignorant. The former means to strive to reach the secrets of Mohammed and 'Alee, for the blessed Prophet has said, "I and 'Alee are made of the same light," and to *see* that they are made of one light, and the All-Just at the same time. Do not, therefore, understand like those who wear the crown of the ignorant. And yet God knows all with goodness.

THE "KHIRKA," OR MANTLE.

It is related that the Imâm Ja'fer having been interrogated on this point of spirituality, and what is the true faith of this garment—its *Kibleh* and *Ghusl*, its "existence," "prayers," and "divine obligation," its "duty" as prescribed by the Prophet (*Sunnet*); its "soul," as well as the proper method of putting it on the body, its collar, and interior and exterior, he replied as follows:—

"Its point of faith is to regard it as a covering for the faults and weaknesses of others;

"Its *Kibleh* is the Peer;

"Its *Ghusl* the ablution from sins;

"Its prayers are manhood (among the Dervishes, I am informed, there are male and female characteristics, from which a man is called 'manly,' and also 'feminine');

"Its 'obligations' are the forsaking of the sin of cupidity;

"Its 'duty,' to be easily contented and satisfied with one's lot in life;

"Its 'soul,' to give one's word, and keep it sacredly;

"Its 'key,' the *Tekbeer;*

"Its 'putting on, or tying,' an inducement to serve others;

"Its 'perfection,' uprightness and correctness of conduct;

"Its 'border' is the condition of a Dervish;

"The 'edges of its sleeves,' the *Tareekat*, or Order;

"Its 'collar,' submission to God's will;

"Its 'exterior,' light; and

"Its 'interior,' secrecy."

On the collar is written *Yâ! 'Azeez, Yâ! Lateef, Yâ! Hakeem.* On its border, *Yâ! Vaheed, Yâ! Ferd, Yâ! Samad.* On the edges of its sleeves, *Yâ! Kabool, Yâ! Shukur, Yâ! Kereem, Yâ! Murshid.* Also the "visible" and the "invisible." The former alludes to those who are visibly submerged in the goodness and mercy of God, and the latter seclusion.

A real Dervish is he who desires for himself nothing, has no egotism, and is meek and lowly, and willing to accept all things as coming from God. The gains of a Dervish are seclusion and retirement, refraining from the utterance of all profane language, reflection, contentment, patience, silence, and resignation, and to watch and obey the will of Allah; to keep the commands of the *Murshid;* to war with his own wild passions; to change his evil feelings for those which are good, and to be faithful to his Order, according to Koran, xxix. 69: "We lead in our paths all those who are jealous in propagating our faith, and God is with those who do good. We make the lesser war (of this world), and also the greater (upon our own wild passions), and this is the true word of God."

The better conduct is that of the pious, and the worse that of the impious. The Man is he who serves (girds up his loins). To serve the Peer, for the science of the Lord, is half of the path of a Dervish, according to the axiom, "The service of kings is one half of the path," "To gird up the loins," is to serve the Peer in such a manner as never to neglect his orders so long as he lives, so that both in this world and in the other he may protect and guard him.

THE "PALENK," OR STONE WORN IN THE GIRDLE.

This stone signifies contentment and resignation to hunger. A *Khirka* cut short means to have given up the world. To wear the *Tennoor*, or the full and wide skirts of the *Mevlevees*, means to have drawn his head out of the oven of misfortune. (The word *Tennoor* means an oven.

The numerical value of the eternal path (*Târik Ebedee*) is ten.

1. To grow old in the science of the Peer.
2. To sow seeds of knowledge.
3. To tell the joys of the Dervish heart, of the pleasures of the path which has been pointed out to him.
4. To reap in the field of abstinence.
5. To be well bred, and to follow this rule in a meek and lowly manner.
6. To pronounce the *Kelimeh Tevheed* to the Mureed until he becomes satiated.
7. To reap with the sickle of Humility.
8. To beat out the grain in the barn of Divine acquiescence.
9. To blow away the tares with the mind of alacrity.
10. To measure with the bushel of Love.
11. To grind in the mill of godly fear.
12. To knead with the water of Reply (this refers to the replies made by the *Peer* to the dreams of his disciples).
13. To bake in the oven of Patience.
14. To burn therein all evil feelings, and come out purified by the fire.

THE POST, OR SEAT.

The *Post* (or skin seat of the *Peer*), with its head, feet, right and left side, has its condition, middle, soul, law, truth, &c.

The head signifies submissiveness.

The feet service.

The right—the right hand of fellowship, at initiations.

The left, honour.

The east, secrecy.

The west, religion.

The condition (obligatory) to bow the head before the *Erens*.

The middle is love.

The *Mihrâb* is to see the beauty of God.

The soul is the *Tekbeer*.

The law is to be absorbed in Divine Love and adoration, so that the soul leaves the heart (body), and wanders away among the other spirits with whom it sympathises.

The *Tarecket* is to enter into that which has been established.

The *Me'rifet* is the fear of the *Peer*.

The *Hakeeket* is whatever the Peer orders to be done, and is the indubitable duty of his disciples.

CHAPTER X.

THE ORDER OF THE MEVLEVEES.

THE founder of this eminent order of Dervishes is *Molânâ Jellâl ed Deen Mohammed el Balkhee er Roomee.* It is commonly called by foreigners, "The Dancing or Whirling Dervishes," from the peculiar nature of the devotions.

He was, as his name designates, a native of the city of Balkh, and was born in the 6th day of the month of Rebee' ul Evvel, A.H. 604. In the work aforequoted, called the *Nafahât el Uns*, by Mollâ Jâmee, it is stated that the spiritual powers of this celebrated Peer were developed at the early age of six years, and that those spiritual forms and hidden figures, viz. those angelic beings who inscribe the acts of mankind, and the pious *Jinns* and illustrious men who are concealed beneath the domes of Honour, became visible to his sight, and drew allegories before his eyes. *Molânâ Behâ ed Deen Veled* writes, as an example of the circumstance, that once on a Friday, Jelâl ed Deen was at Balkh, on the roof of a house, in company with some other youngsters of his own age, when one of them asked him whether it would not be possible to jump from the place on which they stood to another house-top. Jelâl ed Deen replied that such a movement would be more suitable to dogs and cats, and other similar animals, but woe to the human being who should attempt to assimilate himself to them. "If you feel yourselves competent to do it, let us jump upwards towards heaven!" and then, setting the example, he sprang upwards, and was immediately lost from their sight. The youths all cried out as he disappeared, but in a moment more he returned, greatly altered in complexion, and changed in figure, and he informed them that whilst he was yet talking with them, a legion of beings clothed in green mantles seized him from amongst them, and carried him in a circle upwards towards the skies; "they showed me strange things of a celestial character, and on your cries reaching us they lowered me down again to the earth."

It is also narrated that during this year he only partook of food once in three or four days. When he went to Mekkeh he communed with the Sheikh *Fereed ed Deen 'Attâr*, then at Nishabor. This Sheikh gave him an *Isrâr-nâmeh*, or "Secret Epistle," in the form of a book, which he always carried upon his person.

The *Hazret i Mevlevee*, viz. Jelâl ed Deen, stated that he was not of the body, which the *'Ashiks*, or Devout lovers of God, beheld; "Perhaps I am that Joy and Delight which the Mureeds experience when they cry out, 'Allah! Allah!' therefore seek that delight, and taste of that joy; hold to it as to riches, and be thankful that it is me." He once is said to have remarked that a bird which flies upward does not reach the skies, yet it rises far above the roof of the house, and so escapes. So it is with one who becomes a Dervish, and though he does not become a perfect Dervish, still he becomes far superior to common men, and far exalted above ordinary beings. He likewise becomes freed from worldly cares and anxieties, and is exhilarated above all ordinary human sensations.

Each *Tekkieh* of every Order of Dervishes has a particular day or days in the week, for the performance of the religious exercises of the brethren. As there are several *Tekkiehs* of the same Order in Constantinople, the brethren of one are thus enabled to visit and take part in the ceremonies of the others. The brethren of other Orders frequently join in the services of the *Tekkiehs* not their own, nothing forbidding it, except, as with the Mevlevees, the want of practice and skill.

A *Kâdiree* who can perform the services of a Mevlevee, on entering a *Tekkieh* of the latter, goes to the *Hujreh*, or cell, of one of the brethren, and receives a cap called

a *Sikkeh*, or cap made in a mould, from which it takes this name. It is made of camel's hair, or otherwise wool; he also receives a *Tennooreh*, which is a long skirt like that of a lady's dress, without arms, and a *Destch Gool* (literally a bouquet of roses), or a jacket with sleeves made of cloth or other material; around his waist is fastened the *Alif-lâm-end*, or girdle of cloth some four fingers in width, one and a half archins in length, edged with a thread (*chârit*), and a piece of the same at its ends serves to tie it round the body; over the shoulders is thrown a *Khirka* or cloak (mantle), with long and large sleeves, and thus equipped he enters into the hall of the Tekkieh, called *Semâ' Khâneh*.

With regard to their services, it may be said—1. that they all perform the usual *Islâm Namâz;* 2. that they offer up certain prayers, of the same character; 3. the Sheikh proceeds to his seat, his book lying in the direction of the *Kibleh* (that of Mekkeh); then standing upright, he raises his hands, and offers a prayer for the *Peer*, asking his intercession with God and the Prophet, in behalf of the Order.

4. The Sheikh then leaves his *Postakee*, or sheepskin seat, and bends his head in humility to the *Peer* (the *Boyun Kesmek* alluded to in the chapter on the *Bektâshees*), towards the side of the *Postakee*, and then makes one step forward, and turning again towards the same seat on his right foot, bows to the same, as that of the *Peer*, were he in existence. After this he continues round the hall, and the brethren, in turn, do the same, all going round three times. This ceremony is called the *Sultân Veled Devree*, after the son of *Hazret i Mevlânâ*, their founder or *Peer*.

5. The Sheikh next takes his position, standing in the *Postakee*, his hands crossed before him, and one of the brethren in the *Mutrib* (upstairs) commences to chant a *Na't i Shereef*, or Holy Hymn, in praise of the Prophet. At its termination the little orchestra in the gallery commences performing on the flutes (called *Nâys*), the *Kemâns* and *Kudoors* (the latter small drums).

6. One of the brethren, called the *Semâ 'Zân*, goes to

the Sheikh, who has proceeded to the edge of his seat, and bows to him, his right foot passing over the other—kisses the hand of the Sheikh, recedes backwards from him, and standing in the middle of the hall, acts as a director of the ceremonies about to commence.

7. The other Dervishes now take off their *Khirkas*,—let fall their *Tennoorees*,—go in single file to the Sheikh, kiss his hand, make an obeisance to the *Postakee*, and commence turning round on the left foot, pushing themselves round with the right. If they happen to approach too near each other, the Semâ 'Zân stamps his foot on the floor as a signal. Gradually the arms of the performers are raised upward, and then extended outward, the left hand turned to the floor, and the right open, upward to heaven; the head inclined over the right shoulder, and the eyes apparently closed. The Sheikh, in the meantime, stands still on his *Postakee*. The brethren, whilst turning round, continually mutter the inaudible *Zikr*, saying *Allah! Allah!* and the musicians play for some twenty minutes or half an hour, chanting a hymn called the *'Ain i Shereef*. Often they perform only some ten minutes, when having reached a certain part of the chant, in which are the words *Hai Yâr!* (O Friend!) they cry it out loudly, and suddenly cease. The Dervishes below at the same time stop in their course, so that the *Tennooreh* wraps around their legs, so as to quite conceal their feet, and all inclining lowly, perform obeisance again to the Sheikh. The Semâ 'Zân, taking the lead, they all march slowly round the Hall, bowing low to the Sheikh, turning completely round as they pass him. If any fall, overcome by the performance, this repose affords them an opportunity to withdraw, which some few do; soon after this the music recommences, and the same performance is renewed until arrested as before. This is done three times, after which they all sit down, and the Semâ 'Zân covers them with their mantles.

8. Whilst thus seated, one of the brethren in the gallery reads or recites a part of the Koran; the Semâ 'Zân rises, and going into the middle of the circle, offers up a prayer for the Sultan, with a long series of titles,

mentioning also a good number of his ancestors. At its conclusion the Sheikh rises from the *Postakee*, and after all have saluted him retires from the *Tekkieh*.

It may be added that the *Kâdirees* and *Khalvetees* have the same form of worship, without music; that is to say, they all take each other's hands, or put their arms over each other's shoulders, and turn round their hall, performing the audible *Zikr*.

Foreigners who are not Mussulmans are admitted into many of the *Tekkiehs* as spectators, either in a particular part of the gallery, or in a small apartment on a level with the hall. In the latter they are expected to stand upright during the performance, and to leave their overshoes or shoes outside the door in charge of a man stationed there for that purpose, and to whom a trifle is handed on departing. They, however, are admitted only after the conclusion of the *Islâm Namâz*.

The apartment of the Sheikh is called the *Sheikh Hujreh*, and the large hall the *Semâ' Khâneh*, or the hall or house where brethren hear celestial sounds, and enter into a state of ecstatic devotion.

The Mevlevees have also another apartment, called the *Ismi Jeleel Hujreh*, where they perform their ordinary morning and evening *Namâz*, or prayers; also the *Ismi Jeleel* (the beautiful name of Allah), or the *Zikr*; and this is not to be found in any other *Tekkieh*. The performance before described is always the third daily prayer, called in Turkish the *Eekindee*, and commences about ten o'clock P.M.

A properly constructed Mevlevee *Tekkieh* should have eighteen chambers, and the vows are also always eighteen. Each occupant of a chamber receives eighteen piastres *per diem*. The Mureed must serve in the kitchens of the convent 1,001 days, and his room is then called the *Chillâh Hudjrehsee*, or "Cell of Retirement," wherein the neophyte is supposed to be under probation, and much occupied in prayer and fasting. They have no other officer than the Sheikh, and perhaps his *Nâib Khaleefeh*, or Deputy, and one who superintends the expenses of the convent, called the *Khâzzeenehdâr*. The office of Sheikh is hereditary, but, in Turkey, as with all the other orders, it requires the confirmation of the Sheikh ul Islâm, or Supreme Head of the Islam religion.

SAKA, OR WATER DISTRIBUTOR.

I have been unable to learn any creditable reason for their peculiar form of worship. The short biographical sketch of the founder, Mevlâ Jelâl ed Deen, shows the facility with which, through his extraordinary spiritual powers, he could become invisible to ordinary sight, and his proneness to rise upward. It is a tradition of the Order that, whenever he became greatly absorbed in pious and fervid love for Allah, he would rise from his seat and turn round, much as is the usage of his followers; and that on more than one occasion he began to recede upward from the material world, and that it was only by the means of music that he could be prevented from entirely disappearing from amongst his devoted companions. His celebrated poem, called "*Methnevee Shereef*," is that kind of poetry which is composed of distichs corresponding in measure, each consisting of a pair of rhymes, and each distich having distinct poetical terminations. It is written in the Persian language, and though it has been commented upon, it is too mystical to permit of a close translation. It is, in fact, filled with the most mystical reflections—mostly on the subject of Divine Love, and breathes in every line the most ecstatic rapture. These raptures are supposed to be holy inspirations, which carry the creature aloft to the Creator, with whom he holds spiritual communion. The soft and gentle music of the *Nây*, or mystical flute of the Mevlevees, is made from a cane or reed, this being the music

of nature, and is used also for the purpose of exciting the senses.

Sir William Jones gives the following translation of a few lines of the *Methnevee Shereef* of this Order :—

"Hail, Heavenly Love ! true source of endless gains !
Thy balm restores me, and thy skill sustains.
O ! more than Galen learnèd, than Plato wise !
My guide, my law, my joy supreme, arise !
Love warms this frigid clay with mystic fire,
And dancing mountains leap with young desire.
Blest is the soul that swims in seas of love,
And longs for life sustained by food above.
With forms imperfect can perfection dwell ?
Here pause, my song, and thou, vain world, farewell."

Regarding the tall felt *Kulah* or cap of the Mevlevees, it is stated that, before the world was created as an abode for man, another one existed, known as the *'Alem i Ervâh*, or spirit-world. A soul is supposed to be a *Noor*, or light, without bodily substance, and consequently invisible to the mirror-like eyes of humanity. During the previous state, the soul of Mohammed is said to have existed, and that the Creator placed it in a vase also of light, of the form of the present cap of the Mevlevees.

The author of the work called the "*Shekaik Numânieh*," already alluded to, says, in regard to this Order :—"The Mevlevees are those who join together as brethren, and by the love of Allah, worshipping Him in a house of love, to the melodious sound of the flute, which expresses the harmony of His creation, and revolve round like His empyrium, dancing for joy, and uttering the soft sound of affectionate sighs and lamentations, the result of their ardent desire to be united to Him. Revolving round and round the *Semâ' Khâneh* of sinful abandonment and spiritual isolation, they free themselves from all unworthy passions, and are detached from all the subtile minutiæ and associations of religion."

The usual services of the Mevlevees are as follows :—

1. The usual *Namâz*. Before commencing it they make what is called the *Niyet*, or vow, to go through the appropriate prayers.

2. The *Allâhu Ekber*, the *Subhânnekeh*, the *Auzoo*

Billâhee, one *Bismillah*, one *Fâtiha*, the *Zamee Sureh* or any other *Sureh* (verse of the Koran), which may be selected.

The *Allâhu Ekber* is made standing upright at first, and at the close is repeated kneeling, saying three times, *Subhân Rebee el 'Azeem*, &c., "Blessed be Thou, O great Lord God," and adds, *Semi'a Allâhu*, &c., "Hear us, O Lord God, whilst we offer up to Thee our praises, for Thou art the greatest of all gods!" and then prostrates himself upon the floor.

After this performance, which composes the *Namâz*, they recite the *Evrâd*. In the morning, before the sun has risen, they perform the *Sabâh Namâzee*, and as it rises above the horizon, some ten minutes or so after it is up, perform two *Rik'ats* (prostrations), called the *Ishrâkieh*, or the sun-rising,—another called the *Vird Ishrâk*. At noon they perform the usual *Namâz* of all Mussulmans, generally of ten *Rik'ats*, four of which are *Sunneh*, four *Farz*, and two also *Sunneh* (the former ordered by the Prophet, the second a Divine ordinance, and the third also by the Prophet, with peculiar injunctions). At the *Eekindee*, or third prayer of the day, they perform eight *Rik'ats*, four of which are *Sunneh*, those said to have been performed by the Prophet himself, four more *Farz*. The evening service is composed of five *Rik'ats*, three being *Farz* and two *Sunneh*. After this latter prayer, they perform another called the *Ism i Jeleel*, which consists of three *Tevheeds*, and as many *Ism i Jeleels* as they who are present please to recite.

Previous to the commencement of their sectarian devotions, the Mureeds are all seated, piously engaged in meditating on their Peer, which occupation is called the *Murâkebeh* and the *Tevejjuh*, whilst those in the gallery, named the *Naizen* (musicians), chant a holy hymn. This gallery is called the *Mutreeb* (place of excitement), and those stationed there are attentive to the directions made by their Sheikh with his hands.

As the whole principle of the Order is the *'Eshk Ullah*, or Love for God, their usual compliment is, for instance after drinking, *'Eshk olsoon* (may it be love.)

None are allowed to beg, but many are seen in the streets (see page 202) bestowing water on the thirsty, *Fee Sebeel* and *Li 'Eschk Ullah* (in the path of God, and for the love of God).

In a small treatise by a learned Sheikh of the Mevlevee Order, lately deceased, there is a clear and distinct explanation of the "spiritual existence" as believed by them. He explains and draws his proofs from the Koran,

A MEVLEVEE ORCHESTRA.

that all mankind were created in heaven, or in one of its celestial spheres, long before God created the present one, and perhaps any of the planets; that in this world they continue to exist in varied conditions before assuming that of humanity; and that moreover they will continue hereafter to exist in other forms before they finally return to their original ones in the sphere of blessedness, near to the Creator from whom they emanated. He shows from a verse of the Koran, wherein God says in reference to the Prophet, "Had it not been for you I would not have created the world," that he pre-existed, and only became human in this world. Adam, he says, was created from earth—a mineral, and corporeally returned to it, though his spirit proceeded on its course of existence elsewhere. He, as well as all Mussulmans, maintain that Jesus Christ was of a Divine origin, that is to say, that He was the *Rooh Allah*, or the Spirit of God, though not God in any manner, as this would necessarily imply a plurality of Gods, which Mohammed constantly denied. He declares that the spirit of man has no knowledge in this life of its condition or existence in any previous one, nor can it foresee its future career, though it may often have vague impressions of past occurrences which it cannot define strongly resembling those happening around it.

CHAPTER XI.

MR. D'OHSSAN, in his celebrated work on the Ottoman Empire, gives the following account of the rise and spread of the Dervish Orders:—

"The enthusiasm with which Mohammed was able to inspire his disciples, exalting their imagination by the picture of the voluptuous enjoyments which he promised them in the other world, and by the victories with which he sustained in this his pretended mission, gave rise among all the believers in the Koran to a host of cenobites whose austerity of life seemed to render them, in the eyes of a credulous people, entire strangers to the earth.

"In the first year of the Hegira forty-five citizens of Mekkeh joined themselves to as many others of Medineh. They took an oath of fidelity to the doctrines of their Prophet, and formed a sect or fraternity, the object of which was to establish among themselves a community of property, and to perform every day certain religious practices in a spirit of penitence and mortification. To distinguish themselves from other Mohammedans, they took the name of *Soofees*. This name, which later was attributed to the most zealous partizans of Islamism, is the same still in use to indicate any Mussulman who retires from the world to study, to lead a life of pious contemplation, and to follow the most painful exercises of an exaggerated devotion. The national writers do not agree as to the etymology. Whilst some derive it from the Greek word *Sophos* (sage), others say it is from the Arabic word *Soof* (coarse camel's wool or hair cloth), or stuff used for clothing by the humble penitents of the earlier days of Mussulmanism; others from the Arabic word *Safâ*, the name of one of the stations around the *Ke'bbeh* of Mekkeh, where many of the neophytes passed whole days and nights in fasting, and prayer, and macerations. To the name of *Soofee* they added also that of *Fakeer* (poor), because their maxim was to renounce the goods of the earth, and to live in an entire abnegation of all worldly enjoyments, following thereby the words of the Prophet, *El fakr fakhree*, or 'Poverty is my pride.'

"Following their example, Abu Bekr and 'Alee established, even during the lifetime of the Prophet, and under his own eyes, congregations over which each presided, with peculiar exercises established by them separately, and a vow taken by each of the voluntary disciples forming them. On his decease, Abu Bekr made over his office of president to one Selmân Fârsee, and 'Alee to Hasan Basree, and each of these charges were consecrated under the title *Khaleefah*, or successor. The two first successors followed the example of the caliphs, and transmitted it to their successors, and these in turn to others, the most aged and venerable of their fraternity. Some among them, led by the delirium of the imagination, wandered away from the primitive rules of their society, and converted, from time to time, these fraternities into a multitude of monastic orders.

"They were doubtlessly emboldened in this enterprise by that of a recluse who, in the thirty-seventh year of the Hegira (A.D. 657) formed the first order of anchorites of the greatest austerity, named *Uwais Karanee*, a native of Karu, in Yamin, who one day announced that the archangel Gabriel had appeared to him in a dream, and in the name of the Eternal commanded him to withdraw from the world, and to give himself up to a life of contemplation and penitence. This visionary pretended also to have received from that heavenly visitor the plan of his future conduct, and the rules of his institution. These consisted in a continual abstinence, in retirement from society, in an abandonment of the pleasures of innocent nature, and in the recital of an infinity of prayers day and night. *Uwais* even added to these

practices. He went so far as to draw out his teeth, in honour, it is said, of the Prophet, who had lost two of his own in the celebrated battle of Ohod. He required his disciples to make the same sacrifice. He pretended that all those who would be especially favoured by heaven, and really called to the exercises of his Order, should lose their teeth in a supernatural manner; that an angel should draw out their teeth whilst in the midst of a deep sleep; and that on awakening they should find them by their bedside. The experiences of such a vocation was doubtless too severe to attract many proselytes to the Order; it only enjoyed a certain degree of attraction for the eyes of fanatic and credulously ignorant people during the first days of Islamism. Since then it has remained in Yamin, where it originated, and where its partisans were always but few in number.

Notwithstanding its discredit, this singular association contributed greatly to the institution of other Monastic Orders, all of which originated in the two great congregations of Abu Bekr and 'Alee,—the founders of which were the most ardent and ambitious of their successors. Each gave his name to the Order which he thus instituted,—taking the title of *Peer*, synonymous to that of *Sheikh*, both words meaning "Deacon" or "Elder." Their disciples bore the name of *Dervish*, a Persian word, the etymology of which signifies the "sill of the door," and metaphysically indicates the spirit of humility, of retirement, and perseverance, which should form the principal characteristic of these anchorites. Each century gave birth, in all Mussulman states, to some of these societies, nearly the whole of which still exist in the Ottoman Empire,—the most distinguished of which are some thirty-two in number. The following is the chronology, with the names of their founders, and the year of their decease.

Sheikh Olwân died at Jedda, in the 149th year of the Hejra (A.D. 766); he is the founder of the *Olwânees*.

Ibrahim Edhem died at Damascus, in the 161st year of the Hejra (A.D. 777); founded the *Edhemees*.

Bayazid Bestâmee died at Jebel Bestâm, in Syria,

A.H. 261 (A.D. 874), and was the founder of the Order of the *Bestâmees.*

Sirree Sâketee died at Baghdad, A.H. 295 (A.D. 907), and founded that of the *Sâketees.*

'Abd ul Kâdir Ghilânee died at Baghdad, A.H. 561 (A.D. 1165), and founded the Order of the *Kâdirees.* He was the *Zawaïdâr*, or Guardian of the Tomb of the Imâm A'zam Abu Haneefeh, the Islam jurisconsult, in Baghdad.

Sa'eed Ahmed Rufâ'ee died in the woods between Baghdad and Bassora, A.H. 578 (A.D. 1182), and founded the Rufâ'ees (called by the public the "Howling Dervishes").

Shahâb ed Deen Suherwerdee died at Baghdad, A.H. 602 (A.D. 1205), founder of the Order of the *Suherwerdees.*

Nejim ed Deen Kubrâ died at Khawerzem in A.H. 617 (A.D. 1220), and founded the *Kubrâwees.*

'Abd ul Hosain Shahzelee died at Mekkeh in A.H. 656 (A.D. 1258), founder of the *Shahzelees.*

Jelâl ed Deen er Roomee Mevlânâ, called the Mollâ Khonkiâr, died at Koniah, A.H. 672 (A.D. 1273), and founded the *Mevlevees*, generally called the "Turning," or "Dancing Dervishes."

'Abd ul Fetan Ahmed Bedâwee died at Tanta, in Egypt, in A.H. 675 (A.D. 1276), and founded the *Bedâwees.*

Peer Mohammed Nakshibendee died at Kasri 'Arifân, in Persia, A.H. 719 (A.D. 1319); founded the *Nakshibendees.* He was a cotemporary of 'Othman I., the founder of the Ottoman Empire.

Sa'd ed Deen Jebrâwee died at Jebba, near Damascus, in A.H. 736 (A.D. 1335), founder of the *Sa'dees.*

Hajee Bektâsh Khorassânee, called the *Walee*, or "Saint," died at Kir Shehr, Asia Minor, in A.H. 759 (A.D. 1357), founder of the *Bektâshees.* He lived several years at the court of Orkhan I., and it was he who blessed the Janissaries on the day of their creation.

'Omer Khalwettee died at Kaiserieh in A.H. 800 (A.D. 1397); founded the *Khalwettees.*

Zain ed Deen Abu Bekr Khâffee died at Koofa, A.H. 838 (A.D. 1438); founded the *Zainees.*

'Abd ul Ghânee Peer Bâbâyee died at Adrianople in A.H. 870 (A.D. 1465); founded the *Bâbâyees.*

Hâjee Bairâm Ankarawee died at Angora, A.H. 876 (A.D. 1471); founded the *Bairâmees.*

Sa'eed 'Abdallah Eshref Roomee died at Chin Iznik in A.H. 899 (A.D. 1493); founded the *Eshrefees.*

Peer Abu Bekr Wafâyee died at Aleppo in A.H. 902 (A.D. 1496); founded the *Bekirees.*

Sunbul Yoosuf Bolawee died at Constantinople in A.H. 936 (A.D. 1529); founded the *Sunbullees.*

Ibrahim Gulshenee died at Cairo in A.H. 940 (A.D. 1533); founded the *Gulshenees.* This Order is called the *Rooshenee,* from the name of Dedda 'Omar Rooshenee, preceptor and consecrator of Ibrahim Gulshenee.

Shems ed Deen Ighith Bashee founded the Order of the *Ighith-Bashees,* and died at Magnesia in Asia Minor A.H. 951 (A.D. 1544).

Sheikh Umm Sinân died at Constantinople in A.H. 959 (A.D. 1552); founded the *Ummi Sinâns.*

Peer Uftadeh Mohammed Jelwetty died at Broosa A.H. 988 (A.D. 1580), and founded the *Jelwettees.*

Husain ed Deen 'Ushâkee died at Constantinople in A.H. 1001 (A.D. 1592); founded the *'Ushâkees.*

Shems ed Deen Siwassee died in the environs of Medineh in A.H. 1010 (A.D. 1601), and founded the *Shemsees.*

'Alim Sinân Ummee died at Elwaly in A.H. 1079 (1668); founded the *Sinân Ummees.*

Mohammed Niyâzee Misree died at Lemnos in A.H. 1106 (A.D. 1694); founded the *Niyâzees.*

Murad Shâmee died at Constantinople in A.H. 1132 (A.D. 1719); founded the *Muradiehs.*

Noor ed Deen Jerrâbee died at Constantinople in A.H. 1146 (A.D. 1733); founded the *Noor ed Deens.*

Mohammed Jemâl ed Deen Edirnawee died at Constantinople in A.H. 1164 (A.D. 1750); founded the *Jemâlees.*

Three of the Orders—the *Bestâmees,* the *Nakshibendees,*

and the *Bektâshees*—descend from the congregation of Abu Bekr (the first Caliph). The fourth Caliph, 'Alee, gave birth to all the others. Their affiliation is seen in the tables drawn up by different Sheikhs. They are called the *Silsileh ul Evlià Ullah*, or the "Genealogy of the Saints of God." The most recent and highest esteemed is that of 'Abdee Efendi, the Sheikh of the *Jemâlees*, who died at Constantinople, in A.D. 1783. We have drawn it up in a more methodical order, and present it to our readers as an object of curiosity. Some of the Sheikhs are omitted, who were not founders of Orders, because writers who have noticed their genealogies do not agree as to their real names. This, however, does not change at all the exactitude which reigns in the original, or the series and general organization found in the list.

In this multitude of Monastic Orders, the Nakshibendees must be distinguished. The successful establishment of the first of these Orders caused the insensible extinction of the two fraternities out of which they originated. But in the commencement of the eighth century of the Hejra, Peer Mohammed Nakshibendee made a merit of restoring it. With this view, he instituted the Order which bears his name, and which is only a religious association. It is based upon the principles of the two ancient ones, and particularly upon that of the Caliph Abu Bekr. Like them, this new congregation was composed only of men of the world. Devotion engaged citizens of all the Orders and men of the highest rank then, as it does even now, in all parts of the empire. The first duty of the members of this Order is to recite, daily, particular prayers, called the *Khatem Kohjagiân*; once, at least, the *Istaghfâr*; seven times the *Salâmat*; seven times the *Fâtiha* (first chapter of the Koran); and nine times the chapter (of the Koran) called the *Elem Neshr'aleika*, and the *Ikhlâs i Shereef*. To these are added certain practices wholly voluntary, consisting of the recital of the common prayers, or rather, in the meeting together of a certain number of the brethren, once a week. Ordinarily, this is on Thursday, and after

the fifth *Namâz* of the day, so that it occurs after nightfall. In each city, each suburb, each quarter, the members of this new association, divided into different bodies, assemble at the house of their respective deacon or Sheikh, where, seated on the sofa, they perform this pious exercise with the most perfect gravity. The Sheikh,

A BESTAMEE SHEIKH.

or any other brother in his stead, chants the prayers which constitute the association, and the assembly respond in chorus "Hoo!" or "Allah!" In some cities, the Nakshibendees have especial halls, consecrated wholly to this purpose, and then the Sheikh only is distinguished from the other brethren by a turban, in form like that of the Sheikhs of the mosques.

Each of the other Orders is established on different principles. Each founder gave to his Order a distinctive character, with rules, statutes, and peculiar practices. These characteristics extend even to the garments worn by their followers. Each Order has, in fact, a particular dress, and amongst the greater part of them this is chosen so as to mark a difference in that of the Sheikh from that of the ordinary Dervishes. It is perceived principally in the turbans, the shape of the coat, the colours, and the nature of the stuff of which the dresses are made. The Sheikhs wear robes of green or white cloth; and any of those who in winter line them with fur use that kind called *petit gris*, and zibaline martin. Few Dervishes use cloth for their dress. Black or white felt, called 'Abbâ, such as is made in some of the cities of Anatolia, are the most usual. Those who wear black felt are the Jelwettees and the Kâdirees. The latter have adopted it for their boots, and the muslin of their turbans. Some, such as the Mevlevees and the Bekirees, wear tall caps called Kulahs, made also of felt; and others, such as the Rufâ'ees, use short caps called Tâkkieh, to which is added a coarse cloth. The headdress of almost all the other Dervishes is called Tâj, which signifies a crown. There are turbans of different forms, either from the manner in which the muslin is folded, or by the cut of the cloth which covers the top of the head, and is in several gores. Some are of four, as the Edhemees; some of six, as the Kâdirees and the Sa'dees; the Gulshenees have eight; the Bektâshees, twelve; and others even eighteen, such as the Jelwettees.

Generally, all the Dervishes allow their beards and mustachios to grow. Some of the Orders—the Kâdirees, Rufâ'ees, Sa'dees, Khalwettees, Gulshenees, Jelwettees, and the Noor ed Deeniehs—still wear long hair, in memory of the usage of the Prophet, and several of his disciples. Some allow their hair to fall over their shoulders; others tie it up in the form of a Hoo, and put it up behind their turban. These Cœnobites are distinguished under the name of Sâchlees, or the "Long-haired," and they live separate, even in their convents. If private Mussulmans are in the habit of holding rosaries of beads as a pastime, the Dervishes do the same, only in a spirit of religion and piety. These must have thirty-three, sixty-six, or ninety-nine beads, which is the number of the attributes of the Divinity. Some have them always in their hands, others in their girdles; and all are required to recite, several times during the day, the particular prayers of their Order.

Whilst attending upon the fastidious details respecting the particular spirit of each one of these Orders, we will limit ourselves to an exposition of the principal rules and practices on which they are based. The statutes of nearly all require the Dervish to repeat often, during the day-time, the seven first attributes of the Divinity, called by them the Esâmee Ilâhee, consisting of the following words:—

1. Lâ ilâha ill' Allah! (There is no God but Allah,) a confession of His unity.

2. Yâ Allah! (O God,) an exclamation referring to Him, the Almighty.

3. Yâ Hoo! (O Him,) He who is. An authentic acknowledgment of His eternal existence; the Jehovah of the Hebrews.

4. Yâ Hakk! (O just God.)

5. Yâ Hay! (O living God.)

6. Yâ Kayyoom! (O existing God.)

7. Yâ Kâhhâr! (O revenging God.)

These words allude to the seven heavens, called the Seb'a Semâ, and the seven Divine lights, called the Envâr Ilâhee, from which, they say, emanate the seven principal colours, viz. white, black, red, yellow, blue, deep green, and light green.

It is by means of these mysteries that they proceed to the initiation of the Dervishes in the greater Orders. The individual who desires to enter an Order is received in an assembly of the fraternity presided over by the Sheikh, who touches his hand and breathes in his ear three times the words "*Lâ ilâha ill' Allah*" (there is no God but Allah), commanding him to repeat them 101, 151, or 301 times each day. This ceremony is called the *Telkeen*. The recipient, faithful to the orders of his chief, obligates himself to spend his time in perfect retirement, and to report to the Sheikh the visions or dreams which he may have during the course of his novitiate. These dreams, besides characterising the sanctity of his vocation, and his spiritual advancement in the Order, serve likewise as so many supernatural means to direct the Sheikh regarding the periods when he may again breathe in the ear of the neophyte the second words of the initiation, *Yâ Allah!* (O God,) and successively all the others to the last, *Yâ Kâhhâr!* (O avengeful God.) The full complement of this exercise, which they call *Chilleh*, requires six, eight, or ten months, sometimes even longer, according to the dispositions, more or less favourable, of the candidate. Arrived at the last grade of his novitiate, he is then supposed to have fully ended his career, called *Tekmeel Sulook*, and acquired the degree of perfection for his solemn admission into the corps to which he has devoted himself. During all his novitiate, the recipient bears the name of *Köchak*, and the Sheikh who directs him in this pretended celestial career takes the title of *Murshid*, which is equal to "Spiritual guide."

The founder of the *Olwânees* laid out the first rules of this novitiate; they were subsequently perfected by the institution of the *Kâdirees*, and more so by the *Khalwettees*. The Dervishes of these two last societies are distinguished from all others by the decoration of their turban, on the top of which are embroidered the words "*Lâ ilâha ill' Allah*."

The tests of the novice among the *Mevlevees* seem to be still more severe, and the reception of these Dervishes is attended with ceremonies peculiar to their Order. The aspirant is required to labour in the convent or *Tekkieh* for 1,001 successive days in the lowest grade of the kitchen, on which account he is called the *Karra Kolak* (Jackal). If he fails in this service only one day, or is absent one night, he is obliged to recommence his novitiate. The chief of the kitchen, or *Ashjibashee*, one of the most notable of the Dervishes, presents him to the Sheikh, who, seated in an angle of the sofa, receives him amid a general assembly of all the Dervishes of the convent. The candidate kisses the hand of the Sheikh, and takes a seat before him on a mat which covers the floor of the hall. The chief of the kitchen places his right hand on the neck and his left on the forehead of the novice, whilst the Sheikh takes off his cap and holds it over his head, reciting the Persian distich, the composition of the founder of the Order:

"It is true greatness and felicity to close the heart to all human passions; the abandonment of the vanities of this world is the happy effect of the victorious strength given by the grace of our holy Prophet."

These verses are followed by the exordium of the *Tekbeer*, after which the Sheikh covers the head of the new Dervish, who now rises and places himself with the *Ashjibashee* in the middle of the hall, where they assume the most humble posture, their hands crossed upon the breast, the left foot over the right foot, and the head inclined towards the left shoulder. Then the Sheikh addresses these words to the head of the kitchen:

"May the services of the Dervish, thy brother, be agreeable to the throne of the Eternal, and in the eyes of our Peer (the founder of the Order); may his satisfaction, his felicity, and his glory grow in this nest of the humble, in the cell of the poor; let us exclaim 'Hoo!' in honour of our Mevlânâ."

They answer "Hoo!" and the accepted novice, arising from his place, kisses the hand of the Sheikh, who at this moment addresses to him some paternal exhortations on the subject of the duties of his new condition, and closes by ordering all of the Dervishes of the meeting to recognise and embrace their new brother.

Among the Bektâshees the novitiate is also required to be 1,001 days; but the practices observed in the reception of the candidates are different.

Each institution imposes on its Dervishes the obligation to recite certain passages at different times of the day in private, as well as in common with others. Several have also practices which are peculiar to themselves, and which consist in dances, or rather religious circular movements.

In each convent there is a hall, all of wood, consecrated to these exercises. Nothing is simpler than its construction; it contains no ornaments of any nature; the middle of the hall, turned towards Mekkeh, contains a niche which serves as an altar; in front of it is a small carpet, mostly made of the skin of a sheep, on which the Sheikh of the community reclines; over the niche the name of the founder of the Order is written. In some halls this incriptions is surmounted by two others,—one containing the confession of faith, and the other the words "Bismilleh," &c. (In the name of God, the Most Clement and Merciful). In others are seen on the wall to the right and the left of the niche tablets on which are written in large letters the name of God (Allah), that of Mohammed, and those of the four first caliphs. At others are seen the names of Hasan and Husain, grandsons of the Prophet, and some verses of the Koran, or others of a moral character.

The exercises which are followed in these halls are of various kinds, according to the rules of each institution; but in nearly all they commence by the recital, by the Sheikh, of the seven mysterious words of which we have spoken. He next chants various passages of the Koran, and at each pause, the Dervishes, placed in a circle round the hall, respond in chorus by the word "Allah!" or "Hoo!" In some of the societies they sit on their heels, the elbows close to those of each other, and all making simultaneously light movements of the head and the body. In others, the movement consists in balancing themselves slowly, from the right to the left, and from the left to the right, or inclining the body methodically forward and aft. There are other societies in which these motions commence seated, in measured cadences, with a staid countenance, the eyes closed or fixed upon the ground, and are continued on foot. These singular exercises are consecrated under the name of *Murâkebeh* (exaltation of the Divine glory), and also under that of the *Tevheed* (celebration of the Divine unity), from which comes the name *Tevheed Khâneh*, given to the whole of the halls devoted to these religious exercises.

In some of these institutions—such as the Kâdirees, the Rufâ'ees, the Khalwettees, the Bairâmees, the Gulshenees, and the 'Ushâkees—the exercises are made each holding the other by the hand, putting forward always the right foot, and increasing at every step the strength of the movement of the body. This is called the *Devr*, which may be translated the "dance" or "rotation." The duration of these dances is arbitrary,—each one is free to leave when he pleases. Every one, however, makes it a point to remain as long as possible. The strongest and most robust of the number, and the most enthusiastic, strive to persevere longer than the others; they uncover their heads, take off their turbans, form a second circle within the other, entwine their arms within those of their brethren, lean their shoulders against each other, gradually raise the voice, and without ceasing repeat "*Yâ Allah!*" or "*Yâ Hoo!*" increasing each time the movement of the body, and not stopping until their entire strength is exhausted.

Those of the Order of the Rufâ'ees excel in these exercises. They are, moreover, the only ones who use fire in their devotions. Their practices embrace nearly all those of the other Orders; they are ordinarily divided into five different scenes, which last more than three hours, and which are preceded, accompanied, and followed by certain ceremonies peculiar to this Order. The first commences with praises which all the Dervishes offer to their Sheikhs, seated before the altar. Four of the more ancient come forward the first, and approach their superior, embrace each other as if to give the kiss of peace, and next place themselves two to his right, and two to his left. The remainder of the Dervishes, in a body, press forward in a procession, all having their arms crossed, and their heads inclined. Each one, at first, salutes by a profound bow the tablet on which the name of his founder is inscribed. Afterwards, putting his two hands over his face and his beard, he kneels before the Sheikh, kisses his hand respectfully, and then they all go on with a grave step to take their places on the sheep-skins, which are spread in a half-circle around the interior of the hall. So soon as a circle is formed, the Dervishes together chant the Tekbeer and the Fâtiha. Immediately afterwards the Sheikh pronounces the words "*Lâ ilâha ill' Allah*," and repeats them incessantly; to which the Dervishes repeat "Allah!" balancing themselves from side to side, and putting their hands over their faces, on their breasts, and their abdomen, and on their knees.

RUFA'EE DERVISHES RECITING THE EVRAD OR PRAYERS TO THE PROPHET.

The second scene is opened by the Hamdee Mohammedee, a hymn in honour of the Prophet, chanted by one of the elders placed on the right of the Sheikh. During this chant the Dervishes continue to repeat the word "Allah!" moving, however, their bodies forward and aft. A quarter of an hour later they all rise up, approach each other, and press their elbows against each other, balancing from right to left, and afterwards in a reverse motion,—the right foot always firm, and the left in a periodical movement, the reverse of that of the body, all observing great precision of measure and cadence. In the midst of this exercise, they cry out the words "*Yâ*

Allah!" followed by that of "*Yâ Hoo!*" Some of the performers sigh, others sob, some shed tears, others perspire great drops, and all have their eyes closed, their faces pale, and the eyes languishing.

A pause of some minutes is followed by a third scene. It is performed in the middle of an Ilâhee, chanted by the two elders on the right of the Sheikh. The Ilâhees, as has already been said, are spiritual *cantiques*, composed almost exclusively in Persian by Sheikhs deceased in the odour of sanctity. The Dervishes then hasten their movements, and, to prevent any relaxation, one of the first among them puts himself in their centre, and excites them by his example. If in the assembly there be any strange Dervishes, which often happens, they give them, through politeness, this place of honour; and all fill it successively, the one after the other, shaking themselves as aforesaid. The only exception made is in favour of the Mevlevees; these never perform any other dance than that peculiar to their own Order, which consists in turning round on each heel in succession.

After a new pause commences the fourth scene. Now all the Dervishes take off their turbans, form a circle, bear their arms and shoulders against each other, and thus make the circuit of the hall at a measured pace, striking their feet at intervals against the floor, and all springing up at once. This dance continues during the Ilâhees chanted alternately by the two elders to the left of the Sheikh. In the midst of this chant the cries of "*Yâ Allah!*" are increased doubly, as also those of "*Yâ Hoo!*" with frightful howlings, shrieked by the Dervishes together in the dance. At the moment that they would seem to stop from sheer exhaustion, the Sheikh makes a point of exerting them to new efforts by walking through their midst, making also himself most violent movements. He is next replaced by the two elders, who double the quickness of the step and the agitation of the body; they even straighten themselves up from time to time, and excite the envy or emulation of the others in their astonishing efforts to continue the dance until their strength is entirely exhausted.

The fourth scene leads to the last, which is the most frightful of all, the wholly prostrated condition of the actors becoming converted into a species of ecstasy which they call *Halet.* It is in the midst of this abandoment of self, or rather of religious delirium, that they make use of red-hot irons. Several cutlasses and other instruments of sharp-pointed iron are suspended in the niches of the hall, and upon a part of the wall to the right of the Sheikh. Near the close of the fourth scene, two Dervishes take down eight or nine of these instruments, heat them red-hot, and present them to the Sheikh. He, after reciting some prayers over them, and invoking the founder of the Order, Ahmed er Rufâ'ee, breathes over them, and raising them slightly to the mouth, gives them to the Dervishes, who ask for them with the greatest eagerness. Then it is that these fanatics, transported by frenzy, seize upon these irons, gloat upon them tenderly, lick them, bite them, hold them between their teeth, and end by cooling them in their mouths! Those who are unable to procure any seize upon the cutlasses hanging on the wall with fury, and stick them into their sides, arms, and legs.

Thanks to the fury of their frenzy, and to the amazing boldness which they deem a merit in the eyes of the Divinity, all stoically bear up against the pain which they experience with apparent gaiety. If, however, some of them fall under their sufferings, they throw themselves into the arms of their *confrères*, but without a complaint or the least sign of pain. Some minutes after this, the Sheikh walks round the hall, visits each one of the performers in turn, breathes upon their wounds, rubs them with saliva, recites prayers over them, and promises them speedy cures. It is said that twenty-four hours afterwards, nothing is to be seen of their wounds.

It is the common opinion among the Rufâ'ees that the origin of these bloody practices can be traced back to the founder of the Order. They pretend that one day, during the transport of his frenzy, Ahmed Rufâ'ee put his legs in a burning basin of coals, and was immediately cured by the breath and saliva and the prayers of 'Abd ul Kâdir Ghilânee; they believe that their founder received this same prerogative from heaven, and that at his death he transmitted it to all the Sheikhs his successors. It is for this reason that they give to these sharp instruments, and to these red-hot irons, and other objects employed by them in their mysterious frenzy, the name of *Gül*, which signifies "Rose," wishing to indicate thereby that the use made of them is as agreeable to the soul of the elect Dervishes as the odour of this flower may be to the voluptuary.

These extraordinary exercises seem to have something prodigious in them, which imposes on common people, but they have not the same effect on the minds of men of good sense and reason. The latter believe less in the sanctity of these pretended thaumaturges than in the virtue of certain secrets which they adroitly use to keep up the illusion and the credulity of the spectators, even among the Dervishes themselves. It is thus, perhaps, that some assemblies of these fanatics have given, in this age of light, and in the heart of the most enlightened nation, the ridiculous spectacle of those pious and barbarous buffooneries known by the name of convulsions. At all times, and amongst every people of the earth, weakness and credulity, enthusiasm and charlatanry, have but too frequently profaned the most holy faith, and objects the most worthy of our veneration.

After the Rufâ'ees, the Sa'dees have also the reputation of performing miracles, pretty much of the same sort as the preceding. One reads in the institutes of this Order, that Sa'd ed Deen Jebâwee, its founder, when cutting wood in the vicinity of Damascus, found three snakes of an enormous length, and that, after having recited some prayers and blown upon them, he caught them alive, and used them as a rope with which to bind his fagot. To this occurrence they ascribe the pretended virtue of the Sheikhs and the Dervishes of this society, to find out snakes, to handle them, to bite them, and even to eat them without any harm to themselves. Their exercises consist, like those of the Rufâ'ees and other Orders, at first in seating themselves, and afterwards in rising upright; but in often changing the attitude, and in redoubling their agitation even until they become overcome with fatigue, when they fall upon the floor motionless and without knowledge. Then the Sheikh, aided by his vicars, employs no other means to draw

RUFA'EE DERVISH IN AN ECSTATIC STATE.

them out of this state of unconsciousness than to rub their arms and legs, and to breathe into their ears the words "*Lâ ilâha ill' Allah.*"

The Mevlevees are distinguished by the singularity of their dance, which has nothing in common with that of the other societies. They call it *Sem'a* in place of *Devr*, and the halls consecrated to it are called *Sem'a Khânehs.* Their construction is also different. The apartment represents a kind of pavilion, sufficiently light, and sustained by eight columns of wood. These Dervishes have also prayers and practices peculiar to themselves. Among them the public exercises are not ordinarily made by more than nine, eleven, or thirteen individuals. They commence by forming a circle, seated on sheep-skins spread upon the floor at equal distances from each other; they remain nearly a half-hour in this position, the arms folded, the eyes closed, the head inclined, and absorbed in profound meditation.

The Sheikh, placed on the edge of his seat on a small carpet, breaks silence by a hymn in honour of the Divinity; afterwards he invites the assembly to chant with him the first chapter of the Koran. "Let us chant the *Fâtiha*," he says, "in glorifying the holy name of God, in honour of the blessed religion of the prophets; but above all, of Mohammed Mustapha, the greatest, the most august, the most magnificent of all the celestial envoys, and in memory of the first four caliphs, of the sainted Fâtimah, of the chaste Khadeeja, of the Imâms Hasan and Husain, of all the martyrs of the memorable day, of the ten evangelical disciples, the virtuous sponsors of our sainted Prophet, of all his zealous and faithful disciples, of all the Imâms, Mujtahids (sacred interpreters), of all the doctors, of all the holy men and women of Mussulmanism. Let us chant also in honour of Hazreti Mevlânâ, the founder of our Order, of Hazreti Sultan ul 'Ulemâ (his father), of Sayid Burhân ed Deen (his teacher), of Sheikh Shems ed Din (his consecrator), of Vâlideh Sultan (his mother), of Mohammed 'Allay ed Deen Efendi (his son and vicar), of all the Chelebees (his successors), of all the Sheikhs, of all the Dervishes, and all the protectors of our Order, to whom the Supreme Being deigns to give peace and mercy. Let us pray for the constant prosperity of our holy society, for the preservation of the very learned and venerable Chelebee Efendi (the general of the Order), our master and lord, for the preservation of the reigning Sultan, the very majestic and clement Emperor of the Mussulman faith, for the prosperity of the Grand Vizier, and of the Sheikh ul Islâm, and that of all the Mohammedan militia, of all the pilgrims of the holy city of Mekkeh. Let us pray for the repose of the soul of all the institutors, of all the Sheikhs, and of all the Dervishes of all other Orders;

for all good people, for all those who have been distinguished by their good works, their foundations, and their acts of beneficence. Let us pray also for all the Mussulmans of one and the other sex of the east and the west, for the maintenance of all prosperity, for preventing all adversity, for the accomplishment of all salutary vows, and for the success of all praiseworthy enterprises; finally, let us ask God to deign to preserve in us the gift of His grace, and the fire of holy love."

After the *Fâtiha*, which the assembly chant in a body, the Sheikh recites the *Fâtiha* and the *Salawât*, to which the dance of the Dervishes succeeds. Leaving their places all at once, they stand in a file to the left of the superior, and, approaching near him with slow steps, the arms folded, and the head bent to the floor, the first of the Dervishes, arrived nearly opposite the Sheikh, salutes, with a profound inclination, the tablet which is on his seat, on which is the name of Hazreti Mevlânâ, the founder of the Order. Advancing next by two springs forward, to the right side of the superior, he turns toward him, salutes him with reverence, and commences the dance, which consists in turning on the left heel, in advancing slowly, and almost insensibly making the turn of the hall, the eyes closed, and the arms open. He is followed by the second Dervish, he by the third, and so on with all the others, who end by filling up the whole of the hall, each repeating the same exercises separately, and all at a certain distance from each other.

This dance lasts sometimes for a couple of hours; it is only interrupted by two short pauses, during which the Sheikh recites different prayers. Towards the close of the exercises, he takes a part in them himself, by placing himself in the midst of the Dervishes; then returning to his seat, he recites some Persian verses expressive of good wishes for the prosperity of the religion, and the state. The general of the Order is again named, also the reigning Sultan, in the following terms:—

"The emperor of the Mussulmans, and the most august of monarchs of the house of 'Othman, Sultan, son of a sultan, grandson of a sultan, Sultan . . . . . , son of Sultan . . . . . , Khan," &c.

Here the poem mentions all the princes of blood, the Grand Vizier, the Muftee, all the Pashas of the empire, the 'Ulemâs, all the Sheikhs, benefactors of the Order, and of all the Mussulman peers, invoking the benediction of heaven on the success of their arms against the enemies of the empire.

"Finally, let us pray for all the Dervishes present and absent, for all the friends of our holy society, and generally for all the faithful, dead and living, in the east, and in the west."

The ceremony terminates by chanting the *Fâtiha*, or first chapter of the Koran.

All these different exercises, in each institution, ordinarily take place once or twice in a week. Among the Rufâ'ees it is on Thursday, the Mevlevees Tuesday and Friday, others on Monday, &c. All meet at the same hour, viz. immediately after the second *Namâz*, or noonday prayer. It is only the Nakshibendees who meet at night, at the close of the fifth (evening) *Namâz;* and the Bektâshees, who only perform during the night. These Bektâshees follow the usage of celebrating their ceremonies, like the Persians, on the anniversary of Kerbelâ, the 10th of Moharrem, a day consecrated among them under the title of *Yevmi 'Ashoorâ* (tenth day). At the close of a solemn prayer, all the Dervishes of the Order anathematize the race of the Mu'âwiya as having been the implacable enemy of that of 'Alee, the fourth caliph, and the nephew and son-in-law of the Prophet.

It must not, however, be imagined that these dances are everywhere exercised in silence. In some of the Orders they are performed to the sound of soft music. Sa'd Shems ed Deen, the immediate successor of 'Abd ul Kâdir Ghilânee, founder of the Order of the Kâdirees, was the first to give an example of this kind. In 1170, he allowed his Dervishes to use tambourines, only, however, to mark the measure of their steps, and to sustain the vivacity of their movements. This practice, though repressed by Islamism, was, nevertheless at length, adopted by the Rufâ'ees, the Mevlevees, the Bedâwees, the Sa'decs, and the Eshrefees. The Mevlevees have added the flute, which is open at either end, called by them the *Nay;* the greater number of the Dervishes of this Order play on it exquisitely; they are the only ones whose exercises are accompanied by various airs, all of a soft, tender, and pathetic expression. The convent of the general of this Order is distinguished from all others by a band of music composed of six different instruments. Besides the Nay and the tambourines, the Dervishes of the house (convent) established at Koniah play on the psalterim, the sister of the bass-viol, and the drum of the Basque.

As in each institution these public exercises are performed at different days, several Dervishes have the habit of visiting and assisting each other reciprocally in their religious dances. They, moreover, hold it as a duty to take part in them, so as to participate, as much as possible, in the merit of the good deed. The Dervishes who are the musicians are almost always attentive to join their *confrères* with their instruments; and those even which are the most scrupulous about the use of music are good enough to allow them to play during their services. This compliance is the more remarkable with reference to the Mevlevees, who never visit any other Order without taking their flutes with them. They are, however, very strict in not allowing the brethren of any other Order to join in their dances; and the Bektâshees are the only ones who hold their services with closed doors, whilst they, on the other hand, are free to assist in those of all the other Orders.

Such is the spirit or general system of these different congregations. If the prayers which are there recited are analagous to the principles of Islamism, and the high idea which the sectarians of the Koran possess of the Supreme Being, the practices which accompany them lead them, nevertheless, away from the maxims of their Prophet, and prove how much the human mind is susceptible of being misled when it gives itself up, without rule and measure, to the illusions of an enthusiastic zeal, and the promptings of an exalted imagination. It is probable that these innovations had their origin, among Mussulmans, in the sacred dances of the Egyptians, the Greeks, and the Romans of the Lower Empire.

But these practices, common to and obligatory on the Dervishes of all the Orders, are not the only ones which their devotion exercises. The more zealous amongst them devote themselves voluntarily to the most austere acts; some shut themselves up in their cells, so as to give themselves up, for whole hours, to prayer and meditation; the others pass, very often, a whole night in pronouncing the words *Hoo* and *Allah*, or rather the phrase, *Lâ ilâha ill'Allah.* The seven nights reputed as holy, as also those of Thursday and Friday, and of Sunday and Monday, sanctified among them by the conception and the nativity of the Prophet, are especially consecrated to these acts of penitence. So as to drive away sleep from their eyes, some of them stand for whole nights in very uncomfortable positions. They sit with their feet on the ground, the two hands resting upon their knees; they fasten themselves in this attitude by a band of leather passed over their neck and legs. Others tie their hair with a cord to the ceiling, and call this usage *Chilleh.*

There are some, also, who devote themselves to an absolute retirement from the world, and to the most rigid abstinence, living only on bread and water for twelve days successively, in honour of the twelve Imâms of the race of 'Alee. This peculiar exercise is called *Khalwet.* They pretend that the Sheikh 'Omar Khalwetee was the first to follow it, and that he often practised it. They add that, one day, having left his retirement, he heard a celestial voice saying, "O 'Omar Khalwetee, why dost thou abandon us?" and that, faithful to this oracle, he felt himself obliged to consecrate the rest of his days to works of penitence, and even to institute an Order under the name of *Khalwetees*, a name signifying "retirement." For this reason, Dervishes of this Order consider it their duty, more than any others, to live in solitude and abstinence. The more devoted among them observe sometimes a painful fast of forty days consecutively, called by them the *Erba'een* (forty). Amongst them all their object is the expiation of their sins, the sanctification of their lives, and the glorification of Islamism; the prosperity of the state, and the general salvation of the Mohammedan people. At each occasion, they pray heaven to preserve the nation from all public calamities, such as war, famine, pests, sins, earthquakes, &c. Same of them, especially the Mevlevees, have it also as a maxim to distribute water to the poor, and for this reason are called *Sakkâs*. With a vessel of water on their backs, they walk about the streets crying out, *Fee sebeel illah*, which means, "In the path of God," or rather in the view of pleasing God, and give water to all those who wish it, without asking for any payment. If they, however, receive anything, it is only for the poor, or, at least, to be partaken of with them.

The most ancient and the greatest of the Orders, such as the Olwânees, the Edhemees, the Kâdirees, the Rufâ'ees, the Nakshibendees, the Khalwetees, &c. are considered as the cardinals; for which reason they call themselves the *Usools*, or "Originals." They give to the others the names of the *Furoo'*, or "Branches," signifying thereby secondary ones, to designate their filiation or emanation from the first. The Order of the Nakshibendees and Khalwetees hold, however, the first rank in the temporal line; the one on account of the conformity of its statutes to the principles of the ten first confraternities, and to the lustre which causes the grandees and principal citizens of the empire to incorporate themselves in it; and the other, because of its being the source of the mother society which gave birth to many others. In the spiritual line, the Order of the Kâdirees, Mevlevees, Bektâshees, Rufâ'ees, and the Sa'dees, are the most distinguished, especially the three first, on account of the eminent sanctity of their founders, of the multitude of the miracles attributed to them, and of the superabundance of the merit which is deemed especially attached to them.

Generally, all these societies of anchorites are to be found spread over the different portions of the empire. They have, moreover, everywhere convents called Tekkehs, Khânakâhs, and Zâwiyehs; they are occupied each by twenty, thirty, or forty Dervishes, subordinate to a Sheikh, and nearly all are endowed by benefactions, and continual legacies left them by charitable persons. Each community only gives, however, to its Dervishes food and lodging. The former consists only of two dishes, rarely ever three. Each one takes his meal in his own cell, though they are nevertheless allowed to unite and dine together. Those who are married have permission to have a private dwelling; but they are obliged to sleep

in the convent once or twice a week, particularly the night preceding their dances or religious exercises. The monastery of the general of the Mevlevees is the only one which allows any deviation from this universal usage. It is not even allowed to the married Dervishes to pass the night there. As to the dress and other necessaries of life, they must provide them for themselves; and it is for this reason that many among them follow a trade or profession. Those who have a fair handwriting copy books, or the more *recherché* works. If any one among them has no resource whatever, he is sure to find aid from his relations, the generosity of the great, or in the liberality of his Sheikh.

Although all of them are considered as mendicant Orders, no Dervish is allowed to beg, especially in public. The only exception is among the Bektâshees, who deem it meritorious to live by alms; and many of these visit not only private houses, but even the streets, public squares, bureaux, and public houses, for the purpose of recommending themselves to the charity of their brethren. They only express their requests by the words *Shayid Ullah*, a corruption from *Sheyun l'illah*, which means "Something for the love of God." Many of these make it a rule to live only by the labour of their hands, in imitation of Hâjee Bektâsh their founder; and, like him, they make spoons, ladles, graters, and other utensils of wood or marble. It is these also who fashion the pieces of marble white or veined, which are used as collars, or buckles for the belts of all the Dervishes of their Order, and the *Keshguls*, or shell cups in which they are obliged to ask alms.

The wealthier convents are held to aid the poorer of the same Order. The Mevlevees are the best endowed of all. The monastery of the general possesses considerable lands, given him as *Wakfs*, or pious legacies, by the ancient Seljukide sultans, and confirmed by the house of 'Othman, or the Ottoman princes when they conquered Karamania. Murad IV. added more liberalities to those of his ancestors. In A.H. 1044 (A.D. 1634), when marching against Persia, and passing through Koniah, in Asia Minor, he bestowed many favours and distinctions upon the general of this Order, and gave to his community, as a perpetual *Wakf*, the full amount of the poll-tax of the tributary subjects established in that city. Considerable as the resources of a convent may be, its superiors never allow for themselves any luxury or ostentation. The surplus of the revenues is distributed among the poor, or is employed in the establishment of private and charitable buildings. The Sheikhs and Dervishes are scrupulously attached to this inviolable principle of their Order. Habituated from their youth to all sorts of privations, they are all the more faithful in the observance of its statutes.

Although in no wise bound by any oaths, all being free to change their community, and even to return to the world, and there to adopt any occupation which may please their fancy, it is rarely that any one makes use of this liberty. Each one regards it as a sacred duty to end his days in the dress of his Order. To this spirit of poverty and perseverance, in which they are so exemplary, must be added that of perfect submission to their superior. This latter is elevated by the deep humility which accompanies all their conduct, not only in the interior of the cloisters, but even in private life. One never meets them anywhere but with the head bent and the most respectful countenance. They never salute any one, particularly the Mevlevees and the Bektâshees, except by the names *Ya Hoo!* The words *Ay b'Allah* (thanks to God) frequently are used in their conversation; and the more devout or enthusiastic speak only of dreams, visions, celestial spirits, supernatural objects, &c.

They are seldom exposed to the trouble and vexations of ambition, because the most ancient Dervishes are those who may aspire to the grade of Sheikh, or superior of the convent. The Sheikhs are named by their respective generals, called the *Rais ul Meshâikh* (Chief of Sheikhs). Those of the Mevlevees have the distinctive title of *Cheleby Efendi.* All reside in the same cities which contain the ashes of the founders of their Orders, called by the name of *Asitânieh*, signifying "the court." They are subordinate to the Muftee of the capital, who exercises absolute jurisdiction over them. The superior head of the Mussulman religion, called the Sheikh ul Islâm, has the right of investing all the generals of the various Orders, even those of the Kâdirees, the Mevlevees, and of the Bektâshees, although the dignity be hereditary in their family, on account of their all three being sprung from the blood of the same founders of their Orders. The Muftee has likewise the right to confirm the Sheikhs who may be nominated by any of the generals of the Orders.

To arrive at the grade of Sheikh, the rights of seniority must also be sustained by talents, virtues, and an exemplary life. The person must even be reputed as holy, and especially favoured by heaven. In nearly all the Orders the generals never name any one to the office of Sheikh except after having prayed, fasted, and asked light of the Most High. They then consider the choice made as being the effect of a supernatural inspiration, which they owe to the powerful intercession of the Prophet, as the founder of the Order, sometimes even of the venerable Sheikh 'Abd ul Kâdir Ghilânee. These considerations, strengthened by prejudices, are the motives which decide the Mufftee (Sheikh ul Islam) to respect the choice made by the generals, and never to refuse to invest the persons proposed to him by them.

On these grounds also the generals are at liberty to name Sheikhs without monasteries and functions. These titular officers, who may be called *in partibus*, go to the city, or the suburb, which, according to the visions of the general, are considered as predestined to possess a convent of such and such an Order, and there wait the period of its being established. Their hopes are never deceived; a noble emulation leads its more wealthy and pious citizens to join in so meritorious a work. Some erect the building at their own expense, others provide for its support by the donation of perpetual *Wakfs*, others uniting their zeal to that of the Sheikh (*in partibus*), do all they can to strengthen the new institution. It is in this manner that formerly the greater part of these institutions were got up, and such even now is the case in various parts of the empire.

In former times the preference was given to those of the Orders which sanctioned neither dances nor music. The others, far from being famed by such acts of benevolence, experienced, on the contrary, much ill-will from many of the citizens. They were even the objects of malice, and were openly accused of following practices forbidden by religion and law; their exercises were regarded as profane acts, and their halls as so many temples devoted to the maledictions of heaven; all were scrupulous about entering them; such was even the effervescence of the public mind that under several reigns, particularly that of Mohammed IV. rigid Mussulmans proposed the abolition of all of these Orders, and the entire destruction of all of their convents and dancing halls. But those who were armed with the principles of religion so as to combat against these institutions, were, in turn, combated with other principles, drawn from the same source. The majority of the nation has always regarded these Sheikhs, the Dervishes, and, above all, their founders, as so many beloved sons of heaven, and in intimate relations with the spiritual powers, these opinions having for basis the belief (still in vogue at the present time) that the different Orders originated in the two congregations of Abu Bekr and 'Alee (the second and fourth Caliphs); the grace which these had received from the Prophet, both as his relatives and vicars, was transmitted, miraculously, down to the series of Sheikhs, who from age to age have governed the monastic societies. It is also generally believed that the legion of 356 saints, who, according to the Mussulmans, perpetually exist among mankind, and who form, in an invisible manner, that spiritual and celestial Order, sacred in the nation under the august name of the *Ghaws i 'Alem*, is principally composed of the members of these different fraternities, and so to abandon, condemn, and destroy them, as was the unanimous voice at the period of the crisis alluded to, would be but to call upon them and the whole empire the anathemas of all the holy saints who have lived, and still live, in pious retirement. The less enthusiastic, or the less favourable to the cause of the Dervishes, did not dare to declare themselves against them; they held this mixture of religious practices and profane exercises to be a mystery which all Mussulmans should adore in silence. The superstitious ideas which the Dervishes themselves have the talent to perpetuate in their nation have always served as their shield; they have maintained their institutions by drawing upon them the veneration and the generosity of credulous souls.

It is for this reason, according to these opinions, that a host of citizens hasten to join the different Orders. If, in the beginning, they preferred those which have no dancing nor music, for some time past they have incorporated themselves indistinctively with all of them. There are some who, not content with the advantages of belonging to one of them, cause themselves to be admitted into several. Some believe that they can add to the merit of their initiation, by joining in the dances of the Dervishes: others go so far as to mix up with them, and take part in their exercises. Those whose zeal is restrained by their occupations, and the regard due to their position in life, are satisfied with the recital, in their own houses, of a portion of the prayers used in the society to which they belong; and so as to purchase, in some manner, this involuntary absence from the convent, they wear two or three times a week, if only for a few minutes at a time, the cap of the order.

The grandees seem to have a preference for the Mevlevees, and those who are of that order never fail to leave off their turban when alone, and to wear the great *Kulah* of these Dervishes. This practice goes back as far as the time of Soliman Pasha, son of Othman I. It has already been seen that this prince addressed himself to the general of the Mevlevees, at Koniah, to ask the blessings of heaven in favour of the expedition which he was about to make against the Greeks of the Lower Empire; that this prelate covered the head of the prince with one of his caps, reciting prayers, and assuring him that victory would accompany his steps; that Soliman Pasha had this cap covered with embroidery of silver, and ordered turbans of nearly the same form for himself and all the officers of his army; and finally, that this cap, which became the ceremonial turban of all of the grandees of the court, and also of the sultans, who wore theirs embroidered in gold, was abandoned by Mohammed, and given up to the officers of the staff of the Janissaries. The opinion which was entertained of the happy influences of this head-dress is still retained by all the grandees who protect the Mevlevees. They consider it as a duty to associate with them, and to wear now and then this cap, in all its primitive simplicity.

The militia, especially the Janissaries, have a particular devotion for the Order of the Bektâshees, on account of the circumstance that, on the day of their creation, under Orkhan I., Hâjee Bektâsh, the founder of the Order, spread the border of his cloak over their heads, and showered his blessings on them. This is the cause of the veneration which the Janissaries have for that institution. On this account they are also called Bektâshees, and the title of the colonel of the Ninety-fifth Oda, or chamber of that force, called *Jemâ'at*, is borne by all of the generals of this order. From this also arose the custom of those troops of lodging and boarding eight Bektâshee Dervishes in the barracks of Constantinople. These have no other duty than to pray, morning and evening, for the prosperity of the empire, and the success of its arms. In all the ceremonies of the Janissaries, and above all, during the days of the Divan of the Seraglio, they marched on foot before the horse of the Aga of the corps, all dressed in green cloth, their hands closely crossed over their stomachs. The elder of them cried out incessantly, with a loud voice, the words, *Kereem Allah!* "God is merciful!" to which the others responded, *Hoo!* and this gave rise to the distinctive name of *Hoo Keshâns*, or "Him scatterers," borne by the Janissaries.

As to the rest of the citizens, though their feelings are pretty much the same with regard to all of the orders, many, nevertheless, appear to make a distinction in favour of the Khalwetees, the Kâdirees, Rufâ'ees, and the Sa'dees. The greater portion of those who do not care to incorporate themselves in these Orders are still attentive to assist occasionally at their dances. One sees among these simple spectators people of every condition of life, of both sexes. The custom is to take places in the corners of the halls, or in separate tribunes; those to the right are for the men, and those to the left for the women. The first are exposed, whilst the latter are covered with blinds. Christians, who in other respects are not allowed to enter the mosques during the holy service, are admitted, without any difficulty, among these Dervishes,—particularly strangers and people of distinction. One of the elders receives and shows them into the tribunes. As I have frequently assisted at these exercises, in several convents of Constantinople, I can vouch for their urbanity.

After these very general opinions as to the sanctity oi these religious Orders, one must not be astonished if the greater portion of the people have so much veneration for the Sheikhs of the Dervishes. Whenever they appear they receive the most distinguished tokens of welcome, and though, from principle, they never ask for anything, they nevertheless never scruple to accept the liberal donations of charitable individuals. There are some who reserve their alms for these pious recluses. Others, who hold it as a duty to seek for such as are the most recommendable in the Orders, form acquaintances with them, see them often, and supply their wants. Many even lodge and board some in their own houses, in the hope of drawing upon themselves, their families, and fortunes, the blessings of heaven. In time of war, this devotion becomes more general and more fervent. One sees Pashas, Beys, and officers, as well as high functionaries of the court, engage one or more of these cœnobites to follow them during the campaign. They pass whole days and nights in their tents, wholly occupied in offering up vows for the success of the Mussulman arms.

Moreover, whenever a warlike expedition is to be got up, a host of Sheikhs and Dervishes of nearly all the Orders hasten to follow the army as volunteers. The Government encourages them, as, by their presence, their example, and the mortifications to which they subject themselves, they animate the courage of the troops, and maintain a religious enthusiasm among them on the eve of an action: they spend the night in prayers and tears, go among the ranks, exhort the officers and soldiers to perform well their duty, or in calling to their minds the ineffable benefits promised by the Prophet to all Mussulmans who fight for the defence of the faith, or who die in arms. Some cry out, "Yâ Ghâzee!—Yâ Shâhid!" ("O ye victorious!—ye martyrs!") Others repeat the words, "Yâ Allah!" or "Yâ Hoo!" More than once, when they thought the Sanjâk Shereef, or holy standard (made out of the garments of the Prophet), was in danger, they have been seen to press around this holy object, strengthen the lines of the Emirs and officers stationed as its guard, sustain their efforts, and even themselves perform prodigies of valour.

Independent of these general considerations, which render the whole corps of the Orders so commendable to the nation, the miraculous virtues attributed to the greater part of their Sheikhs inspire especial devotion to them. They claim the power of interpreting dreams, and of healing, by means of spiritual remedies, both mental and bodily diseases. These remedies consist in exorcisings and prayers. Ordinarily, they put their hand on the head of the invalid, make mysterious breathings on his person, touch the suffering parts, and give the individual small rolls of paper, on which hymns have been written of their own composition, or passages taken from the Koran—generally from the two chapters which refer to the work of malevolence, enchantments, witchcraft, &c. They order some to throw them into a cup of water, and to drink the liquid some minutes afterwards; to others they recommend that they should carry them on their persons, in their pockets, or to hang them around their necks for fifteen, thirty, or sixty days, reciting, now and then, certain prayers.

They believe that these exorcisms may be traced back to the time of the Prophet. Indeed, the historian Ahmed Efendi relates that, in the tenth year of the Hejra, 'Alee, the fourth Caliph, having to march against the province of Yamin, the army of which was superior to his own, expressed some anxiety as to the success of his expedition; that Mohammed, to reanimate the courage of his son-in-law ('Alee), covered his head with one of his own turbans, and then pressed his hands on his breast, adding these words—"O my God! purify his tongue, strengthen his heart, and direct his mind." Since then religious traditions have sanctified these words as a fruitful source from which all the exorcising Sheikhs draw the virtue and efficacy of their remedies. It is not only to the sick that they give these cabalistic writings; they distribute them to persons in good health, as so many preservatives against physical evils and moral afflictions. Those who have recourse to these talismans flatter themselves that they have the virtue of curing the plague (small-pox), and generally all kinds of evils, even the wounds of an enemy. Some retain them on their person all their lives in small trinkets of gold and silver; others festoon them on their arms, place them on the upper part of their caps, or on their turbans; others again suspend them around their necks with a cord of gold or silk, and between the shirt and the vest.*

All these rolls are called *Yâftas*, *Nuskhas*, or *Hammâils*, and possess virtue, so say the Sheikhs, only when given by their own hands. The superstitious of all classes, men and women, zealously call upon them, and they never fail to bestow upon the former (the Sheikhs) marks of their generosity in the shape of silver, stuffs, or provisions of all kinds. Whatever may be the success of these remedies, nothing changes the faith of the meek-minded, because those who administer them require as the chief condition the strongest faith on the part of those who ask for them; so that, by accusing them of failing in this point, they are always able to screen themselves from the reproaches which the recipients might feel disposed sometimes to utter against their efficacy.

The public attribute to some of the Sheikhs the secret faculty of charming snakes, of discovering their nests in houses, of indicating thieves and pickpockets, of destroying the magical tie (*Bâgh*), which, it is believed, prevents newly-married husbands from consummating their marriage; finally, of preventing the unhappy effects of every sort of malevolence by drawing with collyrium the letter Elif (*a*) on the foreheads of women, and especially of children.

If, on the one hand, these reveries, which are prescribed by Islamism, attract at the same time the devo-

* Kara Mustapha, whose head is in the Museum of Armour at Vienna, wore a shirt covered with cabalistic Dervish writings, as a preservative.

tion and money of the superstitious, on the other they only serve to discredit them in the minds of people of reason and good sense. What adds still more to this personal disfavour, is the immorality of many of these same Sheikhs and Dervishes. It is observed that they unite together debauchery and the most severe acts of austerity, giving to the public the scandalous example of intemperance, dissoluteness, and the most shameful excesses. The least reserved of all are those travelling Dervishes, called *Seyyâhs*, or travellers, about whom something remains to be said.

These recluses adopt the system of wandering over all Mussulman countries in the three portions of the globe, and are divided into three classes. One, principally Bektâshees and Rufâ'ees, travel for the purpose of making collections, and of recommending their Orders to the liberality of the pious and charitable. The others are individuals expelled from their Order for misconduct, and who, retaining the garb of a Dervish, beg a subsistence from town to town. The third are foreign Dervishes, such as the 'Abdallees, the 'Ushshâkees, the Hindees, &c., for whom the Ottomans entertain but little devotion, on account of their not descending, like the others, from the original congregations during the life-time of the Prophet.

To this latter class belong also the *Uwaisees*, the most ancient of all, and the *Kalenderees*, whose founder was Kalender Yoosuf Andaloosee, a native of Andalusia, in Spain. He was for a long time a disciple of Hâjee Bektâsh, but, having been dismissed from his Order on account of his haughty and arrogant character, he made vain efforts to be admitted into the Mevlevees, and ended by establishing on his own authority an Order of Dervishes, with the obligation of perpetually travelling about, and of entertaining an eternal hatred against the Bektâshees and the Mevlevees.

The title of *Kalender*, which he himself assumed, and afterwards gave to his disciples, signifies pure gold, in allusion to the purity of the heart, to the spirituality of the soul, and to the exemption from all worldly contamination which he required of his proselytes. The rules of his Order compelled them to live wholly upon alms, to travel about mostly without shoes, and to practise the severest acts of austerity, so as to merit the favour of Heaven, especially in a state of ecstacy, of light, of perfect sanctity, which makes, he declared, the portion of every Cœnobite, renders him truly worthy of his vocation, of the name of a Kalenderee, or that of a Mevlevee. It is, therefore, given to all the Dervishes of the other Orders who are distinguished by their brethren for acts of supererogation, for revelations, and for supernatural grace. It is this class of enlightened beings of

A WANDERING DERVISH OF THE KALENDEREE ORDER.

the various Orders which has produced so many fanatics in every age of Mahommedanism. From it came the assassin of Sultan Byazid II., and of many ministers and grandees of the empire. Out of it came, under various reigns, so many false *Mehdees*, who, under this name, have got up the most audacious enterprises, and desolated entire countries by misleading the minds of the public through their impositions, their revelations, and pretended prophecies.

To secure the State and public from similar calamities, the light of the age in which we live should penetrate into this nation where vulgar prejudices have prevailed, as yet, even over the laws, and, at the same time, triumphed over all the projected reforms made from time to time by wise, enlightened men, though, it must be added, with feeble and tremulous hands. But, if fanaticism has its schools, irreligion has also its precipices. If, then, it is in the destiny of the Ottomans to return at some future day to a better order of things, we entertain the hope (and it is only humanity which inspires us), that he who shall undertake this salutary reform, will avoid, with prudence, extremes equally disastrous, by combining with his plan the principle of wise moderation. This is the only means whereby, in point of policy, abuses of religion, and vices of government among any people, may be corrected, and effect a concurrence of legal authority and doctrinal tenets in favour of the prosperity of the State, the glory of its chiefs, and the happiness of all individuals.

CHAPTER XII.

As Egypt contains many Dervishes, I cannot offer a better account of them than by quoting the remarks of Mr. Lane, in his excellent work called "the Modern Egyptians," which I do in his own language. I preserve also his own pronunciation of Arabic words.

"Durweeshes are very numerous in Egypt, and some of them who confine themselves to religious exercises, and subsist by alms, are much respected in this country, particularly by the lower orders. Various artifices are employed by persons of this class to obtain the reputation of superior sanctity, and of being endowed with the power of performing miracles. Many of them are regarded as welees.

"A direct descendant of Aboo-Bekr, the first Khaleefeh, having the title of '*Esh-Sheykh el Bekree*,' and regarded as the representative of that prince, holds authority over all Orders of Durweeshes in Egypt. The present Sheykh el Bekree, who is also descended from the Prophet, is *Nackeeb el Ashrâf*, or chief of the Shereefs. I may here add that the second Khaleefeh 'Omar has likewise his representative, who is the Sheykh of the 'Enáneeyeh, or Owlád 'Enán, an Order of Durweeshes so named from one of their celebrated Sheykhs, Ibn 'Enán. 'Osmán has no representative, having left no issue. The representative of 'Alee is called Sheykh es Sâdât, or 'Sheykh of the Seyyids' or 'Shereefs,' a title of less importance than that of Nackeeb of the Shereefs. Each of these three Sheykhs is termed the occupant of the 'seggádeh' (or prayer carpet) of his great ancestor. So also the Sheykh of an Order of Durweeshes is called the occupant of the seggádeh of the founder of the Order. The seggádeh is considered as the spiritual throne. There

Persians here all affect to be Sunnees. The Turks are the most intrusive of the two classes."

Mr. Lane thus describes a scene which he witnessed at Cairo, and which is much the same as I have seen at Constantinople. I suppose the Dervishes described belong to the Order of the Rifâ'ees, or one of their branches.

"The 'Zikkeers' (or performers of the Zikr,) who were about thirty in number, sat cross-legged upon matting extended close to the houses on one side of the street, in the form of an oblong ring. Within this ring, along the middle of the matting, were placed three very large wax-candles, each about four feet high, and stuck in a low candlestick. Most of the Zikkeers were Ahhmedee Durweeshes, persons of the lower orders, and meanly dressed: many of them wore green turbans. At one end of the ring were four Moonshids (or singers of poetry), and with them was a player on the kind of flute called *Náy*. I procured a small seat of palm-sticks from a coffee-shop close by, and, by means of a little pushing and the assistance of my servant, obtained a place with the Moonshids, and sat there to hear a complete act, or *Meglis* of the Zikr; which I shall describe as completely as I can, to convey a notion of the kind of Zikr most common and most approved in Cairo. It commenced at about three o'clock (or three hours after sunset), and continued two hours.

"The performers began by reciting the Fáthhah altogether; their Sheykh (or chief) first exclaiming, 'El Fáthhah!' They then chanted the following words:—'O God, favour our lord, Mohammed, among the latter generations; and favour our lord, Mohammed, in every time and period; and favour our lord, Mohammed, among the most exalted princes (the angels in heaven), unto the day of judgment; and favour all the prophets and apostles among the inhabitants of the heavens and of the earth; and may God (whose name be blessed and exalted), be well pleased with our lords and our masters, those persons of illustrious estimation, Aboo Bekr, and 'Omar, and 'Osman, and 'Alee, and with all the favourites of God. God is our sufficiency, and excellent is the Guardian! And there is no strength, nor power, but in God, the High, the Great! O God! O our Lord! O Thou liberal of pardon! O Thou most bountiful of the most bountiful! O God! Amen!' They were then silent for three or four minutes, and again recited the Fáthhah, but silently. This form of prefacing the Zikr is commonly used by almost all Orders of Durweeshes in Egypt. It is called *Istiftáhh ez Zikr.*

"After this preface, the performers began the *Zikr.* Sitting in the manner above described, they chanted, in slow measure, *Lá iláha illa 'lláh* (there is no deity but God), to the following air:—

bowing the head and body twice on each repetition of 'Lá iláha illa 'lláh.' Thus they continued about a quarter of an hour, and then, for about the same space of time, they repeated the same words to the same air, but in a quicker measure, and with correspondingly quicker motions. In the meantime, the Moonshids frequently sang, to the same or a variation of the same air, portions of a Ckaseedeh or of a Mooweshshahh, an ode of a similar nature to the 'Song of Solomon,' generally alluding to the Prophet as the object of love and praise.

"I shall here give a translation of one of these Mooweshshahhs which are very numerous, as a specimen of their style, from a book containing a number of these poems, which I have purchased during the present *Moolid* (birthday) from a Durweesh who presides at many Zikrs. He pointed at the following poem as one of those most common at Zikrs, and as one which was sung at the Zikr which I have begun to describe. I translate it verse for verse, and imitate the measure and the above Orders. Among the most celebrated of them are the 'Hhefnáweeyeh,' the ''Afeefeeyeh,' the 'Dimurdásheeyeh,' the 'Nuckshabendeeyeh,' the 'Bekreeyeh,' and the 'Leyseeyeh.'

"It is impossible to become acquainted with all the tenets, rules, and ceremonies of the Durweeshes, as many of them, like those of the Freemasons, are not to be divulged to the uninitiated. A Durweesh with whom I am acquainted thus described to me his taking the 'Ahd, or initiatory covenant, which is nearly the same in all the Orders. He was admitted by the Sheykh of the 'Dimurdásheeyeh.' Having first performed the ablution preparatory to prayer (the woodoo), he seated himself upon the ground before the Sheykh, who was seated in like manner. The Sheykh and he, the Mooreed, or canditate, then clasped their right hands together in the manner which I have described as practised in making the marriage contract: in this attitude, and with their hands covered by the sleeve of the Sheykh, the candidate took the covenant, repeating after the Sheykh the following words, commencing with the form of a common oath of repentance:—

"'I beg forgiveness of God the Great' (three times), 'than whom there is no other Deity; the Living, the Everlasting. I turn to Him with repentance, and beg His grace and forgiveness, and exemption from the fire.'

"The Sheykh then said to him: 'Dost thou turn to God with repentance?' He replied, 'I do turn to God with repentance, and I return unto God; and I am grieved for what I have done (amiss), and I determine not to relapse:' and then repeated after the Sheykh, 'I beg for the favour of God, the Great and the Noble Prophet; and I take as my Sheykh and my guide unto God (whose name be exalted), my master 'Abd er Rahheem ed Dimurdáshee el Khalwetee er Rifá'ee en Nebawee, not to change nor to separate; and God is our witness; by God, the Great' (this oath was repeated three times); 'there is no deity but God' (this also was repeated three times). The Sheykh and the *Mooreed* then recited the

Fáthhah together, and the latter concluded the ceremony by kissing the Sheykh's hand.

"The religious exercises of the Durweeshes chiefly consist in the performance of *Zikrs*. Sometimes standing in the form of a circular or oblong ring, or in two rows, facing each other, and sometimes sitting, they exclaim or chant, 'Lá iláha illa 'lláh' (There is no deity but God), or 'Alláh! Alláh! Alláh!' (God, God, God), or repeat other invocations, &c. over and over again, until their strength is almost exhausted, accompanying their ejaculations or chants with a motion of the head, or of the whole body, or of the arms. From long habit they are able to continue these exercises for a surprising length of time without intermission. They are often accompanied at intervals by one or more players upon a kind of flute called *náy*, or a double reed pipe called *arghool*, and by persons singing religious odes; and some Durweeshes use a little drum called *Báz*, or a tambourine, during their *Zikrs;* some also perform a peculiar dance, the description of which, as well as of several different *Zikrs*, I reserve for a future chapter.

"Some of the rites of the Darweeshes (as forms of prayer, modes of *Zikr*, &c.) are observed only by particular Orders; others by members of various Orders. Among the latter may be mentioned the rites of the 'Khalwetees' and 'Sházilees,' two great classes, each of which has its Sheykh. The chief difference between these is that each has its particular form of prayer to repeat every morning, and that the former distinguish themselves by occasional seclusion, whence their appellation of 'Khalwetees;' the prayer of this class repeated before daybreak, is called 'Wird Sahar;' that of the 'Sházilees,' which is called 'Hhezbesh-Sházilee,' after daybreak. Sometimes a Khalwetee enters a solitary cell, and remains in it for forty days and nights, fasting from daybreak till sunset the whole of this period. Sometimes also a number of the same class confine themselves, each in a separate cell, in the sepulchral mosque of the Sheykh of 'Ed Dimurdáshee,' on the north of Cairo, and remain there three days and nights, on the occasion of the *moolid* of that saint, and only eat a little rice and drink a cup of sherbet in the evening. They employ themselves in repeating certain forms of prayer, &c. not imparted to the uninitiated; only coming out of their cells to unite in the five daily prayers in the mosque, and never answering any one who speaks to them but by saying, 'There is no deity but God.' Those who observe the forty days' fast, and seclude themselves during that long period, practise nearly the same rules, and employ their time in repeating the testimony of the faith, imploring forgiveness, praising God, &c.

"Almost all the Durweeshes of Egypt are tradesmen or artisans, or agriculturalists, and only occasionally assist in the rites and ceremonies of their respective Orders; but there are some who have no other occupations than those of performing *Zikrs* at the festivals of saints, and at private entertainments, and of chanting in funeral processions. These are termed *Foockara*, or 'Fackeers,' which is an appellation given also to the poor in general, but especially to poor devotees. Some obtain their livelihood as water-carriers, by supplying the passengers in the streets of Cairo and the visitors at religious festivals with water, which they carry in an earthen vessel or a goat's skin, on the back. A few lead a wandering life and subsist on alms, which they often demand with great importunacy and effrontery. Some of these distinguish themselves in the same manner as certain reputed saints before mentioned, by the 'Dilck,' or coat of patches, and the staff with shreds of cloth of different colours attached to the top; others wear fantastic dresses of various descriptions.

"Some Rifá'ee Durweeshes (besides those who follow the occupation of charming away serpents from houses) pursue a wandering life, travelling about Egypt, and profiting by a ridiculous superstition which I must here mention. A venerated saint, called See Da'ood El 'Azab (or Master David the Bachelor), who lived at Tefáhineh, a village in Lower Egypt, had a calf which always attended him, brought him water, &c. Since his death, some Rifá'ee Durweeshes have been in the habit of rearing a number of calves at his native place, or burial place above named, teaching them to walk upstairs, to lie down at command, &c.; and then going about the country each with his calf, to obtain alms. The calf is called ''Egl el 'Azab' (the calf of El 'Azab, or of the Bachelor). I once called into my house one of these Durweeshes with his calf, the only one I have seen; it was a buffalo-calf, and had two bells suspended to it, one attached to a collar round its neck, and the other to a girth round its body. It walked up the stairs very well, but showed that it had not been very well trained in every respect. The 'Egl el 'Azab is vulgarly believed to bring into the house a blessing from the saint after whom it is called.

"There are numerous wandering Turkish and Persian Durweeshes in Egypt; and to these, more than to the few Egyptian Durweeshes who lead a similar life, must the character for impudence and importunacy be ascribed. Very often, particularly in Rumadán, a foreign Durweesh goes to the mosque of the Hhasaneyn, which is that most frequented by the Turks and Persians at the time of the Friday prayers; and when the Khateeb is reciting the first *Khootbeh*, passes between the ranks of persons who are sitting upon the floor, and places before each a little slip of paper upon which are written a few words, generally exhortative to charity, (as 'He who giveth alms will be provided for,'—'The poor Durweesh asketh an alms,' &c.); by which proceeding he usually obtains from each, or almost every person, a piece of five or ten *fuddahs*, or more. Many of the Persian Durweeshes in Egypt carry an oblong bowl of cocoa-nut or wood, or metal, in which they receive their alms, and put their food, and a wooden spoon; and most of the foreign Durweeshes wear dresses peculiar to their respective Orders: they are chiefly distinguished by the cap. The most common description of cap is of a sugar-loaf or conical shape, and made of felt. The other articles of dress are generally a vest, and full drawers or trousers, or a shirt and belt, and a coarse cloak or long coat. The are four great seggádehs of Durweeshes in Egypt, which are those of four great Orders about to be mentioned.

"The most celebrated Orders of Durweeshes in Egypt are the following :—1. The 'Rifá'eeyeh' (in the singular 'Rifá'ee'). This order was founded by the Seyd Ahhmad Rifá'ah el Kebeer. Its banners and the turbans of its members are black, or the latter are of a very deep blue, woollen stuff, or muslin of a very dark greenish hue. The Rifá'ee Durweeshes are celebrated for the performance of many wonderful feats. The ''Ilwáneeyeh,' or 'Owlád 'Ilwán,' who are a sect of the Rifá'ees, pretend to thrust iron spikes into their eyes and bodies without sustaining any injury; and in appearance they do this in such a manner as to deceive any person who can believe it possible for a man to do such things in reality. They also break large masses of stone on their chests, eat live coals, glass, &c.; and are said to pass swords completely through their bodies, and packing-needles through both their cheeks, without suffering any pain, or leaving any wound; but such performances are now seldom witnessed. I am told that it was a common practice for a Durweesh of this Order to hollow out a piece of the trunk of a palm-tree, fill it with rags soaked with oil and tar, then set fire to these contents, and carry the burning mass under his arm in a religious procession (wearing only drawers), the flames curling over his bare chest, back, and head, and apparently doing him no injury. The 'Saadeeyeh,' an Order founded by the Sheykh Saad ed Deen El Gibáwee, are another and more celebrated sect of the Rifá'ees. Their banners are green, or of the dark hue of the Rifá'ees in general. There are many Durweeshes of this Order who handle with impunity live venomous serpents and scorpions, and partly devour them. The serpents, however, they render incapable of doing any injury by extracting their venomous fangs, and doubtless they also deprive the scorpions of their poison. On certain occasions, as for instance on that of the festival of the birth of the Prophet, the Sheikh of the Saadeeyeh rides on horseback over the bodies of a number of his Durweeshes and other persons, who throw themselves on the ground for the purpose, and all assert that they are not injured by the tread of the horse. This ceremony is called the Doseh. Many Rifá'ee and Saadee Durweeshes obtain their livelihood by going about to charm away serpents from houses. Of the feats of these modern Psylli an account will be given in another chapter.

2. "The 'Ckádireeyeh,' an Order founded by the famous Seyd 'Abd el Ckádir el Geelánee. Their banners and turbans are white. Most of the Ckádireeyeh of Egypt are fishermen; these, in religious ceremonies, carry upon poles nets of various colours (green, yellow, red, white, &c.) as the banners of their Order.

3. "The 'Ahhmedeeyeh,' an Order of the Seyd Ahhmad el Bedawee, whom I have lately mentioned. This is a very numerous and highly respectable Order. Their banners and turbans are red. The 'Beiyoomeeyeh' (founded by the Seyd 'Alee el Beiyoomee), the 'Shaaráweeyeh' (founded by the Sheykh 'Alee Esh-Shaaráwee), the 'Shinnáweeyeh' (founded by the Seyd 'Alee Esh Shinnáwee), and many other Orders are sects of the Ahhmedeeyeh. The Shinnáweeyeh train an ass to perform a strange part in the ceremonies of the last day of the *moolid* of their great patron saint, the Seyd Ahhmad el Bedawee at Tunta; the ass, of its own accord, enters the mosque of the Seyd, proceeds to the tomb, and there stands, while multitudes crowd around it, and each person who can approach near enough to it plucks off some of its hair, to use as a charm, until the skin of the poor beast is as bare as the palm of a man's hand. There is another sect of the Ahhmedeeyeh, called the 'Owlád Noohh,' all young men; who wear *turtoors* (or high caps), with a tuft of pieces of various-coloured cloth on the top, wooden swords, and numerous strings of beads; and carry a kind of whip (called firckilleh), a thick twist of cords.

4. "The 'Baráhimeh,' or 'Boorhámeeyeh;' the Order of the Seyd Ibraheem ed Desoockee, whose *moolid* (birthday) has been mentioned above. Their banners and turbans are green. There are many other classes of Durweeshes, some of whom are sects of one or other of

of his thumb upon the reptile's back, as he grasped it, at a point about two inches from the head, and all that he ate of it was the head and the part between it and the point where his thumb pressed, of which he made three or four mouthfuls; the rest he threw away. Serpents, however, are not always handled with impunity even by Saadees. A few years ago, a Durweesh of this sect, who was called 'El Feel,' or the elephant, from his bulky and muscular form and great strength, and who was the most famous serpent-eater of his time, and almost of any age, having a desire to rear a serpent of a very venomous kind, which his boy had brought him among others that he had collected in the desert, put this reptile in his basket, and kept it for several days without food to weaken it. He then put his hand into the basket to take it out for the purpose of extracting its teeth; but it immediately bit his thumb. He called out for help; there were, however, none but women in the house, and they feared to come to him, so that many minutes elapsed before he could obtain assistance; his whole arm was then found to be swollen and black, and he died after a few hours."

Mr. Lane thus describes the performances of another Order of Dervishes, called the "'Eesáweeyeh" of Moscow.

"Before I describe the performances of the 'Eesáweeyeh, I should mention that they are a class of Durweeshes of whom all, or almost all, are Mughrebees, or Arabs of Northern Africa, to the west of Egypt. They derive their appellation from the name of their first Sheykh Seedee Mohammad Ibn 'Eesá, a Mughrebee. Their performances are very extraordinary, and one is particularly remarkable. I was very anxious that they should perform this night what I allude to, and I was not disappointed, though I was told that they had not done it in Cairo for several years before.

"I found about twenty of these Durweeshes, variously dressed, sitting upon the floor, close together, in the form of a ring, next to the front wall of the building. Each of them, excepting two, was beating a large '*tár*' (or tambourine), rather more than a foot in width, and differing from the common *tár*, in being without the tinkling pieces of metal which are attached to the hoops of the latter. One of the two persons mentioned as exceptions, was beating a small *tár* of the common kind, and the other a '*báz*,' or little kettle-drum. Before this ring of Durweeshes, a space rather larger than that which they occupied was left by the crowd for other Durweeshes of the same order; and soon after the former began to beat their tambourines, the latter, who were six in number, commenced a strange kind of dance; sometimes exclaiming 'Allah,' and sometimes, 'Allah Mowlána' (God is our Lord). There was no regularity in their dancing; but each seemed to be performing the antics of a madman;—now moving his body up and down, the next moment turning round, then using odd gesticulations with his arms, next jumping, and sometimes screaming; in short, if a stranger, observing them, was not told that they were performing a religious exercise, supposed to be the involuntary effect of enthusiastic excitement, he would certainly think that these Durweeshes were merely striving to excel one another in playing the buffoon; and the manner in which they were clad would conduce to impress him with this idea. One of them wore a *ckuft'an*, without sleeves, and without a girdle, and had nothing on his head, which had not been shaved for a week: another had a white skull-cap, but was naked from the head to the waist, wearing nothing on his body but a pair of loose drawers. These two Durweeshes were the principal performers. The former of them, a dark, spare, middle-aged man, after having danced in his odd manner for a few minutes, and gradually become more wild and extravagant in his actions, rushed towards the ring formed by his brethren who were beating the *társ*. In the middle of this ring was placed a small chafing-dish, of tinned copper, full of red-hot charcoal. From this, the Durweesh just mentioned seized a piece of live charcoal, which he put into his mouth; then he did the same with another, another, and another, until his mouth was full; then he deliberately chewed these live coals, opening his mouth very wide and distressing exertions of the performers at the close of the Zikr, and their calm gravity and solemnity of manner at the commencement, was particularly striking. Money was collected during the performance for the Moonshid. The Zikkeers receive no pay.

"An *Ishárah* passed during the meglis of the Zikr above described. This Zikr continues all night until the morning call to prayer, the performers only resting between each meglis, generally taking coffee, and some of them smoking."

The same celebrated Oriental scholar thus describes what is called the *Dosch*, or "treading" on the prostrate Dervishes by the horse of the Sheikh,—a spectacle only to be witnessed, I believe, in Egypt :—

"The Sheykh of the Saadeeyeh Durweeshes (the seyd Mohhammad El Menzeláwee), who is Khateeb (or preacher) of the mosque of the Hhasaneyn, after having, as they say, passed a part of the last night in solitude, repeating certain prayers and secret invocations and passages from the Koran, repaired this day (being Friday) to the mosque above mentioned, to perform his accustomed duty. The noon-prayers and preaching being concluded, he rode thence to the house of the Sheykh El Bekree, who presides over all the Orders of Durweeshes in Egypt. This house is on the southern side of the Birket El Ezbekeeyeh, next to that which stands at the south-western angle. On his way from the mosque, he was joined by numerous parties of Saadee Durweeshes, from different districts of the metropolis; the members from each district having a pair of flags. The Sheykh is an old grey-headed man, of an intelligent and amiable countenance, and fair complexion. He wore, this day, a white *benish*, and a white *ckaoock* (or padded cap, covered with cloth), having a turban composed of muslin of a very deep olive colour, scarcely to be distinguished from black, with a strip of white muslin bound obliquely across the front. The horse upon which he rode was one of moderate height and weight; my reason for mentioning this will presently be seen. The Sheykh entered the Birket El Ezbekeeyeh preceeded by a very numerous procession of the Durweeshes, of whom he is the chief. In the way through this place, the procession stopped at a short distance before the house of the Sheykh El Bekree. Here a considerable number of the Durweeshes and others (I am sure that there were more than sixty, but I could not count their number), laid themselves down upon the ground, side by side, as close as possible to each other, having their backs upwards, their legs extended, and their arms placed together beneath their foreheads. They incessantly muttered the word 'Allah!' About twelve or more Durweeshes, most without their shoes, then ran over the backs of their prostrate companions; some beating '*bá'zes*,' or little drums of a hemispherical form, held in the left hand, and exclaiming 'Allah!' and then the Sheykh approached; his horse hesitated for several minutes to tread upon the back of the first of the prostrate men; but, being pulled and urged on behind, he at length stepped upon him; and then, without apparent fear, ambled, with a high pace, over them all, led by two persons, who ran over the prostrate men; one sometimes touching on the feet, and the other on the heads. The spectators immediately raised a long cry of '*Alláh Lá' lá lá láh!*' Not one of the men thus trampled upon by the horse seemed to be hurt; but each, the moment the horse had passed over him, jumped up and followed the Sheykh. Each of them received two treads from the horse; one from one of his forelegs, and a second from a hind leg. It is said that these persons, as well as the Sheykh, make use of certain words (Yestaameloo asmâ), that is, repeat prayers and invocations, on the day preceeding this performance, to enable them to endure without injury the tread of the horse; and that some, not thus prepared, having ventured to lie down to be ridden over, have, on more than one occasion, been killed, or severely injured. The performance is considered as a miracle, effected through supernatural power, which has been granted to every successive Sheykh of the Saadeeyeh. It is said that the second Sheykh of the Saadeeyeh (the immediate successor of the founder of the Order) rode over heaps of glass bottles, without breaking any of them. Some persons assert that the horse is unshod for the occasion; but I thought I could perceive that this was not the case. They also say that the animal is trained for the purpose; but if so, this would only account for the least surprising of the circumstances; I mean, for the fact of the horse being made to tread on human beings, an act to which, it is well known, that animal is very averse. The present Sheykh of the Saadeeyeh refused, for some years, to perform the *Doseh*. By much entreaty he was prevailed upon to empower another person to do it. This person, a blind man, did it successfully, but soon after died; and the Sheykh of the Saadeeyeh then yielded to the request of his Durweeshes, and has since always performed the *Doseh* himself.

"After the Sheykh had accomplished this extraordinary performance, without the slightest appearance of any untoward accident, he rode into the garden, and entered the house of the Sheykh el Bekree, accompanied by only a few Durweeshes. On my presenting myself at the door, a servant admitted me, and I joined the assembly within. The Sheikh having dismounted, seated himself on a *seggádeh* spread upon the pavement against the end wall of a tukhtabosh, or wide recess, of the court of the house. He sat with bended back and downcast countenance, and tears in his eyes, muttering almost incessantly. I stood almost close to him. Eight other persons sat with him. The Durweeshes who had entered with him, who were about twenty in number, stood in the form of a semicircle before him upon some matting placed for them, and around them were about fifty or sixty other persons. Six Durweeshes advancing towards him, about two yards from the semicircle, commenced a Zikr, each of them exclaiming at the same time, 'Alláhu hhei' (God is living), and at each exclamation beating with a kind of small and short leather strap, a báz, which he held by a boss at the bottom in his left hand. This they did only for a few minutes. A black slave then became melboos, and rushed into the midst of the

Durweeshes, throwing his arms about, and exclaiming, 'Alláh! lá! lá! lá! lá! láh!' A person held him, and he soon seemed to recover. The Durweeshes, altogether, standing as first described, in the form of a semicircle, then performed a second Zikr, each alternate Zikkeer exclaiming, 'Allahu hhei' (God is living), and the others, 'Yá hhei' (O thou living), and all of them bowing, at each exclamation, alternately to the right and left. This they continued for about ten minutes. Then, for about the same space of time, in the same manner, and with the same motions, they exclaimed, "Dáïm" (Everlasting), and 'Yá Dáïm!' (O Everlasting!) I felt an irresistible impulse to do the same, if I could, without being noticed as an intruder, and accordingly joined the semicircle, and united in the performance, in which I succeeded well enough not to attract observation; but I worked myself into a most uncomfortable heat. After the Zikr just described, a person began to chant a portion of the Koran; but the Zikr was soon resumed, and continued for about a quarter of an hour. Most of the Durweeshes there present then kissed the hand of the Sheykh, and he retired to an upper apartment.

"It used to be a custom of some of the Saadeeyeh, on this occasion, after the *Doseh*, to perform their celebrated feat of eating live serpents before a select assembly, in the house of the Sheykh El Bekree; but their present Sheykh has lately put a stop to this practice in the metropolis, justly declaring it to be disgusting, and contrary to the religion, which includes serpents among the creatures that are unfit to be eaten. Serpents and scorpions were not unfrequently eaten by Saadees during my former visit to this country. The former were deprived of their poisonous teeth, or rendered harmless by having their upper and lower lips bored and tied together on each side with a silk string to prevent their biting, and sometimes those which were merely carried in processions had two silver rings put in place of the silk strings. Whenever a Saadee ate the flesh of a live serpent, he was, or affected to be, excited to do so by a kind of frenzy. He pressed very hard with the end system of rhyme of the original, with this difference only, that the first, third, and fifth lines of each stanza rhyme with each other in the original, but not in my translation.

'With love my heart is troubled;
  And mine eyelid hindreth sleep:
My vitals are dissevered;
  While with streaming tears I weep.
My union seems far distant,
  Will my love e'er meet mine eye?
Alas! did not estrangement
  Draw my tears, I would not sigh.

By dreary nights I'm wasted:
  Absence makes my hope expire:
My tears, like pearls, are dropping;
  And my heart is wrapped in fire.
Whose is like my condition?
  Scarcely know I remedy.
Alas! did not estrangement
  Draw my tears, I would not sigh.

O turtle-dove! acquaint me
  Wherefore thus dost thou lament?
Art thou so stung by absence?
  Of thy wings deprived, and pent?
He saith, "Our griefs are equal:
  Worn away with love, I lie."
Alas! did not estrangement
  Draw my tears, I would not sigh.

O first, and sole Eternal!
  Show Thy favour yet to me.
Thy slave, Ahhmad El Bekree
  Hath no Lord excepting Thee.
By Tá' Há! * the Great Prophet!
  Do Thou not his wish deny.
Alas! did not estrangement
  Draw my tears, I would not sigh.'"

After repeating the 'Lá iláha' in various times and measures, Mr. Lane adds—

"They next rose, and standing in the same order in which they had been sitting, repeated the same words to another air. During this stage of their performance. they were joined by a tall, well-dressed, black slave, whose appearance induced me to inquire who he was:

* "Ta Ha" is the name of the Arabian Prophet.

I was informed that he was a eunuch, belonging to the Basha. The Zikkeers, still standing, next repeated the same words in a very deep and hoarse tone, laying the principal emphasis upon the word *Lá'*, and the first syllable of the last word, *Allah*, and uttering, apparently with a considerable effort: the sound much resembled that which is produced by beating the rim of a tambourine. Each Zikkeer turned his head alternately to the right and left at each repetition of 'Lá iláha illa 'llah.' The eunuch above mentioned, during this part of the Zikr, became what is termed, *melboos*, or 'possessed.' Throwing his arms about, and looking up, with a very wild expression of countenance, he exclaimed, in a very high tone, and with great vehemence and rapidity, 'Allah! Allah! Allah! Allah! Alláh! la! la! la! la! la! la! la! la! la! la! la! la! la! láh! Yá 'ammee! Yá 'ammee! Yá 'ammee! Ashmáwee! Yá Ashmáwee! Yá Ashmáwee!' (Yâ 'ammee signifies O my uncle!) His voice gradually became faint, and when he had uttered those words, though he was held by a Durweesh who was next him, he fell on the ground, foaming at the mouth, his eyes closed, his limbs convulsed, and his fingers clenched over his thumbs. It was an epileptic fit. No one could see it and believe it to be the effect of feigned emotions; it was, undoubtedly, the result of a high state of religious excitement. Nobody seemed surprised at it, for occurrences of this kind at Zikrs are not uncommon. All the performers now appeared much excited; repeating their ejaculations with greater rapidity, violently turning their heads, and sinking the whole body at the same time, some of them jumping. The eunuch became melboos again, several times, and I generally remarked that his fits happened after one of the Moonshids had sung a line or two, and exerted himself more than usually to excite his hearers. The singing was, indeed, to my taste, very pleasing. Towards the close of the Zikr, a private soldier, who had joined through the whole performance, also seemed, several times, to be melboos; growling in a horrible manner, and violently shaking his head from side to side. The contrast presented by the vehement every moment to show its contents, which, after about three minutes, he swallowed; and all this he did without evincing the slightest symptom of pain; appearing, during the operation and after it, even more lively than before. The other Durweesh, before alluded to as half-naked, displayed a remarkably fine and vigorous form, and seemed to be in the prime of his age. After having danced not much longer than the former, his actions became so violent that one of his brethren held him; but he released himself from his grasp, and rushing towards the chafing-dish, took out one of the largest live coals, and put it into his mouth. He kept his mouth wide open for about two minutes; and during this period, each time he inhaled, the large coal appeared almost of a white heat; and when he exhaled, numerous sparks were blown out of his mouth. After this, he chewed and swallowed the coal, and then resumed his dancing. When this performance had lasted about half-an-hour, the Durweeshes paused to rest.

"Before this pause, another party of the same sect had begun to perform, near the centre of the great portico. Of these, I now became a spectator. They had arranged themselves in the same order as the former party. The ring composed by those who beat the tambourine consisted of about the same number as in the other company, but the dancers here were about twelve, sometimes less. One of them, a tall man, dressed in a dark woollen gown, and with a bare shaven head, took from the chafing-dish, which was handed to the dancers as though it had been a dish of cakes or sweetmeats, a large piece of brilliantly hot coal, placed it between his teeth, and kept it so for a short time, then drew it upon his tongue, and keeping his mouth wide open for, I think, more than two minutes, violently inhaled and exhaled, showing the inside of his mouth like a furnace, and breathing out sparks as the former Durweesh had done, but with less appearance of excitement. Having chewed and swallowed the coal, he joined the ring of the tambourine players, and sat almost close to my feet. I narrowly watched his countenance, but could not see the least appearance of his suffering any pain. After I had witnessed these extraordinary performances for about an hour, both parties of Durweeshes stopped to rest; and, as there was nothing more to see worthy of notice, I then quitted the mosque.

"Sometimes, on this occasion, the *'Eesáweeyeh* eat glass as well as fire. One of them, the Hhagg Mohhammad Es Seláwee, a man of gigantic stature, who was lamp-lighter in the mosque of the Hhasaneyn, and who died a few years ago, was one of the most famous of the eaters of fire and glass, and celebrated for other performances. Often when he appeared to become highly excited, he used to spring up to the long bars, or rafters, of wood, which extend across the arches above the columns of the mosque, and which are sixteen feet or more from the pavement, and would run along them, from one to another; then, with his fingers wetted in his mouth, he would strike his arm and cause blood to flow, and by the same means staunch the blood."

On describing the "Procession of the Kisweh," or holy covering for the temple, called the *Ka'beh*, at Mekkeh, Mr. Lane further adds, on the subject of the ceremonies of the Dervishes:—

"But the most remarkable group in this part of the procession consisted of several Durweeshes of the sect of the Rifá'ees, called Owlád 'Ilwán, each of whom bore in his hand an iron spike, about a foot in length, with a bell of the same metal at the thick end, having a number of small and short chains attached to it. Several of these Durweeshes, in appearance, thrust the spike with violence into their eyes, and withdrew it without showing any mark of injury; it seemed to enter to the depth of about an inch. This trick is well performed. Five *fuddahs*, or even a pipeful of tobacco, seemed to be considered a sufficient recompense to the religious juggler for this display of his pretended miraculous power. The spectators near me seemed to entertain no suspicion of any fraud in this singular performance; and I was reproached by one who sat by me,—a man of very superior information,—for expressing my opinion that it was a very clever piece of deception."

The Rifá'ee and Sa'dee Dervishes seem, by Mr. Lane's account, to be the principal charmers of serpents. I have witnessed in Tunis the performance of certain individuals, who I did not suppose at the time were members of any other order than that of ordinary jugglers, but who were evidently allied to one of the above. These, after letting free several snakes of about a yard in length, from a bag, so that they crawled over the ground to the alarm of the spectators, would seize one at a time, by the head or tail, I do not now remember which, and, as the performers danced round in a circle to the music of one or more little drums, raise each a serpent above their heads, and putting one end in their mouth, permit the whole of it to disappear down the throat. After allowing the snake to remain there a few moments, it would be withdrawn, and restored to the bag, and the same operation would be repeated with others. Whether the snake coiled itself away in the man's mouth, or actually went down his throat, I am unable to say; but there is not the least doubt that the entire body entered his mouth. There are Dervishes at Constantinople who pretend to the power of charming adders; and a friend lately related to me the following anecdote:—

Near his establishment in Stamboul, a house had remained vacant for a considerable length of time, from the supposition that it was haunted by an evil spirit, which, at times, made so extraordinary a noise as to frighten away every one who attempted to live in it. Having mentioned the circumstance to a Dervish, he determined to visit and examine the house. After a cursory examination, this person declared that it had adders in it, and promised to charm and destroy them. To effect this, he spent some time in singing a soft air in several parts of the house, without, however, any results, no serpents appearing. My friend, who was present, asked the Dervish what he would do in case one or even more adders made their appearance, and he assured him that he should at once catch them in his hands, and either kill them or abstract their stings. It is said that adders, after being deprived of their stings, are used in Stamboul as medicine, and that large numbers are imported for this purpose from Adrianople, where they abound. To put the Dervish to the test, my friend, unknown to him, sent his servant to a part of the city where adders are sold, with directions to purchase for him half-a-dozen in the poisonous state, at the same time telling the Dervish to continue his charms. The servant soon after returned, bringing with him a box, such as the adders are preserved in; on seeing which the Dervish became extremely agitated, and in expectation of these being let loose in an apartment with himself, begged my friend to allow him to go to his own house for a charm, which he assured him would enable any one to seize the most poisonous adder with impunity. Seeing his anxiety, he was allowed to depart, and although his return was awaited for some time, he did not again reappear.

Having made allusions to charms for self-preservation, I may add another anecdote thereon.

A Mussulman friend informed me that he was once visited by a Dervish, who told him that he possessed a charm by which the wearer would be preserved against a bullet fired at him, and which he desired to dispose of to him, as a particular favour, for a consideration. My friend appeared to believe in the efficacy of the charm, and so as to be able to admire more fully its extraordinary power, requested the Dervish to do him the favour to put it on his person, and step down into his garden, where he could fire at him one or two shots with his rifle. The Dervish, without any hesitation, returned to the foot of the stairs, as he said, to procure his overshoes, but finding the street door open, he took "French leave," much to the amusement of my friend, who is one of the best rifle-shots in the capital.

Mr. Lane's account of these snake-charming Dervishes is the following:—

"Many Rifá'ee and Saadee Durweeshes obtain their livelihood, as I have mentioned on a former occasion, by going about to charm away serpents from houses. A few other persons also profess the same art, but are not so famous. The former travel over every part of Egypt, and find abundant employment, but their gains are barely sufficient to procure them a scanty subsistence. The charmer professes to discover, without ocular perception (but perhaps he does so by a peculiar smell), whether there be any serpents in a house, and if there be, to attract them to him, as the fowler, by the fascination of his mice, allures the birds into his net. As the serpent seeks the darkest place in which to hide itself, the charmer has, in most cases, to exercise his skill in an obscure chamber, where he might easily take a serpent from his bosom, bring it to the people without the door, and affirm that he had found it in the apartment; for no one would venture to enter with him after having been assured of the presence of one of these reptiles within; but he is often required to perform in the full light of day, surrounded by spectators, and incredulous persons have searched him beforehand, and even stripped him naked; yet his success has been complete. He assumes an air of mystery, strikes the walls with a short palm-stick, whistles, makes a clucking noise with his tongue, and spits upon the ground, and generally says, 'I adjure you by God, if ye be above or if ye be below, that ye come forth. I adjure you by the most great Name, if ye be obedient, come forth; and if ye be disobedient, die, die, die!' The serpent is generally dislodged by his stick from a fissure in the wall, or drops from the ceiling of the room. I have often heard it asserted that the serpent-charmer, before he enters a house in which he is to try his skill, always employs a servant of that house to introduce one or more serpents; but I have known instances in which this could not be the case, and am inclined to believe that the Durweeshes above mentioned are generally acquainted with some real physical means of discovering the presence of serpents without seeing them, and of attracting them from their lurking places. It is, however, a fact well ascertained, that the most expert of them do not venture to carry serpents of a venomous nature about their persons until they have extracted the poisonous teeth. Many of them carry scorpions also within the cap, and next the shaven head; but doubtless first deprive them of the power to injure; perhaps by merely blunting the sting. Their famous feats of eating live and venomous serpents, which are regarded as religious acts, I have before had occasion to mention, and purpose to describe particularly in another chapter."

CHAPTER XIII.

MUSSULMAN SAINTS.

I AM somewhat deviating from the object of the present work, by devoting a chapter, however small, to the subject of Mussulman Saints. These, nevertheless, are so intimately connected with the spiritualism of the Dervishes, that I do not see how it can be properly avoided. The subject has already been alluded to in Chapter III., and I avail myself of the information given in Mr. Lane's "Modern Egyptians," for details which confirm what I there stated.

"The Mooslims of Egypt, in common with those of other countries, entertain very curious superstitions respecting the persons whom they call *Welees*. I have often endeavoured to obtain information on the most mysterious of these superstitions, and have generally been answered, 'You are meddling with the matters of the Tareeckah' (*Tareekat*), or the religious course of the Durweeshes; but I have been freely acquainted with general opinions on these subjects, and such are perhaps all that may be required to be stated in a work like the present; I shall, however, also relate what I have been told by learned persons, and by Durweeshes, in elucidation of the popular belief.

"The Egyptians pay a superstitious reverence not to imaginary beings alone; they extend it to certain individuals of their species, and often to those who are justly the least entitled to such respect. An idiot or a fool is vulgarly regarded by them as a being whose mind is in heaven, while his grosser part mingles among ordinary mortals; consequently he is considered an especial favourite of Heaven. Whatever enormities a reputed saint may commit (and there are many who are constantly infringing precepts of their religion), such acts do not affect his fame for sanctity; for they are considered as the results of the abstraction of his mind from worldly things, his soul, or reasoning faculties, being wholly absorbed in devotion; so that his passions are left without control. Lunatics who are dangerous to society are kept in confinement; but those who are harmless are generally regarded saints. Most of the reputed saints of Egypt are either lunatics, or idiots, or impostors. Some of them go about perfectly naked, and are so highly venerated, that the women, instead of avoiding them, sometimes suffer these wretches to take any liberty with them in a public street; and, by the lower orders, are not considered as disgraced by such actions, which, however, are of very rare occurrence. Others are seen clad in a cloak or long coat composed of patches ot various coloured cloths, which is called a *Dilck*, adorned with numerous strings of beads, wearing a ragged turban, and bearing a staff with shreds of cloth of various colours attached to the top. Some of them eat straw, or a mixture of chopped straw and broken grass, and attract observation by a variety of absurd actions. During my first visit to this country, I often met in the streets of Cairo a deformed man, almost naked, with long matted hair, and riding upon an ass led by another man. On these occasions he always stopped his beast directly before me, so as to intercept my way, reciting the Fáthhah (or opening chapter of the Koran), and then held out his hand for alms. The first time that he thus crossed me, I endeavoured to avoid him; but a person passing by remonstrated with me, observing that the man before me was a saint, and that I ought to respect him, and comply with his demand, lest some mischief should befall me. Men of this class are supported by alms, which they often receive without asking for them. A reputed saint is commonly called 'Sheykh,' 'Moorábit,' or 'Welee.' If affected with lunacy or idiotcy, or of weak intellect, he is also, and more properly, termed 'Megzoob,' or 'Mesloob.' 'Welee' is an appellation correctly given to an eminent and very devout saint, and signifies a favourite of heaven; but it is so commonly applied to real or pretended idiots, that some wit has given it a new interpretation, as equivalent to 'beleed,' which means a 'fool,' or 'simpleton,' remarking that these two terms are equivalent both in sense and in the numerical value of the letters composing them; for 'Welee' is written with the letters 'wáoo,' 'lám,' and 'ye,' of which the numerical letters are 6, 30, and 10, or together, 46; and 'beleed' is written with 'be,' 'lám,' 'ye,' and 'dál,' which are 2, 30, 10, and 4, or, added together, 46. A simpleton is often called a 'Welee.'

"In the first place, if a person were to express a doubt as to the existence of true Welees, he would be branded with infidelity; and the following passage of the Ckoran would be adduced to condemn him: 'Verily, on the favourites of the God no fear shall come, nor shall they grieve.' This is considered as sufficient to prove that there is a class of persons distinguished above ordinary human beings. The question then suggests itself, 'Who, or of what description are these persons?' and we are answered, 'They are persons wholly devoted to God, and possessed of extraordinary faith; and according to their degree of faith, endowed with the power of performing miracles.'

"The most holy of the Welees is termed the *Ckootb;* or, according to some persons, there are ten who have this title; and again, according to others, four. The term 'Ckootb,' signifies an axis; and hence is applied to a Welee who rules over others; they depending upon him, and being subservient to him. For the same reason it is applied to temporal rulers, or any person of high authority. The opinion that there are four Ckootbs, I am told, is a vulgar error, originating from the frequent mention of 'the four Ckootbs,' by which expression are meant the founders of the four most celebrated Orders of Durweeshes (the Rifá'eeyeh, Ckádireeyeh, Ahhmedeeyeh, and Baráhimeh), each of whom is believed to have been the Ckootb of his time. I have also generally been told that the opinion of there being two Ckootbs is a vulgar error, founded upon two names, 'Ckootb el Hhackeeckah' (or the Ckootb of truth), and 'Ckootb el Ghos' (or the Ckootb of invocation for help), which properly belong to but one person. The term 'el Ckootb el Moo'tawellee' is applied, by those who believe in but one Ckootb, to the one ruling at the present time; and by those who believe in two, to the acting Ckootb. The Ckootb who exercises a superintendence over all other Welees (whether or not there be another Ckootb—for if there be, he is inferior to the former) has under his authority Welees of different ranks, to perform different offices,—'Nackeebs,' 'Bedeels,' &c., who are known only to each other, and perhaps to the rest of the Welees, as holding such offices.

"The Ckootb, it is said, is often seen, but not known as such; and the same is said of all who hold authority under him. He always has a humble demeanour and mean dress; and mildly reproves those whom he finds acting impiously, particularly those who have a false reputation for sanctity. Though he is unknown to the world, his favourite stations are well known; yet at these places he is seldom visible. It is asserted that he is almost constantly seated at Mekkeh, on the roof of the Kaabeh; and, though never seen there, is always heard at midnight to call twice, 'O thou most merciful of those who show mercy!' which cry is then repeated from the mád'nehs of the temple by the Mooeddins: but a respectable pilgrim, whom I have just questioned upon this matter, has confessed to me that he himself has witnessed that this cry is made by a regular minister of the mosque, yet that few pilgrims know this: he believes, however, that the roof of the Kaabeh is the chief Murkaz (or station) of the Ckootb. Another favourite station of this revered and unknown person is the Gate of Cairo, called Báb Zooweyleh, also called Báb Mootawellee. Though he has a number of favourite stations, he does not abide solely at these; but wanders through the world, among persons of every religion, whose appearance, dress, and language he assumes; and distributes to mankind, chiefly through the agency of the subordinate Welees, evils and blessings, the awards of destiny. When a Ckootb dies, he is immediately succeeded in his office by another.

"Many of the Mooslims say that Elijah, or Elias, whom the vulgar confound with El Khidr, was the Ckootb of his time, and that he invests the successive Ckootbs; for they acknowledge that he has never died, asserting him to have drank of the fountain of life. This particular in their superstitious notion respecting the Ckootbs, combined with some others which I have before mentioned, is very curious when compared with what we are told in the Bible of Elijah, of his being transported from place to place by the Spirit of God; of his investing Elisha with his miraculous powers and his offices, and of the subjection of other prophets to him and to his immediate successor." El Khidr, according to the more approved opinion of the learned, was not a prophet, but a just man, or saint, the Wezeer and councillor of the first Zoo'l Karneyn, who was a universal conqueror, but an equally doubtful personage, contemporary with the patriarch Ibráheem, or Abraham. El Khidr is said to have drunk of the fountain of life, in consequence of which he lives till the day of judgment, and to appear frequently to Muslims in perplexity. He is generally clad in green garments, whence, according to some, his name of Khidr.

I may here add that in a work which I possess in MS., entitled "Hadeeket el Jevâmi'," or "An account of the mosques, tekkiehs, &c. of Constantinople," it is stated in the description which it gives of the mosque of St. Sophia, that "in the centre of the holy mosque, under the Top Kandil, and between the Muslâ gate and the Minber, there is a picture of a door in the wall, marking the Mokâm, or place of Khidr; and that by the command of Hazreti Khidr, the grandson of the celebrated pious Mussulman Divine Ak Shems ed Deen, named Hamdi Efendi, translated the tale of Yoossuf and Zuleikhâ of Mollâ Jâmee, in the centre of the mosque." (See 1 Kings xviii. 12, and 2 Kings ii. 9—16.)

Much veneration is shown in the East for the tombs

of Walees, Sheikhs, and other deceased pious persons. Throughout Constantinople one frequently meets with similar tombs, on which a lamp is kept suspended and lit at nightfall. Others are within *Turbehs*, or mausoleums, more or less splendid, covered with costly shawls or embroidered silks, and, either on the tombstone or on a framed inscription, the names and titles of the deceased are narrated at length. On the windows are seen pieces of rags, tied there by those who believe they may profit by the spiritual powers and holiness of the deceased. These petty native offerings are called *Nezr*, or vows. On this subject Mr. Lane says :—

"Over the graves of most of the more celebrated saints are erected large and handsome mosques; over that of a saint of less note (one who by a life of sanctity or hypocrisy has acquired the reputation of being a Walee or devout Sheykh) is constructed a small, square, whitewashed building, crowned with a cupola. There is generally directly over the vault in which the corpse is deposited an oblong monument of stone or brick (called *Turkeebeh*), or wood (in which case it is called *Táboot*), and this is usually covered with silk or linen, with some words from the Ckorán marked upon it, and surrounded by a railing or screen of wood or bronze, called 'Mucksoorah.' Most of the sanctuaries of saints in Egypt are tombs; but there are several which only contain some inconsiderable relic of the person to whom they are dedicated, and there are few which are mere cenotaphs. The Egyptians occasionally visit these and other sanctuaries of their saints, either merely with the view of paying honour to the deceased, and performing meritorious acts for the sake of these venerated persons, which they believe will call down a blessing on themselves, or for the purpose of urging some special petition, such as for the restoration of health, or for the gift of offspring, &c., in the persuasion that the merits of the deceased will insure a favourable reception of the prayers which they offer up in such consecrated places. The generality of the Mooslims regard the deceased saints as intercessors with the Deity, and make votive offerings to them. The visitor, on arriving at the tomb, should greet the deceased with the salutation of peace, and should utter the same salutation on entering the burial ground. In the former case the visitor should front the face of the dead, and consequently turn his back to the Ckibleh. He walks round the 'mucksoorah,' or the monument, from left to right, and recites the Fáthhah inaudibly, or in a very low voice, before its door, or before each of its four sides. Sometimes a longer chapter of the Ckorán than the first (Fáthhah) is recited afterwards; and sometimes a Khutmeh (or recitation of the whole of the Ckorán) is performed on such an occasion. These acts of devotion are generally performed for the sake of the saint, though merit is likewise believed to reflect upon the visitor who makes such a recitation. He usually says at the close of this, 'Extol the perfection of thy Lord, the Lord of Might, exempting Him from that which they (the unbelievers) ascribe to Him' (namely, the having a son or a partaker of his Godhead); and adds, 'And peace be on the Apostles, and praise be to God, the Lord of all creatures. O God! I have transferred the merit of what I have recited from the excellent Ckorán to the person to whom this place is dedicated,' or 'to the soul of this Welee.' Without such a declaration, or an intention to the same effect, the merits of the recital belongs solely to the person who performs it. After this recital the visitor, if it be his desire, offers up any prayer for temporal or spiritual blessings, generally using some such form as this—'O God! I conjure Thee by the Prophet, and by him to whom this place is dedicated, to grant me such and such blessings;' or, 'My burdens be on God and on thee, O thou to whom this place is dedicated.' In doing this, some persons face any side of the mucksoorah and the Ckibleh; but I believe that the same rule should be observed in this case as in the salutation. During the prayer the hands are held (raised upwards and open) as in the private supplications after the ordinary prayers of every day, and afterwards they are drawn down the face. Many of the visitors kiss the threshold of the building, and the walls, windows, mucksoorah, &c. This however, they disapprove, asserting it to be an imitation of a custom of the Christians. The rich, and persons of easy circumstances, when they visit the tomb of a saint, distribute money or bread to the poor, and often give money to one or more water-carriers to distribute water to the poor and thirsty for the sake of the saint. On these occasions it is a common custom for the male visitors to take with them sprigs of myrtle: they place some of these on the monument, or on the floor within the mucksoorah, and take the remainder, which they distribute to their friends. At almost every village in Egypt is the tomb of some favourite or patron saint, which is generally visited on a particular day of the week by many of the inhabitants, chiefly women, some of whom bring thither bread, which they leave there for poor travellers, or any other persons. Some also place small pieces of money on these tombs. These gifts are offerings to the Sheykh, or given for his sake. Another custom common among the peasants is to make votive sacrifices at the tombs of their Sheykhs. For instance, a man makes a vow (nezr) that, if he recover from a sickness, or obtain a son, or any other specific object of desire, he will give to a certain Sheykh (deceased) a goat, or a lamb, or a sheep, &c.: if he obtain the object, he sacrifices the animal which he has vowed at the tomb of the Sheykh, and makes a feast with its meat for any persons who may happen to attend. Having given the animal to the saint, he thus gives to the latter the merit of feeding the poor. It is a custom among the Mooslims, as it was among the Jews, to rebuild, whitewash, and decorate the tombs of their saints, and occasionally to put a new covering over the turkeebeh or táboot; and many of them do this from the pharisaic motives which actuated the Jews."

Besides the care taken to keep up, and in good order, the tombs of deceased holy Sheikhs, Dervishes, &c. in the East, these are frequently watched over by a pious living brother Dervish, who abandons the world and its attractions for this purpose. Himself of undoubted purity of conduct and character, his prayers are solicited by those in need of religious and spiritual consolation and aid—often of a purely worldly nature—such as the procuring of office, the favour of the Sultan, or other person high in office. These guardians of holy tombs may themselves be Sheikhs, and have with them one or more Mureeds, to whom they give "spiritual" instruction. They are of various Tareeks or "Paths," Nakshibendee, Bedâwee, Khalwetee, or Kâdiree, &c.; and considerable rivalry exists among them, which degenerates into calumny and ridicule.

A humorous story has been told me regarding a Sheikh near one of the larger cities of Asia Minor, who for many years had watched over the tomb of a deceased Dervish saint, attended by a youth, or Mureed, to whom he was supposed to impart his spiritual knowledge. The Sheikh possessed an extensive reputation for piety, and even spiritual power and influence, and was consequently much frequented by the peasantry, and even the neighbouring gentry—especially the female part of the community. The Turbeh over the grave was a conspicuous object, and contained two or three small rooms, in which lodged the Sheikh and his disciple, and served as a dormitory for any wandering Dervish who, on his way to and from places of pilgrimage in various parts of Asia Minor, might claim his hospitality. A lamp hung suspended at the head of the grave, and this was always kept burning at night, and even on certain days—such as, for instance, that of the birth of the deceased—and on Fridays, when visitors were most apt to frequent the Sheikh for the purpose of presenting various gifts, of imploring his prayers and blessings, and of offering prayers over the sainted remains. The windows of the little mausoleum were literally covered with bits of rags tied there by the many persons who made vows or "nezrs" to the saint; and the reverence shown for both the living and the dead saint, brought quite a revenue to the former and his humble Mureed or disciple. The Sheikh for many years had possessed a comely ass, on which he was wont to make visits to his friends in the vicinity, and a small amount of the veneration bestowed on its master, was even vouchsafed to his humble animal. As to the Mureed, he became well versed in the routine of the affairs of the Turbeh, and was supposed to exercise considerable influence with his principal. He wore the cap of the Tareek or Order of the Sheikh, though the rest of his costume was rather the worse for long years of wear; but this by no means affected his reputation—indeed, on the contrary, poverty is so well known an attribute of the "poor Dervish," and gives so much interest to his career, that it forms the chief capital of the fraternity, and enables them to wander over the world free from all fear of robbery, or of a want of daily subsistence. It formed the "pride" of the blessed Prophet, and therefore might readily do as much for a humble Dervish, who, though generally sadly deficient in cash, never had occasion to complain of the want of food, as this flowed into the Turbeh in abundance, especially on Fridays, through the benevolence and piety of the visitors. As to the Sheikh himself, he wore the full costume of his Order, and even added the green turban which designates descent from the family of the Prophet, through his only child and daughter Fâtimah, the wife of 'Alee, the nephew as well as son-in-law of the Prophet, and who finally succeeded him as the fourth of the direct Caliphs of Islamism. This turban constituted him a Said—*Emir* or a *Shereef*—of the family of Mohammed, and tended to add greatly to his claims to popular veneration. Whether he possessed the necessary *Sened*, or *Silsilch-nameh* (Genealogical Register), to support his assumed descent from so honoured a source might have been questioned; but no one cared or perhaps dared to entertain, much less put in doubt, such a matter with regard to the honoured Sheikh who passed his days, and even much of his nights, in prayers over the sainted tomb of the Dervish, whose name and good character were fully described in the epitaph at its head.

The disciple, whose name was 'Alee, had never been much remarked for any superior intelligence: but for piety, and acquaintance with the duties of his position, no fault could possibly be found with him. He had gradually assumed the sedate and calm exterior of a pious Dervish, and always possessed a dignity of demeanour which was quite impressive on the minds of the visitors of the *Turbeh.* It was predicted that some day he would be sure to figure as an eminent Sheikh, and destiny seemed to press him strongly in that direction already. Quite as little was known of his origin and parentage as of those of the Sheikh, his superior; but these are of little use to a Dervish, who, it is well understood, has no claims to celebrity other than those acquired by his own spiritual powers and personal reputation. The Sheikh was his immediate spiritual director, or *Murshid*, and all the knowledge which he possessed was due to the oral instruction received from him. From him he had taken the *Be'at*, or initiation; he had spent long nights in prayer and meditation, and the visions of the latter had been duly reported to and interpreted by him, much to his own satisfaction and encouragement. The time had therefore fully arrived when, according to the rules of the Order, he must set out on his travels, for the purpose of performing pilgrimages to various holy tombs situated throughout Islam Lands, or to extend his wanderings as far even as that of the blessed Prophet and the Ke'beh, or the shrines at Kerbelay, where are interred the remains of the grandsons of the Prophet, Hasan and Hosain, and others of the victims of the cruel usurpers of the Caliphat, after the death of the fourth Caliph, 'Alee.

One Friday evening, after the visitors had all departed, and the Sheikh and his pupil remained quite alone in the *Turbeh*, the former renewed a topic which had already been slightly touched upon on some previous occasions, viz., of the necessity which existed for the latter setting out upon his travels. This time a decision was come to, and it was mutually agreed upon that on the following Sunday the young neophyte should take his departure. "I have instructed you with much care, my son," said the Sheikh, "and taught you all that it is necessary for you to know, and your further continuance here is not only of no use to you, but even detrimental to your career. As you well know, I possess but little of the world's goods, but of what I have you shall receive a bountiful share. You have now grown up to manhood, and will be able to make your way in the world, and by your pious appeals to the benevolent and the wealthy, not fail to receive all the assistance of which you may stand in need. On the morning aforenamed I will be prepared to equip you for your long and tedious journey, and to bestow upon you my blessing." So much goodness deeply impressed the heart and mind of young 'Alee, and so overcame him, that, in place of any answer, he devoutly pressed his Sheikh's hand to his lips, and retired to meditate upon his future prospects, and cultivate whatever spiritual visions might be sent him by the *Peer* of the Order, or even by the blessed Prophet himself.

Early on Sunday morning 'Alee arose, and awaited the conclusion of the Sheikh's slumbers. The latter was not long behind him, and after the usual salutations and morning prayers, he gave his pupil some excellent advice, and then quite overcame him by the declaration that he had decided to offer him an evidence of the great friendship which he had always entertained for him, by the gift of his own long-treasured companion the ass, on which he had rode for so many years, with its pack-saddle, one of his own *khirkas*, or mantles, and a wallet of provisions sufficient for some days' use. Besides these, he presented him with a *keshgool*, or alms-cup, a *mu'een*, or arm-rest, made of iron, in which was concealed a goodly dagger with which to defend himself against wild animals or in any other danger—for it was not to be supposed that it could possibly ever be used as a means of offence in the hands of a pious Dervish like himself, travelling over the world only for the most peaceful and honest motives—and a tiger's skin to throw over his shoulders, as some protection against the heat of the sun and the colds of winter. But the most precious of all his gifts was a *nuskha* or *hamileh* (amulet), which the Sheikh had long worn suspended to his own neck in a small metal cylinder, which seemed to be of some precious metal, much resembling silver, greatly admired and revered by the visitors of the Turbeh, in which so many of his days had been spent. As to the ass, it had peculiar claims to his consideration on account of its age and truly venerable appearance. They had long served together, and often suffered, especially during the winter season, from the same cause, viz., a want of food; and even now its lean condition seemed to indicate that pasture was scarce, and a more nourishing diet decidedly on the decline. Whether this was the case, or rather that its teeth were imperfect, cannot be now stated with any degree of accuracy; but there was one thing quite apparent to 'Alee, and which he now remembered with reflections to which the coming future gave rise, that he and the ass were nearly about the same age, and therefore could readily sympathize with each other in whatever lot their lives might hereafter be cast during their united pilgrimage.

The ass was soon got ready for the journey, and its load now consisted only of the wallet, the *keshgool*, and the mantle, for 'Alee decided to start on his wanderings on foot, like any ordinary Dervish, and so not accustom himself, at the outset, to the luxury of a conveyance. The Sheikh took a deep interest in all his preparations, and when these had been got ready for the departure, he accompanied his pupil some half a mile or so from the *Turbeh*, and then, coming to a stand-still, took his hand in his own and devoutly blessed him, reciting the *Fâtiha*, or first chapter of the Koran, with a tone of peculiar benevolence. Then, bidding him farewell, he slowly returned to the *Turbeh*, and 'Alee bent his way, not to the town, but across the neighbouring valley, and towards the distant mountain range which bordered the horizon.

For some days 'Alee journeyed onwards over the public route, without much regard to its possible termination, and with a very vague idea of the direction which he was taking. His provisions were becoming low, and his companion's strength was failing from the want of a better nourishment than that offered by the way-side. His nights had been spent in true Dervish style, under the cover of a hospitable tree, or beside a bountiful spring of water, and few had been the alms which he, thus far, had received from passers-by. Hunger, however, had not as yet rendered it necessary for him to appeal to the benevolent for assistance; and as he was naturally of a timid disposition, he rather had avoided than sought companionship on his way. Indeed, it is so usual to meet with wandering Dervishes in the great routes of Asia Minor, that his appearance attracted no particular notice. But one day, towards nightfall, 'Alee was much fatigued by the exertions which he had been compelled to make to induce his companion to proceed: and, indeed, the ass had several times actually lain down by the way-side from sheer exhaustion. The day had been extremely warm, and little shelter or pasture had been found for their relief. Finally, age and its infirmities overcame the animal, and falling down, it seemed to fail rapidly. A few minutes of heavy breathing, then a quivering of all its limbs, a gurgling in its throat, and a reversion of its eyeballs, and all was over. 'Alee was left alone in the world by the side of a dead ass, with no one to sympathize with him in his loss, or from whom to seek consolation in his grief. Overcome by his feelings, he folded his arms across his breast, and gave vent to his sorrow in a copious flood of tears. The vast plain in the midst of which he stood now appeared to him peculiarly desolate, and his thoughts reverted to the distant *Turbeh* in which so many years of his life had glided away, free from care or anxiety. To this he could, however, no more return, and the dead ass served as the last link which connected him with his deserted home and venerated instructor, its pious Sheikh. It might be said, that this was the first time he had ever experienced real grief, and his lonely condition added to its poignancy.

Whilst the young Dervish was thus situated, he beheld on the distant horizon a small cloud of dust rise, which indicated the approach of visitors, and gave to him the reflection that, lest he should be held responsible for the decease of his late companion, he would do well to drag him away from the public road ; and, as well as he was able, under the circumstances, to conceal his remains beneath its sandy soil. It did not take him long to put this plan into effect, and so, in a short space of time, he had succeeded in digging a hole sufficiently deep to contain the thin body of the deceased animal. When this was done he sat down by the side of the newly-made grave, and indulged in a fresh flow of tears.

In the meantime, the small cloud of dust which 'Alee had seen in the distance, and which had excited his apprehensions, gradually increased, and speedily approached him. Seated by the grave of his late companion, the ass, his mind became filled with reflections of a desolate and alarming nature ; friendless and alone in the wide and desert world that surrounded him, he watched the arrival of the coming interruption to his grief with no ordinary interest. Although not very near to the road, he was not so distant as to be able to hope to escape the notice of those who were approaching, and a vague feeling of danger greatly agitated him. He began to regret that he had buried the ass from view, and half determined to disinter it, so that there could be no misapprehension as to the truth that the deceased was only an ass, dead from sheer age and exhaustion, and not a human being, whose death might be attributed to violence. In case of suspicion, thought he, they can readily remove the thin cover of earth which conceals its remains, and so verify the fact of my assertion of innocence. With this reflection he had almost recovered his composure, and modified somewhat his grief, when, the dust rising higher and higher in the air, he could distinctly perceive emerge from it quite a numerous cavalcade of Mussulman travellers, none of whom, as yet, seemed conscious of his existence. In advance of the group was one who seemed to be the most prominent of the company; either from the unpleasantness of the heat and atmosphere, or from fatigue, the party hastily rode on in silence, and he hoped that it would pass him by unnoticed. From, however, an intuitive impulsion of respect, common to all the people of the East in the presence of even possible superiors, as it neared him he rose to his feet, and so, perhaps, attracted the attention of the whole company. Surprised by so sudden an apparition, their faces were all immediately directed towards 'Alee, some nods were exchanged amongst them, and the leader of the group, having suddenly come to a halt, he turned to one of his attendants and directed him to ride up and see who the lonely individual was.

Now the party in question was that of a wealthy Bey of the neighbourhood, returning from a distant visit to the governor of the province, attended by a numerous retinue of his own servants, and by several of the principal inhabitants of the little town in which he resided, not many miles off, among the hills, which, in a clearer atmosphere, were visible from the spot on which 'Alee stood. Though somewhat fatigued by the ride over the dusty plain, and overcome by the heat of the day, now almost spent, the Bey was not insensible to the wants of others, and thought that the individual in question might be some wayfaring traveller in need of assistance. Mussulman hospitality and generosity is never more prominent than on those occasions when it is asked for by silent respect; and to have passed 'Alee by unnoticed would have been a strange deviation from this noble characteristic of the Eastern gentleman. The attendant had only to approach 'Alee to discover, from his Dervish cap, his tiger skin, and the keshgool suspended at his side, that he belonged to one of the fraternities of the Islam Orders. So, turning back to the Bey, he informed him that the stranger was a poor Dervish. On hearing this, the whole company followed its leader to the spot where 'Alee stood, trembling with apprehension, and his countenance still showing the grief which he had so recently felt for the loss he had sustained.

After the exchange of the usual Mussulman salutation, the Bey was struck by the circumstance that the poor fellow was standing beside a newly made grave, undoubtedly that of a recently deceased brother Dervish; and he was struck with the strange fate or providence that had led them to so desolate a spot, the one to die there, and the other to inter his remains, where neither water could be procured for the requisite ablutions of the dead prescribed by Islam holy law, nor an Imâm to assist at so touching a ceremony. He made inquiry of 'Alee as to the time of the decease, and learned that it had even occurred during the present day; and to the question as to how long they had been companions, 'Alee, with much emotion, added that, from his earliest youth, they had almost been inseparable. Deeply touched by so tender an attachment and devotedness between two brothers, the Bey deemed it unnecessary to make any more inquiry as to the history of the deceased. After a few words exchanged between him and one or two of the better dressed companions of his journey, turning towards 'Alee, he stated to him that he regarded the whole circumstance as one of a particularly providential character, intended as a blessing to the whole neighbouring country, which had never possessed, he added, any of the advantages always derived from the protection and spiritual influence of the grave of an holy man; and that one such was greatly needed by the community. We beg you, therefore, he continued, to consent to remain amongst us; and if you do so, we will, without any loss of time, have a goodly *Turbeh* constructed over the sainted remains of your deceased brother, which shall remain under your own especial care. Too much affected by the recent occurrence of the day to enter into any explanations of the real facts of the case, or perhaps fearful that an exposition of the truth might be so mortifying to the Bey, as to result in an immediate and severe exhibition of arbitrary power upon his own person, for having conferred the honours of burial upon an ass, which are only due to a human being, 'Alee was unable to utter a word of remark. Perhaps, also, he was not dissatisfied with the favourable turn which had thus, unexpectedly, occurred to his fortunes, and found that silence neither committed him to a falsehood, nor betrayed imprudent truth. He, therefore, said nothing, and only by his countenance and a low salutation, consented to sacrifice any private desire he might entertain for the prolongation of his travels, and pilgrimages to holy tombs, for the spiritual benefit to the pious Mussulmans of the surrounding country. "Remain here, and watch over the remains of your deceased brother," said the Bey, "and we will have the *Turbeh* commenced without delay. I will even, to-night, have some provisions and drink sent you from my own family, and you shall, henceforth, be in want of nothing necessary for your comfort."

With these parting words, the Bey turned his horse again towards his route, followed by all of his company, and gradually receded from sight. In the course of an hour or two he reached his home, and the news of the decease of a pious Dervish on the plain, and of the intention of the Bey to erect a *Turbeh* over his hallowed remains, soon became known over the little town or village in which he and his companions resided.

As to 'Alee, he made a frugal meal from the now almost empty wallet bestowed upon him by his venerated Sheikh; and as the sun was descending behind the hills of the distant horizon, devoutly spread his tiger skin (the hair of which, from long use, was quite worn off) upon the earth, beside the grave of his lamented companion, and performed the *Namâz* appropriate to the fourth period of the day prescribed by the Islam Prophet. Having no water with which to perform the requisite *Ghoosl*, or ablutions, he, according to usage, made use of sand for that purpose, and so acquitted himself of his religious duties. These he had been instructed never to omit, and to perform them as strictly in a crowd as in a desert place—in the *Turbeh*, or by the way-side—and thus leave no room to doubt his piety and strict observance of all the injunctions of the "*Path*," or Order to which he belonged, and to religion in general. Then placing his *keshgool* under his head, and his *mu'een* by his side, as a means of defence in case he should be attacked by any wild animal during the night, his skin serving him for a bed, and his mantle for a cover, he sought relief and calmness in sleep from the sorrows and anxieties of the past day. Some time before midnight he was roused by the sound of a human voice and the noise of an animal's feet, and, jumping up, he was addressed by a Mussulman peasant, sent by the Bey, with an abundant supply of food and water for his use. The bearer stayed but a short time, and on delivering the provisions, told 'Alee that he had also been directed to repeat to him the desire of the Bey, that he should continue to watch by the remains of his deceased brother, over which a *Turbeh* was to be commenced as soon as possible. Then devoutly kissing 'Alee's hand, and pressing it to his forehead, in token of deep respect, he begged his blessing and prayers, and set off for the place from which he came.

On the following day 'Alee had occasion to review the labours of the previous one, and to place the remains of his late companion considerably deeper in the ground than he had primitively done, and also to raise the earth above them in such a manner as to give to the spot more the appearance of a properly constructed grave. He also threw some water over the fresh earth, either as an oblation or to harden the surface. Whilst thus engaged, he was not surprised to perceive in the distance the approach of visitors, perhaps of travellers, perhaps of workmen, sent for the construction of the *Turbeh*. With more calmness and composure than on the previous occasion, he quietly watched their approach, which was but slow; and perceiving that the company was formed of waggons heavily laden, drawn by oxen and buffaloes, and the drivers pointing to himself, he became convinced that he was the object of their visit. Lest he should not have time to perform them, after their arrival, he now spread his skin beside the grave of his lost friend, and was busily engaged in the performance of his *Namâz* when the waggons drew near, and out of respect for his evident piety, the drivers stood at some little distance from him, until their completion. It was readily seen how forcible was the impression which this simple act of piety made upon them, for, after saluting 'Alee, they each came forward and kissed his hand. A little group was soon formed around the newly-made grave, and two pieces of plank were at once erected at its head and foot by one of the workmen. The loads were next discharged, the circumference of the building was laid out, and the construction of the *Turbeh* at once commenced.

We must now pass over a period of several years. The *Turbeh*, or mausoleum, had long since been constructed, and 'Alee been constituted the *Turbehdâr*, or keeper of the holy tomb of the deceased, whose venerated remains rested peacefully beneath its little dome. The structure seemed to be formed much after the model of the other one, in which he had spent so many days of comfort with his Sheikh ; and if he had really any part in shaping it, there is no doubt but that the resemblance was intentional. In place of two pieces of wood, an equal number made of marble now marked the grave of the deceased. On the one at its head was inscribed an epitaph, commencing as usual with "Him, the Creator and the Eternal," and adding, "This is the tomb of the celebrated *Kootb*, or Axis, of eminent piety, the renowned Sheikh 'Abdul Kâdir, of the *Tareek*, or Order, of the Kâdirees. Say a *Fâtiha* (the opening chapter of the Koran) for his soul." As if so eminent a Santon could not possibly be equalled in stature by ordinary humanity, the length of the grave was considerably extended, and full ten feet of space showed the size of the great man whose bones were considered so great a blessing to the locality in which they reposed. The tomb was surrounded by a wire network, to keep it from the pollution of impure hands ; and not unfrequently a costly shawl, or a rich silk article of apparel was spread over this, to remain there, however, only for some days, and receive for its future wearer the benefit of the spiritual powers of the revered and holy deceased. A lamp hung suspended within the enclosure, which at nightfall was carefully lighted, and a pious lady of the neighbouring town had, just before her decease, appropriated a sum of money as a *Wakf*, or votive offering, from which to support the expense of keeping up this lamp. Other *Wakfs* had also been left for the support of the *Turbeh* generally, and to ensure the comfort of the pious individual who watched over the tomb. In the windows of the *Turbeh* could be seen innumerable pieces of cloth and cotton fabrics tied there in evidence of the *nezrs*, or vows of the visitors who had come to ask spiritual aid from the deceased ; many of them from young Mussulman maidens, who, not being able orally to make known their affection for the objects of their preferences, sought, through the spiritual powers of their renowned Sheikh, to reach their hearts in an indirect manner—an usage unknown to or unpractised by the now Islam world ; or from married ladies, to secure the wavering affections of their husbands—or acquire the cares of maternity—through his intercession. Few persons ever passed by the *Turbeh* without stopping to offer a prayer at its tomb, and such visits were a source of no little emolument to 'Alee, who now bore the full title of "'Alee the Sheikh." It was not uncommon for persons highly placed in official as well as social position throughout the neighbouring country, to send him a present, and ask his intercession with the deceased saint in their behalf, and for the promotion of their worldly interests. The Sheikh 'Alee, much to the dissatisfaction and mortification of sundry maidens and wealthy widows of the neighbourhood, had refused to join his lot in life with theirs, and change his solitary position for one more in harmony with their own desires and regard for his welfare. Following the example of the Sheikh by whom he had been educated, he preferred passing his life in a state of celibacy, his only companion being a comely youth, then of some twelve or fourteen years of age, whom he had found destitute and an orphan, in one of the villages of the vicinity.

Sheikh 'Alee's renown had spread far and wide over the surrounding country. His eminent piety, and the innumerable miraculous occurrences at the *Turbeh*, all attributed to his prayers and the spiritual powers of the holy Santon over whose tomb he presided, tended greatly to acquire for him and it an enviable celebrity. News of it had reached even as far as the *Turbeh* in which he had been educated, and created no little surprise in the mind of its Sheikh. He had never heard of the presence nor of the decease of any eminent member of his own fraternity, much less of the existence of so pious a Sheikh as the one must be who presided at his tomb. Curiosity, as well perhaps as jealousy, deeply penetrated his heart, and finally decided him to make a pilgrimage in person to a tomb so renowned for its sanctity. One fine autumn day the now venerable old Sheikh closed his *Turbeh*, and set out on a journey, which, at his time of life, was not free from much inconvenience and fatigue. The object in view, however, was so important to his own interests, both temporal and spiritual, that he considered it quite providential, and worthy of his declining days. At least, so he gave out to the usual visitors at his own shrine; and the painful effort which it required greatly enhanced his own already high reputation. He therefore set out, with the prayers and blessings of all his friends and admirers. Travelling by easy stages, the aged Sheikh finally reached the object of his little pilgrimage, and on Friday noon arrived at the *Turbeh* by the way-side.

There were many visitors present on the occasion in question. Ladies had come there in such wheeled conveyances as the country furnished; others rode there on horseback, quite in the same fashion as the men: not a few bestrode gentle donkeys, especially the more aged and infirm; and men came, some on horseback, and some even on foot. A few trees, which had grown up under the care of Sheikh 'Alee and the protection of the holy tomb, afforded these visitors some shade during the heat of the day, and copious draughts were imbibed from a well which had been sunk in close proximity to the tomb, the waters of which had become widely celebrated for their healing qualities. Mingling among the crowd, the old man attracted but little attention, and after the performance of the usual prayers at the holy tomb, he sat down in quiet beside it, his mind filled with pious meditations on the Prophet, the Peer of his Order, and the holy deceased in general. As Sheikh 'Alee passed frequently by him, he had abundant opportunity of seeing his features, now considerably changed by time, and a goodly beard which ornamented his features, and greatly added to the venerableness of his appearance. Although his head was covered by a green turban of considerable dimensions, showing his direct descent from the blessed Prophet, more than once it flashed across the mind and memory of the old man that he had seen him under other circumstances and in some other part of the world. Indeed, he at one moment almost thought that he had some resemblance to his former pupil, but as he had never heard from, or of him, since his departure, he concluded that it was only accidental, and that 'Alee must have long since joined the list of the deceased. Gradually the visitors departed, and towards nightfall the two eminent Sheikhs remained alone at the *Turbeh*, attended only by the comely youth afore alluded to. It was only then that any communication took place between them, and very soon the old man became fully convinced that the younger Sheikh was none other than his former pupil. The former made no difficulty in admitting the fact, and an intimacy soon was renewed between them. The flourishing condition of his late élève was a source of much satisfaction to the old man, and dispelled any feelings of envy which he might have previously entertained. Sheikh 'Alee, on his part, seemed to be extremely happy on receiving the visit of his former master, and treated him with much respect and consideration. They freely talked over the interests of their particular *Turbehs*, and the old man admitted that the growing celebrity of the newer one had considerably affected that of the old. The old man, being now no longer able to restrain his curiosity, begged Sheikh 'Alee to be so good as to inform him who was the revered member of their Order whose remains were interred in the *Turbeh*. But on this point his former pupil made some objection to enlighten him. Pressed, however, to inform him of what so deeply interested the character and welfare of their common Order, 'Alee, after exacting a most formal promise of secrecy, narrated to his late master the entire history of his journey thus far, on the pilgrimage on which he had originally set out, its sudden termination, with the untimely death of the aged ass which he had so generously bestowed upon him, and the manner in which its remains had been canonized by popular favour, he having only to offer no opposition to what he verily believed was brought about by a direct intervention of Providence for some wise purpose, the ass having perhaps been the receptacle of the soul of some re-embodied saint. To this frank avowal the old man did not make even a show of surprise, and received the information with his usual calm and dignified demeanour. At this 'Alee was somewhat astonished and alarmed, lest it might prove ominous to the continuance of his heretofore most peaceful and prosperous career as a Sheikh. With this reflection he thought he would venture to inquire, for the first time in his life, what holy man was interred at the *Turbeh* of the old Sheikh, his former master, but found him equally uncommunicative on such a subject. As a matter of reciprocity and mutual confidence, he pressed him for information on so deeply interesting a subject; and it was only after having given him a most solemn pledge of secrecy, that he learned, with no little surprise, that the deceased saint over which the venerable Sheikh had presided for so many years, and to which so many of his own earlier prayers and supplications had been offered, were those of none other than the father of his own once so lamented companion, and now so highly venerated saint, the ass, which had been bestowed upon him by his master, with his blessing.

CHAPTER XIV.

It has been heretofore shown that the principles entertained by the more modern *Tareeks*, or Orders of the Dervishes, first became prominent in Persia and Bokhara, though it is scarcely to be doubted that they originated in Arabia. From thence they travelled into Turkey, Syria, and Egypt, and even along the shores of the Mediterranean, as far as Morocco.

In Malcolm's "History of Persia" are found some interesting details of the original Orders of the Soofees, taken from Persian manuscripts, which may be fully depended upon for their accuracy. It is therein stated that the original sects were two in number, viz., the *Haloolieh*, or the "Inspired," and the *Itihâdieh*, or the "Unionists," out of which grew five branches. Of these, the first is the *Vusoolieh*, or the "United;" the second, the *'Ashkieh*, or the "Loving;" the third, the *Telkeenieh*, or the "Learned;" the fourth, the *Zureekieh*, or the "Penetrating;" and the fifth, the *Vahdetieh*, much resembling the *Itihâdieh*, the chief principle being the great primitive dogma of mankind, the Unity of the Deity.

The first branch maintains that God has entered, or descended into man, and that the Divine Spirit enters into all those who are of a devout and intelligent mind.

The second believes that God is one with every enlightened mind, and that the immortal part forms its union with God, and becomes God. They say that the divine nature of Christ, who is called by all Mussulmans the *Rooh Allah*, or "Spirit of God," was derived from the Spirit of the Deity having entered the womb of the Virgin Mary.

The third and fourth have no very distinct dogma.

The fifth maintains that God is in everything, and that everything is in God. They admit that their principles are the same as those of the ancient Greek philosophers of Greece, especially of Plato, who, they assert, maintains that God created all things with his own breath, and that everything is thus both the Creator and the created. This principle, in many of the modern writings of the Dervishes, is called the *Nufs*, or "breath of God," and, as applied to man, is deemed to be the human part of animated nature, and distinct from the *Rooh*, or "soul," the immortal part.

There are many Dervish Orders in Bokhara, nearly all of the *Sunnee*, or orthodox kind, more closely attached to the dogmas of the Koran and its Prophet than those of Persia, which are almost all *Shee'a*, and advocates of the Caliph 'Alee. The people of these two countries are much divided by their religious sentiments, though with 'Othman those of Bokhara have a strong sympathy. I regret to be unable to give any account of the Dervish Orders of the latter country, and believe that they are particularly fanatic and hostile to all non-Mussulmans.

M. Le Cte. A. de Gobineau, formerly secretary of the French Embassy in Persia, in 1859 published a small work called "Three Years in Asia," and on the subject of the religion of the people of Persia, gives some interesting accounts, from which I borrow the following summary.

"The first sovereign of the dynasty of the *Sefâvees*, who mounted the throne in the 16th century, was not a Mussulman. He was a *Soofee.* The partiality of the Persians for 'Alee had already given birth to several sects, which extended as far even as Syria, the greater part of which were *Sheeites.* The Mollahs of Persia had always a tendency in that direction. The new dynasty, in accordance with them, made it the religion of the State, modified considerably the oral doctrine (of the *Hadees*, or traditions), and broke off from the rest of Islamism. From this moment, the interpretation given by the Persians to the law of Mohammed, received a consecration. They became Legitimists. The existence of an ecclesiastical body, the exaggerated cult of the

Imâms—a theology as refined and exuberant in developments as the Koran is simple—and the veneration of saints, out of whom they made demi-gods, was all formed into a doctrine, now not only tolerated and favoured, but even commanded. The Mollahs, in fact, became the absolute masters of the empire. These, however, having assumed a despotic sway over the people, they became the object of satire and invectives, out of which grew a struggle; and the sovereign having taken the part of the latter, these prevailed, and increased the civil power at the expense of the religious."

The Eastern idea that the spirit or soul returns to this world, and lives again in a new body, long after the decease and decay of its primitive corporal form, is held as true by many of the modern Sheikhs of Persia. With them the belief in the re-existence of the Imâm Mehdee is stronger than among any other Mohammedans. They are, as aforementioned, with few exceptions, '*Aleeides*, and attach the greatest importance to all of the members of his family—the twelve Imâms. The transmigration of the soul from one body to another is fully developed in their estimation of the Mehdee. It is, perhaps, borrowed from a parallel in Christianity, or may even be traced to the Old Testament.* The Mehdee, according to them, still lives, and will again reappear in a new body. It forms the chief principle of the religion of the Druzes, who hold that the great apostle of their faith, *Hakeem bi emr Illah*, possessed the soul of the 12th Imâm. The Persians place but small faith in some of the dogmas of the Koran, and having superseded its founder by the person of 'Alee, are disposed even to doubt the authenticity of certain portions of it, or at least to interpret it after the manner of the Sunnees. The Dervish Orders of Persia are less good Mussulmans than the people at large, and carry the principle that the "spiritual part of man emanated from God, and will return to Him," and will as that man, through a state of extreme piety and religious fervour, becomes re-united, or near to God, to an extreme degree.

* Elias.

This same approach to the Divinity is supposed by them to give to the pious Dervishes great "spiritual power," so as to enable them to overcome the ordinary laws of nature, and therefore to perform superhuman, or otherwise "miraculous" acts. The most remarkable of these Dervishes, however, are not actually Persians, but come from India. M. de Gobineau describes one of these, who visited Teheran, from Cashmere, as "dressed in a cotton robe, much torn, his long and thin arms penetrating two sleeves, which scarcely held to the body; he was barefooted; his head covered with a mass of black shaggy hair; his eyes of a surprising brilliancy, and teeth of the greatest whiteness, offering a striking contrast to his dark Eastern complexion. He had travelled all over India, Turkistan, and the whole Eastern world; and public report declared that he was possessed of the most extraordinary secrets.

The Nosairees of Persia seem, from M. de Gobineau's account of them, to be those who entertain the most extreme principles of the 'Aleeide Dervishes. They call their religion that of the *Ehl el Hakk*, or the "People of Truth." The Arabs and Turks call them *Nosairees*, the Persians, the *'Alee Ilâhees*. The former assimilate them to the Christians of the East, whilst the latter suppose that they consider 'Alee as God, and so adore him. There are numbers of this sect in Constantinople, mostly from Persia, and the same exist in various parts of Asia Minor. He states that the *'Alee Ilâhees* (believers in the divinity of 'Alee) are different from the *Ehl el Hakks*, inasmuch as the former distinctly declare that the son-in-law of the Prophet was an incarnation of the Deity, and it is for this reason that they are considered by the more rigid Mussulmans as assimilated to the Christians, who attribute the same divine character to Jesus Christ, whilst the *Ehl el Hakk* consider that every one may, by superior piety and love of God, become joined to Him, or even become God.

I make special mention of these two sects of Persia, whence came almost all of the Dervish Orders now in the Ottoman Empire—and refer particularly to the principles entertained by the Bektâshees before described. They have but little respect for Islamism, though they hold themselves to be Mahommedans. The Ehl el Hakk carry the dogmas of the Bektâshees to an extreme degree; they consider the Koraishite Prophet (Mohammed) as an impostor, and do not either frequent the mosques nor perform the prayers, except when it is absolutely necessary. They pretend to a purely spiritual religion, and are very tolerant to other religions. They differ from ordinary Mussulmans by not believing in any legal impurity, and so have no need of the ablutions prescribed by the former. They divide themselves into the Ehli Sheri'at, or those of "religious legal law;" the Ehli Me'ârifât, or those of "religious knowledge or wisdom;" the Ehli Târikât, or those of the "destructive orders;" and the Ehli Hakeekât, or Ehli Hakk, or those of the "true faith," or "truth." By their theory, the first are those who follow the ordinances of the religious law, and among them are considered the Jews and Christians; the second are those who still seek for higher and more extensive knowledge, among whom are the Soofees, whose beliefs are quite pantheistic; and by considering each human soul as a Divine emanation, expose themselves to much persecution by an assumption which would, *in extensis*, place them superior to ordinary humanity. As this incarnation of man originates in India, this doctrine may be considered semi-Hindoo—semi-Ghebre. The second (Ehli Me'ârifet) are those who seek for divine knowledge, and, having obtained it, are superior to the ignorant; whilst the third (Ehli Târikât) are those who have found and entered upon the true path, which leads to divine inspiration.

Malcolm, in his "History of Persia," on the subject of the Dervish principles (Soofeeism) also says:—"So as to secure fidelity and secrecy, the Mureed or Novice is required to place himself under the guidance of a Sheikh or Master of the Order, who is regarded as possessing a peculiarly holy character, and to place implicit confidence in his tuition, as well as to submit to his will, quite—to use the Dervish expression—"like a dead body in the hands of an Imâm."

Dervishes represent themselves as entirely devoted to *Hakk*, or "the Truth," and as being incessantly occupied in the adoration of Allah—a union with whom they desire with all the ardour of a Divine love. The Creator is, according to their belief, diffused over all His creatures. He exists everywhere and in everything. They compare the emanations of His Divine Essence and Spirit, to the rays of the sun, which they conceive to be continually darted forth and reabsorbed. It is for this reabsorption into the Divine Essence—to which their immortal parts belong—that they continually aspire. This return to the Deity is fully carried out in a verse of the Koran (2d Chap.), which says:—"All mankind are *of*, and will return *to*, Him." This verse is the basis of much of what is peculiar to the Dervish doctrine. They believe that the soul of man, and the principle of life, which exists throughout all nature, is not *from* God, but *of* God. In their sophistry they use the term *'Alem i Khiyâl* ("delusive world") to signify that we are continuously in a state of delusion with regard to the *Mâddeh*, or *Matter*, of which the universe is formed; that the "Light of God" is the animating principle which enables us to see the latter—viz. the "matter"—just as would be the case did not light shine upon all objects, and so render them visible to the eyes; and that God having poured His Spirit over the universe, its light became diffused everywhere, and intelligence beamed upon the mind of man. This is also called the *Vahdet el Vujood*, or "unity of being"—the One God being everywhere and in all things.

Their doctrine teaches that there are four stages or degrees, called the four columns of the Order, through which living man must pass before he can attain to the highest grade—that of "Divine Beatitude"—when his corporeal veil will be removed and his emancipated soul will rejoin the glorious Essence from which it had been *separated*, but not *divided*. The first of these stages is that of humanity, called the Shee'at, or that of "holy law," which supposes the Mureed or disciple to live in obedience to the written law, and to be an observer of all the established rites, customs, and precepts of the (Islam) religion, which are admitted to be useful in regulating the lives and restraining the vulgar mass within the proper bounds—as souls cannot reach the heights of Divine contemplation, and might be corrupted and misled by that very liberty of faith which tends to enlighten and delight those of superior intellect and more fervent devotion.

The second stage is called the Târikât, or "Paths," which may be called that of the "Mystical Rites," in which the Mureed or disciple attains power or strength. He who arrives at this leaves that condition, in which he is only admitted to admire and follow a Murshid, or "spiritual teacher," and enters the pale of the mystical *Soofeeism* beforementioned. He may now abandon all observance of strictly religious form and ceremonies, because he exchanges *practical* for *spiritual* worship. But this cannot be attained without great piety, virtue, and fortitude, as the mind cannot be trusted in the neglect of religious or legal usages and rites necessary to restrain it, whilst yet weak, until it has acquired strength from habits of mental devotion, grounded on a perfect knowledge of its own dignity, and of the divine nature of the Almighty.

The third stage is that of the Me'ârifât, or "Knowledge," and the disciple who arrives at, or is deemed to have attained to supernatural knowledge—or, in other words, to have become as one inspired—and he is supposed when he reaches it to be on an equality with the angels in point of knowledge.

The fourth and last stage or degree is called the Hakeekât, or that of the "Truth," at which the disciple is supposed to have arrived when he has become completely united to the Deity.

In these four degrees the disciple must be under the guidance of a Murshid, who on his part must be of great piety and virtue, and himself reached them, through the spiritual teachings of another. For this purpose he attaches himself to a learned Sheikh, and seeks instructions from his wisdom, just as, in the times of the Greek philosophers, young men, anxious to learn the principles of a particular master, attached themselves to him and sought knowledge from his mouth—or like St. Paul at the feet of the learned Jewish teacher Gamaliel.

The Mureed must, mystically, always bear his Murshid in mind, and become mentally absorbed in him, through a constant meditation and contemplation of him. The teacher must be his shield against all evil thoughts. The spirit of the teacher follows him in all his efforts, and accompanies him wherever he may be, quite as a guardian spirit. To such a degree is this carried that he sees the master in all men and in all things, just as a willing subject is under the influence of the magnetizer. This condition is called "self-annihilation" into the Murshid or Sheikh. The latter finds, in his own visionary dreams, the degree at which the Mureed has reached, and whether or not his soul or spirit has become bound to his own.

At this state of the disciple, the Sheikh passes him over to the spiritual influence of the Peer, or original founder of the particular Tareek or "Path" to which they belong, long since deceased, and he sees the latter only by the spiritual aid of the former. This is called "self-annihilation" into the Peer. He now becomes so much a part of the Peer as to possess all of his spiritual powers, and may perform even all of his supernatural acts.

The third grade also leads him, through the spiritual aid of the Sheikh, up to the Prophet himself, whom he now sees in all things. This state is called, like the preceding, "self-annihilation" into the Prophet.

The fourth degree leads him even to God. He becomes a part of the Divinity, and sees Him in all things. Some, in this state of ecstacism, have gone so far, in Persia, as to declare themselves to be the Deity, and for this have forfeited their lives,—such as Mansoor and Neseem, both celebrated mystical Dervishes. It is related that Junaidee of Bagdad, the Peer of all the modern 'Aleeide Orders, believed himself to be in this state, and allowed his disciples to cut at him with a sword. It is said that they could not hurt him, but made, nevertheless, so many wounds on their own persons.

The Sheikh, after this remarkable proof of spiritual teaching, next brings the Mureed back to his original state, like the physician, who, after reducing the patient, by natural remedies restores him to health, and puts upon him the Tâj, or cap of his Order, or confers upon him the grade of *Khaleefeh*, which, in his case, is an honorary degree. He now again performs all of the rites of ordinary Islamism. Few ever reach the fourth degree, though many do the second. Although, in all the various Orders there are differences of usages and forms of worship, still, in the chief principles they agree with each other,—particularly in those which inculcate the necessity of an absolute obedience to inspired teachers, and the possibility, through fervent piety and enthusiastic devotion, of attaining (for the soul, even when the body inhabits this world) to a state of celestial beatitude. Among the first acts required of the Mureed, or disciple, is that of spending much of his time—with some forty days and nights—in retirement and prayer, invoking the name of Allah, after which he will see visions, the spiritual interpretation of which he receives from the Sheikh of his *Tekkieh*. Among their points of belief are the following. Some maintain that God has entered or descended into the Devout, and that the Divine Spirit enters into all those who are of a truly pious and intelligent mind.

Some believe that God is as one with every enlightened mind, and that the immortal part forms its union with God, and becomes God. They say, as before stated, that the Divine nature of Christ, who is called by all Mussulmans, the *Rooh Allah*, or "Spirit of God," was derived from the Spirit of the Deity entering the womb of the Virgin Mary. Others, as before stated, hold that God is in all things, and that everything is God. They say that the Prophet was a Soofee, or believer in mystical religion, of a high order, and quote many of his *Hadeesât*, or "Traditional sayings," to sustain the same. They declare that the caliph 'Alee was thoroughly acquainted with their doctrines, and deputed two of his sons, Hasan and Hosain, and two other holy men of his time, named Kumâil ibn Zead, and Hasan el Basree, to teach and perpetuate them. From these, they maintain, many of the principal founders of Tareeks or Paths received their intuition, and their *Khirkas*, or mantles, as symbols of their spiritual orders. This symbol reminds us of the mantle of Elijah which descended upon Elisha, and the cloak or garment of Christ.

I may also add a fact of some significancy. As among the more recent Orders of Dervishes, the head of the Tekkieh is called the Sheikh, or Murshid, and his successor the Khaleefeh, or Caliph, so is it with regard to the political head of the State who has received the mantle of the Prophet, and becomes his Caliph, or successor. Sultan Selim I. received the *Khirka Shereef*, or holy mantle, from Mohammed, the last of the Abbassides, of the Prophet's lineage, when he conquered Egypt; and this revered relic is carefully preserved in the old seraglio at the present time, under the charge, I am assured, of a descendant of the As-hâb, or friendly companions of the Prophet, named *Rais*, on whom he bestowed it.

To arrive at the second grade or degree of office in a Tekkieh, that of Khaleefeh, it is, as before stated, necessary to spend much time in fasting and prayer, and in complete abstraction from all worldly pursuits. The man must die, so to say, before the saint can be born. To this degree of spiritual perfection, as well as to his supposed familiarity with all the mystical dogmas and tenets of the Order, he must possess the respect, reverence, and entire submission of all of the Mureeds. By constant prayer, his breath, even his touch, must possess a sanctifying influence, and be believed to have the superhuman power of performing miracles. This is peculiarly the case with the Rufâ'ee, or "Howling Dervishes." If, in the course of his devotional probation, the Mureed who seeks advancement succeeds in seeing a vision, the Peer of his Order, by whom its import is interpreted, may terminate his seclusion; and, though much reduced in bodily strength (but strengthened spiritually), his trial has not ended. He must wander from place to place; visit holy tombs, at which to seek further inspiration, perform the pilgrimage to Mekkeh and Medinah, and even proceed to the revered tombs of Kerbeleh, near to Bagdad.

Among some of the Orders, the Sheikh is free to leave his mantle of succession, at his death, to whomever of his Mureeds he deems most worthy of it. But in the Ottoman Empire, the office of Sheikh has generally become hereditary in the family of the Murshid, though in default of a son and heir, the members may elect a successor from among themselves; or all the Sheikhs of the same Order meet, and select one, subject however to confirmation by the Sheikh ul Islâm, or head of the Islam Faith, who resides at Constantinople, and is appointed by the Sultan.

The Zikr, or repetition of God's Name by the Dervishes and Moslems generally, which has been explained elsewhere, may be traced to the habit of the Prophet himself, who frequently recited various portions of the Koran, with an audible voice, both in moments of prayer, and in those of danger, to his followers. To the efficacy of this recitation, he evidently attached great importance, and believed in their merit with the Creator. During several of his battles, he observed this custom, either designing thereby to encourage his forces, or to obtain a Divine manifestation through the pious act. As he, doubtlessly, fully believed in his own inspiration, and that the verses which he recited had come to him from the Creator, through the medium of a celestial messenger, whom he called the Angel Gabriel during his periods of pious fervour and ecstasy; he also believed in their value near Him from whom they emanated. It is not, therefore, surprising that his followers should still entertain the same conviction. Such a belief finds some confirmation in the practice of pious Christians, when they call upon God and Christ in the language of the Old and New Testaments. In his last illness, the Prophet often recited various Sooras, or chapters, some of the longest of the Koran, especially in the quiet of the night, in praise of the Lord. It is related that he suffered greatly during his periods of mental excitement and agitation attending the reception of the revelations conveyed to him by the Angel,—such as the chapters called the "Hood," the "Inevitable," and the "Striking," designated as the terrific Sooras; and he is said to have attributed his grey hairs to them. It is difficult to suppose that he composed these long chapters, and committed them at the same time to memory, and yet such must have been the case. He pretended to no super-human powers at such seasons, nor did he ever recite them in the view of imposing on his friends, disciples, or any others, differing widely from the Dervishes.

I would refer the curious reader to the "Life of Mahomet," by William Muir, Esq., of the Bengal Civil Service, for the most interesting and truthful biography ever written of this wonderful man. I regret not to have found in it any allusion to the origin of the Tareeks, or "Paths" of the Dervishes.

Whenever the origin of these Tareeks cannot be found in the practices of the Prophet, or in the interpretation of the verses of the Koran by their Peers or Founders, it may be taken for granted that it is contained in the Hadees, or traditions, collected in the first and second centuries of the Hejreh. So far as I know, no collection of these has been translated into Turkish, or any European language. They would, doubtlessly, well repay the labour of translation, especially could they be arranged chronologically, and with reference to the historical events which gave rise to them.

SPIRITUAL EXERCISES.

The ordinary state or condition of pious contemplation and prayerfulness is called Murâkabeh. This is possessed in wakeful moments, when the soul and body are united, and the senses of the latter are enfeebled by superior powers of the soul. There is, however, another condition, called Insilâ, when, it is held, the soul of man leaves the body, and wanders about without regard to time or space. It was in this latter that the Prophet is supposed to have ascended in the spirit to heaven, borne there on an imaginary celestial animal, called the Berrâk.

The celebrated Sheikh, Muhee ed Deen el 'Arabee relates regarding the Insilâ:—"Once when I was in the vicinity of the holy and reverend Ke'beh (Caaba), it happened that, absorbed in mental reflections on the four great jurisconsults of Islamism, I beheld a person who continuously made the Tawâf or circuit of that holy building. His height was quite as elevated as the Ke'beh itself. Two other individuals were engaged in the same occupation, and whenever these were near to each other, the power would pass between them, without, however, separating them. From this I concluded that the individual must belong to spiritual bodies only. As he continued his circuits, he recited the following: 'Truly, we have been, for many long years, engaged in walking round this holy house, but you only are doing it now' (Koran cxxiii).

"On hearing these words, I formed a desire to know who he was, and to what tribe he belonged. So I fixed him with my eyes, after the manner called Habs i Nazr, and when he had ended his circuit, and desired to depart, he was unable to do so. Finally, he came to my side, and feeling that I was the cause of his detention, begged me to allow him to depart. I answered him with the words, 'Bismillah er Rahmân er Raheem,' 'In the name of God, the merciful and the clement,' and added, 'I will allow you to go only after you have let me know what kind of a being you are, and to what tribe or people you belong.' He replied, 'I am of Mankind.' I next asked him how long it was since he left this world. He replied, 'It is now more than forty thousand years.' Surprised, I added, 'You say it is so long, whilst it is only six thousand years since Adam's time, and yet you state that you are of mankind.' He answered, 'The Adam you speak of was the father of the Human race, and though since his time only six thousand years have elapsed, thirty other worlds preceeded him. In the Traditions of the Pride of all Beings (the Prophet), and the Sovereign ('Alee), it is said, 'Certainly God created the Adam (Man) you know of, after the creation of an hundred thousand others, and I am one of these.'"

The principles of this writer are peculiarly spiritual. He believes that the world was inhabited by many other species of human beings previous to the creation of Adam and Eve, all differing from each other, and some of them also of various degrees of stature and spiritual faculties. The spirits of mankind, separated by death from the body, continue to people the vast space which surrounds the world on which we dwell, but are wholly invisible to the ordinary organs of vision; that some persons of a high spiritual power are, however, able to behold them, and that a superior spiritual faculty possesses an influence and power over an inferior one; and that visions are not connected with the ordinary senses of the body, but are wholly spiritual, so that often times during our corporeal slumbers, when the senses are lulled into repose, the soul leaves the body and wanders over the world, with a velocity which knows neither time nor space, and can see objects extremely distant; whilst ordinary dreams are but an effect of the senses—such, for instance, as memory—when in a state of half repose, and are common to all animated nature, in which expression are understood those animals which do not possess immortal souls or spirits.

In connexion with the preceding account of the principles of Muhee ed Deen, of arresting any one by a "spell," it may not be out of the way to add the following summary of a little work by Ibn Isay, as an explanation of what has only been given as a theory.

Ibn Isay was born, so says the MS., at Ak Seeay, in Asia Minor, and emigrated thence to Tripoli of Barbary, where he founded the Order ot the Isâvees. He was originally of the Order of the Bairamees.

An abridged account of his theory:—

Tâlib signifies the Dervish.

Matloob is the person whom you wish to appear before you.

Mulâhaza is the action of thinking of the latter in such a manner as to make him appear.

Tevejjuh is the producing of the person in question.

Ehli Hâl, those who have the power of making others appear.

Ehli Tesarruf are the holy people who possess that power.

Murâkebeh is much the same as the Tevejjuh.

Hâl is the state of ecstasy into which the person goes who makes the absent appear to him.

Kâl is the condition of perfect submission of the person thus appearing to the power of the Hâl.

Shüghl is the performance of this act of power.

Vifk is the science of mystical numbers.

Istidrâj is the acquisition of certain illegal and diabolical powers, by the abandonment of the purifications and prayers required by religion.

In the fourteenth chapter of his work he explains the spiritual powers of "Fascination," viz. the producing of an effect upon an absent individual for a good or an evil purpose. He calls it that faculty of the soul of the Tâlib, or active agent, which by the power of the will, or profound contemplation (Mulâhaza), can produce the Matloob, or passive object, before him. The method of exercising this peculiar power, he says, can best be taught practically by a Mushaikh (Sheikh). One of the rules, however, is for the Tâlib to place himself in operation (Shüghl); the name of the Tâlib and the Matloob must be drawn up according to the science of the Vifk (or the mystical numerical value of the letters of their respective names) calculated and placed upon the left knee; he must gaze upon them with deep fixedness, and think constantly on the figure and form of the Matloob; he must blow, as it were, at the mouth of the Matloob and recite his incantation, and so continue to bring the figure nearer and nearer to his vision. After this he must look at the Vifk and recite the Verd (an Islam prayer); now and then close his eyes, and blow at the mouth of the Matloob; then recite the Fâtiha (2nd chapter of the

Koran), without, however, for a moment allowing the figure to escape from his sight. To thus gaze upon the Vifk is the same as to gaze upon the Matloob; to gaze upon the figure is an evidence of the Hâl, and to neglect to follow this rule is a proof that the Tâlib is in a state of Istidrâj. When the figure is by this means brought near to the Tâlib, he can describe it to any persons who may be present.

It is related that Nemrood, who, Orientals say, was a great apostate, was once desirous of affecting an evil upon a king, and for this purpose had his portrait made and placed before him. By continuously gazing upon this figure, and by the exercise of his "power of the will," he so seriously affected the health of the king, that he would certainly have died, had he not sent and begged him to cease, offering to submit entirely to his will.

The Tevejjuh is produced by the Ehli Sulook (the Dervish) fixing his gaze upon the heart of the Matloob. If he looks upon the left breast, he will perceive the figure appear from out of the heart; then the act of the Tâlib is completed. He must then look upon the left breast whilst in a dark and quiet apartment; many erroneous thoughts will arise in his own mind, and after they have vanished, a Ref'at, or true state, will come upon him; the figure of the Matloob will rise before him, and as it will be perfectly submissive to his will, he can readily effect whatever purpose he may have in view.

Another mode of the Tevejjuh is the following: This is not by looking at the heart, but by turning the thoughts to the Almighty. You must pray to Him, and give yourself up entirely to Him. Whether the figure of the Matloob appear or not, the Tâlib must persist in his act of the Shüghl, and pray and weep with much warmth, until it does finally appear. The moment it begins to show itself, he must blow, as it were, in its mouth, recite the invocation, lament and beg, and excite his own feelings excessively. The Tâlib, nevertheless, must be calm in mind, and not suffer his fervour to overcome him. Besides this, he must never have any doubt of the efficacy of his effort, but place entire faith in its certainty.

Every Daireh, or "Mystic Circle," has its Tevejjuh; that of the Tâlib, who seeks the right path, is called "Of the Heart." When once attained, its possessor can perform spells over the feebler wills of others, especially of females. When he reaches the Daireh of the Spirit, he can bewitch men and lovers; on reaching that of the "Mind," he can bewitch aged persons, the 'Ulemâ (doctors of law), the Fuzelâ (pious), the Zâhid (the devout). By the Secret Circle, he can enchant the learned, poets, and those who spend their lives in the pleasures of love. By it, also, he can ensorcillate Sheikhs, people in a state of ecstatic fervour, the Tesavvuf, and even the Ehli Sulook (Dervishes). In the Circle of the Jelâl (Name of the Deity), these powers are used for purposes of revenge; in that of the Jemâl (beauty), for purposes of kindness; and all of these are known to the Ehli Hâl. As it sometimes happens that through the power of the Tâlib, the figure of the third person is produced, this one is apt to suffer from it, and may even die; it is, therefore, necessary that the operator be made thoroughly acquainted with the process, lest danger be incurred. Should the Tâlib produce the figure of a fiend, or of his beloved, he must cease and recite the Ikhlâs (a Moslem prayer), and so preserve him or her from any injury. At other times the Tâlib effects the Tevejjuh and the Tesevvur (imagining), and when the figure of the Matloob appears, he can arrest it by a spell, by simply crying out its name, blowing in its mouth, and, looking fixedly at its heart, reciting a prayer.

The powers of the Sheikh Ibn Isay, were certainly thus most extraordinary, for after reciting the Verd, he would gaze fixedly upon the Vifk, so as to produce, before his own vision, the figure of the person desired. He could so affect any person present, as to perfectly subdue him or her to his will, and then take any revenge on him or her that he pleased. No one could withstand the ardour of his gaze, and he could impress any one so as to hold him completely under his control.

Another Tevejjuh is when the Tâlib is desirous of bestowing something upon a Matloob, and he can then so influence the latter by his powers, as to impress him beneficially. This is generally done to the Sâliks, or neophytes under his instruction. The Sheikh Ibn Isay, during the course of his instructions, would bestow the benefit of the prayers of his circle upon his pupils, and so enable them to produce the same results on others. This he could do from a distance, as well as near, and he could so influence them, that they assumed whatever condition he pleased, of joy or grief.

The preceding is quite sufficient to show the nature of the "Spiritual Powers" of this Sheikh, who is quite renowed in Tunis and Tripoli, where there are many adherents of his Order. They seem to be of a magnetic character, and resemble those of Muhee ed Deen el 'Arabee, mentioned in a preceding part of this chapter.

HASHEESH.

Heretofore I have endeavoured to explain how, among the Dervishes, the mental excitement and enthusiastic germ is ascribed by them entirely to divine inspiration, growing out of the Zikr, or invocation of the Diety. Among some of them, however, material means are also resorted to for the purpose of exciting, if not the mental faculties, at least the brain, so as to produce visionary glimpses of what is considered by them at least a foretaste of future happiness and enjoyment, in that existence which, the more sensible, hold to be entirely of a "spiritual" character. On this subject, a writer in the *Levant Herald*, of Constantinople, makes the following observations :—

"The peculiar pleasures affecting especially the nerves, and produced by narcotics, tobacco, and opium, belong apparently to modern times—that is to say, that it is only in modern times that we find them in general use. Amongst the ancients there is very little doubt of their existence, but they were the secrets of the priests, or of the initiated. We read, for instance, of certain temples in Cyprus or in Syria, to which the votaries thronged from all parts of the world, in expectation of having their wishes gratified.

Those wishes generally were in such cases interviews with some beloved object, or visions of future happiness. The votary was bathed, dressed in splendid robes, given some peculiar food, after which he inhaled a delicious odour, and was then laid on a couch strewn with flowers. Upon this he probably went to sleep; but in all events such an intoxication of the mind was produced that the next morning he rose satisfied that in the night all his desires had been realised. The worship of the Paphian Venus, of the "Syrian Goddess," be she Astarte, or known by whatever other name, and of other mystical divinities, was full of these rites, in which the effects on the mind could only have been produced by narcotic stimulants.

The first intention of Hasheesh was evidently not as a stimulant. It was intended as a "spiritual" soporific, producing that quiescence of soul so dear to Orientals, and known throughout all the regions under Arabian influence by the name of "Kaif." But this stolid annihilation of ideas was not sufficient for the more exalted natures; these found a higher power in the drug—that of raising the imagination until it attained to a beatified realization of the joys of a future world. This last effect could only be produced by mixing other noxious ingredients with hasheesh, already sufficiently noxious of itself, and the effect of the delirium was mentally worse than that of opium itself. The mind (brain), utterly prostrate after the effect had ceased, required still more imperatively than in the case of the opium-eater a fresh supply to the deceased imagination; the dose was heightened as the craving for beatitude became stronger, and half-a-year's indulgence ended in a madness of the most moody and miserable kind—all the more miserable that, unlike the opium-eater, the inhaler of hasheesh in this form preserves his corporal strength and activity. The lovers of this vice present few of the hideous forms of humanity exhibited by a Chinese opium-house; but, on the other hand, the mental effect is wilder, more terrible, and yet more difficult of cure.

The use of hasheesh prevails in the Levant to an extent very little suspected by the common observer, so carefully is it concealed, or veiled under the pretence of ordinary smoking. The word "hasheesh" is of Egyptian or Syrian origin (Khoshkhosh in the Arabic language signifies simply the poppy). At Constantinople it is known by the name of "esrâr," which word means a secret product or preparation; the name of hasheesh in European Turkey being confined to the poppy from which the product is obtained. The cultivation of this plant is carried on with much activity in many parts of the Ottoman dominions; it thrives best and in most abundance in the provinces of Asia Minor, and especially Nicomedia, Broosa, and in Mesopotamia, near Mosul. The dealers in esrâr repair to these countries towards the end of May, in the first place, to examine the state of the vegetation and to suggest improvements in its cultivation; and in the second, to overlook the harvest, and themselves to collect the dust which forms the staple of this commodity. The merchant, as soon as he arrives at the spot, sends the company he brings with him into the fields to cut off the heads of the plants, in order that the leaves which contain the precious material may have more force. Fifteen days after this operation the plants are gathered in, after care has been taken to ascertain that the leaves are large, and feel viscous to the touch. The plants are cut down, not rooted up, for fear of damaging the leaves; they are then taken into a shed, where the leaves are carefully picked off, and spread out to dry upon a long, coarse carpet, made of wool, and called Kileem. When the leaves are sufficiently dry, they are collected together upon one half of the carpet,

A BEKTASH DERVISH INHALING HASHEESH.

the other half being left free for the purpose of beating the leaves till they are reduced to dust. The first product is immediately collected, forming the choicer portion of the esrâr, and is called Sighirmâ. The fibres of the leaves are then, by means of a second and third pounding, reduced to dust. This dust, called "Honarda," is in less esteem; so much so that, while the first dust sells at forty francs the kilogramme, the second is not worth more than ten, it being not only as the refuse, but lying under the suspicion of adulteration. It is sent to Constantinople in double sacks—the outside one of hair, the inner one of skin; the entire quantity is not there consumed, much of it being sent to Egypt and Syria. Before being brought into the market, the esrâr is differently prepared, according to the tastes of the different countries. In Egypt and Syria the extract is preferred in a fatty form, prepared with butter. At Constantinople the rancid and viscous flavour produced by this process is greatly disliked, and the esrâr is sold in the form of syrup, or in pastiles to be smoked with tombeki (in the Narghili or water-pipe). The simple syrup still retains something of the fatty and viscous flavour, and for that purpose some aromatic productions, as bahârâb, are introduced into the preparation. This last addition is of great importance, as by the nature of its excitement it impresses the mind of the imbiber, in addition to the ecstatic delirium of the pure hasheesh, with a series of visions of the joys of paradise and other scenes of future life, much prized on this account by the true believer. This last preparation is extremely expensive, and is therefore only in the reach of the rich; it is chiefly used by the grandees of Asia Minor, who, being more devout than those of Europe, carefully abstain from fermented liquors, but consider hasheesh, which produces the same effects in a very aggravated form, to be in perfect accordance with the law of the Prophet.

The inhabitants of the capital (Constantinople) are less impulsive, and for the purpose of producing that state of mind so desirable, and known in the East by the name of "kaif," they add the effects of râki and other fermented liquors. The pastiles for smoking are thus prepared. A certain quantity of esrâr is put into an iron pot, and warmed slowly over a brazier. A peculiar acrid odour is then given forth, upon which the operator puts his hand, enclosing a portion of the dust, into a vase full of a strong infusion of coffee, with which he carefully moistens and kneads the dust. After having been thus mixed, the dust becomes a paste, having the smell and colour of coffee; it is then taken from the fire and put upon a marble table, where it undergoes a long process of manipulation until it is made thoroughly homogeneous; it is then cut in pieces, and moulded into the form of small cylinders or rolls. Pastile cylinders, weighing four grammes, are sold for a piastre (or four cents), and one is more than enough to throw any person not habituated to the practice into the most complete delirium. This last form of hasheesh is the most common and the best appreciated in the country. The reason of the preference is partly the cheapness and partly its colour and form, which allow it to be carried about and used without discovery. The pastiles are commonly soaked for use in the narghilâ with the tombeki, or Persian tobacco, but those who require a more decided action, prefer the mixture with common tobacco, for which reason the dealers in esrâr sell cigars impregnated with this substance to those who are not used to it. According to precise returns, the quantity of esrâr dust collected in the aforenamed localities commonly exceeds 25,000 kilogrammes.

THE OCCULT SCIENCES.

Education in the East is removing from the minds of Moslems many of the superstitious ideas which they attached to what may be called the "hidden arts," and to the value of amulets, talismans, charms, &c. I have found, however, that these are still cherished by most of the lower classes, and especially among the Dervishes. Mr. Lane, in his excellent work, afore-quoted, called the "Modern Egyptians," gives a minute account of these, and I would recommend the curious and patient reader to refer to it for what I spare him in the present humbler book.

So much sanctity is attached by Moslems generally, and Dervishes in particular, to particular verses of the Koran as to lead them to believe in certain "spiritual powers" possessed by each one of these, differing according to their application. On many of the more magnificent palaces and konâks, or the dwelling-houses of the wealthy, it is usual to suspend a writing for the protection of the same. Sometimes a few words are written on an angle of the building, and in these cases the words are generally some of the names of the Deity, or a pious invocation, such as "Yâ! Hâfiz!" "Oh! protector!" at others the writing is composed of several words, or even of a full verse of the Koran. In addition to these, it is not at all uncommon to see suspended from an angle of the same edifice—even a royal one—an old shoe or a bunch of garlic, the latter sometimes painted blue. Even an old horse-shoe is supposed to possess certain vague powers of protection against fire and ill-luck; and, as it cannot be supposed that the intelligent owner of the konâk really believes in its efficacy, it must be attributed to a "popular superstition," against which he does not care to offend. The "pious invocation" arises from a higher motive, inasmuch as it is a part of that strong principle of Islamism which teaches its disciple a perfect submission to the will and providence of God, and to look to Him only for protection and preservation under all the circumstances of life. The religious amulets or "tilsims" generally known as "talismans" are stones of various kinds, such as agates and cornelians, or even those of a more precious character. On these are engraved various verses of the Koran, or even some of its shorter chapters, and vary according to the peculiar belief of the engraver or the wearer. These are suspended to the neck, attached to the arm, or worn as a ring. Sometimes they are also an invocation of the Caliph 'Alee, or of all of the four direct caliphs—of even the Prophet; and when the former are sectarian, they generally are of a Persian or Dervish character. Verses of the Koran are also written on parchment or paper, and are worn in the same manner and for the same purpose. These are called "nuskhas," or amulets, and are worn by an immense number of Mussulmans of every position in life.

There are, however, another class of talismans, which are entirely of a mystical or cabalistic character, drawn up according to what is called the "'Ibm Vifd," or "Science of Calculation." To these the public, and especially the Dervishes, still attach extraordinary powers.

This is the science of drawing up figures in a mystical manner. All the letters of the Arabic alphabet have a numerical value, like in our own, V is 5, X is 10, &c. and it is therefore easy to draw up an invocation or a prayer in figures; chronograms are written in a similar manner, and in most public inscriptions the last line, though written and possessing a signification of a poetical character, if calculated, also gives the date of the writing. In this manner, if I am not mistaken, the inscription on the marble slab sent by the late Sultan, 'Abd ul Mejid to the Washington Monument explains the period of the contribution in the last line. It is only necessary to ascertain the numerical value of each letter, and these when added together form the date. The letters "Bektâsh" make the date of his Order, A.H. 738.

It is also believed that each letter of the alphabet has a servant appointed by Allah to attend upon it. These, it is supposed, may be invoked in case of need. Particular writings are equally attended by mysterious beings, who, though they may not actually appear when invoked, are nevertheless present, and are supposed to obey implicitly the commands of the invoker. Some of these writings in numerals are for evil as well as for good purposes. They must be drawn up on certain days and hours, at certain periods of the moon, or on certain positions of the stars, without which their powers are lost. They are also engraved upon stones taken from certain localities, such as in the vicinity of the holy cities of Mekkeh and Medineh, in Arabia, or near the tombs of celebrated saints or founders of the Dervish Orders. Those from the neighbourhood of the grave of Hâjee Bektâsh are highly esteemed. Besides verses from the Koran, are often seen invocations to 'Alee or the other caliphs, and to the Prophet; and mystical numerical calculations inscribed in and on drinking-cups, so that they may arrest the eye of the drinker. In case a charm is drawn up for the purpose of inspiring some one with the divine passion (love), the servants, or, as they are called, the "Jins," attendant upon the letters which compose it meet together and devise a series of influences, which, though invisible, are believed to have the power of compelling the devoted person to obey them. The only means of protection to be used in such cases, is to draw up a counter charm, the jins attendant upon which either overcome the others or come to a compromise, and so relieve the afflicted object.

Various calculations are made of an abstruse nature, involving a series of cubes and squares, subtractions and divisions, multiplications, and additions, of a conventional character, to learn a result, either odd or even. If odd, the result is considered unfortunate, whilst if even, it is fortunate.

The Tesbeeh, a Mussulman rosary, composed of ninety-nine beads (some of those of the Dervishes are much greater), represent so many names of the Deity, which are invoked by the devout. Its use is taken from the 41st verse of the 33d chapter of the Koran, viz.:—

"O, believers (in the unity of Allah, and the mission of His Prophet), repeat the name of Allah, and count His names, night and morning."

Another peculiar belief has been thus explained to me by a Dervish friend, in connexion with the mystical character of Letters, based upon the principle, that the faculties of reason and speech being peculiarly Divine gifts bestowed upon man, letters also were given to him as a means of expressing himself, and of perpetuating knowledge, and were practically used by God himself, in His communications to some of the prophets, as in the writing of the Ten Commandments.

The four elements, viz. Water (Ab), Earth (Turâb), Fire (Nâr), and Air (Havâ), possess twenty-eight letters, as follows:—

A, 1; B, 2; J, 3; D, 4; H, 5; V, 6; Z, 7; H, 8; T, 9; Y, 10; K, 20; L, 70; M, 40; N, 50; S, 60; 'A, or 'Ayin, 70; F, 80; Z, or Zâd, 90; K, 100; R, 200; Sh, or Shin, 700; T, 400; Th, or Thay, 500; H, or Heh, 600; Z, or Zeh, 700; Dz, 800; Zh, 900; and Gh, or Ghayin, 1,000.

These are divided into four classes, each of a different temperament. Fire has seven letters, *i.e.* A, H, T, M, F, Sh, and Dz, all supposed to be of a hot temperament. Earth has seven letters, *i.e.* D, H, L, 'Ayin, R, Khah or K, and Gh or Ghayin, which are of a dry temperament. Air has seven letters, *i.e.* B, V, Y, T, S, N, and Dz, all of a cold temperament. Water also has seven letters, *i.e.* J, Z, S, K, Kaf, T, and Th, all of moist temperaments. The letters of the element Water are considered as being the principal ones, and all the others as their branches; for God says, in the Koran, "All things have been made by us from water."

These are called the *'Anâsir i Erbe'â*, or the four elements of Nature, and are much considered in many of the modern sciences, such even as medicine and chemistry, among not only the Dervish Orders, but even among the more educated classes of Mussulmans generally.

A List of all of the Dervish Convents, or *Tekkiehs*, at Constantinople, and the days in which they perform their exercises, for the guidance of curious visitors.

FRIDAY.

The *Mevlevees*, or "Turning Dervishes," in Pera.

The *Sumbulees.*—Convent at Kojah, "Mustapha Pasha," Stambool.

The *Jelvetees.*—Convent of Azees Mahmood Efendi, in Scutary.

The *Nakshibendees.*—Emir Bokhara Convent, near the Mosque of Sultan Mohammed, the conqueror of Constantinople.

The *Kâdirees.*—Yahya Efendi Convent, at Beshik Tosh.

The *Nakshibendees.*—Convent of Kioshgiâree 'Abdullah Efendi, at "Idris Kiosk."

The *Nakshibendees.*—A Kalender Khaneh, at Eyub.

The *Jelvetees.*—Convent of Ak Shems ed Deen, at Zayrek.

The *Rufâ'ees.*—Convent, called "Kubbeh," near Sultan Mohammed the II.'s Mosque, in Constantinople.

The *Nakshibendees.*—Convent of the "Sheikh ul Islâm," at Eyub.

The *Jelvetees*—Convent of "Amee Zinân," at Shehr Eminee.

The *Jelvetees.*—Convent, called "Tekkieh," at Topee Capu.

The *Jelvetees.*—Convent, called "Banderwâlee Zâdeh," at the place called "Inadieh," in Scutary.

The *Nakshibendees.*—Convent, called the "'Othman Efendi," in Scutary.

The *Sumbulees.*—Convent of "Sinan Erdebelee," near the Mosque of St. Sophia.

The *Sa'diehs.*—Convent of "Kara Mustapha," near Ak Seray, Stambool.

The *Kâdirees.*—Convent, called the "Hakeem Oghloo 'Alee Pasha," Stambool.

The *Kâdirees.*—Convent, called "Fevree," at "Bulbul Deresee," near Eyub.

The *Nakshibendees.*—Convent, called "Hindeeler Tekkiehsee," at Khorkhor, near Ak Seray, Stambool.

The *Kâdirs.*—Called "Pialee Pasha Tekkiehsee," near the Oke Maidân, behind the Navy Yard.

The *Kâdirs.*—"Resmee Tekkiehsee," near to the Adrianople Gate, Stambool.

The *Sumbulees.*—"Bâllat Tekkiehsee," near the Ballât Mosque, Stambool.

The *Kâdirs.*—"'Alee Baba Tekkiehsee," near Pialee Kosha.

The *Kâdirs.*—"Terabee Tekkiehsee," near the Navy Yard.

The *Nakshibendees.*—"Beshir Aga Tekkiehsee," near to the Sublime Porte, in Stambool.

The *Nakshibendees.*—"Usbek Tekkiehsee," near to Bulbul Deresee, Scutary.

The *Khalvetees.*—"Kallanjee Sheikh Emin Efendi Tekkiehsee," at the Otakfilar, in the Chayir bashee meadow.

The *Bairamiehs.*—"'Abdee Baba Tekkiehsee," near Eyub.

The *Khalvetees.*—"Sheikh Nusuhee Efendi Tekkiehsee," at the Toganjilars, Scutary.

The *Nakshibendees.*—Us "bekler Tekkiehsee," at the ascent of the Mohammed Pasha Yokashee, Stambool.

The *Rufâ'ees.*—"Alaja Mesjid Tekkiehsee," near to the Lenkeh Bey Gate, at Merjemek.

The *Khalvetees.*—"Aideen Oghlou Tekkiehsee," near to the Sublime Porte, Stambool.

The *Nakshibendees.*—"Izzet Mehmet Pasha Tekkiehsee," Eyub.

The *Nakshibendees.*—"Emir Bokhara Tekkiehsee," just outside the Adrianople Gate, Stambool.

The *Sa'diehs.*—"Sheikh Ghanee Tekkiehsee," near the Tabutjilars, Scutary.

The *Khâlvetees.*—Called the "Khalvettieh Tekkiehsee," inside the mosque of "Kuchook Aya Sofieh" (*small* St. Sophia), Stambool.

The *Khalvetees.*—"Faizee Efendi Tekkiehsee," near "Agach Kakan."

The *Khalvetees.*—"Sachlee Husain Efendi Tekkiehsee," near to the Ahmedieh meadow.

The *Sa'diehs.*—"Châkir Aga Tekkiehsee," near the Salma Tomrook, Stambool.

The *Sa'diehs.*—"Kantarji Tekkiehsee," at Dolma Bakcha.

The *Jelvetees.*—"Divanee Mustapha Efendi Tekkiehsee," in the Sheikh Jâmee (mosque), at Scutary.

The *Khalvetees.*—"Ujeeler Tekiehsee," at the Silivree Gate. Stambool.

The *Khalvetees.*—"Cholak Hasan Efendi Tekkiehsee," at Idris Kuskee.

The *Rufâ'ees.*—"Sherbetdâr Tekkiehsee," in the quarter called *Fenâee,* at the Khassakee meadow.

The *Kâdirs.*—"Kiurukji Tekkiehsee," at the Asmalee Zokak, in the Lalazar meadow.

The *Khalvetees.*—"Chellak Tekkiehsee," in the Men keuch meadow.

SATURDAYS.

The *Mevlevees.*—"Mevlevee Khaneh Tekkiehsee."

The *Khalvetees.*—"Said Velâet Hazreteree Tekkiehsee," near the plain or meadow, called Ashik Pasha Arzassee.

The *Sumbulees.*—"Keshfee Ja'fer Efendi Tekkiehsee," at Fundukli.

The *Jelvetees.*—"Selamee 'Alee Efendi Tekkiehsee," at Ajee Badem, in Scutary.

The *Khalvetees.* — "Ordoo Sheikhee Hâfiz Efendi Tekkiehsee," near Hamam Chelebee Mehmed Aga.

The *Sa'diehz.*—"Balchik Tekkiehsee," at Defterdar Eskalasee, near Eyub.

The *Rufâ'ees.*—"'Alee Kuzee Tekkiehsee," at Telurkluk, in Kasim Pasha.

The *Kâdirees.*—"Peshmakji Tekkiehsee," at Kuchook Pialee Pasha.

The *Khalvetees.*—Sa'dullah Chaush Tekkiehsee," at Ainalee Bakal, near the Silivree Gate.

The *Rufâ'ees.*—"Sheikh Kiamil Efendi Tekkiehsee," near Avret Bazaar, Stambool.

The *Rufâ'ees.*—"Birbirler Sheikhee 'Ottoman Efendi Tekkiehsee," at Bayazid Aga Mahalassee Top Kapu.

The *Bairamiehs.*—"Mehmed Aga Tekkiehsee," in the aforenamed mosque.

SUNDAYS AND WEDNESDAYS.

The *Khalvetees.*—"Bulbulji Zâdeh Efendi Tekkiehsee," in the mosque of Nishanji Pasha Jedeed.

The *Kâdirs.*—"Yarmaji Baba Tekkiehsee," at Liman Pasha, Sentary.

The *Kâdirs.*—"Sheikh Mehmed Khifâf Tekkieshee," at Balji Yokushee, in Kuchook Haman.

The *Khalvetees.*—"Sheikh Faiz Ullah Efendi Tekkiehsee," at Ahmedieh, in Scutary.

The *Sumbulees.*—" Bairam Pasha Tekkiehsee," near the Khassakee Mosque, Stambool.

The *Khalvetees.*—" Emirler Tekkiehsee," at the Silivree Gate.

The *Kâdirs.*—" Gavsee Efendi Tekkiehsee," near to the convent called " Mimararzassee."

The *Kâdirs.*—" Hamdee Efendi Tekkiehsee," at Sinâan Pasha.

The *Sa'diehs.*—" Yagji Zâdeh Tekkiehsee," at the Wharf of Bulban, in Scutary.

The *Sa'diehs.*—" Kirpassee Mustapha Efendi Tekkiehsee," at Eyub.

SUNDAYS.

The *Mevlevees.*—" Kasim Pasha Mevlevee Khâneh see."

The *Nakshibendees.*—"Sheikh Murad Tekkiehsee," near the Ortakjilars.

The *Nakshibendees.*—" Murad Molla Tekkiehsee," in the market of Chaharshenbee.

The *Nakshibendees.*—" Emir Bokhara Tekkiehsee," near the Egree Kapu Gate.

The *Nakshibendees.*—" Salamee Efendi Tekkiehsee," in the place called Baba Hyder, near Eyub.

The *Khalvetees.*—" Jemâlee Zâdeh Tekkiehsee," outside of Egree Kapu.

The *Nakshibendees.*—" Mustapha Pasha Tekkiehsee," outside the Adrianople Gate, Stambool.

The *Rufâ'ees.*—" Sachlee Efendi Tekkiehsee," near to the fountain, called Chirâgji, at Katchuk Mustapha Pacha.

The *Sa'diehs.*—" Sheikh 'Alee Efendi Tekkiehsee," near to the Otagjilar Bedavee Tekkiehsee, at Tatavla.

The *Khalvetees.*—" Yildiz Tekkiehsee," near Bakcha Capusee, in Stambool.

The *Sa'diehs.*—" Sanjakdar Hyred Deen Tekkiehsee," near the Tchinar Mosque.

The *Kâdirs.*—" Hyder Dede Tekkiehsee," near to Serâch Khâneh.

The *Rufâ'ees.*—"Kukji Zâdeh Tekkiehsee," at the New Gate. It is the "Tarsoos Tekkieh."

The *Nakshibendees.*—"Selim Baba Tekkiehsee," near Chinar.

The *Khalvetees.*—"Sheikh Saliman Efendi Tekkiehsee," near to the Soofeeler.

The *Khalvetees.*—"Amee Sinan Tekkiehsee," near the Kurkji Mosque, at Top Kapu.

The *Nakshibendees.*—"Nooree Efendi Tekkiehsee," near the Top Kapu.

The *Nakshibendees.*—"Vannee Ahmed Efendi Tekkiehsee," at Lallazar.

The *Sumbulees.*—"Meer Akber Tekkiehsee," near the "Seven Towers."

The *Khalvetees.*—"Hâjee Kadin Tekkiehsee," at Samathia.

The *Khalvetees.*—"Khamza Zâdeh Tekkiehsee," near to Nishanji Pasha Jedeed.

The *Nakshibendees.*—"Rakam Efendi Tekkiehsee," at Zinjirlee Küyoo, in Stambool.

The *Sa'diehs.*—"'Arab Hassan Efendi Tekkiehsee," near to the "Bâb Mevlevee Khaneh."

The *Khalvetees.*—"Hafiz Efendi Tekkiehsee," Beykos.

The *Rufâ'ees.*—"Toygar Tepésee Tekkiehsee," Scutary.

The *Kâdirees.*—"Hilim Gulem Tekkiehsee." Zingirlee Kuyu, at Scutary.

The *Nakshibendees.*—"Erdek Tekkiehsee," near Daoud Pasha.

The *Kâdirees.*—"Jedid Hâjee Dede Tekkiehsee," in Tunus Bâgh, at Scutary.

The *Kâdirees.*—"'Abd ul Selâm Tekkiehsee," in Khoss Kiöy.

The *Khalvetees.*—"Sheikh Hâfiz Efendi Tekkiehsee," near Karaja Ahmed, Scutary.

The *Khalvetees.*—"Khalvetee Tekkiehsee," in the Kinissa Mosque, near to the Kiosk of the Kallijilar.

The *Kâdirees.*—"Tâshji Tekkiehsee," at Kossim Pasha, in the lot called "Bâb i Sail."

The *Sumbulees.*—"Safvettee Tekkiehsee," at the Aga Chair, near to the Selivria Gate.

The *Khalvetees.*—"Öksizja Bâbâ Tekkiehsee," near the lot called Akarja.

The *Khalvetees.*—"Sir Târik Zâdeh Tekkiehsee," at Eyub, near the Nishanjlar.

The *Kâdirees.*—"Sheikh Khaleel Efendi Tekkiehsee," near the Alti Mermer.

The *Nakshibendees.*—"Mybekler Tekkiehsee," at Salamieh, in Scutary.

The *Bairamiehs.*—"Yanez Tekkiehsee," at Salajik, in Scutary.

The *Khalvetees.*—"Kavserah Mustapha Bâbâ Tekkiehsee," at the Chaush Déré, Scutary.

The *Sa'diehs.*—"Saif ed Deen Efendi Tekkiehsee," in Chaush Déré, Scutary.

The *Nakshibendees.*—"Sheikh Said Efendi Tekkiehsee," at Kandillee, in the valley.

The *Nakshibendees.*—"Jân Fidâ Tekkiehsee," at Kubbeh Tosh.

MONDAYS.

The *Mevlevees.*—"Yani Kapu Mevlevee Khanebsee."

The *Khalvetees.*—"Noor ed Deen Jerahee Tekkiehsee," near to the Kara Gumruk, Stambool.

The *Sa'diehs.*—"'Abd ul Selâm Tekkiehsee," near Hasan Pasha Khan. It is well known under the title Koghajee Sheikh Tekkiehsee.

The *Rufâ'ees.*—"Yahya Efendi Tekkiehsee," at Eyub. It is also known as the "Haseeb Efendi Tekkiehsee."

The *Rufâ'ees.*—"Kara Sariklez Tekkiehsee," near Muftee Hamam.

The *Nakshibendees.*—"Dulger Zâdeh Tekkiehsee," at Beshik Tosh.

The *Sumbulees.*—"Hâjee Avhed Tekkiehsee," near Yadi Koolee, or "Seven Towers."

The *Shazellees.*—"Shazellee Tekkiehsee," near 'Alee Bey village.

The *Jelvetees.*—"Selâmee 'Alee Efendi Tekkiehsee." Beshik Tosh.

The *Kâdirees.*—"Nizâmee Zâdeh Tekkiehsee," near the Shehr Emeenee.

The *Khalvetees.*—"Matehka Tekkiehsee," at Beshik Tosh.

The *Sa'diehs.*—"Finduk Zâdeh Tekkiehsee," at Yuksik Kalderim.

The *Khalvetees.*—"Altoonjee Zâdeh Tekkiehsee," at Ekshee Karâ Toot.

The *Kâdirees.*—"Paik Dede Tekkiehsee," at the Selivria Gate.

The *Khalvetees.*—"'Alâ ed Deen Tekkiehsee," near Hamam Soofeeler.

The *Kâdirees.*—"Chekeh Zâdeh Tekkiehsee," near Eski 'Alee Pasha.

The *Bedâvees.*—"Haseeb Efendi Tekkiehsee," near Top Tâshee, Scutary.

The *Khalvetees.*—"Bazurgian Tekkiehsee," at Khoja Mustapha Pasha.

The *Sa'diehs.*—"Jigerim Dede Tekkiehsee," near the Marine Barracks.

The *Rufâ'ees.*—"Jindi Harem Tekkiehsee," at "Alti Mermer."

The *Nakshibendees.*—"Nakshibendee Tekkiehsee," in the Mosque of Kurshundee Mahsen, Galata.

The *Kâdirees.*—"Sheikh 'Omer Efendi Tekkiehsee," at Hâjee Elias, near to the Egri Kapusu, Stambool.

The *Khalvetees.*—"Hasan Efendi Tekkiehsee," in the Mosque of Jihângeer.

The *Khalvetees.*—"Ishak Karamanee Tekkiehsee," at Sudlija.

The *Sa'diehs.*—"'Abd ul Bakee Tekkiehsee," at Kadi Kiöy.

The *Khalvetees.*—"Fazlillahee ât Bazâree 'Othman Efendi Tekkiehsee," at the ât Bazaar, Stamboul.

The *Kâdirees.*—"Tashjee Tekkiehsee," near Daoud Pasha Eskalasee.

The *Gulshenees.*—"Tâtâr Efendi Tekkiehsee," at Top Khaneh.

The *Khalvetees.*—"Fenâ'ee Tekkiehsee," at Mollâ Kiovanee.

The *Khalvetees.*—"Mu'bir Hasan Efendi Tekkiehsee," near to Eski 'Alee Pasha.

The *Nakshibendees*.—"Karilar Tekkiehsee," at Idris Kuskee.

The *Sa'diehs*.—"Beder ed Deen Zâdehler Tekkiehsee," Psamatia.

The *Kâdirees*.—"Kâdiree Tekkiehsee," near Chagala Zâdeh Seray.

The *Khalvetees*.—"Toghramaji Tekkiehsee," behind the Zindân (prison) of the Arsenal.

The *Bairamiehs*.—"'Abd ul Samed Efendi Tekkiehsee," at Khagid Khanah.

TUESDAYS.

The *Kâdirees*.—"Ismail Roomee Hazreteri Tekkiehsee," Top Khanah, called also "Bakadir Khanah."

The *Sumbulees*.—"Shah Sultan Tekkiehsee," at Baharieh, called likewise "Nijâtee Efendi Tekkiehsee."

The *Bedâvees*.—"Sheikh Mustapha Efendi Tekkiehsee," near Tatavala in Uzun Yol.

The *Sa'diehs*.—"Mehmed Efendi Tekkiehsee," at Kara Gumruk, called also "Ejder Efendi Tekkiehsee."

The *Gulshenïehs*.—"Kiorji Sheikh 'Alee Efendi Tekkiehsee," near Molla 'Ashkee.

The *Jelvetees*.—"Sir Târik Zâdeh Tekkiehsee," at Kamerillee, in the vicinity of the Mosque of Mohammed II.

The *Nakshibendees*.—"Keshfee Efendi Tekkiehsee," in the Kéffélee Mosque, at Deragman.

The *Sumbulees*.—"Ibrahim Pasha Tekkiehsee," at Kum Kapu, in the Mosque Nishamji.

The *Sumbulees*.—"Koruk Tekkiehsee," near Molla Kuranee.

The *Khalvetees*.—"Ismail Efendi Tekkiehsee," at Yanee Kiöy.

The *Sa'diehs*.—"Kapu Agassee Ismail Aga Tekkiehsee," near to Aga Hamam, Scutary.

The *Bairamiehs*.—"Bezji Zâdeh Muhee Efendi Tekkiehsee," at Diyunjilee, Scutary.

The *Kadirs*.—"Kartal Ahmed Efendi Tekkiehsee," at Bazârbashee, Scutary.

The *Gulshenees.*—"Halvee Efendi Tekkiehsee," at Shehr Emeenee.

The *'Ushshâkees.*—"Mahmud Efendi Tekkiehsee," at Gechajiler.

The *Kâdirees.*—"Mahmud Efendi Tekkiehsee," at Eyub, near the Dabag Khaneh.

The *Bairâmiehs.*—"Taveel Mehmed Efendi Tekkiehsee," near to the Alti Mermer.

The *Sa'diehs.*—"Sheikh Jevher Tekkiehsee," at the Oke Maidân.

The *Khalvetees.*—"Shevkee Mustapha Efendi Tekkiehsee," near Mimar.

The *Sa'diehs.*—"Kullamee Tekkiehsee," in the Chârsoo, and at the Yailâ.

The *Nakshibendees.*—"Saleeh Efendi Tekkiehsee," near to Deragman.

The *Sa'diehs.*—"Sheikh Emeen Efendi Tekkiehsee," in the Pashmakji Chair.

The *Khalvetees.*—"Mimar Sinan Tekkiehsee," at 'Ashik Pasha.

The *Jelvetees.*—"Badjilar Tekkiehsee," near 'Azeez Mahmood Efendi, Scutary.

The *Khalvetees.*—"Khoja Zâdeh el Hâjee Ahmed Efendi Tekkiehsee," at Zairek.

WEDNESDAYS.

The *Mevlevees.*—"Beshiktâsh Mevlevee Khanehsee."

The *Khalvetees.*—"Umee Sinan Tekkiehsee," at Eyub in the Dökmajilar.

The *Sa'diehs.*—"Hâziree Zadeh Tekkiehsee," at Suduljâ.

The *Rufâ'ees.*—"Sheikh Halvaee Tekkiehsee," at the Boztaghan Kemeree.

The *Sumbulees.*—"Isa Zâdeh Tekkiehsee," near Deragman.

The *Kadirs.*—"Sheikh Resmee Tekkiehsee," at the Kara Gumruk, in Stambool, also called "Kubbeh Kollak."

The *Khalvetees.*—"Ak Bayik Tekkiehsee," at Akhor Kapussu.

The *Sumbulees.*—"Sirkaji Tekkiehsee," at Jeballee, Yeni Kapussu.

The *Nakshibendees.*—"Chakir Dede Tekkiehsee," at Shahzâdeh Bashee.

The *Khalvetees.*—"Keshfee Tekkiehsee," near Shahzâdeh Bashee.

The *Khalvetees.*—"Turmish Dede Tekkiehsee," at Roomali Hissar.

The *Kâdirees.*—"Remlee Tekkiehsee," near Shehr Emeenee.

The *Kâdirees.*—"Yannik Tekkiehsee," at Ferhad Aga in Kassim Pasha.

The *Khalvetees.*—"Iskender Bâbâ Tekkiehsee," near Aga Hamam, in Scutary.

The *Rufâ'ees.*—"Sheikh Nooree Tekkiehsee," in the Dabaglar Maidân, Scutary.

The *Jelvetees.*—"Ibrahim Efendi Tekkiehsee," in the Kizil Mesjid, Bulgarlee.

The *Khalvetees.*—"Umee Ahmed Efendi Tekkiehsee," near to the Chinilee Mosque, Scutary.

The *Khalvetees.*—"Idris Efendi Tekkiehsee," in Chaush Dere.

The *Gulshenees.*—"Said Efendi Tekkiehsee," in the Yashji Mosque, at Khassakee.

The *Kâdirees.*—"Kâdirieh Tekkiehsee," at Top Khaneh.

The *Jelvetees.*—"Salâmee 'Alee Efendi Tekkiehsee, at Chamlidja.

The *Jelvetees.*—"Jelvettee Tekkiehsee," at Top Khaneh, near Akarja.

The *Khalvetees.*—"Yahya Kethoda Tekkiehsee," at Kasim Pasha, near Jumâ' Bazaar.

The *Jelvetees.*—"Fenâ'ee Tekkiehsee," at Allâjâ Minareh, in Scutary.

The *Bairâmiehs.*—"Jesim Lateef Tekkiehsee," at Akseray.

The *Khalvetees.*—"'Alee Efendi Tekkiehsee," at Ajee Cheshmeh, near the Adrianople Gate.

The *Rufâ'ees.*—"Khoja Zâdeh Tekkiehsee," near Top Khaneh, at Firooz Aga.

The *Sumbulees.*—"Mimar Tekkiehsee," at Mimar Chârsoo.

The *Khalvetees.*—"Said Khalifeh Tekkiehsee," at Fanâ'ee.

The *Kâdirees.*—"Nebatee Tekkiehsee," at Top Khaneh.

The *Kâdirees.*—"Mu'bir Hasan Tekkiehsee," at Kasim Pasha.

The *Kâdirees.*—"Dibilee Kala Ahmed Efendi Tekkiehsee," near to the new Mevlevee Khaneh.

THURSDAYS.

The *Mevlevees.*—"Yani Kapu Mevlevee Khanehsee."

The *Sumbulees.*—"Merkez Efendi Hazreteree Tekkiehsee," outside the Mevlevee Khaneh.

The *Nakshibendees.*—"Yahya Efendi Hazreteree, Tekkiehsee," at the same place.

The *Nakshibendees.*—"Ahmed el Bokharee Tekkiehsee," at the Kaban Dakeek, Stambool.

The *Shazalees.*—"Shazalee Tekkiehsee," at the same place.

The *Rufâ'ees.*—"Al Yanak 'Alee Efendi Tekkiehsee," in the Mosque of Zehkerjee, at Lallazar.

The *Nakshibendees.*—"Beshikji Zâdeh Tekkiehsee," near the Mosque of Bikir Pasha.

The *Sa'diehs.*—"'Abid Chelebee Tekkiehsee," near Kazee Cheshmeh.

The *Khalvetees.*—"Iplikjee Mehmed Efendi Tekkiehsee," near Otlâgji Yokushee.

The *Nakshibendees.*—"Samanee Zâdeh Tekkiehsee," at the same place.

The *Sa'diehs.*—"Tashlee Buroon Tekkiehsee," near Eyub.

The *Nakshibendees.*—"Uluklu Bayir Tekkiehsee," at Eyub.

The *Nakshibendees.*—"Emeer Bokhara Tekkiehsee," at the Otâgjilar.

The *Nakshibendees.*—"Silimieh Tekkiehsee," at Scutary.

? .—"Khussam ed Deen 'Ushshâkee Tekkiehsee," at Kasim Pasha.

The *Khalvetees.*—"Suklee Mehmed Pasha Tekkiehsee," at the At Maidân in Stambool.

The *Nakshibendees.*—"Sâdik Efendi Tekkiehsee," at the Alaja Mi'mâree, in Scutary.

The *Nakshibendees.*—"Mudaniehlee Zâdeh Tekkiehsee," near to the *Bâb i Humayun*, in Stambool.

The *Bairâmiehs.*—"Himet Zâdeh Tekkiehsee," near Nakkash Pasha.

The *Rufâ'ee.*—"Mehmed Shemsee Efendi Tekkiehsee," near Yanee Bakcheh.

The *Nakshibendees.*—"Tâhir Aga Tekkiehsee," near Kasâsb Bashee Cheshmassee.

The *Sa'diehs.*—"At Yamez Tekkiehsee," near Psamathia, Stambool.

The *Nakshibendees.*—"Aga Sheikh Tekkiehsee," near the Jebbeh Khaneh.

The *Nakshibendees.*—"Said Bâbâ Tekkiehsee," near Khassakee.

The *Kadirs.*—"Sheikh Tay Efendi Tekkiehsee," near Khassakee.

The *Nakshibendees.*—"Deroonee Tekkiehsee," near Kemer Boz Tagan.

The *Nakshibendees.*—"Na'lber Mehmed Effendi Tekkiehsee," at Roomalee Hissar.

The *Nakshibendees.*—"Bâbâ Hyder Tekkiehsee," near Eyub.

The *Khalvetees.*—"Tellonee Tekkiehsee," near Inadieh, at Scutary.

The *Sa'diehs.*—"Khaleel Pasha Tekkiehsee," near the wharf of Daoud Pasha, Stambool.

The *Khalvetees.*—"Hakeekee 'Othman Efendi Tekkiehsee," near Egree Kapoo.

The *Khalvetees.*—"Khalvetee Tekkiehsee," near Arpa Cheshmasee, Eyub.

The *Nakshibendees.*—"Alta Efendi Khaleefehsee Tekkiehsee," in Anadolee Hissar.

The *Rufâ'ees.*—"Rufâ'ee Tekkiehsee," at the Eskee Menzil Khaneh, at Scutary.

The *Nakshibendees.*—"Mehmed Alta Allah Efendi Tekkiehsee," at Kanlijik.

The *Nakshibendees.*—"Saidee Bey Tekkiehsee," near Yuksek Kalderim.

The *Bairâmiehs.*—"Hashmee 'Othman Efendi Tekkiehsee," at Kalaksiz in Kasim Pasha.

The *Khalvetees.*—"Chamlijalee Mehmed Efendi Tekkiehsee," near Chaush Dere, Scutary.

The *Nakshibendees.*—"Ya'kub Zâdeh Tekkiehsee," near Baila.

The *Nakshibendees.*—"Selim Baba Tekkiehsee," at Sultan Tépésee, Scutary.

The *Kâdirees.*—"Hâjee Ilias Tekkiehsee," near Egree Kapoo, at Batgan.

The *Khalvetees.*—"Roofee' Efendi Tekkiehsee," at Toganjilar, Scutary.

The *Khalvetees.*—"Safvettee Efendi Tekkiehsee," (same place).

The *Khalvetees.*—"Kara Bash 'Alee Efendi Tekkiehsee," in Eski Jâmee Vâlideh, at Scutary.

The *Khalvetees.*—"Sarmashik Tekkiehsee," near the Adrianople Gate, Stambool.

The *Nakshibendees.*—"Dulger Oghlu Tekkiehsee," near the Khaffâf Khaneh.

The *Khalvetees.*—"Kush 'Adâlee Ibrahim Efendi Tekkiehsee," at the Senglee Bakkâl.

The *Khalvetees.*—"Sheikh Suliman Efendi Tekkiehsee," at Beycos.

The *Sa'diehs.*—"Sultan 'Othman Tekkiehsee," at Seera Serveeler, in the Otâgjiler.

The *Khalvetees.*—"Sivassee Tekkiehsee," near Sultan Selim's Mosque, in Stambool.

The *Nakshibendees.*—"Agvanlar Tekkiehsee," near the Chinilee Mosque, at Scutary.

The *Khalvetees.*—"Karabash Tekkiehsee," in the Roomalee Hissar.

The *Khelvetees.*—"Karabash Tekkiehsee," at Top Khaneh.

CHAPTER XV.

ONE of the most interesting and correct writers on the "East," Mr. M. A. Ubicini, devotes a chapter in his book, entitled "Letters on Turkey," to the subject of the Dervishes. I should commit an act of injustice did I not mention the valuable statements it contains. This author says:—

"If the *Ulemâ* (of Turkey) in its actual condition represent on the one side the secular clergy, the Orders of the Dervishes may also be assimilated, on the other, to the regular clergy of our own ecclesiastical society. Spread, from the Atlantic to the Ganges, over a vast space, under the name of Dervishes, Santons, Sofies, and Fâkirs, they are the religious members of Islamism, in the same manner as the *Ulemas* are its theologians, and form, with these latter—although they be irreconcilable enemies to each other—the opposing force in Turkey.

"It is necessary, however, not to carry this assimilation too far. The Dervishes are individuals who voluntarily deprive themselves of their worldly goods for the purpose of devoting them to the benefit of the poor. The word *Dervish*, according to the Persian etymology, signifies a beggar (*der* signifies door, and *vich* spread, or extended, meaning, in fact, the poor, who, having no asylum, stretch themselves at night upon the sill of doors to sleep), thus denoting the poverty of the profession, and also one who reduces himself to mendicity for the purpose of aiding others.

"The Khalife Alee was the first among Mussulmans who gave the example of this voluntary renunciation of worldly store, not, as might be supposed, as an act of penitence, but to accomplish literally the maxim of the Koran, which says, 'The best of men is he who is useful to mankind.' His example led a large number of Mussulmans in the same path, who formed an association, of which he became the chief. These were called the *Safasahibi*, from the Arabic adjective *safi*, 'pure,' to express the poverty of their lives and conformity to the moral law of the Koran. Little by little, however, the Dervishes departed from their original design; attracted by the charms of contemplative life and the example of the solitary individuals of India and Greece to the practice of acts of benevolence, they substituted the ravings of ecstacism, and began to withdraw from the rest of society. Soon afterwards they formed communities, which adopted practices, some of an austere, and some of a fantastical character; and it was then, that under the double influence of rules and mysticism, there was developed amongst the Dervishes the character which assimilates them to our religious Orders.

"Two things must be distinguished among the Dervishes—doctrine and institution. The first is nothing else than the Sofeism which existed in the East long previous to the coming of Mohammed. Perhaps, if we wish to trace it to its origin, we must go back even to the most remote theocracies of Egypt and India, through the secret schools of the Pythagorians, and the Neo-Platonism of Alexandria. It is easy to convince oneself, if attention be paid, that under the confusion of fantastical names, times, and often of doctrines, the Greek trace does not cease to be visible in the Arabian philosophy alongside of an Indian impression. It is thus that we see, more than a century before Mohammed, the ten great sects which divide it:—the *Meschaïouns* (the walkers), and the *Ischrachaïouns* (contemplators), reminding us, by the similarity of the names, of a certain point, and by the conformity of doctrines of the two great philosophical schools of Greece, represented by their illustrious chiefs (*Muallim eyel Aristhatlis*), 'the grand master Aristotle,' and *Aflathoun elahi* ('the divine Plato'); nor is it less true, notwithstanding this title of Divine, which has been religiously preserved in the ὁ θεῖος Πλάτων of the Greeks, that Plato, seated amidst his disciples, and rising to the highest practical truths of morality and religion, was but a Plato doubled up by Diogenes, bent up in a tub, and causing virtue to consist in absolute inaction, and the annihilation of all the faculties. The almost simultaneous apparition of the Koran, and the writings of the ancient philosophers, which as yet were only known through tradition, marks a new era in the history of Arabian philosophy. The religious element joined the rational element which had, until then, reigned without partition; and, under the combined influence of these causes, the two primitive sects, becoming each transformed in the sense of its doctrine—the *Meschaïouns* continued in the *Mutekelim*, or metaphysicians, and the *Ischrachaïouns* in the *Sofis*. What is the correct origin of the name of *Sofis*, on which so many dissertations have been written? Does it come, as well as the word given to the association of which Alee declared himself to be the head, from the Arabic adjective *safi*, or from *sâfâ*, one of the stations around the Keabèh, or from *sof* (wool, or that which is made from wool), in allusion to the woollen garment adopted by this new sect, either through humility, or so as to distinguish it from the other rival sects? Or rather must it be attributed, more naturally, to a corruption of the Greek word *σοφοί*? This question of etymology merits less our attention than the examination of Sofeism itself."

The beginning of Soofeeism is nothing else than pantheism, as shown in the exclamation of Mevlânâ Zelâleddeen, addressed to his spiritual master, "O my master, you have completed my doctrine by teaching me that you are God, and that all things are God." Whilst the philosophers of India and Greece limited themselves to teaching, under a diversity of myths and systems, the immortality of the soul, the emancipation of Divine intelligence, its fall, its terrestrial condition, and reunion to its source, the Soofees had reached only to the sight, in material forms, of the emanations of the Divine essence, resembling, they say, the rays of the sun, which are continuously darted forth and re-absorbed; applying thus to the entire creation that which Seneca had said in magnificent terms regarding the soul, in which a particle of the Divinity,—"Quemadmodum radii solis contingunt quidem terram, sed ibi sunt undè mittuntur: sic animus magnus et sacer. . . . conversatur quidem nobiscum, sed hæret origini suæ."—Sen. *Epist.* xl. Comparisons of this nature abound in the books of the "Spirituality of the Soofees." I will cite a few of those which are the most familiar.

"You say 'the sea and waves,' but in that remark you do not believe that you signify distinct objects, for the sea when it heaves produces waves, and the waves when they settle down again become sea; in the same manner men are the waves of God, and after death return to His bosom. Or, you trace with ink upon paper the letters of the alphabet, *a*, *b*, *c*; but these letters are not distinct from the ink which enabled you to write them: in the same manner the creation is the alphabet of God, and is lost in Him."

The Cheik Choubli, contemporaneous with Murad II., whose disciple Amededdin was condemned by a sentence of the Ulema to be skinned alive, publicly taught that the human soul absorbed in God, mixed with Him, just as rain does with the water of the sea.

Spinoza undertook at a later period to show in proper terms the identity of God with matter. From that comes the necessity of a perpetual adoration of the Creator in His works. The Soofees inculcate the doctrine, "Adore God in His creatures." It is said in a verse of the Koran which I have already cited—"It is not given to man that God should speak to him; if He does so it is by inspiration, or through a veil." Thus all the efforts of man should tend to raise up the veil by the force of divine love and the annihilation of the individuality which separates him from the Divine essence; and this expression, "raise up the veil," has remained in the language of the East as expressive of the greatest intimacy. Must one say, however, that the Soofees, by leaning upon the passage of the Koran, and upon another where it is said that "God made the creation as an emanation, and will afterwards cause it to re-enter Himself" (Koran v. 4), pretend to the consecration of this dogma? On the contrary, the dogma had perished in their hands. They did not deny the divine mission of the Prophet, but they reduced his precepts to an allegorical sense, the key of which alone could give the interpretation. In our times even the Wahabites, whom Sultan Mahmood could not wholly destroy, and who are still spread over the Persian Gulf, admit no other authority than that of the Koran as interpreted by human individual reason, and without any submission to the prophets or the Imâms.

Moreover, the Soofees regained in the beginning all that such a doctrine could possess of the dangerous by teaching the strictest morality. They incessantly preached union, sobriety, universal benevolence, and offered in themselves an example. They said that evil only came into the world through ignorance, and is the cause of error and disunion among men. Some of them cited on this subject the following tale:—"Four travellers—a Turk, an Arab, a Persian, and a Greek, having met together, decided to take their meal in common, and as each one had but ten paras, they consulted together as to what should be purchased with the money. The first said *Uzum*, the second *Ineb*, the third decided in favour of *Inghur*, and the fourth insisted upon *Stafilion*. On this a dispute arose between them, and they were about to come to blows, when a peasant passing by happened to know all four of their tongues, and brought them a basket of grapes. They now found out, greatly to their astonishment, that each one had what he desired."

"I do not know," adds M. Ubicini, "for my part any more abominable doctrine than this deceptive idealism which tends to substitute the creation for the Creator, and arrives by an irresistible slope at the destruction of all faith and all morality; all the more dangerous as it veils its corruption under the most amiable exterior, and so it misleads, unknown to themselves, the best minds: '*eo perniciosior, quod abundans dulcibus vitiis*,' as Quintilian said of the diction of Seneca. The materialism in which it finally terminates, with the unheard-of niceties of sensuality, is a hundred times less to be feared, because it at once revolts the secret instincts of the human conscience, whilst mystical reveries so full of seductions are a snare laid for the inclinations of the most unsuspecting and the most noble of our nature. It is this point which gives so much authority to the words of Bossuet, combating, in the name of the immutability of dogma, and the integrity of morality, the quietism of Fénelon. These fermentations of dissolution, which Sofeism had thrown into the bosom of Mussulman society, did not at once manifest themselves, tempered moreover, as I have just said, by the ardent, though sincere, enthusiasm, and the austerity of morals of its first adepts. But they gradually gained ground, and little by little entered the veins of the social body. In fact this spirit of holy abstraction upon which Sofeism is based; this ardent mysticism so marvellously adapted to the imaginations, at the same time wildly unsteady and sensual, of Orientals, and of which the Bible offers more than one trace, could not fail to gain for him many proselytes. Egypt, once the cradle of monastic life, after the folly of the desert had succeeded, among the first Christians, to the folly of the cross, was again filled with Thebaides. With the only substitution of the name of Allah for that of Jesus, it was the same life, or rather the same absence of life, '*Vitæ mori ac uivere morti*,'—the same austerities, the same exaggerations. Mount Olympus, on the Asiatic coast, nearly opposite Mount Athos, where there were erected innumerable Greek monasteries, held thousands of these solitarians, lost in the contemplation of themselves and of nature, and whose memory is still venerated as that of holy persons. From thence they passed over into Arabia, to Persia, as far as the extremity of India, wherever there was Mohammedan power. Always this enthusiasm, like that of the earlier times of Christianity, spread towards the desert, fleeing from the world in contempt of temporal things; it neither strove to reverse authority nor to invade established powers. Sofeism did not take this character until when, from being a doctrine, it became an institution."

It was in the second century of the Hejra, near 129, that a Soofee reputed for his virtue and knowledge, Sheikh Olwan, founded the first religious Order, to which he gave his name. This innovation met with great opposition on the part of the legislators and the truly orthodox of Islâmism, who recalled the formal declaration of Mohammed, "No Monkery in Islâmism." Though this sentence, because in some sort proverbial, was received at the same time as an article of faith by all Mussulmans, the inclination of the Arabs for a solitary and contemplative life carried it against orthodoxy. Other Orders were soon founded in imitation of the first. The number grew rapidly from the second to the seventh century, and also in subsequent epochs. Hammer counts up thirty-six, which he enumerates according to D'Ohsson. Of this number twelve are subsequent to the Ottoman monarchy, the eighteen others arose from the commencement of the fourteenth to the middle of the eighteenth century.

Soofeeism modifies itself, like all systems, by passing from theory to action. There were, as has been always practised in the divers schools of Theosophists and Thaumaturgists, two doctrines—the one public, which precedes the initiation; and the other secret, for the adepts only. A strict observance of religion and of all the social virtues was required of the candidate for his initiation. Later, when by a long suite of proofs and mortifications, above all by the absolute annihilation of his individuality, he was supposed to have arrived at the desired degree in which to contemplate the truth face to face, and the veil, until then spread over his vision, suddenly fell, they taught him that the Prophet in his book had only presented, under the veil of allegory, maxims and political precepts; that the Koran without the interpretation was only an assembly of words void of sense; that once the habit of mental devotion contracted, he could reduce his worship to a purely spiritual one, and abandon all forms and external ceremonies.

"When one is out of the Ke'beh (the Ke'beh in the allegorical language of the Dervishes is 'Divine Love'), it is good to direct our regards towards it; but for him who is in the Ke'beh, it imports little to what direction he turns." This is the language of Jelâleddeen in his Mesnevi Shereef. The whole passage is too remarkable not to be cited here entire.

"Moses once met with a shepherd, who, in the fervour of his soul, addressing God, exclaimed, 'O my Master! my Lord! where art Thou, that I may become Thy servant,—that I sew Thy shoes,—that I comb Thy hair, —that I wash Thy robes,—that I serve up to Thee the milk of my goats,—to Thee whom I revere? Where art Thou, that I may kiss Thy beautiful hand,—that I rub Thy beautiful feet,—that I sweep out Thy chamber before Thou retirest to rest?' Thus spoke the simple shepherd. Moses, warmed by zeal for the religion which he had been sent to proclaim, reproached this man for blasphemy, telling him that God has no body, that He has no need of clothing, of nourishment, or of a chamber, and ended by declaring that he was an infidel. The shepherd, whose intelligence could not rise to the comprehension of a Being who had not, like himself, a body subject to all the same wants, was stunned by the reproaches of the envoy of God, gave himself up to despair, and renounced all adoration. God addressed Moses, and said, 'Thou hast driven My servant away from Me; I had sent thee to draw others near to Me, and not to divide them. Each being has received a mode of existence, and a different means of expressing himself. What thou findest blameable, is praiseworthy in another. What thou callest poison, is honey in his sight. Purity, impurity, slowness, precipitation,—all these distinctions are beneath Me. The Indian language alone is good for the Indian, the Zend for the Zend. Their expressions cannot stain Me; they, on the contrary, are purified by the sincerity of the homage which they offer to Me. Words are nothing to Me; I regard the heart, and if it is humble, what do I care if the tongue tells the contrary? The heart is the substance of love—words are only accidents. My servant embraces the heart of My love, and cares nothing for thought, nor for expressions. The compass only serves to direct the prayers of those who are outside of the Ke'beh, whilst within it no one knows the use of it."

M. Ubicini, in giving this beautiful extract of the Methnevi Shereef of the founder of the Mevlevee Order of Dervishes, which shows in a very clear manner the purity of its Spiritualism, adds the following note:—

"Saint Theresa, in her ecstatic rapture, cries out in the same manner; 'O my Friend! my Lord! my well-beloved! O life of my life!' When she beholds Jesus Christ during her devotional exercises, that which strikes her above all others, is the incomparable beauty of His hand, the whiteness of His feet, the penetrating softness of His voice, of His look, &c. The language of the mystical of all religions is the same."

I may here add another somewhat similar quotation from the writings of Jelâl ed Deen er Roomee.

"During the reign of an Eastern sovereign, he remarked that the learned and pious men of his times differed widely in their estimate and comprehension of the Deity, each ascribing to Him characteristics differing the one from the other. So that this prince had an elephant brought in secret to his capital, and encircled in a dark chamber; then, inviting these learned men, he told them that he was in possession of an animal which none of them had ever seen. Descending with them to the dark abode of the elephant, he requested them to accompany him. On entering it, he said the animal was before them, and asked them if they could see it. Being answered in the negative, he begged them to approach and feel it, which they did, each touching it in a different part. After returning to the light, he asked them if they believed the animal really existed, and what it was like. One declared it was a huge column; another, that it was a rough hide; a third, that it was of ivory; a fourth, that it was huge flaps of some coarse substance, &c., but not one could correctly state what the animal was. Now, returning to the same chamber, to which the light of heaven fully penetrated, these learned men beheld, for the first time, the object of their curiosity, and learned that, whilst each one was correct in what he had said, all differed widely from the truth.

"Such, now, said the prince, is God; men judge of Him according to their sensual capacities, differing from each other, but all equally true, when they feel and search for the truth, without doubting of His existence."

Similar doctrines came to light in the fourteenth century, in Christendom, among the Beguins, condemned by the Council of Vienna, in Dauphiny, and which taught, among other anti-social principles, that the practice and the observance of the law is only for the imperfect, and that the perfect are exempt from it. Like these latter, the Dervishes tend to the overthrow of all authority, political or religious. "Men who conduct themselves according to the laws of society form one class,—those who consume the love of God form another. The lovers of God are the people of no other than God."

"The last fragment of the dogma had thus departed, at the same time that the foundation of all morality was destroyed. One only principle remained, and marked the ruin of religious enthusiasm and sacerdotal imposture. This was submission to their inspired institutor (the *Pir*), which took the place amongst the Dervishes of the individual interpretation, which is the basis of Sofeism. I have already cited the narration of the Founder of the Mevlevees, regarded by all the Dervishes, indistinctively, as one of the greatest masters of the spiritual life. 'O my master, you have completed my doctrine by teaching me that you are God, and that all is God.' Already nearly four centuries previous, Bayazid of Bestamee, the founder of the Bestamees, had identified himself with the Divinity, when he cried out, in the presence of his disciples, alluding to his own person, 'Glory to me! I am above all things!'—a formula which, in the language of Orientals, is applied exclusively to God. The adoration of the Master replaces also for the Dervishes the worship of the Divinity; the end of the being no longer dwelt in the intimate union of the soul with the Creator, but in an absolute conformity to the thoughts of the Sheikh. 'Whatever you may do, whatever you may think, have always your Sheikh present in your mind.' Such is the first obligation, the only one, so to speak, imposed on the Dervish, and expressed by this species of mental prayer, called *Rabouta*, to which he is not less exact in the performance than the ordinary Mussulman is to his Namâz."

"The consequences of such a doctrine did not fail to be soon felt, and produced these sectarians, half religious, half political, who call themselves, according to the places, the *reds*, the *whites*, the *masked* (borkay), the *intimates* (bâtinee), the *allegorists*, or *interpreters* (muteewwil), *Karmathites, Ismailites*, &c., and of which traces in history, from the second to thes eventh century of the Hejra, are marked with blood and ruins. The orthodox designate them by the generic name of *Moulhâd* (rascals), or of *Sindeek* (strong minds). The most celebrated were the Ismailites, or assassins (derived from *Hashâsheens* (eaters of the Hasheesh), who originated, as is well known, in Persia; the remains of whom are still to be seen in the mountains above Tripoli (of Syria) and of Tortosia. In fact, Persia was the classic land of Dervishism, both from the decided inclination to mysticism, which always distinguished its inhabitants, and from the effect of the Shee'ite dogma, where the belief in the hidden Imâm (the Mehdee), and who is still expected, like the Messiah among the Jews, favours the ambition of the impostures of the sectarians. Add to this the *éclat* of the names of Sa'di and Hâfiz, and the great number of the celebrated poets of Persia, who were all either Dervishes or affiliated to their Orders, and whose works are placed in the highest rank of the books on Spirituality. They represented, moreover, in their writings, rather the philosophical than the political side of the doctrine. These are dreamers, inspired songsters, moralists sometimes of a singular character; they are neither ambitious sectarians nor repining hypocrites. But one must read their *gazels* (odes), each line of which is filled with ecstatic ravings, to comprehend how far mysticism may be carried in poetry, to surpass by the sensuality of expression and the crudity of images, the material paintings of a most voluptuous nature. Nothing of this kind, not even the invocation to Venus by Lucretius, equals the passage of the *Mesnevi*, where the poet shows us, in the soft Persian idiom, all Nature filled with that Divine love, by which the humble plant even is excited to seek after the sublime object of its desires. The adoration of the creature, under that of God; the terrestrial love taught as the bridge over which all must pass who seek for the beatitude of divine love; the apotheosis of matter under the glorification of the mind: such are the familiar reveries of the Persian poets. These are Sofies rather than Dervishes. At the same time, they show themselves careful, for the most part, to preserve the purity and sincerity of the doctrine. The eighth chapter of the Gulistan of Sa'di is full of instruction for Dervishes, and of reprimands for those who make of spiritual life an act of hypocrisy. These austerities and mortifications—this dirty and neglected exterior—this affected contempt of all ordinary decency, does not inspire him with any confidence. 'Have,' he says, 'the virtues of a true Dervish, and afterwards, in place of a cap of wool, take, if you choose, the felt of a Tartar,' for the Turks have a proverb which says, 'Dervishlik khirkâdan belli deghildir,' *i.e.* 'The Dervish is not known by the mantle which he wears.'"

He next seeks to describe and define the ecstasy which he regards, in the same manner as all of the Soofees, as the end of the being, and the last effort of our nature. "But how render, with the language of man, that which is beyond human powers? The words which we use cannot express other than what is common to our material and gross ideas. He who enjoys ecstasy and returns again to his ordinary state, does not retain any idea of it, because he has again become man, whilst previously Divine love had consumed in him all that belonged to human nature. The poet comments thus upon his idea with the aid of an allegory. 'A Dervish, interrogated with decision by one of his brethren, as to what marvellous gift he brought back with him from the garden of delights out of which he had come, replied:

"I intended, on arriving at this rose-bush (the sight of God), to fill the skirt of my robe with roses, so as to offer them as a present to my brethren; but when I was there, the odour of the rose-bush so intoxicated my senses that the border of my robe escaped from my hands." The tongue of that man is dulled who has known God.'

"Such was the favour which the Dervishes enjoyed in Persia, that one of them, Shâh Ismail Sefevee, who pretended to be descended from Moosâ, the seventh revealed Imâm, reached the throne in the tenth century of the Hejra (A.D. 1501), and founded the dynasty of princes, known in Europe under the name of the *Sophees*. The Ottoman Sultans, and the Khalifs their predecessors, had only waited until then to act against the Dervish system; and, justly alarmed at its progress, took it upon themselves to do all in their power to suppress it. The 'Ulemâs, in turn, also excited, under the plea of defending Mussulman orthodoxy, but in reality to maintain its spiritual supremacy, became their auxiliaries in a struggle wherein the altar and the throne, the power of the sovereign and that of the mosque, were equally in danger. It even happened that the people, at certain moments, adopted the same, as the result of the deep antipathy which the *Sunnees* entertained against the *Shee'ees*. This triple intervention of political power, of the 'Ulemâs, and of popular instinct, presents the matter under three different aspects.

"Political power acted directly, by brute force,—as, for example, on the occasion of the attempt made, in 1656, under the Grand Vizirat of Mohammed Kuprulee, to destroy entirely the Mevlevee Dervishes, the Khalvetees, Jelvetees, and the Shemisees. But in general these attempts proved unsuccessful, and only served to show more and more the impotency of the Government and the growing credit of the religious Orders. One remarks that the first is afraid; its acts of violence, even, accuse its pusillanimity, or at least embarrass its situation; it fears revolts, defections; it fears, above all, the Janissaries, who were united by a kind of fraternity, to the Dervishes,—especially to the Bektâshees. This fraternity dated back even to the origin of this militia. When the second Sultan of the Ottomans, Orkhân, created, in 1328, the *Yenicherees*, (new troops) —the name which Europeans have changed into 'Janissaries,'—he wished, conformably with the same political principles which led the Khalifs to have their ordinances sanctioned by the *Fetvâ* of the *Muftee*, to impress a religious seal upon this military institution. Hâjee Bektâsh, a venerable Sheikh, and founder of the Bektâsh Dervishes, blessed the troops by putting on the heads of the principal officers the sleeve of his robe, which has since then figured in the head-dress of the Janissaries, as a piece of felt which hung down behind their cap; and since then, also, an indestructible solid feeling was established between the Dervishes and the Janissaries, who considered themselves as possessing a common origin; and that, as a double expression of the same idea, they were, at the same time, both a religious and a military body.

"The intervention of the 'Ulemâs was more pacific in its form, yet more hostile, more constant, and more systematic. There existed, in point of fact, not only a rivalry of interests, but also one of doctrines. Ambition, pride, fanaticism, *amour propre*,—all the human passions were brought into play. It was both a battle and a dispute. The 'Ulemâs being unable to attack the basis of the Dervishes, so long as it continued to remain secret, fought, in the name of the Koran and the Sunna, the principles which served as a basis to the Institution,—such as abstinence, vows, music and dances, used in the Tekkiehs, the gift of miracles and communication directly with God, claimed by the Sheikhs, as contrary to the letter and spirit of Islamism. They recalled the example of the first disciples of the Prophet, of Osman, 'Alee, and 'Abd er Rahman, who was the first to vow not to approach his wife Esmeh, from one sunrise to another; the second, not to sleep until morning; the third, not to take any food for twenty-four hours; and the Prophet reprimanded them for it with a *Hadees*, since become celebrated. Soon after this, as it happens, the Dervishes abating in the prudence and severity which form a rule of their Orders, as their influence increased, let out the last word of their doctrine. This last word, the dominant idea of the Institution, was nothing less, one may say, than an attempt at a Christian priesthood, and a divine church, clearly designated by the Living God, who figures among the seven attributes of the Dervish symbol, viz.

1. There is no God, except God.
2. The Omnipotent God.
3. The Eternal God.
4. The Judging God.
5. The Living God (upon Earth).
6. The Existing God (in Heaven).
7. The All Omnipotent God ;—

attributes figured in the seven firmaments, and the seven principal colours, *i.e.*, white, black, red, yellow, blue, deep green, and light green. At the same time, it became known that it terminated with certain prayers anathematizing the Ommaide Khalifs, and glorifying 'Alee. Then their adversaries could knowingly accuse them, not only of wishing to introduce a new dogma, but also of mixing up impious dogmas and abominable practices; to give themselves up to orgies of every kind, in the Tekkiehs; to blaspheme the Koran; to deny even the existence of God; to preach disobedience to all established temporal powers, and to trample upon all divine and human laws. The Middle Age has put upon record similar accusations, which public opinion proclaimed against the Templars before their condemnation.

"Popular opposition held, as I have said, to the puritanism of Sunnite orthodoxy, and to the horror which zealous Mussulmans have professed at all times against the Shee'ites, whose doctrines they willingly confounded with those of the Dervishes; but this was neither general nor regular; its habitual mode of expressing it was by mockery. Turkish literature is full of tales and satires upon the Dervishes, in which they are little better treated than our monks were in the fables of the tenth and eleventh centuries. These consist in jocosity and drolleries, so to speak, in entire freedom of thought and language. One author says, in allusion to the Dervishes, 'An ill-dressed body, hands without a farthing, and an empty stomach, are the characteristics of those whom God honours with His intimate friendship.'—'If you wish to know,' says another, 'some of the qualities of a good Dervish, they are the following: he must have ten of those which are peculiar to the dog, viz., always hungry, homeless, sleepless at night, no heirs after death, to bark at passers-by,' &c. Moreover, by a contrast which confirms the reconcilement which I have just pointed out, one does not see that these constant jokes at the expense of the Dervishes, affect in any manner their credit with the people, and matters go on exactly in Turkey as they did in France and Italy during the Middle Ages, where the monks were never more powerful than when they were the object of public raillery.

"It is thus that the Dervishes continued to exist, notwithstanding the odium and ridicule with which it was attempted to cover them, having, at the same time, the *Firmâns* of the Sultan, the Fetvâs of the Muftees, the jeers and curses of the public, whilst daily they beheld their authority increase, in the face even of all the vain efforts of their enemies to destroy them. Sultan Mahmood was the first to strike them a severe blow, by the abolition of the Janissaries; but this was only a prelude to a more precise and personal attack. Twenty-six days after, the 10th of July, 1826, he took advantage of a revolt which occurred in consequence of the suppression of the Janissaries, and in which the Bektâshees were accused of being mixed up, to finish with these fanatics. After having consulted with the Muftee and the principal 'Ulemâs, the three chiefs of the congregation were publicly executed, the Order was abolished, the Tekkiehs were reduced to ruins, the greater part of the Dervishes exiled, and those who were allowed to remain in Constantinople, were made to leave off their distinctive costume. This bold step spread terror among the Dervishes. At one moment they thought that all of their Orders would be immediately dispersed, and they remained noiseless, waiting the advent of their last day, 'devoured with anguish, and their backs leaning against the wall of stupefication.'

"Unfortunately Sultan Mahmood hesitated. 'He who had not feared;' so says the historian of the massacre of the Janissaries, 'to open with the sword a road to public happiness, cutting away the thorny bushes which obstructed his way and tore his Imperial mantle,' stopped before the sole measure which could insure success to the completion of his work. The opportunity once passed, could not be regained. The Dervishes renewed their audacity with their hopes, and silently recommenced to agitate the public. Even the Sultan came near falling a victim of the fanatic zeal of one of them. One day, in 1837, whilst he was crossing, surrounded by his guards, the bridge of Galata, a Dervish, known by the name of Sheikh Sâchlu (the Hairy Sheikh), and whom the people venerated as a saint, sprang forward in front of his horse, and cried out in a fury, 'Ghiour Pâdishah' (infidel sovereign), 'art thou not yet satisfied with abominations? Thou wilt answer to Allah for all your impieties; thou destroyest the institutions of thy brethren; thou revilest Islamism, and drawest the vengeance of the Prophet upon thyself, and upon us.' The Sultan, who feared the effect of such a scene upon the public, commanded one of his officers to rid the way of such a man, whom he declared was a fool. 'Fool!' screamed out the Dervish with indignation, 'me a fool? it is yourself and your unworthy councillors who have lost your senses. To the rescue, Mussulmans! The spirit of God which anoints me, and which I obey, compels me to declare the truth, and promises me a recompense given to the saints.' He was arrested and put to death, and the next day news spread over the whole city that a brilliant light had been visible during the whole night, over the tomb of the martyr.*

* It is, however, well known that Sultan Mahmood was an affiliated member of the Mevlevee Tekkieh of Pera, and frequently visited it. He also frequently visited a Nakshibendee Tekkieh at

"It is by the pretended miracles which are daily renewed under the eyes of the authority that the Dervishes keep alive in the public mind their ancient superstitions and the idea of their supernatural powers. An Ottoman filling an eminent position in the state once remarked to me, 'Our ministers labour in vain for that civilization which will never enter Turkey so long as the turbehs (holy tombs) are in existence.' We were at the time at Scutary, where we had assisted at a representation of the 'Howling Dervishes.' We had observed various individuals brought into the Tekkieh from without, sick and infirm, women, aged persons, and even children as young as two or three days, who were laid on their backs before the Sheikh for him to cure them, not by the imposition of his hands, but of his feet. When he had finished and left the inside of the Tekkieh, not only did the crowd prostrate themselves before him and kiss his robes, as they would have done to a saint, but the guards actually presented arms and beat their drums in honour of him. 'See,' said my companion, 'the Government which hates the Dervishes, and only desires to get rid of them, not only tolerates them and keeps well with them, but even aids them to be powerful by causing military honours to be shown them. You can scarcely imagine, after what you have seen, the impudence of these rascals. Lately, a Dervish of Bokhara (you must know that these surpass all others in fanaticism) presented himself before Reshid Pasha, and there publicly, in the path itself, heaped upon him abuse and threats, calling him a dog, an infidel and disbeliever, and invoking upon his head the lightning of heaven and the dagger of every true Mussulman. The Vezir, so as to remove all pretext for a commotion, which began to show itself, had to content himself with putting him out of his room by a Kavas; and that, too, politely, as he would have done

Fondukli, where he witnessed the ecstatic swoon of the Sheikh. The latter on one occasion revived, much to his amusement, on learning that the Sultan was about to leave, so as to secure a royal present.

to any poor fellow who had lost his senses. You are astonished? There is scarcely a month or a week that some of the ministers have to submit to the remonstrances of any Dervish who is pleased to push himself forward at his audiences for the purpose of abusing and threatening him. It is the effect of this fanaticism, nourished by the Dervishes, and this freedom of language, which the people use in the presence of public authority, that creates the explosions during the month of Ramazan. Here this is nothing, where the Government has its eyes upon them; but in certain provinces, at Bagdad, in Arabia, in Egypt, their daring and cynicism is carried beyond all limits. Will you believe that I saw at Cairo, in full daylight, one of these miserable creatures who run about the streets half-naked, stop a woman in the street and glut his brutality upon her, in the presence even of passers-by, who turned their faces away, some out of respect, others from disgust, without one calling upon the aid of the police. I do not know which carries the palm among these bandits, hypocrisy or fanaticism, two things which seem, however, to exclude each other. May God preserve you from ever meeting one of them in the public road, for these vagabond Dervishes who, under the name of Seyyâhs (travellers) infest most of the routes, where they live by begging and robbery. Many of the most dangerous of them are strangers; they travel by the order of their superiors to collect money, or have been dismissed from their convents for grave causes: these are Kalenders whose statutes do not allow them to have any fixed abodes—in fact, they are no better than unknown individuals or criminals, who, under the cover of a Dervish cloak, escape punishments richly merited by their actions.'

"My interlocutor added many things on the difficulties of the position of the case in general. I was struck with the consideration which he finally expressed: 'What we lose is the want of faith in our work; some are discouraged into inertia, others hasten to arrive at a goal which has no stability. You say that God is patient because He is eternal; but we are impatient because we fear that we have but a few hours to live, and we feel the future fly away from us.'

"But let us return to the subject of the Dervishes by attempting to resume the idea of this latter and the preceding one. The two bodies of which religious society in Turkey is composed—the 'Ulemâ and the Dervishes—are the enemies of all reform. The danger, however, is not equal on both sides, neither for the Government nor for society. The 'Ulemâ speak in the name of the law, of which they pretend to be guardian and the depository; they say, 'Touch nothing which has been established, borrow nothing from the infidels, because the law forbids it.' The Sheikh says, 'There is no law,' or rather, 'The law is I; all is good that I commend, all is evil that I forbid. You must kill your mother, your sovereign, if I bid it, for my sentence is the sentence of God.' One thus sees the difference between the two doctrines. On the one hand, the Government may hope to have the 'Ulemâ on its side; many of them are not wanting either in acquired information or in natural light. The example of the Sheikh-ul-Islâm and the principal chiefs of the magistracy in Turkey, who form a part of the Government, may do much with them. Old prejudices commence to lose ground, especially among the 'Ulemâs of Constantinople in contact with Europeans. One of them—a most wonderful thing—has actually allowed himself to be sent to Paris by the Diwân, which desired to show him that civilization which he and his brethren reject without possessing any knowledge of it. This new attempt on the part of Reshid Pasha will do more, if it succeeds, for the emancipation of Turkey than has been as yet done by the mission to Paris and London of many young Turks to study there; and who, having left there without any direction or fixed rule of action, have badly answered in general to the hopes placed upon them. The 'Ulemâs may be thus brought to comprehend that, even by sacrificing their privileges, there still remains to them a fair place in the State, and that their interests are actually the same as its own. But this cannot be said of the Dervishes; between them and it there is a mortal conflict."

As it has been my object throughout the present little work to enable the curious and patient reader to judge of the Dervishes both by what they say of themselves and by what others say regarding them, I would not terminate my extracts without placing before their eyes the words of that eminent Orientalist, Sir William Jones—than whom, perhaps, no greater has ever lived—on the subject of the leading principles of the Dervishes, *alias* Sufaism. In his lecture "On the Philosophy of the Asiaticks," this wonderful Eastern linguist says:—

"From all the properties of man and of nature, from all the various branches of science, from all the deductions of human reason, the general corollary admitted by Hindus, Arabs, and Tartars, by Persians, and by Chinese, is the supremacy of an all-creating, and all-preserving Spirit, infinitely wise, good, and powerful, but infinitely removed from the comprehension of his most exalted creatures; nor are there in any language (the ancient Hebrew always excepted) more pious and sublime addresses to the Being of beings, more splendid enumerations of His attributes, or more beautiful descriptions of His visible works than in Arabic, Persian, and Sanscrit, especially in the Koran, the introductions to the poems of Saadi, Nizami, and Firdausi; the four Vedas, and many parts of the numerous Purânas; but supplication and praise would not satisfy the boundless imagination of the Vedânti and Sufi theologists, who, blending uncertain metaphysics with undoubted principles of religion, have presumed to reason confidently on the very nature and essence of the Divine Spirit, and asserted in a very remote age—what multitudes of Hindus and Mussulmans assert at this hour—that all spirit is homogenous, that the Spirit of God is in *kind* the same with that of man, though differing from it infinitely in *degree*, and that as material substance is mere illusion, there exists in this universe only one generic spiritual substance the sole primary cause, efficient, substantial, and formal of all secondary causes and of all appearances whatever, but endowed in its highest degree with a sublime providential wisdom, and proceeding by ways incomprehensible to the spirits which emanate from it; an opinion which Gotama never taught, and which we have no authority to believe; but which, as it is grounded on the doctrine of an immaterial Creator supremely wise, and a constant Preserver supremely benevolent, differs as widely from the pantheism of Spinoza and Toland as the affirmation of a proposition differs from the negative of it; though the last-named professor of that insane philosophy had the baseness to conceal his meaning under the very words of St. Paul, which are cited for a purpose totally different by Newton, and has even used a phrase which occurs, indeed, in the *Veda*, but in a sense diametrically opposite to that which he would have given it. The passage to which I allude is in a speech of Varuna to his son, where he says, 'That Spirit from which these created beings proceed, through which having proceeded from it they live; towards which they tend and in which they are ultimately absorbed; *that* Spirit study to know; *that* Spirit is the Great One.'"

In the "Sixth Discourse on the Persians," he says :—

"I will only detain you with a few remarks on that metaphysical theology which has been professed immemorially by a numerous sect of Persians and Hindus, was carried in part into Greece, and prevails even now among the learned Mussulmans, who sometimes avow it without reserve. The modern philosophers of this persuasion are called *Sufis*, either from the Greek word for a *sage*, or from the *woollen* mantle which they used to wear in some provinces of Persia; their fundamental tenets are, that nothing exists absolutely but God; that the human soul is an emanation from His essence, and though divided for a time from its heavenly source, will be finally reunited with it; that the highest possible happiness will arise from its reunion, and that the chief good of mankind in this transitory world consists in as perfect an *union* with the Eternal Spirit as the incumbrances of a mortal frame will allow; that, for this purpose, they should break all connexion (or *taâlluk*, as they call it) with extrinsick objects, and pass through life without attachments, as a swimmer in the ocean strikes freely without the impediment of clothes; that they should be straight and free as the cypress, whose fruit is hardly perceptible, and not sink under a load like fruit-trees attached to a trellis; that, if mere earthly charms have power to influence the soul, the *idea* of celestial beauty must overwhelm it in ecstatick delight; that, for want of apt words to express the divine perfections and the ardour of devotion, we must borrow such expressions as approach the nearest to our ideas, and speak of *beauty* and *love* in a transcendant and mystical sense; that, like a *reed* torn from its native brook, like *wax* separated from its delicious honey, the soul of man bewails its disunion with melancholy *musick*, and sheds burning tears like the lighted taper, waiting passionately for the moment of its extinction, as a disengagement from earthly trammels, and the means of returning to its only beloved. Such in part (for I omit the minuter and more subtil metaphysicks of the Sufis which are mentioned in the *Dabistan*) is the wild and enthusiastick religion of the modern Persian poets, especially of the sweet Hafiz and the great Maulavi (Mevlevee); such is the system of the Vedanti philosophers and best lyrick poets of India; and, as it was a system of the highest antiquity of both nations, it may be added to the many other proofs of an immemorial affinity between them."

"On the Philosophy of the Asiaticks," he says:—

"I have already had occasion to touch on the Indian metaphysicks of natural bodies according to the most celebrated of the Asiatic schools, from which the Pythagoreans are supposed to have borrowed many of their opinions; and, as we learn from Cicero, that the old sages of Europe had an idea of centripetal force and a principle of universal gravitation (which they never indeed attempted to demonstrate), so I can venture to affirm, without meaning to pluck a leaf from the never-fading laurels of our immortal Newton, that the whole of his theology and part of his philosophy may be found in the Vedas, and even in the works of the Sufis; that *most subtil spirit* which he suspected to pervade natural bodies and lying concealed in them, to cause attraction and repulsion, the emission, reflection, and refraction of light, electricity, calefaction, sensation, and muscular motion, is described by the Hindoos as a *fifth element* endowed with those very powers; and the Vedas abound with allusions to a force universally attractive, which they chiefly ascribe to the sun, thence called *Aditya*, or the attractor, a name designed by the mythologists to mean the child of the goddess Aditi; but the most wonderful passage in the theory of attraction occurs in the charming allegorical poem of "Shirin and Ferhad, or the Divine Spirit and a Human Soul disinterestedly pious," a work which from the first verse to the last is a blaze of religious and poetical fire. The whole passage appears to me so curious that I make no apology for giving you a faithful translation of it:—

"'There is a strong propensity which dances through every atom, and attracts the minutest particle to some peculiar object; search this universe from its base to its summit, from fire to air, from water to earth, from all below the moon to all above the celestial spheres, and thou wilt not find a corpuscle destitute of that natural attractibility; the very point of the first thread in this apparently tangled skein is no other than such a principle of attraction, and all principles beside are void of a real basis; from such a propensity arises every motion perceived in heavenly or in terrestrial bodies; it is a disposition to be attracted which taught hard steel to rush from its place and rivet itself on the magnet; it is the same disposition which impels the light straw to attach itself firmly to amber; it is this quality which gives every substance in nature a tendency toward another, and an inclination forcibly directed to a determinate point.'"

From the preceding extracts of this learned scholar, and those of the first chapter of the present work, the intelligent reader will readily perceive the strong affinity which exists between the principles of the Vedas of India and the metaphysical and philosophical writings of the Soofees. The religion of Brahma has been carried into Persia and even Arabia, and been engrafted upon that of Islâmism by the Dervishes. It would be interesting to trace the connexion which existed between the ideas of the sages of Greece and those of India. Whilst with these the original oneness of the Deity became extended into an infinity of secondary gods, Islâmism has retained the purity of the Mosaic principle of a One Supreme, Omniscient, and Omnipotent Creator, possessing a great number of *attributes*, which are not personified as with the Hindoos and the Greeks. In the religion of the former it is impossible not to perceive traces of the creation, of the history of man as revealed to Adam, handed down to his posterity, and chronicled by the earliest historian of the human race—Moses.

In support of this assertion I would add the following extract from Sir William Jones's lecture "On the Gods of Greece, Italy, and India."

"That water was the primitive element and first work of the creative power is the uniform opinion of the Indian philosophers; but as they give so particular an account of the general deluge and of the creation, it can never be admitted that their whole system arose from traditions concerning the flood only, and must appear indubitable that this doctrine is in part borrowed from the opening of *Birásit*, or Genesis, than which a sublimer passage from the first word to the last never flowed, or will flow, from any human pen.

"'In the beginning God created the heavens and the earth. And the earth was void and waste, and darkness was upon the face of the deep, and the Spirit of God moved upon the face of the waters. And God said, Let light be, and light was.'

"The sublimity of this passage is considerably diminished by the Indian paraphrase of it, with which Menu, the son of Brahmâ, begins his address to the Sages, who consulted him on the formation of the universe.

"'This world,' says he, 'was all darkness, undiscernible, undistinguishable, altogether as in a profound sleep, till the self-existent, invisible God, making it manifest with five elements, and other glorious forms, perfectly dispelled the gloom. He, desiring to raise up various creations by an emanation from His own glory, first created the waters, and impressed them with a power of motion.'

"To this curious description, with which the Mânava Sàstra begins, I cannot refrain from subjoining the four verses which are the text of the Bhâgavat, and are believed to have been pronounced by the Supreme Being to Brahmâ.

"'Even I was, even at first, not any other thing (existed), that which exists unperceived, supreme; afterwards, I am that which is; and He, who must remain, am I.

"'Except the first cause, whatever may appear, and may not appear in the mind, know that to be the mind's *Mâyâ* (or delusion) as light and darkness.

"'As the first elements are in various beings, entering, yet not entering (that is, pervading, not destroying), thus am I in them, yet not in them.

"'Even thus far may inquiry be made by him who seeks to know the principle of mind, in union and separation, which must be everywhere always.'

"The Hindoos believe that when a soul leaves its body, it immediately repairs to *Yamapur*, or the city of *Yama*, when it receives a just sentence from him, and either ascends to *Swerga*, or the first heaven, or is driven down to *Nârac*, the region of serpents, or assumes on earth the form of some animal, unless its offences had been such that it ought to be condemned to a vegetable, or even to a mineral poison."

THE HINDEE, OR THE WANDERING DERVISHES OF INDIA.

In the list of the various *Tekkiehs* of Constantinople given previously, mention is made of that called the Hindeeler Tekkiehsee. This is also a Mesjid, or chapel, situated near the Mosque of Murad Pasha Jiamassee. It is the refuge of all those wandering Dervishes who, from the distant clime of Hindostan, visit Stambool.

A Dervish friend informs me that the greater part of these belong to the Order of the Nakshibendees, Kidârees, Cheshtees, Kubravees, Ni'metullahees, and Kalenderees.

These natives of India, after performing the *Be'at*, or initiation required by the Order of their profession, and receiving the blessing of its Sheikh, set out on their travels, depending upon the alms and charities of the public for a subsistence. But few make the journey by land, and mostly take passage from Bombay to Jiddeh, in the Red Sea, on their way to the holy cities of the Hejâs. They there perform the usual *Hajj*, or pilgrimage of all Mussulmans, and next proceed across the country by land to Bagdad. Some re-embark at Jiddeh for Basserah, in the Persian Gulf. The object of this journey is to visit the holy graves of Hazreti 'Alee, Hazreti Husain, Imâm 'Abbâs, and the other sons of the fourth Caliph 'Alee. At Bagdad they remain at the Tekkieh and Jiâmee of Hazret, Sheikh 'Abdul Kâdir Ghilânee, the founder of the Kâdirees. Some of them sit as night-watchers (Bekjees) in the bazaars of Bagdad, and do not beg. At other times their home is the great establishment of the Kâdirees aforementioned. At the entrance to this is the grave of Hazreti 'Abdul Jebbâr, son of the founder, before which the newly-arrived Hindee spends three days, as a trial of his faith, and if he prove to be a Majoosee, or Idolater in disguise, it is said that he cannot possibly support the ordeal of prayer and fasting. A superior spiritual influence is supposed to be exercised against him, and before the termination of that period, he is self-condemned, and flies from exposure and ill-treatment.

It is only after he has visited the other sacred tombs, and performed all the devotionary exercises required, that he really begins his career of mendicity. By some he is called a Fakeer (poor man), and it may be added that the greater number are not affiliated in any particular Order or Tareek, but simply indigent Mussulmans, who have vowed to make a visit (Ziyâret) to certain holy tombs in the distance, and difficulties in which he finds religious merit. To do this, these Fakeers abandon father, mother, wife, children, and friends, and all they may possess. This abnegation of all the pleasures and comforts of life places them above the ordinary *convenances* of society, and they affect to respect no one, whatever may be his official position; and their poverty and miserable appearance preserves them from punishment when their remarks are insolent.

Among the anecdotes relating to Dervishes of this category, I add the following:—

"Once, when a king was passing near a Dervish, the latter, who was seated on the ground, neither arose to his feet nor otherwise offered any tokens of respect; so that the king, being of an irascible temper, was offended by his want of regard, and exclaimed, 'These ragged individuals are no better in manners than so many wild beasts.' The Vizir, or minister of the king, cried out to the Dervish, and asked him why he thus failed in respect to the king? 'Tell your master,' replied the Dervish, 'to look for respect from those who need his bounties, and that, as sovereigns are for the protection of the people, the latter are under no obligation to court their duties by external marks of respect.' On this reply, the King directed the Vizir to ask the Dervish what he could do for him, and, in reply, the latter said that all he wished was to be let alone."

"A Dervish, speaking to a king who entertained but little respect for persons of his condition, said: 'We have neither the strength, nor the power, which you possess in this world; but I am sure we are all the happier for it. After death, we are all equals; and after the day of judgment, we are your superiors.'"

"A thief once asked a *Fakeer*, if he was not ashamed to stretch out his hand and beg alms of passers-by? The latter replied, that it was better to do that, than have his hand cut off for thieving."

"A king had vowed that, if he should succeed in an affair which he was about to undertake, he would distribute a handsome sum of money among the poorer Dervishes of his capital. Having met with the desired success, he confided the distribution of the money to one of his officers. The latter, not being favourably impressed with the character of the Dervishes, kept the money until nightfall, and then returned it to the king, remarking, that he had not been able to find any such in his capital. The king was much surprised, and said that there must be several hundreds; but the officer replied, 'Dervishes do not accept money, and those who do are not Dervishes.'"

A Dervish, as above said, should possess ten of the characteristics of a dog, viz.: he should be always hungry; he should have no home; he should not sleep even at night; he should leave no inheritance at his death; he should never forsake his master, even if the latter illtreat him; he should be satisfied with the lowest and most humble place; he should give up his place to whoever wishes it, and take another; return to whoever beats him, when he offers him a piece of bread; he should remain at a distance when food is served up; and he should never think of returning to the place he has left, when he is following his master.

Conformably with the preceding, a Dervish, after having been frequently invited to a great man's house, was often driven away by his servants; and when the master, to whom the fact became known, apologized for such illtreatment, and expressed his admiration for the humility and patience which he had shown, the Dervish remarked that it was not a merit, but only one of the characteristics of a dog, which always returns, when driven away.

CHAPTER XVI.*

ON THE TESAVVUF, OR SPIRITUAL LIFE OF THE SOOFEES.

TRANSLATED FROM THE TURKISH OF MOHEMMED MISSIREE.

THE word "soof" signifies in Arabic "wool," and Mr. Lane, in his 102d note on the 10th chapter of the "Arabian Nights," says that the so-called Soofees derive their title either from their wearing woollen garments, or from the Greek word σοφός, because of their philosophical tenets. He adds, that "there is an Order of Muslim Darweeshes called Soofees, 'who make profession of a more regular and more contemplative life than Darweeshes in general; and many of this class have written books of spirituality, of devotion, and of contemplation, which mostly bear the title of "Tasowwuf," that is, of spiritual life.' . . . The Sunnee Soofees are in a great degree mystical and latitudinarian; but not so much so as the Soofees of the Persian sect."

In all the tekkiehs, or convents, of the various sects which I have visited the members sit on sheep-skins, called postakees. Many also wear white felt caps made of wool, and even their cloaks are of an uncoloured stuff of the same material.

The Order of the Bektâshees, which was intimately connected with the Yanicherees, wear white felt caps, and believe in the *tenassuh*, a system of metempsychosis.

TRANSLATION.

"A few remarks on the subject of the *tesavvuf* (lit., profession of Soofeeism, or spiritual life), by the learned

* This chapter originally appeared in the Journal of the American Oriental Society.

and pious Mohemmed Messiree—may his precious grave be blessed!

"In the name of the Clement and Merciful God.

"Praise be to the Lord of the Universe (lit., the present and future world). Prayers and Peace [from his people] be upon our Sayd (Lord) Mohemmed [the Prophet], and 'Alee [his cousin and son-in-law], and all other prophets, and the family and Ashabs (Companions) of Mohemmed.

"[*Question.*]—Should any person ask what is the beginning of the *tesavvuf*, the answer is:

"[*Answer.*]—Faith, which has six columns, to wit: 'The existence of God,' 'His Unity,' 'the Angels,' 'the Prophets,' 'the Day of Resurrection,' and 'Good and Evil through His Predestination'—all of which are to be spoken with the tongue, and acknowledged with the heart.

"[*Q.*]—What is the conclusion and end of the *tesavvuf*?

"[*A.*]—It is the pronouncing with the tongue of faith the six preceding columns, and the confirming of them with the heart, as was said by Junaydee, in answer to an interrogation on the subject of the end of the *tesavvuf*.

"[*Q.*]—What is the distinction between the *Soffa* (lit., the clarified) and common people?

"[*A.*]—The knowledge [which is the foundation] of the faith of the latter is only an imitation of these six columns, whilst the faith of the *Soffa* is the true, as is shown by the evidences of the *ulema i uzama* (doctors of the sects).

"[*Q.*]—In what does this imitation consist?

"[*A.*]—This imitation is what has been learned from their fathers, the *imaams* (preachers) of the quarters in which they live, or from one of the *ulema*, and so believed; but they do not know why it has become a fundamental rule to believe in these Columns of Faith, nor how salvation is obtained thereby. It is not known that, whilst walking in the public streets, one has found a jewel which many sovereigns sought after unsuccessfully—conquering the world from one end to the other, and finding everything else but it. He who has found it, has found a light brighter than the sun, when it obscures the lesser lustre of the moon, and found an alchemy which converts copper of a thousand years old into pure gold. The finder, however, knows not its real value, and considers it only as a false jewel, which its possessor, if thirsty, might give away for a drink of water.

"[*Q.*]—What is the proof of faith?

"[*A.*]—The proof consists in a search made for the origin of each of the six columns above named, and one's arrival at the truth (*hakkikat*). The *ilm i tarikat* (science of the sects) is the distinctive path existing between a *taklid* village and a *taklid* city [*i.e.* only leads from one authority to another]. Many persons follow on that path for ten, others for twenty, others thirty, others forty years, wandering away from the truth, and entering each upon a different road of error. Some become Ehlee Jebree (persons who believe that God compels each action of man, and leaves no room for free will); some become Ehlee Kaderee (persons who hold that man has power to do good and evil); others are Ehlee Mutazelee; some again become Mujessemmees (Anthropomorphists); and others, Mushebbahees (those who define the appearance of God by portraits or otherwise). There are, in all, seventy-three ways or sects; each one following one of these wanders off, without ever arriving at the city of the true faith; only one of these seventy-three parties is in the right, called the Firkaï Najieh (Party of Salvation), and it is those alone who follow this way that reach the proper goal. Through their perfect subjection to the directions of the blessed Prophet, these know the real value of the jewel found by them. Their faith is manifest; and whilst proceeding, as it were, with a lamp, they have reached the sun. Though at first only imitators, they have finally found the truth. After finding the true faith, they turn their attention to the imitation (or semblance), and familiarize themselves with its interior. They find that the *tarikat* (paths of the Dervishes) and the *sheryat* (laws of Islam) are coincident. They have as yet only received sufficient inspiration from God to enable them to see the truth, which is hidden from those who still wander in the path of imitation. Comparing the two with each other, they consider them as being like the soul and the body, according to the words of the blessed Prophet: 'Whoever is deficient in one of his faculties, is deficient in one of his parts,' from which it is clear that whoever is deficient in the *sheryat* cannot be perfect in the *hakkikat.*

"[*Q.*]—In matters of faith and forms of worship, to what sect are the *Soffa* attached?

"[*A.*]—Most of them are of the Muslim faith, and of the sect of the Ehlee Sunneh (those who observe the traditionary precepts of the blessed Prophet), and accept the *jemâat* (prescribed forms of public prayer), according to the *mezheb* (creed) of the celebrated Sheikh Abu Mansur Matureedee. Most of the Arabs are of the creed of the Sheikh Abul Hassan el Esharee, and are Ehlee Sunneh, and accept the *jemâat*, as understood and practised in conformity with one or other of the four Rites, adopted in the country to which they belong (*i.e.* either the Haniffee, Hanballee, Shâfee, or Malekee). For instance, those of the country of Room are Haniffees, so called from Abu Haniffeh, who derived his articles of faith from the Koran and the *hadisat* (traditional sayings) of the blessed Prophet; those in Arabia, Egypt, and Aleppo, as well as in the two holy cities are Shâfees; all the people of Tunis and Morocco, and as far as Andalusia, as well as some in Arabia, are Malekees; most of the people of Bagdad, Iraak, and a part of Arabia, with some of the inhabitants of the holy cities, follow the Hanballee Imaam. There are some differences between these, but only such as refer to forms of worship; as regards dogmas, they all agree. The blessed Prophet designated those who observe the *sunneh* and *jemâat* by the title of Ehlee Vejah (the Saved), and these four are all of this kind. All the *Soffa* belong to the Ehlee Vejah. It is a point of belief among the *Soffa* that it is not for every one who is of the Ehlee Allah, or a *keramat sahibee* (*i.e.* either a believer in the Divinity, or particularly gifted by the Divinity), to attain to the character of sanctity belonging to the four great doctors of the holy law, much less to that of one of the Ehlee Kuzeen (the Twelve Imaams). The only means of arriving at their degrees of perfection would be to follow their creed until one surpassed it, and then to establish, by God's sanction, a new one superior to theirs—which, as yet, no one has ever been able to do.

"[*Q.*]—When Bayazid el Bestamee was asked of what sect he was, he replied: 'I am of the sect of Allah.' What did he mean by this answer?

"[*A.*]—All of the sects of Allah are those just mentioned. They are called [for example] the sects of the Greater Imaam (Numan ibin Sabit el Kuffee) and of the Shâfee Imaam, but are in reality sects of Allah; and so Bayazid spoke truly when he said he was of His sect.

"[*Q.*]—Most of the Soffees, in their *kassidehs*, use certain words which we hear and understand as showing that they were of the Ehlee Tenassuh (Metempsychosians). They say: 'I am sometimes Lot, sometimes Rayu, sometimes a vegetable, sometimes an animal, at other times a man.' What does this mean?

"[*A.*]—Brother! the blessed Prophet has said: 'My people, in the eternal life, will rise up in companies'—that is, some as monkeys, others as hogs, or in other forms—as is written in a verse of the Koran (chap. lxxviii. v. 18) which has been commented on by Kazee Beyzavee (this commentator cites a tradition to the effect that, at the resurrection, men will rise up in the form of those animals whose chief characteristics resemble their own ruling passions of life: the greedy, avaricious man, as a hog; the angry, passionate man, as a camel; the tale-bearer, or mischief-maker, as a monkey); because, though these men, while in this life, bore the human form externally, they were, internally, nothing different from the animals whose characters are in common with their own. The resemblance is not manifest during one's life, but becomes so in the other existence, after the resurrection. Let us avoid such traits; repentance before death will free any one from these evils. The blessed Prophet said with regard to this: 'Sleep is the brother of Death.' The dying man sees himself in his true character, and so knows whether or not he is, by repentance, freed from his ruling passion of life. In like manner, he will see himself during his slumbers, still following in the path of his passion. For instance, the money-calculator, in sleep, sees himself engaged in his all-absorbing occupation; and this fact is a warning from God, not to allow himself to be absorbed in any animal passion or degrading occupation. It is only by prayerful repentance that any one can hope to see himself, in his sleep, delivered from his ruling carnal passion, and restored to his proper human, intellectual form. If in your slumbers you see a monkey, consider it as a warning to abandon or abstain from the passion of mischief; if a hog, cease to seize upon the goods of others; and so on. Go and give yourself up to an upright *murshid* (spiritual guide), who will, through his prayers, show you in your slumbers the evil parts of your character, until one by one they have passed away, and have been replaced by good ones—all through the power of the name of God, whom he will instruct you to invoke: at length you will only see in your slumbers the forms of holy and pious men, in testimony of that degree of piety to which you will have attained.

"This is what is meant by that expression of certain poets, referring to one's condition previous to the act of repentance, when the writer says: 'I am sometimes an animal, sometimes a vegetable, sometimes a man;' and the same may be said by the Soffees, in application to themselves, of any other part of creation, for man is called the *akher i mevjudat* (the climax of beings): in him are comprised all the characteristics of creation. Many mystical books have been written on this subject, all showing that man is the *nuhaï kubra* (the larger part,) and the world, the *nuhaï sogra* (the smaller part), of God's creation. The human frame is said to comprise all the other parts of creation; and the heart* of man is

* Orientals consider the heart as the seat of mental capacity: and the liver, of the affections.

supposed to be even more comprehensive than the rainbow, because, when the eyes are closed, the mental capacity can take in the whole of a vast city: though not seen by the eyes, it is seen by the capacious nature of the heart. Among such books is the *Haoz el Hayat* (Well of Life), which says that, if a man closes his eyes, ears, and nostrils, he cannot take cold; that the right nostril is called the sun, and the left the moon; that from the former he breathes heat, and from the latter cold air. There is also a treatise entitled *Nuskhaï Kubra*, wholly on the subject of the superiority of man, which is one of the favourite works of the Soffees.

"[*Q.*]—Explain the distinctive opinions (*mezhebs*) of believers in the tenassuh, and of the Soffees.

"[*A.*]—We say that this system of metempsychosis has nothing to do with the *barzakh* (a name given to the intermediate period between death and the resurrection, mentioned in the 23d chapter of the Koran, 102d verse, in which departed souls receive neither rewards nor punishments: here, however, it means only a state of total indifference to all future life, into which some men fall in consequence of the vicious nature of their lives, or their spiritual demoralization). It is believed to be operative in eternity, or in the future state; it is declared, that it does not exist in the present life. For example, it is said that some men take the character of certain animals, not their forms, and that, when they die, their souls enter the bodies of such animals as they already resembled in character, and so, by natural propagation, they become the animals themselves, visible to the eye, and never again really die, or cease to exist in this world. In this manner, mankind leave the human form, and become, in turn, various animals, either through natural propagation, or by one animal devouring another, perpetually. Such is the belief of the Metempsychosians, and it is wholly inconsistent with the true faith. On this point Omar ibin el Farid has said: 'He who believes in transformation and transmigration stands in need of God's healing—keep thyself far removed from his belief!'

"O brother, keep far from such a belief, and have no

connexion with it. Of the seventy-two erring sects, before alluded to, this is the worst. God preserve us, in this life and the one to come, from participating with, or even beholding, such sectaries!

"[*Q.*]—These persons regard certain things as legally proper, which are forbidden. For instance, they command the use of wine, wine-shops, the wine-cup, sweethearts; they speak of the curls of their mistresses, the moles on their faces, cheeks, &c.; and compare the furrows on their brows to verses of the Koran. What does this mean?

"[*A.*]—Just as these Soffees leave the true faith for its semblance, so they also exchange the external features of all things for the internal (the corporeal for the spiritual), and give an imaginary signification to outward forms. They behold objects of a precious nature in their natural character, and for this reason the greater part of their words have a spiritual and visionary meaning. For instance, when, like Hafiz, they mention wine, they mean a knowledge of God, which, extensively considered, is the love of God. Wine, viewed extensively, is also love: love and affection are here the same thing. The wine-shop, with them, means the *murshid i kiamil* (spiritual director), for his heart is said to be the depository of the love of God; the wine-cup is the *telkin* (the pronunciation of the name of God, in a declaration of faith, as: There is no God but Allah), or it signifies the words which flow from the *murshid's* mouth respecting divine knowledge, and which, heard by the *sâlik* (the Dervish, or one who pursues the true path) intoxicates his soul, and divests his mind (of passions), giving him pure spiritual delight. The sweetheart means the excellent preceptor, because, when any one sees his beloved, he admires her perfect proportions, with a heart full of love: the Dervish beholds the secret knowledge of God which fills the heart of his spiritual preceptor (*murshid*), and through it receives a similar inspiration, and acquires a full perception of all that he possesses, just as the pupil learns from his master. As the lover delights in the presence of his sweetheart, so the Dervish rejoices in the company of his beloved preceptor. The sweetheart is the object of a worldly affection; but the preceptor, of a spiritual attachment. The curls, or ringlets, of the beloved are the grateful praises of the preceptor, tending to bind the affections of the Dervish-pupil; the moles on her face signify that when the pupil, at times, beholds the total absence of all worldly wants on the part of the preceptor, he also abandons all the desires of both worlds—he perhaps even goes so far as to desire nothing else in life than his preceptor; the furrows on the brow of the beloved one, which they compare to [verses of] the Koran, mean the light of the heart of the *murshid*: they are compared to verses of the Koran, because the attributes of God, in accordance with the injunction of the Prophet: 'Be ye endued with divine qualities,' are possessed by the Sheikh (or *murshid*).*

"[*Q.*]—The *murshid* and other Dervishes say: 'We see God.' Is it possible for any other than the Prophet to see God?

"[*A.*]—It is not possible. What they mean by this assertion is that they know God, that they see His power; for it is forbidden to mortal eyes to behold Him, as is declared in the Koran (ch. vi. v. 103): 'No sight reaches Him: He reaches the sight—the Subtle, the Knowing.' The blessed Prophet commanded: 'Adore God, as thou wouldst didst thou see Him; for, if thou dost not see Him, He sees thee.' This permission to adore Him is a divine favour, and they say that they are God's servants by divine favour. The blessed 'Alee said: 'Should the veil fall from my eyes, how would God visit me in truth!' This saying confirms that no one really sees God, that even the sainted 'Alee never saw Him.

"[*Q.*]—Can it possibly be erroneous to say that, by seeing the traces of any one, he may be beheld?

"[*A.*]—One may certainly be thus seen. When any

* During the wars between Alee and Muavieh, the latter, on being once beaten, elevated the Koran on a lance, and begged for mercy. On this being reported to Alee, he declared that he himself was the living and the speaking Koran, whilst the one raised upon the lance of his enemy was only a painted, or imitated one.

person sees the brightness of the sun, he may safely say that he has seen the sun, though indeed he has not really seen it. There is another example, namely: should you hold a mirror in your hand, you see a figure in it, and you may therefore say that you see your own face, which is really an impossibility, for no one has ever seen his own face, and you have asserted what is not strictly correct.

"[*Q.*]—Since every one sees the traces of God, as every one is able to do, how is it that the Dervishes declare that they only see Him?

"[*A.*]—Those who make this statement do not know what they see, and have never really seen Him. A person who has eaten of a sweet and savoury dish, given to him, but of which he knows not the name, seeks for it again with a longing desire after it, and thus wanders about in search of what has given him so much delight, ignorant of what it is. So are those who seek after God, without knowing Him, or what He is.

[*Q.*]—Some Dervishes declare: 'We are neither afraid of Hell, nor do we desire Heaven—a saying which must be blasphemous. How is this?

[*A.*]—They do not really mean that they do not fear Hell, and that they do not wish for Heaven. If they really meant this, it would be blasphemous. Their meaning is not as they express themselves; probably they wish to say: O Lord, Thou who createdst us, and madest us what we are, Thou hast not made us because we help Thy working: we are therefore in duty bound to serve Thee all the more devotedly, wholly in obedience to Thy holy will; we have no bargaining with Thee, and we do not adore Thee with the view of gaining thereby either Heaven or Hell. "God has bought the goods and persons of the Faithful, and given them Paradise in return" (ch. ix. v. 112, of the Koran), which signifies that His bounty has no bounds, His mercy no end; and thus it is that He benefits His faithful servants. They would say: Thou hast no bargaining with any one; our devotion is from the purity of our hearts, and is for love of Thee only. Were there no Heaven, nor any

Hell, it would still be our duty to adore Thee. To Thee belongs the perfect right to put us either in Heaven or in Hell, and may Thy commands be executed agreeably to Thy blessed will! If Thou puttest us in Heaven, it is through Thine excellence, not on account of our devotion; if Thou puttest us in Hell, it is from out of Thy great justice, and not from any arbitrary decision on Thy part; so be it for ever and for ever! This is the true meaning of the Sofees, when they say as before stated.

"[*Q.*]—Thou saidst that there is no conflict between the *sheryat* and the *hakkikat*, and nothing in the latter inconsistent with the former; and yet these two are distinguished from one another by a something which the Ehlee Hakkikat (believers in the truth) conceal. Were there nothing conflicting, why should it be thus hidden?

"[*A.*]—If it be concealed, it is not because there is a contrariety to the *sheryat*, but only because the thing is contrary to the human mind: its definition is subtle, and not understood by every one, for which reason the blessed Prophet said: 'Speak to men according to their mental capacities,' for, if you speak all things to all men, some cannot understand you, and so fall into error. The Sofees therefore hide some things conformably with this precept.

"[*Q.*]—Should any one not know the science which is known to the Sofees, and still do what the *sheryat* plainly command, and be satisfied therewith, would his faith (*imân*) and *islam* be less than that of the Sofees?

"[*A.*]—No. He would not be inferior to the Sofees; his faith and *islam* would be equal even to that of the prophets, because faith and *islam* are a jewel which admits of no division or separation into parts, and can neither be increased nor diminished, just as the portion of the sun enjoyed by a sovereign and by a fakir is the same, or as the limbs of the poor and the rich are equal in number: just as the members of the body of the sovereign and the subject are precisely alike, so is the faith of the Ehlee Islam the same in all and common to all, neither greater nor less in any case.

"[*Q.*]—Some men are prophets, saints, pure ones, and

others *fassiks* (who know God, but perform none of His commands); what difference is there among them?

"[*A.*]—The difference lies in their *marifeh* (knowledge of spiritual things), but in the matter of faith they are all equal: just as, in the case of the sovereign and the subject, their limbs are all equal, while they differ in their dress, power, and office. As to the humanity of men, that depends upon their dress of knowledge, and their spiritual power; in these only are they men, and not simply animals. The character of the sovereign does not depend upon his humanity, which is the same as that of all other men, but upon his office and rank."

DERVISHES OF THE MEVLEVEE ORDER.

CHAPTER XVII.

A BIOGRAPHY OF THE FOURTH CALIPH 'ALEE.

THE reader will have perceived the intimate connexion existing between the Dervish Orders and the Fourth Direct Caliph 'Alee. Indeed, nearly all of these are 'Aleeides, as if he had been the great originator of them, and the advocate and patron of their peculiar principles. Whether this was the case or not, much that is of a "spiritual" character is attributed to him, and even in those Orders that are *sunnee*, or othodox, 'Alee is held in high respect. I have, therefore, thought it necessary to devote a chapter especially to him, and for this purpose have translated a short biographical sketch of him from the work in the Turkish language, entitled, The *Chehâr Yâr*, or the "Four Friends," by Shems ed Deen Sivâsee (of Siwas, in Asia Minor). From this sketch, the reader will readily imagine why such honour is paid by a large portion of the Islam world, and by the Dervish Orders in particular,—so much so as to give him the sublime title of *'Alee el Ilâhee*, or "'Alee the Divine."

"'Alee bin Abi Tâlib, ibin 'Abd el Matlab, was of the same lineage as the Blessed Prophet, being the son of the uncle of the latter, and therefore his cousin.

"He was born in the revered city of Mekkeh, in the thirtieth year of the era of the Arabs, known as the 'Year of the Elephant,' and the 910th of the Alexandrian era. Perwas (the Sassanian king of Persia), had ceased to reign eight years.

"His mother, Fâtimeh binti Asad bin Hâshim (so it is related), one night saw in a dream that her chamber was filled with light, and that the mountains which surrounded the holy *Ke'beh* (Caaba) were worshipping it;

that she had held in her hands four swords, all of which having fallen out of them, lay scattered before her. One of these swords fell into water; a second flew up into the air, and disappeared from her sight as it rose upwards towards heaven; and a third, as it fell, attempted to do the same, but suddenly became converted into a lion, which fled away towards the mountains, alarming every one by its ferocity, so much so, that no one ventured to approach it, except the Prophet of God,—on whom be the Divine satisfaction!—who, going up to it, seized upon, and so subdued it, that it followed after him, licked his blessed face, and feet, and voluntarily served his wishes.

"Four months after this dream, the Prophet of God visited Fâtimeh, and looking her in the face, exclaimed, 'O mother! what ails thee, for I see a change in thy countenance?' She replied, 'My son, I am pregnant; aid me to have a male child.' The Prophet replied, 'O mother! if you have a son, give him to me, and I will pray for you.' On hearing these words, Fâtimeh vowed to Allah, that in case her child was a son, she would give him to the Prophet. Abu Tâlib (her husband) confirmed the vow, by making one similar to it.

"The Prophet therefore blessed her, and the fruit of her conception was 'Alee el Murtezà, or "'Alee the Agreeable.'

"On the occasion of 'Alee's birth, a light was distinctly visible, resembling a bright column, extending from the earth to the firmament.

"Upon receiving news of his nativity, the Prophet immediately visited the dwelling of his parents. On seeing, for the first time, the little infant, he took some spittle from his own lips, and rubbed it upon those of the child, and it immediately swallowed it. It is believed that from this, 'Alee derived all of his great knowledge and power, as well as miraculous capabilities. By it, he became victorious in all his battles, and a perfect sovereign for conquest and heroic deeds. He also was thus gifted with all of the most eminent qualities of manhood; and the most noble and loveable traits of character were certainly united in him.

"The Prophet also recited in his ears, the Tekbeer and the Tehleel, at the same time giving him the name of 'Alee (the sublime or exalted). His mother, in remembrance of her dream, also called him Hyder (lion), and the Prophet declared that he would become the 'Lion of God.' Taking off his own turban, he wrapped one end of it around the child, and rolled the other about his own head, so that it became a crown of glory to him. None of the Faithful have ever had so great a distinction bestowed upon them as this.

"By some it has been related, that when the mother of 'Alee was about to be confined, she went into the 'Beit i Shereef,' or the holy temple of Mekkeh, for the purpose of there being delivered; and that it being impossible to remove her, the child was actually born within its sainted precincts; but for this, we have only their report.

"Ayisha (the third wife of the Prophet, and daughter of Abu Bekr, the first Direct Caliph)—on whom be the Divine satisfaction!—relates, that one day when the 'Pride and Glory of the World' (the Prophet) was seated, 'Alee happened to pass by him. 'Calling my attention to him, he declared to me, that 'Alee was the Seyd (Cid) of the Arabs. But, I asked, are you not their Seyd? He answered, "I am the Seyd of all, that is, of the Turks, the Tartars, the Hinds, the Arabs, and the 'Ajems; but 'Alee is especially the Seyd of the Arabs."' This favoured lady also adds that the Prophet was fond of rocking the cradle of 'Alee, and would often lift him out of it, and carry him about in his arms; so that even when asleep, on hearing the approaching footsteps of the Prophet of God, he would awake, press his little arms out of their ties, and raise them up towards him. On such occasions, the Prophet would hasten towards the child, take it from its cradle, and press it, with great tenderness and affection, to his breast. Its mother more than once chided him for it, and begged him to allow her to nurse and look after the child, as became her duty; but the Prophet would, as often, remind her that even before its birth she had given it to him, and that, consequently, he must, for the present and the future, consider him as his own. It is related, that one day, the 'Joy of the World' (the Prophet)—on whom be the blessings and salutations of the Most High!—was seated in the Holy Temple, holding the child, 'Alee, on his knees. Many of the most valiant men of the day were assembled there, boasting of their deeds. Pointing to the child, he told them that it would become the most heroic man of his time, and that no one would be his equal on the face of the globe. Surprised and irritated by these words, they expostulated with the Prophet; 'O Mohammed el Emin! we always thought you were a wise and truthful man; pray how can you speak thus of a little child, about whose future career in life you can foresee nothing?' In reply, the Prophet only bade them remember his words, and that in a few years they would see them verified.

"It is related that, at the age of three years, 'Alee would perform the Namâz (prayers) with the Prophet. On seeing this, Abu Tâlib made no remark, regarding the precocity of his child, but the mother was much pleased, and exclaimed, 'See! our child worships the Ke'beh with Mohammed, and does not adore our idols.' Abu Tâlib replied, 'O Fâtimeh! we have given him up to Mohammed,—whatever he does will be right in the sight of the All-Just; he is still a child, and will be of whatever religion Mohammed is; let them be brothers, and inseparable.' One day, also, when the revered Prophet and 'Alee were performing their prayers together, Abu Tâlib approached them on horseback, and remarked that 'Alee was on his right side. Now Ja'fer Tiyâr—on whom be the Divine satisfaction!—was close behind his horse, and Abu Talib, addressing him, bade him go and place himself to the left of the Prophet, and pray with them, 'for in this manner you will become an eminent person.' Ja'fer immediately left Abu Tâlib, and proceeded to the left side of the Prophet, and stood there, on seeing which the latter was much rejoiced, and after prayers, addressing Ja'fer, said, 'Rejoice, O Ja'fer, that the Most High has given you two wings, with which you may fly away to Paradise, and be the companion of the Khoor i Ayeens (Hoories), and be near to the Lord of the Universe.'

"According to some narratives of holy note, it is stated that 'Alee was born thirty years after the era of the elephant, on the thirteenth day of the Moon of Rejeb, which fell on Friday, and that it occurred within the holy Ke'beh; that there was in Yemin a very aged and pious person, named Meerem, whose heart was free from all worldly desires, and who spent the great life of 190 years in adoration and prayer. He cared nothing for worldly wealth, and his only pleasure consisted in pious occupations; he never turned his eyes in any other direction than that of the Minber (the point of Mekkeh). One day, this person prayed to God that He would bless his country with some one from among the residents of the Holy Temple, and those who were eminent among the chiefs of the Ke'beh. His prayer was accepted, and by Divine direction, Abu Tâlib, then one of the most prominent individuals of Mekkeh, was led to travel, and visit his country. After learning who his visitor was, he thanked God for having accepted his prayer, and sent him so distinguished an individual as Abu Tâlib, son of 'Abd ul Matleb, of the tribe of the Benee Hâshim, and a native of the city of Mekkeh. He then told him that from ancient times there was a tradition to the effect that 'Abd ul Matleb would have two grandsons, one from the loins of 'Abd Ulleh, and that he should be a prophet, and the other from those of Abu Tâlib, who would render easy the enigmas of the *velâyet* (spiritual holiness); and that when the Prophet would have reached his thirtieth year, the *Vâlee* would come into the world,—and that a prophet like whom none other had ever yet appeared. To this Abu Tâlib replied, 'Oh! Sheikh, that prophet has been born, and is now in his twenty-ninth year.' Meerem responded, 'Oh! Abu Tâlib, when you return to Mekkeh, and approach the place of prayer, take with you my salutations, and say that Meerem has always borne testimony to the unity of the one universal Creator, who is without any equal, and that he is His prophet. Take also my salutations to the one who is born to you.'

"Abu Tâlib, seeing opposite him a dry pomegranate tree, as a temptation to the Sheikh, requested him to cause it to put forth leaves and fruit, as a proof of the truthfulness of his words. The Sheikh turned his face upwards in supplication to God, and prayed, that for the sake of the *Nebee* (Prophet) and the *Vâlee* ('Alee), about whom he had just declared words of sincerity, there might be a demonstration of Divine power over Nature. In a minute the tree became covered with leaves and fruit, from which he presented his visitor with the fresh pomegranates. Of these the Sheikh gave one to Abu Tâlib, which he broke open and ate two grains. It is related that the juice of these two grains became the source from which sprang the bodily existence of 'Alee el Murtezà.

"Abu Tâlib, much rejoiced with what he had heard from the Sheikh, returned to Mekkeh; and his wife, Fâtimeh binti Asad, soon proved to be pregnant. During her pregnancy (as she stated), 'I was one day engaged in making the turn around the holy house (called the Tawâf), and had an attack of the spleen. The blessed Prophet saw and understood what ailed me, and addressing me, asked whether I had terminated my circuit (the Tawâf). I replied that I had not. He then added, 'Continue, and if you feel fatigued, enter into the Ke'beh.' It is also narrated in the book entitled 'Siyer el Mustafâ,' that whilst Fâtimeh binti Asad was thus engaged in making the Tawâf of the Harâm i Ke'beh, Abbâs ibn el Matleb, and all the Benee Hâshim following behind her, did the same; she suddenly had an attack of the spleen, and, being unable to go out, prayed, 'Oh, Lord, give an easy confinement.' Suddenly the wall opened, and Fâtimeh became lost from sight. In the view of learning something about her, I entered the Ke'beh, but was still unable to do so, because for three days she could not be found; on the fourth day she came out, bearing in her arms 'Alee bin Abu Tâlib,—on whom be the Divine satisfaction!

"The Imâm el Harâmain (Imâm of the ten holy places) states that before this case, never was any one blessed with such a favour; for it has never been heard that any other one was born in the Harâm. Fâtimeh conveyed 'Alee to her dwelling, and bound him in a cradle. Abu Tâlib was present, and, desiring to see the child's face, attempted to raise up the veil which covered it, but 'Alee, with his own hand, prevented him, and even scratched his face. His mother, on observing this, approached, and endeavoured to compel the child to submit, but it still refused, and even wounded her in the face also. Abu Tâlib was much surprised at such conduct, and, asking Fâtimeh what name they should give to their child, she replied, 'Oh, Abu Tâlib, it has the strength of a lion's claws, and if we call it a lion, it will be very proper.' Abu Tâlib answered, 'I wish to name it Zayd.' So soon, however, as the 'Pride of the Universe' heard of the birth of the child, he hurried to the house, and having enquired what name had been decided upon for it, and heard all that was said on the subject, remarked that it was his desire that he should be an honour to the 'elevated people' (elevated signifies 'Alee). Fâtimeh, on hearing this, exclaimed, 'I also heard a voice (Hâtif, is the unknown and mystical voice) saying the same name.'

"Another report is that a dispute occurred between the parents regarding the name to be given to this child; and in the view of asking Divine counsel on the subject, they both went to the Ke'beh, where Fâtimeh prayed: 'O Lord! for the child whom Thou givest me in the Harâm i Shereef, or Holy House, let me beg of Thee a name.' Just then a voice was heard as from the roof the Ke'beh, directing her to call it 'Alee, which they did.

"The blessed Prophet having desired to approach the cradle of the child, Fâtimeh begged him not to do so, for it had all the ferocity of a lion, and might act uncivilly towards him; but to this the blessed Prophet replied, 'O Fâtimeh! this child respects in me the regard due to the True Path.' 'Alee el Murtezà having in the meantime fallen asleep, the Prophet gazed attentively at its face, on which was already impressed the light of Divine Truth. Afterwards he raised it up out of the cradle, and with his own hands washed it, thus performing the religious ablution, called the Ghusl; and when Fâtimeh, with surprise, inquired the cause, the Prophet replied, 'I have now performed this for 'Alee at his birth, and he will do the same for me at the end of my life.' It was thus that he acted towards the child, taking the deepest interest of an uncle in its future welfare.

"When 'Alee was five years old, a great drought occurred in the Hejâz, from which the inhabitants suffered severely. Abu Tâlib had many persons in his family. The Prophet one day remarked to 'Abbâs, 'O! uncle, you are a man of wealth, whilst Abu Tâlib is poor and has a large family; during the present distress we should each take charge of one of his sons and aid him with provisions.' Just then they fell in with Abu Tâlib, and told him what they had designed doing. 'Leave Okail with me, and you may do with the rest of my sons as you please,' was his reply; so 'Abbâs took Ja'fer Tiyâr, and the Prophet took 'Alee el Murtezà, and he remained with him until the angel Gabriel (Jebrâil) gave him permission (to leave this world). He became an acceptant of the Emân (true faith) after Abu Bekr. May God have mercy upon them both, and upon all of the As-hâbs (friends) of the blessed Prophet!"

"The Prophetship was given to the Glory of the World (Mahommed) on the second day of the week (Monday), and on Tuesday the Emân (true faith) was accepted of the Imâm 'Alee. Abu Bekr thus preceded him, and before him no one had accepted it. 'Alee was, as just said, the second, and he was then ten years of age, though some pretend that he was only seven years old. At no time did he ever worship idols, and from this great sin the Almighty preserved him.

"It is related that he once said: 'When I was still in my mother's womb, she went to a church (keneesa) for the purpose of worshipping an idol; but, by special

Divine power, a pain suddenly came upon her, and she was compelled by it to forget her design, and seek relief from her suffering. The Imâm 'Alee was brought up by the Prophet, and Abbas relates that no less than 300 Ayats (verses of the Koran) descended from heaven in honour of him."

"The Imâm 'Alee has several names. One of these is Abu'l Hasan, one Abu'l Husain, one Hyder, one Kerâr, one Emir el Nuhl, one Abu'l Rehanain, one Asad Allah, and one Abu'l Turâb; but he always said that he liked none so well as the last (which signifies 'the Father of Dust'), because it was given him by the 'Glory of the World' himself. The occasion on which he gave it was the following. It happened that one day Fâtimeh el Zehrâ and the Imâm 'Alee had an altercation, and on account of it the latter went to the Mesjid (chapel) and lay down on the dry earth. Much grieved with this, she forthwith went in search of the Prophet, and related to him what had happened, adding that the fault was her own. The Prophet immediately walked around the Mesjid, and observing 'Alee reposing on the ground, addressing him, exclaimed, 'Arise, 'Alee, arise!' 'Alee, on hearing the voice of the blessed Prophet, at once got up, and the latter seeing some earth on his face, with his own blessed hands wiped it off, and said, 'Abu Turâb (father of earth), arise!' But, in the Shevâhid el Nebooveh it is stated that one day the blessed Prophet went to the house of Fâtimeh—on whom be Divine satisfaction!—and, not finding 'Alee there, inquired where he was; Fâtimeh replied that, having been troubled, he had gone out, perhaps to the Mesjid. On hearing which the Prophet forthwith went there, and seeing 'Alee lying on the bare ground, his mantle fallen off, and his body covered with dust, he bade him arise, calling him for that purpose Abu Turâb, and with his own hands wiped the dust off him."

"The marriage of 'Alee with Fâtimeh el Zehrâ (the fair), daughter of the Prophet, occurred as follows:

"The blessed Prophet had six children born to him by Khadeejeh el Kubrâ (the great), two of which were boys and four were daughters; and it was after the birth of Fâtimeh that she left this perishable world for that of eternity. The blessed Prophet nursed this last child until she reached the age of puberty, and himself educated her (morally). One day, whilst she was engaged in serving her father, he remarked that she had reached an age when it was necessary to marry her, and he felt sad to think that he had not the mother, whom she greatly resembled, to attend to the matter for her. It may be added that Fâtimeh had always been a pious and serious-minded girl, and was in consequence much beloved by her parent. Whilst this thought was still in his mind, the messenger of the Most High (the angel Gabriel) appeared before him, and saluting him on the part of the Almighty, said, 'Be not troubled, O! Mahommed; I will prepare a dowry for Fâtimeh out of the treasures of Paradise, and bestow her upon one who is a good and faithful servant to Me.' These words greatly affected the blessed Prophet, and so soon as he had offered up thanks and adoration to God for his great mercies, the angel disappeared from sight but for a moment, for he soon returned, bearing in his hand a golden vessel, covered over with a golden cloth. Behind him followed 1,000 angelic cherubim (Kerubiyoon), with the angel Mekâil (Michael) in their rear, also bearing a similar vessel, covered over like the first; after them came the same number of cherubim, followed by the angel Izrâil, similarly laden, and each laid their burthens as an offering before him.

"On beholding this apparition the Prophet, addressing Gabrâil, said, 'Oh! Brother, tell me what are the commands of the Most High, and what I am to do with these vessels!' The angel replied, 'O! Prophet of God, He salutes thee, and commands that "thy daughter of Paradise, Fâtimeh el Zehrâ, be given to 'Alee; for from the great arch of the heavens I have married them together." He has likewise commanded that you betroth her in the presence of the As-hâbs; let her be dressed in the garments contained in one of the vessels; and make a feast for the guests (As-hâbs) from the food contained in the others.'

"The blessed Prophet, on hearing these divine commands, addressing the angel, exclaimed, 'O! Brother Gabrâil, pray inform me distinctly as to what I must do regarding the wedding.' The angelic messenger replied, 'He has commanded that the gates of Paradise be thrown open; that Paradise be splendidly ornamented; that the doors of the criminals be closed; that all of the angels, Makribeen, Kerubiyeen, and Ruhâneen (those nearest to God, the cherubim, and the blessed spirits), in the seven spheres of heaven and earth, assemble together in the shade of the great arch, under the Tooby trees. He has also commanded that an odoririferous breeze shall blow over the angels, the sweetness of which is indescribable, and that when it blows it put in motion the leaves of the same trees, in such a manner as to create the most pleasant harmony, intoxicating the senses of those who hear them; and He also has commanded the birds of the gardens of Paradise to sing sweetly.' All of which was done accordingly.

"The angel also said to the Prophet: 'O! Friend of God, the Most High has likewise commanded me as follows: "O! Gabrâil, be thou the vakeel (representative at the marriage ceremony) of My lion 'Alee, and I will be the vakeel of My servant Fâtimeh; and these, My angels, be witnesses that I have freely bestowed My servant Fâtimeh in marriage upon My lion 'Alee. Thou, Gabrâil, as his vakeel, accept of the betrothal." In this manner, these two are to be married from heaven; and He (God) has commanded that you assemble here all of the As-hâbs—on whom be the Divine satisfaction!—and proceed to the performance of the nuptial ceremony.' The blessed Prophet again offered up adoration and thanks, and called together all of the As-hâbs, and then addressing the angel, said: 'O! Brother Gabrâil, my thoughts are much occupied with my daughter Fâtimeh; it is not proper that she should wear in this world the clothes of Paradise; take them, therefore, back there.'

"When the As-hâbs came together, they enquired who would be the vakeels of the Prophet and 'Alee. Just then the Angel Gabriel descended, and addressing the Prophet of God, said, 'O Prophet of God! He salutes thee, and commands that 'Alee performs the Khotbeh' (the solemn prayer of noon, on Friday, and in Bairâm). 'Alee thereupon recited this prayer, after which he was married to Fâtimeh, for the dowry of four hundred Akchas (silver pieces). When Fâtimeh received information of her marriage, she was dissatisfied; and the angelic messenger descending again, said, 'O Prophet of God! He commands that in case my servant Fâtimeh be not satisfied with the amount of four hundred Akchas, let it be four thousand.' This change being communicated to Fâtimeh, she still expressed discontent; and Gabriel, again returning, directed that the portion be made four thousand Altuns (gold pieces). As she was still dissatisfied, Gabriel returned, and directed the Prophet to go in person to his daughter, and ask her what she desired. On hearing this, the Prophet arose, and having gone to her, his daughter, asked her what she wished done on the occasion of her marriage; she replied, 'O Friend of God! I wish that in the same manner that you are the intercessor for rebellious men, at the Day of Judgment, to render them faithful, so may I intercede for women, and place them in Paradise' (Jennet). On this, the Prophet withdrew, and made known to Gabriel what his daughter desired. The Angel departed, and conveyed to the presence of the All-Glorious her reply: he soon returned, and reported to the Prophet that her wishes had been acceptable to God; and He had commanded that, at the Day of Judgment, she might intercede for women. He added, that there was a verse in the ancient books, and in the Great Koran, to that effect, serving as a Hojjet or title in her behalf. The Prophet having enquired where the title was, to which he alluded, the Angel begged leave to convey his question to the Most High, and receive His commands,—which he did, and immediately returned, bearing in his hand a roll of white silk, which he handed to the Prophet. The latter, on opening the roll, perceived in it a document, in which was written, 'By this Title, I appoint my servant Fâtimeh to be the intercessor, in the Day of Judgment, in favour of the Mumineh (faithful females).' The Prophet of God now took this roll, and conveyed it to Fâtimeh; she accepted it, and declared that she was now satisfied with her marriage. It is, however, related that the Imâm 'Alee did not put any faith in this title. At the Last Day, he may therefore be asked what became of it. It is also related that when the Prophet married Fâtimeh to 'Alee, he presented to her eighteen Akchas, together with a spotted robe, and that as he wept, she put it on, and enquired the cause of his tears, and he replied by asking her what account she would be able to give of her nuptial presents when she came to appear before the Almighty? He likewise added that if the thoughts of such small presents gave him so much pain, what must be the reflections of those parents who expend hundreds, —perhaps even thousands,—upon the bridal suits of their daughters."

"The Imâm 'Alee was somewhat smaller than the middle size, with broad shoulders, and light coloured eyes; his blessed beard was of a sandy colour, and plentiful in quantity, and his breast was rather large. Whenever infidels beheld his countenance, their hearts failed them, and caused them to tremble like autumn leaves. He not unfrequently remained without food from three to four, five, and even seven and eight days, and so remarkable was this peculiarity, that the blessed Prophet was once questioned as to the cause. He answered that 'Alee possessed a holy strength, which preserved him from the cravings of hunger, so that during the Holy Wars, in which he took an active part, he seldom partook of any food, and occupied himself entirely with the promotion of the war,—the subject of food never for a moment troubling his mind. No such war occurred without his taking part in it; and whenever a fortification held out, or the enemies proved to be strong, the Prophet would give him his own flag, and telling him that he had commended him to the Most High, bade him take the former and conquer it, which he never failed to accomplish."

"There was a very numerous Christian tribe, called the Benee Buhrân, which, notwithstanding the repeated advice of the blessed Prophet, continued dissatisfied, and held out against him. Their pertinacity and rebellious conduct increasing, it was impossible to strive against them. Finally, the illustrious Ayât (verse) of the Ibtihâl (obedience) descended from heaven, and they were thus divinely commanded to submit. It is stated in the *Sureh* (a chapter of the Koran) called the *Al 'Amrân* (chap. iii. and 54th verse): 'To those who shall dispute with thee on this subject, since thou hast received perfect knowledge, reply, "Come, let us call our children and yours, our wives and yours, come, us and you, and let us pray to the Lord, each one apart, and call down curses upon the liars."'

"This signifies, that whosoever disputes with thee on the subject of Jesus,—on whom be peace!—after the knowledge which has come to thee respecting Jesus, who is the servant and apostle of the Most High, know that the expression *Abnâanâ*, of this Ayat, means Fâtimeh, and *Anfusanâ* means the blessed Prophet's pure breath, which is none other than 'Alee himself; because among the Arabs it is customary to call the son of an uncle Nefsee (breath or person). God has said, *Ve lâ telmezoo enfsuikum*, meaning 'your brothers,' in which is understood all those who are of the true religion; and Ibin 'Abbâs,—on whom be Divine satisfaction!—declares that *Thumm nebtahal* signifies, 'Let us pray and implore.' Gulebee (an author) says this means 'to pray and war excessively,' whilst Kesâee and Abu 'Obaideh say it means, 'Let it curse them together,' for *Ibtihâl* signifies, 'the curse,' and *Fe tij'âla la'net Ullah 'alà 'l Kiâzibeen* means, 'Let us, we and you, all of us, call God's curses upon the liars.'

"The Prophet of God read this verse on the people of Bahrân, and invited them not to curse his faith; whilst on their part they replied, 'Let us return to our people, and take counsel together regarding our affairs, and to-morrow we will come.' So they assembled together, and finally the more sensible amongst them said, 'Do you not believe in the words of the Messiah?' To which the Prophet replied, 'Oh! Nazareens, you confirm the congregation (of the Messiah), and that Mohammed is the Prophet sent by the Most High, and yet call upon yourselves His curses. If you thus continue, you will all meet death; so return to your Master, and remain in the belief of His words.'

"On the following day they came with 'Alee before the blessed Prophet, whom they found holding Hosain in his arms, and Hasan by his hand, whilst Fâtimeh followed him. He bade these to exclaim, 'Amen!' whenever he prayed. Now when the Nazareen chiefs approached him, he, addressing them, said, 'Oh! congregation of Nazareens, I of a truth thus view the case: if you ask of God to remove a mountain, He will do so, in honour of Himself; guard against maledictions, or you will meet destruction, and not a Nazareen will remain on the earth's surface from this to the end of time.' On hearing this, the chiefs begged Abu'l Kâsim to advise them what to do, and added that they had decided not to curse Mohammed. 'We will leave you in your religion, and continue firm in our own.'

"The Prophet of God commanded, 'Since you have decided to refrain from curses, become Mussulmans. You are in need of that which they possess, and you will then participate in the same.' This they refusing to do, he added, 'Prepare then to die, for we will certainly put you to death.' They now declared that they were unable to war with the Arabs, and preferred to make peace with them, and have their lives spared. 'Do not,' they said, 'frighten us, nor seek to cause us to abandon our religion, and we will yearly pay you

2,000 suits, 1,000 in the month of Sefer, and 1,000 in that of Rejeb.' So the blessed Prophet consented to their proposal, and made peace with them, and declared, 'My person is in His hands. Punishment has been turned away from the people of Bahrân. Had they cursed, they would have been turned into monkeys and pigs, and been consumed with flashes of fire; in fact, God would have destroyed both Bahrân and its inhabitants; and even the birds on the trees would not have survived one year.'"

"Meer Husain Vâ'iz—on whom be Divine mercy!—in his work in the Persian tongue, a commentary called 'Kesf,' when commenting on the Surah Bakrah (of the Koran, ch. ii. verse 275), 'Those who give alms day and night, in secret and in public, will receive their reward from God; fear will not descend upon them, nor will they be afflicted,' says, in regard to the 'causes of descent,' that 'Alee el Murtezà once had four Dirhems, one of these he publicly gave away in alms; one he gave away secretly, one he bestowed during the darkness of night, and one he bestowed during the light of day. The Most High thereon caused that Ayat to descend, and the blessed Prophet inquired of 'Alee what kind of alms he had been giving. He replied, 'I have not gone beyond these four paths in their bestowal; I took them all upon myself, so that at least one of them may meet with acceptance.'"

"In the Surah 'Alem Sejda (adoration), on the subject of the "Signs of descent" (ch. xxxii. verse 18), 'He who has believed, will he be like he who has given himself up to sin? Will they both be equal?' The commentator, Muhee el Seneh—on whom be mercy!—says, 'This verse descended in favour of 'Alee bin Abi Tâlib, and Veleed bin Abi Ma'eet, who, on his mother's side, was related to 'Othman (the third direct Caliph). A quarrel occurred between 'Alee and Valeed, on which occasion the latter made a remark to 'Alee, and directed the latter to be silent, saying, 'You are but a youth; I for the want of a tongue, am silent, and in point of years am your senior; my heart is more courageous than yours, and in war I am braver.' To this 'Alee replied, 'Be you silent, for you are certainly a wicked man. The Most High has sent down this verse, but said *they*, in the *plural*, and not *they*, in the *dual*, for He did speak of one faithful and one evil-minded, but alluded to *all* the faithful and to *all* the wicked.'"

"On the same subject (the Me'lem Tenzeel), or the 'Signs of the Descent,' the Imâm Bugavee, regarding the chapter lxxvi. verse 1, 'Has much time passed over man without his being thought of?' and the eighth verse of the same chapter, 'Who, though themselves sighing after the meal, give food to the poor, the orphan, and the captive,' says there has been much disputation regarding these verses, and the cause of their descent. Mejâhid and 'Atâ ibn 'Abbâs relate that they came down for 'Alee, and in a succinct manner state the fact; whilst in other commentaries it is narrated in detail. Hasan and Hosain (sons of 'Alee) having fallen ill, the holy and revered Prophet and all of the As-hâbs went to see them, and 'Alee and Fâtimeh were addressed by the Prophet, and requested to make a vow in favour of their beloved children; this was also done by the maiden slaves of the parents, named Suroor and Fezeh, and they all together vowed that if God would restore them to health, they should fast for three days. After they had recovered, they had nothing to eat, and 'Alee went to a Jew and purchased on credit three bushels of barley, which, in performance of the vow, he devoted to their fast. One of the three measures Fâtimeh ground, so as to make five cakes. When their term of fasting had ended, she gave one to 'Alee, one to Hasan, one to Hosain, and another to the maid Fezeh, whilst she kept one for herself. Just then a miserable beggar appeared, and exclaimed, 'Oh! family of the Prophet of God I am a most miserable Mussulman; give me of your food, and God will recompense you by bestowing on you the choicest meats of Paradise." On hearing these words, they gave him the cake that was in their hands, and contented themselves with a cup of water, and fasted till the day following. Fâtimeh again ground another measure, and made five more cakes. When they were about to partake of these, an orphan came along and asked for food, so they gave them to it, rejoicing its heart by the gift, and again contented themselves with a drink of water, and went to sleep. On the day following, she ground the third measure of barley, and made five cakes, and just as they were about to eat them, a captive made his appearance and asked for food, saying, "It is three days that I am without food, and have been kept tied without anything to eat; pray, for God's sake, have pity on me." So they all gave the starving man their cakes, and contented themselves with water. Some say that this captive was a believer in the Trinity, and the narrative goes to prove that to feed a suffering captive, even if he be a Trinitarian, is a good action, and must be so regarded. It is said that on the morning of the fourth day, 'Alee took his ten sons in his hands, and went to the blessed Prophet, who remarked that hunger had reduced them so much that they trembled like young birds; and he said to 'Alee, 'Oh, 'Alee, how deeply you have afflicted me!' Then, taking them with him, he went to Fâtimeh, whom he saw in the *Mihrâb* (pulpit), her stomach stuck to her back, and her eyes were sunken. His grief was thereby greatly increased. Just then the Angel Gabriel, descending, addressed the blessed Prophet, and said, 'Take this from the All-Just,' handing him the chapter entitled *Insân*, or 'man.'

"It is related that when the Prophet once visited Fâtimeh, he said to her, 'My daughter, it is now four days since your father has partaken of any food.' He had, in fact, left Medineh, and met with an Arab engaged in drawing water from a well; and, addressing him, asked whether he would employ him to draw up water for him, and, having consented, an agreement was made by which he was to receive two dates for each bucket of water, so that the most blessed Prophet of the Most High Almighty was actually employed, for a given stipend, to draw water from the well. After drawing as much water as was needed, by Divine providence the cord broke, and the bucket fell into the well: on seeing which the Arab struck his blessed face a blow, and paid him all of the dates which he had earned. The Prophet now reached his hand down into the well and pulled out the bucket, and, after handing it to the Arab, departed to visit Fâtimeh, to whom he now presented the dates. Whilst eating them, she remarked traces of the blow upon her father's face, and asked the cause of it. The Prophet replied that it was nothing, and sought to conceal the fact from her knowledge. Now it happened that when the Arab struck the blessed Prophet, and saw him draw up the bucket from the well, he was greatly surprised, and reflected that if the individual was not God's Prophet he could certainly not have done this. 'The hand which has done such a dishonour to a Prophet must not be mine;' so he at once cut it off, and set out in search of the Prophet whom he had wronged. Knocking at the door, 'Alee was surprised to see before him a man with one hand held in the other, and blood flowing from the arm from which it had been amputated. Having informed the Prophet of the circumstance, he smiled, and said that this was the Arab who had struck him so severely as to leave traces of the blow on his face. He also bade 'Alee permit the man to come in; and on his entrance he was much pained by the sight, and asked the Arab why he had committed such an act? The Arab wept, and implored forgiveness of his fault, and the blessed Prophet, putting the two ends of the arm and hand together, prayed over them, and so they became reunited. By God's providence, thus the Arab recovered the full use of his arm."

"Fâtimeh relates that once the blessed Prophet asked 'Alee whether he loved God. 'Alee replied that he did.

The Prophet next asked him whether he loved him, and 'Alee made the same answer. He next asked him whether he loved Fâtimeh, and he replied again in the affirmative. He then inquired whether he loved Hassan and Hosain, and he answered as before.

"The Prophet now asked him how his heart could contain so much love, and he was unable to reply. Troubled by his want of ability, 'Alee went to Fâtimeh and explained the same to her. She remarked that he did not need to be troubled, for love for God came from the mind; that for the Prophet from faith; love for her came from human passion, and that for their sons from nature.

"'Alee now returned forthwith to the Prophet, and having given him this answer, the latter exclaimed, 'This is not the fruit of faith, but of the prophetship,' thereby meaning that the answer did not proceed from himself, but from Fâtimeh. In fact, her explanations were full of wisdom, merit, and deep reflection."

"Fâtimeh also relates that when 'Alee el Murtezà had captured the fortress of Hyber, and with his *Zul Fikâr* (a sword presented to him by the Prophet) had cut off the heads of the infidels, and returned sound, and with much booty, he told Fâtimeh to remark that he owed the capture to that sword. She answered, 'Oh, 'Alee, I know the Zul Fikâr far better than him. 'Alee went to the Prophet, and repeated to him what had occurred and the words of Fâtimeh; and he arose, and going to see her, asked how it was she knew better the Zul Fikâr than 'Alee. Fâtimeh replied, 'Oh, most excellent and respected parent, the night in which you went up to heaven and saw your Lord, you reposed under a tree of Paradise, from which you gathered two apples, one of which you gave to my mother, and the other you ate. I am the fruit of those two apples. At the time the sword of Zul Fikâr hung upon the tree.'

"The Prophet was much gratified by her answer, and

on leaving her, exclaimed that it was a blessing for any person to have such a daughter."

"In the work entitled the 'Mesâbeeh Shereef,' it is related, as an anecdote, coming from Sa'd ibn abi Vakkâs, that the blessed Prophet once remarked to 'Alee, 'Thou art to me what Aaron was to Moses, and of a truth after me there is no prophet.' Thur Pishtee states that on the occasion of the war of Tebook, the Prophet appointed 'Alee as his Khelifeh (lieutenant) over the people, and directed that he should preside over their affairs. The hypocrites having learned this, declared that he had not appointed 'Alee as Khelifeh, and it was only to rid himself of worry that he so named him. When 'Alee heard of this, he put on his sword, and went directly to the Prophet, then at a place called Jerf, and asked him whether what the hypocrites had said regarding his appointment, viz., that it was only to free himself from worry, was true? The Prophet declared that they were all liars, and that he had named his Khalifeh in consequence of his intended absence from Medineh; that he should return, and act as such for him, even if his own wife (Khadeejeh) and that of 'Alee should refuse to accept of him. 'For you are to me what Aaron was to Moses, just as it is said in the holy Ayat, "And Moses said to his brother, be my Khalifeh among the people."' All commentators and confirmers of this Ayat, held this to be a legal deed in favour of 'Alee. Even the Râfizees and the Shey'ees hold to this, to show that the Caliphat belonged to 'Alee, and that he thus accepted it. At a later period, disagreements arose between them, and the Râfizees declared that the As-hâbs were guilty of blasphemy, and others again accused 'Alee of the same crime. According to their statement, 'Alee had a full right to the Caliphat; and, if so, why did he not arise and demand it? All of this (says the author) I must most surely condemn as entirely erroneous.

"Kâzee states that, 'there is no room to doubt of the blasphemy of those who make such a declaration; for any one who would thus injure his whole people, and debase the highest authorities, denies the holy law itself, and destroys Islamism.' The fact is that the Ayat (before quoted) in no manner served as a deed to their declaration in favour of 'Alee; it can only serve, at best, as a proof of his excellent character, but cannot be quoted to show that he was *the* best, or even equal to the other successors of the blessed Prophet. On the occasion of the war of Tebook, he was named Khalifeh only for the reasons assigned, just as Aaron acted for Moses for a particular period. It is well known that Aaron did not become Khalifeh after Moses, and there is good reason to believe that he died full forty years previous to Moses, and only was appointed to lead the prayers when the latter went to be with the Lord."

"It is also related, as an anecdote in the 'Mesâbeeh,' that 'Alee stated: 'Glory be to that Most High God, who causeth the grain to grow, and who created man, on account of the words which the blessed Prophet used in my behalf, "because he loved only the faithful, and despised the hypocritical;"' the correct signification of which *Hadees* is that the person who only regards 'Alee on account of his connexion with the Prophet, and for the love which the latter bore for him, and from the influence which the acts of 'Alee had upon the conquests of Islamism, and loves him because of them, has in these so many evidences of the healthy faith of the believer. He who is happy on account of the coming of Islamism, and renders obedience to the things which the blessed God and His Prophet have exhibited, but who opposes 'Alee on account of the same, entertains a feeling which is the reverse of what it should be, and is a gross hypocrite; his mystical faith will be evil in the extreme,—from all of which may God preserve us!"

"Tehil bin Sa'd relates that on the occasion of the battle of Hyber, the blessed Prophet said he would provide a standard for the day following, which, in the hands of one who, under God's blessing, would carry it to victory,—a man who is beloved of God and His Prophet, and who also loves them.

"Now the morning of that day came, and the people ran in haste to the Prophet to ask and implore him for the promised flag. The Prophet asked for 'Alee; and being informed that his eyes pained him, he bade them call him. On his arrival, the blessed Prophet of God rubbed his eyes with his own fingers, and the pain at once left them, so that they suddenly became perfectly cured. He then handed him the flag. 'Alee asked him whether he should destroy the infidels, after the usual mode of warfare: and the Prophet directed him to approach their country quietly and gently, and then to invite them to accept of Islamism, or prepare to meet the young lion who advances against them on the part of the Most High God; for it is a good deed, he added, to be the medium of directing even one man in the true faith."

"On the same subject of the qualities of 'Alee, it is related in the *Mesâbeeh*, as coming from 'Amrân bin Hosain, that the blessed Prophet once declared, 'Of a certainty 'Alee is from me, and I am from 'Alee, and he is the *Valee* of all the Faithful.' In the excellent commentators of these words, it is found stated by Kâzee, 'The Shee'â people declare that 'Alee is the *Valee* (possessor), and that the meaning of this *Hadees* is that 'Alee was worthy of possessing all the things that the Prophet possessed. The affairs of the Faithful appertained to these, and 'Alee was therefore their Imâm.' To this we reply that he could not correctly bear the *Imâmet* over their concerns during the life of the Prophet, because he was the Imâm, and, consequently, his *Velâyet* was only one of love and affection.

"The same work states, as coming from Ibn 'Omer, that the blessed Prophet declared the As-hâbs should all be as brethren to each other. 'Alee on learning this, wept, and asked of the Prophet, why, as he had made them to be brethren, he had made him brother to no one? To this, the Prophet replied, 'You are my brother, both in this life and in the life to come.' The Imâm Termezee relates the same as a 'remarkable' Hadees (Hadees Garbee) or one not fully confirmed.

"On the subject of this same Hadees, Inis relates that once the blessed Prophet had a roasted bird before him, of which he was about to partake, and exclaimed, 'O God! send to me him whom Thou lovest most among Thy creatures, so that he may eat of this bird with me.' At that moment 'Alee came to the Prophet, and they ate the bird together. Termezee states that this is a remarkable and beautiful Hadees; and Thur Pishtee, on commenting on it, after alluding to it with much eloquence and excellence, says, 'Innovators have wasted much breath on this Hadees, and have blown the feathers quite off the wings of the bird, making a great deal of very little. Without wishing to cast any blame on the Caliphat of Abu Bekr, this Hadees should, on the decease of the Prophet, have been the first principle on which to unite the Mussulman people together, for it would have consolidated them, and sustained them.'

"To this we reply that the Hadees in question, does not at all strengthen those which are of an obligatory character. As to the precedents, as well as all the good things that arose in the Caliphat of Abu Bekr, they condemn these holy Hadeeses, notwithstanding the most exact information which we possess from the whole of the As-hâbs, whose remarks on them still exist. It is, however, not proper to deny the Hadees in question, and one of these persons, Inis, quotes the fact that it was actually uttered, and no one disputes it. The real sense and signification of it is, therefore, that God should send him one of His most beloved, for his personal excellence, and superior intelligence. There is nothing in the holy law showing that 'Alee was the most beloved of all of God's creatures, for among these was the blessed Prophet himself. We must then only accept what is conformable to the holy oracles of the Koran, and known to the community of the people, then with the Prophet. It must, therefore, be read as we have stated above, or as it was understood by the children of the Prophet's uncle (Abu Bekr) whom he loved very much; because he often spoke freely, but always attentively, and never with negligence. In the Mesâbeeh, it is related, in connexion with this Hadees, that 'Alee himself stated: 'Whenever I asked anything of the blessed Prophet, he would answer me; and if I remained silent, he would commence a conversation explaining his meaning.'

"It is also related in the Mesâbeeh, as subsequent to the preceding Hadees, that the blessed Prophet once said, with regard to 'Alee, 'I am the house of Wisdom, and 'Alee is the door.' Termezee states that this also is a Hadees Garbee; and Muhee el Seneh, who is the author of this book, declares that it was not known to any one of the companions of the Prophet. The Shee'âs say that it was the intention of the Prophet, that instruction in metaphysics (Hikmet) should be peculiar to 'Alee; that no one else had this faculty, and that it could only be acquired by his medium. God, in His own firm words, has said, 'Piety does not consist in your entering your house through a door in its rear; but, in the fear of God, enter therefore by its proper portals' (chap. ii. verse 185). There is, in fact, no need of this at all, for Paradise is widely open to those acquainted with spiritual wisdom (Hikmet), and it has eight portals for their admission. In the Mesâbeeh, it is related as coming from Jâbir, that the blessed Prophet called 'Alee, the day that he sent him to Tâyif, and spake with him secretly. Though this conversation was a lengthy one, he said to his uncle's sons, 'I did not conclude with him, but God did.' Now the expression 'to conclude' signifies to 'converse secretly.' The commentator, Tâyibee, says that these words mean that 'God commanded the Prophet to converse secretly with 'Alee;' and I truly believe that it was by Divine command that he spoke with him of secret things. The same work relates, on the part of Ami Atieh,—on whom be the Divine satisfaction!—that the Prophet of God sent troops in a holy warfare, and that 'Alee was among them. On that occasion, the blessed

Prophet elevated his hand, and prayed, 'O God, do not kill 'Alee, but send him back to me.'

"On one occasion, the As-hâbs inquired of the blessed Prophet the cause and reason of his great love for 'Alee, so that, in conformance with it, they might also increase their affection for him. In reply, he bade them go and call 'Alee to him, and learn the cause from himself. One of them went and called him; and whilst he was gone, the Prophet said, 'O my companions! should anyone do good to you, what would you do in return to him?' They replied that they would do good to him. He then asked them what they would do if anyone did harm to them; and they answered that they would still do him good. The Prophet repeated the latter question, and they bent down their heads, and made no reply. Just then 'Alee appeared, and the blessed Prophet asked him what he would do, if any person should do him evil, in return for his own goodness. 'Alee replied, 'O Prophet of God, I would do him good.' 'Should he again do you evil, what would you do?' added the Prophet; and 'Alee replied as before. This question was put for the seventh time, by the most excellent of prophets, and 'Alee always replied the same, and finally added, 'O Prophet of God, I swear by that Almighty One, and there is none other, that should such a person harm me, a thousand years, in return for my own kindness, I would always continue to do him good.' On hearing these words, the As-hâbs all agreed that the love of the Prophet was well founded, and they offered up a prayer for the object of his affection.

"Beware, from supposing that the question of the As-hàbs was caused by any feeling of jealousy, for it was only so as to know the cause of the particular affections the blessed Prophet bore for 'Alee.

"Once, three persons visited the Prophet of God, one of the people of Ibrahim, one of Moses, and one of Jesus. The first asked the Prophet, 'How shall we know that you are indeed what you declare yourself, *i.e.* the greatest and most excellent of prophets, and the most acceptable of God,—for God said to Ibrahim

(Abraham), Thou art my friend (*Khaleel*)?' To this one the Prophet replied by saying, 'The Most High has said to me, Thou art my beloved friend (*Habeeb*), which therefore is the nearest to any one; His friend (companion or associate), or His beloved?' The individual was amazed, and unable to make any reply. Then, looking upon the blessed face of the Prophet, he, from the bottom of his heart, pronounced the confession, 'I bear testimony that there is no God but Allah. He is unique, and without any associate, and that Mohammed is His servant and apostle.'

"Next came the individual of the people of Moses, and asked, 'Oh, Prophet of God, when you say that your place is the most exalted of all the prophets, and that you are their joy and sovereign, how shall it be known that this is really so? I have heard that the All-Just said to Moses, You are my *Keleem* (interlocutor, or one who speaks with me), and that whenever He was up in Mount Sinai, he spoke with God.' To this the blessed Prophet replied, 'When God called Moses his *Keleem*, He called me His *Habeeb*, and though he went up on Mount Sinai, He sent me the angel *Jebrâil* (Gabriel), with *Berâk*, ornamented with caparisons of Paradise, and, seated on him, in a short space of time I visited the world, the heavens, the celestial vault, the throne, Paradise, and Hell, as well as the whole Universe and all Creation, from the *Kâb Kavsér* (cup of a stream of Paradise called *Kavsér*) to the smallest object. The Most High spoke with me, and showed me the greatest kindness, so much so that there is no cause for modesty with Him on my part. Blessed be God for His great mercy in having chosen this humble and insignificant servant from among His people! God also promised me that whoever should pray every day one hundred times to my pure spirit, and he should never abandon or neglect this habit, He will pardon and have mercy on him one thousand times, and give him an exalted place in Paradise. His sins will a thousand thousand times be more pardoned than if he had given as many alms to the poor.'

"Abu Horaireh relates, on the part of Ibn Malik, that

on hearing the preceding, the individual was quite overcome; that he fell at the feet of the blessed Prophet, and then raising up his hands, recited with great joy the Confession of Faith.

"Next came the individual who was of the people of Jesus, and asked, 'When you say, I am near God, and am beloved of Him, and am the Lord of the beginning and of the ending; and that Jesus was the Spirit of God (*Rooh Allah*), and that he resuscitated the dead in God's name, how are we to know the truth of this?' To this the blessed Prophet and the Apostle of the Oppressed, answered, 'Go and call 'Alee.' On hearing this command, one of the As-hâbs went and bade 'Alee come to the Prophet; and on his arrival the latter directed the individual to point out to 'Alee one of the very oldest cemeteries. This person replied that in such a place there was a grave one thousand years old. 'Go,' said the blessed Prophet to 'Alee; 'go to that grave, and cry out three times, and wait patiently until you see what God will do.' 'Alee proceeded to the spot, and cried out once, 'O Jacob!' The grave immediately opened; he cried out the same once more, and the grave became completely open; on calling the same once more, lo! an aged man, with a bright countenance, came out of the grave, with hair so long that it reached from his head to his feet; and standing upright, he cried out with a loud voice the Confession of Faith. He next accompanied 'Alee to the presence of the Prophet of God, where, at the sight of so extraordinary a miracle, a large number of infidels accepted the true faith. As to the individual of the people of Jesus, he joined the people of the Prophet and became a Mussulman.

"Regarding these traits or sketches of 'Alee's character, it will suffice to add that when the blessed Prophet was commanded by the Most High to emigrate (the Hejreh) from Mekkeh to Medineh, He directed 'Alee to occupy his bed, and that he should be his lieutenant in the holy Ke'beh; to watch over his family, to distribute among their owners all the objects deposited in the keeping of the Prophet, and to take care of such As-hâbs as should remain in the Ke'beh. That same night the miserable infidels attacked the dwelling of the blessed Prophet; but God, in His infinite mercy, sent a sleep upon them. The devil (*Shaitân*)—on whom be maledictions, was with them, and he also fell asleep. 'Alee, together with Abu Bekr, went out of the house, and walked about. The Most High commanded the angels *Mikail* (Michael), and *Izrâfeel* (on whom be the Divine salutation of peace) to hasten to His lion, 'Alee, because the infidels wished to commit a crime. In the wink of the eye these two exalted angels appeared—Michael stood by 'Alee's head and Izrafeel at his feet, where they prayed. Soon afterwards the devil awoke, and cried out aloud, 'Mohammed has escaped.' To the infidels this accursed one having appeared in a human form, they, addressing him, asked, 'How should we know it?' and he replied, 'It is now so many thousand years since I have had any rest that I slept to-night, and it is possible that Mohammed has bewitched me, and put me to sleep.' After this, all of the infidels having fled away, the people entered the house of the Prophet of God; and 'Alee arose from his bed, and standing up they beheld that the Prophet of God was really gone, and that in his place was 'Alee, who came suddenly out. On the following day, he proceeded to the Ke'beh, and took up the place in which the blessed Prophet was used to stand, and from thence cried out that whoever had any objects deposited with the Prophet of God they should come forward and receive them, which, on producing the tokens received for them they did, and took them away, so that not one remained. All of the As-hâbs in the holy Ke'beh sought protection of 'Alee, and not one had reason to complain of any wrong. As the Prophet's dwelling was inside the Ke'beh, 'Alee made it his abode. Some time after this the Prophet commanded that 'Alee should take his family and proceed to Medineh, which he did; and going to the congregation of the infidels of the Koraish, he told them of his intention to set out on the day following, and that if any one had anything to say let him speak. All lowered their heads, and not one had a word to answer.

"After the departure of 'Alee, Abu Jehel (on whom be curses) asked them, 'O, ye great men of the Koraish! why did you not speak out whilst the family of Mohammed was still here, for it can do us no harm?' They then assembled around Abu Jehel and discussed the matter, and finally proceeded to 'Abbâs, and begged him to advise his brother's son ('Alee) not to remove the family of Mohammed, lest trouble should arise in consequence of its departure. 'Abbâs found the *Shâh i Murdân* (the king of men, 'Alee), and spoke with him on the subject; but the latter answered that, 'Inshallah! on the morrow he would remove the family of the Prophet.' This he did, and was followed by four or five of the Koraish mounted on horses. Previous to 'Alee's departure, however, he declared that he would fight whoever attempted to prevent him carrying into effect the orders of the Prophet. On hearing this from 'Abbâs the infidels were greatly troubled. and formed a compact among themselves not to permit 'Alee to leave the city. So that when they met 'Alee and ordered him to return, he refused, and having mounted his charger commenced fighting them, and through Divine assistance was enabled to beat them all. He now continued on his way, and next met with Mikdâd bin Aswad, who also commenced fighting him. But the Imâm 'Alee, in the most fearless manner, withstood the attack, and soon dismounted him. Placing his foot upon this man's breast, he invited him to accept of the true faith, which he at once most cheerfully did, and became a Mussulman. This person's son became a martyr in the defence of the Imâm Hosain ('Alee's son) at Kerbelâ; and beside being a most heroic man, subsequently became one of the most excellent of the As-hâbs. If any one wishes to know more about this story they will please refer to the work entitled the 'Siyer en Nebee' (a biography of the Prophet), where it is given in a detailed manner.

"The Imâm 'Alee, in consequence of having heard the 'Friend of God,' in the Prophet, declared in a Hadees, that 'Poverty was his pride,' became extremely poor. From that moment, he took no interest in worldly concerns, so much so, that if he became possessed of 1,000 pieces of gold, he would, by the morrow, not have one of them, for all would be given away to the poor. The blessed Prophet therefore used to say of 'Alee, that he was the 'Sultan of the Liberal.' 'Alee once said to the pure Fâtimeh, 'O best of women, and the daughter of the Prophet of God, have you nothing to give your husband to eat, for I am extremely hungry?' Fâtimeh replied, 'O father of Hasan, I declare to you by that Allah, beside whom there is none other, I have absolutely nothing; but in the corner of that tomb you will find six *Akchas* (pieces of silver): take them, go to the bazaar, and buy something for yourself to eat, and also some fruits for our sons Hasan and Hosain.' 'Alee departed, and on his way met with two Mussulmans, the one holding the other by the collar of his robe, rudely pulling him, and claiming the payment of a debt, and declaring that he could wait no longer, and must have his money. Approaching them, 'Alee asked how much was the debt, and on hearing that it was just six *Akchas*, he thought to himself that he would free this Mussulman from his affliction, and yet was embarrassed as to what he would say to Fâtimeh, who expected him to return with food. Nevertheless he paid over the sum, and so relieved the Mussulman. He reflected for a moment on the answer which he should give to Fâtimeh, and was much troubled by his painful position. With the idea in his mind that she was the best of women, and the Prophet's daughter, he returned, empty-handed, and had scarcely reached the door, when he saw their sons, Hasan and Hosain, running towards him, in the full expectation that their father had brought them some fruit for food, and, on seeing that he had none, they both wept. He now explained to their mother what use he had made of the money which she had given him, and how he had freed a Mussulman from a most painful predicament. 'You have done well,' she exclaimed, 'and I am delighted that you have done so good an action,' though, at the same time, she was pained at heart; and in place of adding, 'How great are our necessities! and how strangely you have acted!' she only said, 'The Most High and Noble Allah will provide for us.'

"As to 'Alee, remarking that his wife was much afflicted, and that his two sons wept from pure hunger, his heart became troubled, and he left the house, in the design of proceeding to the blessed Prophet of God, to see what would follow; for it was well known that, should any one be oppressed with ten thousand sorrows, the sight of the countenance of the blessed Prophet at once removed them all, and in their stead he became filled with innumerable joys. On his way he met with an Arab leading a fatted camel, who asked him whether he would not purchase it, and 'Alee replied that he did not possess any ready money with which to pay for it. To this the Arab replied that he would credit him for the amount; and as 'Alee requested to learn the price, he added that it was 100 *Akchas*. 'Alee accepted the offer, and the Arab delivered him the animal. Taking its bridle in his hand, he proceeded on his way, and soon met with another Arab, who, addressing him by name, inquired whether he would not sell it. 'Alee replied that he would, and the Arab asked him whether he would accept of 300 *Akchas* for it. Having consented, he handed over the camel to the purchaser, who forthwith counted him out the sum thus agreed upon.

"'Alee, much delighted, proceeded at once to the bazaar, where he purchased an abundance of food and fruit, and thence returned to his house. Opening the door, his children clung to him, delighted with the prospect of partaking of a bountiful meal. Their mother inquired of him how he became possessed of so much money, and 'Alee related to her the preceding occurrence. After satisfying their hunger, they all returned thanks to that Sublime and Blessed Allah who thus provided for their pressing wants. 'Alee then arose, and after telling his wife of his intention, proceeded to the residence of the Pride of the Universe, the most blessed Prophet of Allah. The latter having, however, just left his house, 'Alee met him on the way to his own premises, where he told the As-hâbs near him, he desired visiting his daughter and son-in-law. So soon as the Prophet beheld 'Alee, he smiled, and exclaimed, 'O 'Alee, from whom did you buy the camel, and to whom did you sell it?' and 'Alee replied, 'God and His Prophet know.' The Prophet now informed him that the seller was the angel Gabrâ'il, and the purchaser the angel 'Izrâfil, and that it was one of the camels of Jennet (Paradise); that the all-just Allah had bestowed upon him fifty favours for the one he had granted to that afflicted Mussulman; and that those which were in store for him, in eternity, were only known to God.

"During the *Mijra i Shereef* (or the Ascension) of the blessed Prophet, he beheld a lion in the seventh heaven, of so terrible an appearance, that it was perfectly indescribable. He inquired of the angel Gabrâ'il what lion it was, and was informed that it was not a wild animal, but was the 'spirituality' of the Imâm 'Alee; adding, 'O friend of Allah, remove your ring from off your finger, and cast it in its mouth,' which he having done, the lion, with great humility and many caresses, took and held the ring in its mouth. On the day following the Ascension, the Prophet gave an account of the same to the As-hâbs; and whilst relating the frightful appearance of the lion, and the matter of the ring, 'Alee, who was also present, withdrew the latter from his own mouth and handed it to him, greatly to the surprise of all the spectators. From this remarkable occurrence they were enabled to understand the sublimity of his character, and their love and affection for him became greatly increased.

"Of the *Ayats* (verses of the Koran) sent in honour of 'Alee, one refers to the following occurrence. Some of the learned 'Ulemâ state that the *Emir el Mumineen*, or 'Commander of the Faithful' ('Alee), was once engaged praying in the Masjid, or chapel, when a beggar approached him, and asked for something. 'Alee, turning aside his face, withdrew a ring from off his finger and handed it to the man. This act of generosity having been agreeable to the Most High, the following Ayat descended from heaven, ch. v. 60 :—'Your protectors are God and His Prophet, and those who believe, who perform the prayers exactly, who give alms, and who incline themselves before God.'

"Another Ayât was the subject of a dispute between 'Abbâs and Telha. The former said, 'I am of those excellent persons who supply the pilgrims with water;' and the latter declared, 'I am of those excellent ones who have charge of the key of the holy house (Ke'beh), and, if I choose, I can spend the night therein.' To this 'Alee remarked, 'What do you say? It is now more than ten months since I have turned my face towards this *Kibleh* (the Ke'beh), and you were not here even then.' It was on this occasion that the following Ayât descended from heaven, ch. ix. 19—20: 'Will you place those who bear water to the pilgrims and visit the holy Oratory on the same footing with those who believe in God and in the Last Day, and fight in the path of God? Now, they will not be equal before God; God does not direct the wicked. Those who have left their own country, who fight in the path of God with their property and their persons, will fill a more elevated place before God; they will be the happy.'

"There is another Ayat, commanded by God, relative to 'Alee bin Abi Tâlib, Fâtimeh, and Hasan and Hosain, ch. xlii. 22: 'This is what God promises to His servants who believe and do good. Tell them, All that I ask of you in return for my ministrations is some for my relations. Whoever shall have performed a good deed, we will raise in value; God is indulgent and thankful.' *Katâda*—on whom be the Divine satisfaction—states that the *Mushriks*, at a meeting, declared, 'Let us see whether Mohammed wishes for a recompense?' On these words, that Ayat descended, as is stated by Sa'eed ibn Jebeel. Ibn 'Abbâs remarks that, in the expression 'relations,' is comprised 'Alee, Fâtimeh, and Hasan and Hosain; and no one must ever feel an illwill for them.

"Another Ayat is that in which the Most High shows the purity of the religious sentiments of 'Alee, ch. xv. 47: 'We will remove all falsehood from out of their hearts; living together as brothers, they will repose upon beds, viewing each other face to face.' Some of the learned have said that this Ayat referred to 'Alee, Mu'âvieh, Telha, Zebeer, and the faithful 'Ayisheh.

"Another Ayat of the Most High is (ch. lviii. v. 13): 'O ye who believe: when you go in private to consult the Prophet, prior to your visit, bestow an alms, for this will be better for you, and more suitable; but, if you have not wherewith to do it, know that God is indulgent and merciful.' The champions of Islamism state that no one acted upon this Ayat except 'Alee, who, whenever he desired to consult the Prophet, conformably with this verse, always bestowed something previously in alms.

"Ibn 'Omar relates that 'Alee possessed three things, of which, said he, 'had I only one, it would have made me much beloved.' One of these was the daughter (Fâtimeh el Zehrah) of the Prophet, given to him in marriage; the second, the gift which the Prophet made to him of the standard of victory, at the battle of Khyber; and the third, that he put in performance the holy Ayat, called the *Nejvee.* It is said of 'Alee, that he would take a dinar, divide it into ten dirhems, and so bestow it in alms on ten poor persons; that he also once asked of the Prophet ten questions, confidentially, one of which was, 'How shall I pray?' and the Prophet replied, 'With fidelity and purity;' the next, 'What shall I ask of God?' and the reply, 'Health in this world and in the other;' the next, 'What do I need most?' and the answer was, 'To keep God's laws, and the commands of His Prophet;' 'What, O Prophet of God, must I do to secure my own salvation?' and the former replied, 'Do no wrong to others, and speak the truth.' He next inquired, 'What is truth?' and the blessed Prophet answered, 'Islam, the Koran, and to act correctly up to the close of your life.' He then asked him, 'What is joy?' and he replied, 'Paradise;' 'What is comfort?' he added, and heard that it was 'To behold God.' 'What is rebellion?' he next asked, and the blessed Prophet told him, 'To be a *Kiâfir*' (or otherwise to be unfaithful to the Most High God); and he added the question, 'What is fidelity?' to which he received the reply, 'To bear testimony that there is no God but Allah, and that Mohammed is the Prophet of Allah;' for He is that God who honours and degrades men; and where His Prophet so admonished the people of Mekkeh, they would turn their faces away, and declare otherwise; for it is said in the Great Book (Koran), ch. xli. 25: 'The infidels say, Do not listen to the Koran, and speak loudly so as to drown the voice of those who read it.' In the end, God so elevated him, that He commanded, 'He is most dear to me, and you must hear and obey everything that he directs.' On this head the Ayat says: 'When you visit the Prophet, before entering near him, bestow an alms, for your own welfare' (ch. lviii. 13). 'Do not address him a word until he comes out of his room.' The Ayat says also (ch. xlix. 4): 'Those who call thee with a loud voice, whilst thou art still within thy apartments, are, mostly, people of no sense.' Also (ch. xlix. 4): 'Do not raise your voice above that of the Prophet.' Also (ch. xxxiii. 9): 'He was at the distance of ten arcs, or nearer.' God placed him in so elevated a position, that the angel Gabrâ'il and all the other angels, though they went round it, were unable to reach it. Those who falsely swear, who shout within the limits of the *Harâm i Shereef*, at Mekkeh and Medina, or are deficient in their prayers and fasts, must bestow alms upon the poor, and thus acquire the satisfaction of the Most High. The holy verse says (ch. xlv. 20): 'Those who do evil, think that we will treat them equally with those who believe,—who do good; and that for either life and death is the same: they judge badly.'

"An Ayat descended for 'Alee, whose faith was correct, and all his acts were good and praisable, without hypocrisy, and unheard-of for perfection. The Christians (Mushrikler) said to him: 'If what you declare (about God and His Prophet) be true, you will be greater than we in this world, and in the other.' (Ch. xxxiii. 33). 'Remain quiet in your houses; adopt not the luxuries of the times of Ignorance; observe the hours of prayer; give alms; obey God and His Prophet. God only wishes to free you from abominations, and give you perfect purity.'

"Sa'eed bin Jebeer relates, on the part of 'Abdullah bin 'Abbâs, as coming from Ibn 'Abbâs, that when the holy verse descended, 'Thou givest fear, and to each people there is a director in the true path,' the blessed Prophet stated, 'I am the one who gives the fear, and 'Alee is he who directs in the true path. O 'Alee, those who are directed will be directed by thee.'

"Rebiyat bin Najd relates, 'Alee once stated: 'The blessed Prophet read over me and said, You resemble Jesus, the Son of Mary, inasmuch as the Jews hated him, and calumniated his mother. The Nazareens loved him so greatly as to declare that he had no post or grade among the prophets, but was really God.' To this 'Alee responded: 'Many persons destroy their souls for love of me; some love me very much, and are inimical to the other As-hâbs; I do not love these, and some who love the other As-hâbs hate me; both of which are of the people of hell. I am not a prophet; on me no inspiration descends, and yet, with all the strength given to me, I conform to God's book.' The blessed Prophet now added: 'All that I order you to do is to conform to the will of the Most High, either through your own free will, or from misery and compulsion. If I should ever order you to do what is contrary to this, do not obey it; for who obeys me, obeys Him.'

"Another narrative is that of Kais bin Hârith. An individual asked a question of Mu'âvieh bin Sofyân, and for reply was directed to make the same interrogation of 'Alee; 'for he knows better than myself.' The individual, nevertheless, persisted in receiving an answer from him, 'for I shall love it more,' he added, 'than any that 'Alee can give me.' The Mu'âvieh, however, declined, and said to the individual, 'You speak falsely, and are a wicked man; for you show an aversion for him who enjoys, to an eminent degree, the respect and regard of the Prophet of God, on account of his great knowledge of Him, respecting whom the Prophet has declared: "O 'Alee, after me, you occupy the place of Aaron after Moses:

with the difference that, after me, there will be no other prophet."' I have also observed that 'Omar often took counsel with him; and whenever any doubts arose, he would say, ''Alee is present, let us ask him.' So Mu'âvieh—on whom be the Divine satisfaction—said to the individual, 'Depart, and may the blessed Allah not give any strength to your steps;' and so he departed.

"Another narrative is by Sa'd bin Abi Vakkâs. 'Once, Mu'âvieh came to me, on account of some personal need. He mentioned 'Alee, and I told him that 'Alee had three peculiar characteristics, of which, had I but one, I would be greatly beloved. These I heard stated by the blessed Prophet himself. 1. "'Alee is the *Velee* (friend) of whosoever I am the *Velee*." 2. The Prophet declared, the day of the battle of Khyber, "To-morrow, I will give the standard to one who is beloved of God and His Prophet," and gave it to 'Alee. 3. "You are to me what Aaron was to Moses."'

"Jâbir bin 'Abdallah relates that the Prophet once stated: 'The night during which I went up to heaven (*El Mi'raj*), I passed by the porters, and heard a voice behind them say, "O Mohammed, goodly is your father Ibrahim, and how goodly is your brother 'Alee bin Abi Tâlib; leave him a testimony from you that he had done good."'

"Hasan Bahree relates that Uns bin Malik heard it from the Prophet: 'There are three persons whom Paradise desires ardently to receive, viz. 'Alee bin Abi Tâlib, 'Ammâr bin Yâsir, and Selmân Farsee.'

"Sa'd bin Abi Vakkâs once said, 'Mu'âvieh asked me, "Do you love 'Alee?" and I replied, "Why should I not love him? Have I not heard the Prophet say to him, 'O 'Alee, after me, you are what Aaron was to Moses.'" At the battle of Badr, he came out of the fight, and a voice came forth from his belly, declaring that God would ever be with him; and he never ceased fighting, until he had coloured his sword with the blood of the infidels.'

"'Amir bin Sherbeel el Sha'bee states, 'Alee once remarked, Zaid ibn Serha, at the battle of Jemel, was in the following condition. He had fallen down in his blood; 'Alee stood over his head, and exclaimed to him, 'O Zaid, may the Most High have mercy upon you; I did not know you, except as one recommended to me; I now know you for your good deeds, and as one to whom the Prophet has given the good news (of faith) and paradise.' Zaid was still covered with blood, and raising up his hands, he exclaimed, 'O Emeer of the Faithful, may thine also be good news; for to thee has the Prophet of God given the same assurances. I swear by the truth of God, I have never had an occasion to fight with you in any battle, where I could destroy the ranks of the enemy, on account of the hypocrisy and falsehoods of the public against you; and yet I have heard it as said by the Prophet, 'Alee is a *pathway;* he is the destroyer of wickedness, and has conquered the person who has conquered him, and put to flight him who would not aid him. I am happy at last to have found myself in battle with you, and to fight with you as a friend.' As he terminated these words, his soul left his body.

"'Amru bin el Jemooh states: 'I was once in the presence of the Prophet of God, when he exclaimed, "O 'Amru;" and I answered, "What are thy commands, O Prophet of God?" He answered, "Do you wish me to show you the columns of Paradise?" I replied that I did. Just then 'Alee passed by, and he, pointing to him, said, "The members of this person's family are the columns of Paradise." It is also reported by 'Abd Allah ibn 'Abbâs, that the Prophet declared, "the chief of places was in his own body."'

"'Alee himself relates that the blessed Prophet declared: 'The night of the Mi'raj, the angel Gabrâ'il held my hand, and led me to a splendidly ornamented position in Paradise, where he placed a quince before me. I took it up and smelt it, and whilst turning it round in my hand, it separated into two pieces, and from out of it came a *Hooree.* Never in my life had I seen so beautiful a being as this. So addressing me, she said, "Peace be to thee, O Mohammed." In reply I asked her who she was, and she replied, "My name is *Râzieh* and *Murzieh* (consenting and consented, or satisfying), and the Most Glorious has created me out of three things: the upper part of me is made of ambergris, the middle camphor, and the lower musk; I was joined together with the water of life, and thus was I created by the Sovereign Lord of the universe for your brother 'Alee bin Abi Tâlib."'

"Abu Zerr Ghifâree also relates, as coming from the Prophet of God: 'Whoever is separated from me is separated from God, and whoever, O 'Alee, is separated from you is also separated from me.' Uns bin Malik states that, 'The glory of all beings (the Prophet) mentioned 'Alee bin Abi Tâlib adoringly.' Jâbir bin 'Abdallah mentions from the same source: 'It is written over the door of Paradise, "There is no God but Allah, Mohammed is His Prophet, and 'Alee is the aider of His Prophet;" and that this was so written 2,000 years before the erection of the heavens and the earth.'

"'Abdallah bin Mes'ood relates: 'I was once in the company of the blessed Prophet, when he said of 'Alee, "Wisdom is divided into ten parts, nine of which are given to 'Alee, and one to mankind."' 'Abdallah bin 'Abbâs relates that the Prophet one day came out of his house, holding the hand of 'Alee in his own blessed hand, and exclaimed, 'Beware that no one bear any hostile feelings for 'Alee, for such an one is an enemy of God and His Prophet; whoever loves 'Alee, loves also God and His Prophet.' The same person relates that the Prophet once remarked: 'Whoever wishes to see the meekness of Abraham, the wisdom of Noah, the patience of Joseph, let him look upon 'Alee bin Abi Tâlib.' Uns bin Malik says: 'I was once seated in company with the Prophet, when suddenly 'Alee appeared and seated himself behind him. The Prophet called to him to sit before him, and addressing him, said, "O 'Alee, God has honoured and distinguished you with the gift of four qualities above my own." 'Alee rose to his feet and exclaimed, "May my father and mother be devoted to you; how can a servant be honoured above his Lord?" The Prophet replied, "O

'Alee, when the Most High and Blessed God desires to honour one of His servants, He bestows upon him those things which eye has not seen, ear has not heard, nor which have ever come into the mind of man." Enis says that he observed, on hearing this, "O Prophet of Allah, explain this to us, so that we may understand it;" and he continued, "God has given him such a wife as Fâtimeh, and not to me; He has given him two such sons as Hasan and Hosain, and none to me; and He has given to him such a father-in-law (the Prophet himself), as He has not given to me."'

"Sa'eed bin Jebeer relates that once the Prophet took the hand of 'Abd Allah bin 'Abbâs, and they together walked to the well of Zemzem, where a number of people were seated, indulging in improper remarks about 'Alee. He sent away Ibn 'Abbâs, and approaching them, stood still, and exclaimed, 'Who is it that dares to speak ill of God and the Prophet of God?' They replied, 'None of us have spoken ill of God, nor of His Prophet.' 'Who,' then added he, 'speaks ill of 'Alee bin Abi Tâlib?' and some one answered, 'Yes, such has been spoken.' 'I know it,' he added, 'for I bear testimony that I heard it with my own ears, and whoever speaks ill of him speaks ill of me, and whoever speaks ill of me has spoken ill of the Most High, and He will cast him headlong into hell.'

"Atiet el Avkee relates: 'I once went to see Jâbir bin 'Abd Allah, and found him much advanced in years, his eyebrows covering his eyes. I asked him a question about 'Alee, and on hearing his name, he raised up his head and smiled for joy and love of him, and exclaimed, "In the time of the blessed Prophet the only hypocrites we knew were those who were unfriendly to 'Alee, and we therefore considered them all as enemies."'

"Sha'bee says, 'Once Abu Bekr el Siddeek, on seeing 'Alee, remarked that "Whoever was well thought of by him ('Alee) and met with his favour, would be held in high consideration by the blessed Prophet; and whosoever 'Alee deemed truly spiritual, would be regarded by the Prophet as being near to God (in a spiritual sense)."'

"'Ayescha relates that she once asked the blessed Prophet, 'Who, after him, was the best amongst the people, and he answered, Abu Bekr el Siddeek; after him, I inquired, and he added, 'Omar; and next, I asked, and he said, 'Othmân. Fâtimeh, on hearing this, exclaimed, "O Prophet of God, have you nothing to say for 'Alee?" and he replied, "I am 'Alee, and 'Alee is myself; have you ever heard any one commend his own self?"'

"Zaid el 'Abideen bin 'Alee Hosain relates that he once heard 'Alee bin Abi Tâlib declare, 'The Prophet of God has taught me a thousand doors of knowledge, each one of which has opened to me a thousand others.'

"'Abd Allah 'Alkendi relates, that Mu'âvieh bin Abu Sofyân made the pilgrimage after the death of 'Alee, and coming among the congregation there, seated himself in the presence of 'Abd Allah bin 'Abbâs and 'Abd Allah bin 'Omar. Mu'âvieh placed his hand upon the knee of 'Abd Allah bin 'Abbâs, and said, 'My affair is better than that of your uncle's son.' 'Abd Allah bin 'Abbâs replied, 'Why did he say that about him who stated, "I am the nephew of the Prophet whom they unjustly put to death?" that is to say, 'Othmân bin 'Affân, on whom be the Divine satisfaction.' 'Abd Allah said, 'His presence is better than you for the Caliphet, for 'Alee's relationship is nearer than that of your nephew.' Mu'âvieh, on hearing this, became silent; then turning toward Sa'd bin Abi Wakkâs, he said, 'O Sa'd! do not separate the truth from the obsolete; will you be with or against us?' To this Sa'd replied, 'When I witnessed the darkness of violence committed, I said to myself, I will be patient until the daylight again appears, and then I will depart from here.' Mu'âvieh, on this, exclaimed, 'I swear by Allah that I have read the most glorious Koran, and found nothing of this in it;' and Sa'd added, 'Do you not accept the words which I myself heard from the mouth of the blessed Prophet on the subject of 'Alee bin Abi Tâlib? "Thou art with the truth, and the truth is with me."' Mu'âvieh now bade him produce some person who had also heard these from the Prophet, or, added he, 'You will see what I shall do to you.' Sa'd said that Ami Selmà had likewise heard them, and so, going to him, Mu'âvieh asked, 'O Father of believers! the public say many things which never were spoken by the blessed Prophet, one of which is a Hadees brought forward by Sa'd.' 'What is it?' inquired Ami Selmà. 'What does he quote?' 'He states,' replied Mu'âvieh, 'that the blessed Prophet was heard to say to 'Alee, "Thou art with the truth, and the truth is with me."' Ami Selmà at once exclaimed, 'He quotes correctly, for I heard him use these same words myself in my own house.' On hearing this Mu'âvieh turned away his face, asked pardon of Sa'd and others of the As-hâbs of the blessed Prophet there present, and exclaimed, 'I swear by the Most High God, that had I known this I would have been the servant of 'Alee to the day of my death.'

"Another statement is from the mouth of the blessed Prophet, given by 'Abd Allah bin 'Abbâs. He says that the former also declared, 'I am the scales of knowledge, 'Alee is its weights, Hasan and Hosain are its cords, Fâtimeh is its suspension; after me the Imâms (Hasan and Hosain) are the columns which sustain it, and by these scales do we weigh the deeds of our friends.' Uns bin Malik states that the Prophet also declared, 'I am the city of knowledge, 'Alee is its gate, and Mu'âvieh is its ring or circle.'

"Ma'az bin Jebel states that the Prophet likewise declared, 'The Most High has made a people pure from sins, as the head of a bald man is neat, and 'Alee is the first of that people.' Selmân Farsee (an eminent founder of a Dervish Tareek) stated, ''Alee is the possessor of my secret.'

"'Alee relates that the Prophet of God once directed him, in case his head ever ached, to put his hands on his temples, and recite the Ayat,—'We have caused this book (Koran) to descend from heaven,' from one end to the other, and the pain will cease. One day, when walking in the environs of Mekkeh, the Prophet holding 'Alee by the hand, they met with several fine gardens. 'Alee relates that, having expressed his admiration of them, the Prophet assured him that a finer one awaited him in Paradise. Soon after the Prophet, looking him stedfastly in the face, burst into tears, on seeing which 'Alee was much affected, and also wept; and on inquiring the cause, the Prophet told him that he had a presentiment of his death, through the enmity of a certain tribe. 'I asked him,' adds 'Alee, 'whether the faith which I possessed would not secure me salvation in the life to come, and being assured that it would, I declared that I would then die contented.'

"When the blessed Prophet captured Mekkeh, there were 1,140 idols in it, which he designed to destroy; 360 of these surrounded the *Beyt i Shereef*, and one large one was inside of it. It was made of stone, and was fastened to the wall with strong spikes and chains of iron. When the Prophet entered the *Ke'beh*, he recited a prayer, and commanded 'Alee to mount on his shoulders, and pull out the spikes and chains, and so free that idol from its fastenings; but he declined to profane the person of the Prophet of God by such an act, and it was only on the repeated remonstrances of the latter that he finally consented, and in this manner the great idol of the infidels was destroyed.

"One day the blessed Prophet, calling to 'Alee, exclaimed, 'Good news to thee, O 'Alee! for God has commanded that at the Judgment Day the keeper of the treasure of Paradise shall give a deed (*Temessook*) of entrance there only to such persons as have met with your approval, and shall refuse admission to all others.' On account of this remark, it once happened that Abu Bekr es Siddeek (the first Caliph) falling in with 'Alee, observed that he had learned the preceding, and asked him whether he would not favour him with a document by which he could enter Paradise. 'Alee answered, 'Of a truth the blessed Prophet did make such a statement, but he even also said that I should not give any such deeds of admission without previous consultation with Abu Bekr. This, therefore, gives you a supervision over me in the matter, and you thus do not need to ask me for any permission.' These remarks were made in a kind and jocose manner, and they proceeded on their way together, pleased with the arrangement entered into."

MEVLEVEE DERVISH OF DAMASCUS CROSSING HIS ARMS BEFORE BEGINNING TO DANCE.